XENOP
THE PERSIAN E...

Edited with Introduction,
Notes and Vocabulary by

Jeremy Antrich
(Head of Classics, Godalming Sixth Form College)

&

Stephen Usher
(Senior Lecturer in Classics, Royal Holloway College, University of London)

Bristol Classical Press
(in co-operation with Joint Assn. of Classical Teachers)

First published in 1978 by Bristol Classical Press
in conjunction with the Joint Association of Classical Teachers

Bristol Classical Press
an imprint of
Gerald Duckworth & Co. Ltd
The Old Piano Factory
48 Hoxton Square, London N1 6PB

Reprinted 1984, 1988, 1991, 1992, 1995, 1997

A catalogue record for this book is available
from the British Library

ISBN 0-906515-11-4

Available in USA and Canada from:
Focus Information Group
PO Box 369
Newburyport
MA 01950

Printed in Great Britain by
Booksprint, Bristol

CONTENTS

LIST OF ILLUSTRATIONS

4

LIST OF PASSAGES

PREFACE

Both the style and story of Xenophon's *Persian Expedition*
(*Anabasis*) make it an ideal beginning to the study of Greek literature both for students taking the General Certificate of Education at Ordinary Level and for any student starting out on a
Greek course. This selection contains some 800 to 850 lines of
Greek with summaries in English of the intervening passages. It
should ideally be read as a whole, but reasonably self-contained
selections may be made up as follows: Book 1; Book 1:8:1 - 10:15
and Book 4; Books 2 and 4; Books 3, 4 and 7; Books 4 to 7.

The Notes are designed to give help with both content and language. They assume only basic grammatical knowledge, and students
may safely begin with any of Books 1 to 4, since elementary points
of syntax and accidence (e.g. the forms of -μι verbs) are repeated
in each Book, sometimes with cross-references to earlier Books.

The Notes accompany the text on the same page; occasionally
a note continues on to the following page, where it ends with a
square bracket. Each paragraph of the Notes usually refers to a
single sentence of the text, fresh points within a sentence often
being seperated with an asterisk.

The text is based on that of C. Hude revised by J. Peters
(Teubner, 1972), with minor alterations. The link passages are
intended to summarise the main events of the intervening narrative
and the chief arguments of the speeches and dialogue in order to
preserve the integrity and continuity of Xenophon's story. The
Introduction attempts to set the expedition in its historical context and to assess its significance; to provide an account of Xenophon's life and career both military and literary; and to draw
attention to the main characteristics of his style and language.

The volume is published jointly by Bristol Classical Press
and the Joint Association of Classical Teachers. It is a team
effort, but S. Usher is largely responsible for the Introduction,
Text, Bibliography and linking summaries, J. Antrich for the Notes
and Vocabulary. Acknowledgements are due to Miss H. Deighton for
typing and lay-out; and to Mrs. J. Bees and Mrs. A. Gregory for
the illustrations.

J.A.
S.U.
1978

Notes

(i)   In the Vocabulary, as much assistance as possible is provided with the problems of Greek word forms, especially verbs.
The student will, for example, find εἵλοντο and ἕλοι listed with
cross-references to αἱρέω but may be expected to derive ἀν-εῖλον
and συν-ελόντι for himself from ἀν- and συν-αιρέω respectively.

(ii) Greek names have been given in transliterated rather than
Latinized or Anglicized forms: e.g. Kheirisophos - not Chiriso-
phus, Maiandros - not Maeander. The transliteration is based on
guidelines laid down by K. J. Dover, *Aristophanic Comedy* (London
1972) pp. xii - xiv. A few common names whose transliterated
form might have looked too unfamiliar have been given a Latinized
or Anglicized form: e.g. Aeschylus - not Aiskhylos, Thucydides not
Thoukydides, Phoenicia - not Phoinike, Corinth - not Korinthos. A
Latinized or Anglicized form is also given frequently in brackets
after the transliterated form in both the list of Places and Tribes
and in the Vocabulary.

LIST OF ABBREVIATIONS
(used in Notes and Vocabulary)

acc.	accusative	*lit.*	literally
act.	active	*m.*	masculine
adj.	adjective	*mid.*	middle
adv.	adverb, adverbial	*n.*	neuter
aor.	aorist	*nom.*	nominative
comp.	comparative	*opt.*	optative
dat.	dative	*part.*	participle
dir.	direct	*pass.*	passive
f.	feminine	*perf.*	perfect
fut.	future	*pluperf.*	pluperfect
gen.	genitive	*pl., plur.*	plural
imperf.	imperfect	*pres.*	present
indic.	indicative	*pron.*	pronoun
indir.	indirect	*s., sing.*	singular
inf.	infinitive	*subj.*	subjunctive
intrans.	intransitive	*sup.*	superlative
		trans.	transitive

INTRODUCTION

1. *Xenophon's Life.*

In the year 401, three years after the end of the Peloponnesian
War, an army led by the Persian prince Kyros and including ten thousand Greek mercenary soldiers marched eastward from Sardis into the
heart of the Persian empire. There it won a major battle against
the forces of King Artaxerxes, but Kyros was killed and the purpose
of the expedition - to establish him on the throne - died with him.
Yet neither guile nor force could bar the northward march of the
Greeks. The King had to forego his revenge, and they reached the
Black Sea after many trials. Five out of every six Greeks survived
the expedition, and of those who did not, most died in the snows of
Armenia. It was an achievement of enormous significance for the
future. The superiority of Greek over Persian arms had been recognised since the battles of Marathon, Salamis, Mykale and Plataia;
but now it was the weakness of Persia's imperial defences that was
demonstrated, and by the clearest proof. Twenty years later the political propagandist Isokrates proclaimed to the Greek world that Persia was ripe for conquest, and cited the March of the Ten Thousand
as practical evidence. It was left to the Makedonian Alexander to
unite Greece and overrun Persia, but on at least one occasion the
name of the Ten Thousand passed his lips as he exhorted his men.

But the exploits of the Ten Thousand could not have inspired
later generations as they did without the genius of a historian. The
one whose account has come down to us was a participant and an eyewitness of the story he tells; and the style in which he wrote was
ideally adapted to its different parts: lucid and vivid in narrative,
relaxed and detailed in descriptive passages, rational and cogent in
oratory and dialogue. This man was Xenophon the Athenian. His *Anabasis*
(March Up-Country) is the first extended autobiographical work in
ancient literature, and the author's skill in presenting his own
actions and portraying his own character is one of the major delights
of his story. From it and other sources we can piece together an
account of his life more detailed than that of most ancient authors.

The Peloponnesian War lasted from 431 to 404 B.C. Xenophon was
born within about five years of its beginning, perhaps between 429
and 427. His father Gryllos owned an estate in the deme of Erkheia,
near modern Spata, about ten miles north-east of Athens between Mt.
Hymettos and Mt. Pentelikos. It is unlikely that Xenophon enjoyed
the pleasures of country life without interruption in his early years,
because annual raids from the Peloponnese drove most Attic landowners
to seek protection within the city's walls. Crops were regularly
destroyed and olive-trees and vines damaged. These must have been
hard times for Gryllos and his family; but he probably saved enough
of his resources to enable his son to be enlisted in the cavalry,
supplying his own horse when at the age of twenty he was called upon
to fight. By the end of the war he had seen some three years' ser-

vice in various campaigns. Like many young men of his generation,
he had never known the Greek world at peace; and the prospect of it
in a defeated city suffering the torments of internal revolution can
have inspired him with little enthusiasm. He may have spent some
time in the early exercise of his literary talents, describing the
main events of the war from the point in 411 where the great historian Thucydides abruptly ended his narrative. This work, the *Hellenika*, he eventually carried down to the year 362. But now, in 401,
came an invitation from a Boiotian friend of his family, Proxenos,
to join Kyros in a campaign against some dissident tribesmen in
his *satrapy* (province). This offer of travel, adventure, and perhaps enrichment, seemed to meet all Xenophon's physical and psychological needs at that time of his life. He accepted it. The story
of the next three years (401 - 399) is the story of the *Anabasis*.

Its sequel is full of uncertainties. He was exiled from Athens
around the time of the disbandment of the Ten Thousand. That year
(399 B.C.) was a troubled one for the city. The restored democracy
was hostile to independent thinking, which had, in their view, led
to the cruel oligarchies and the tyranny of the Thirty. An atmosphere
of suspicion and recrimination still hung over the city. It was
against this background that Sokrates was charged with rejecting
the city's gods and corrupting the youth with subversive teaching.
His condemnation endangered his pupils, of whom Xenophon was one.
But his countrymen may already have come to regard Xenophon as a
traitor on two other counts. He had joined an expedition organized
by a Spartan, Klearkhos, on behalf of Kyros, who had been responsible
for supplying Sparta with money to build the fleet with which Lys-
andros had defeated them at the Battle of Aigospotamoi in 405, and so
won the war. Also, Athens was anxious not to antagonize the Persian
king at this time, and Xenophon's action was hardly consonant with
such a policy.

Banishment forced him to remain with his Spartan friends, and
he eventually served on the staff of King Agesilaos. He also married, and sired two sons. We know that his wife's name was Philesia, and that his sons were named Gryllos and Diodoros. He must
have established his family in an Ionian city which was securely
under Spartan control, like Ephesos or Dardanos, while he accompanied
the Spartan king on his Asiatic campaigns against Persia, returning
with him to Greece in 395. Although his account in the *Hellenika* of
the battle of Koroneia (394), in which the Spartans were ranged against the Thebans and Athenians, is impersonal, it may be assumed
that he faced the ranks of his own fellow-citizens in that closely-
fought and indecisive encounter, even though he no doubt did so with
mixed feelings. After Koroneia and perhaps a few more years of campaigning, he retired. The Spartans gave him an estate at Skillous,
by the road to Olympia, and to it he brought his family from Asia.
There they enjoyed some twenty years of idyllic rural life. He sent
his sons to Sparta for their education, expressing his own admiration
for the Spartan discipline in a short tract *On Spartan Institutions*.

Other writings occupied much of the time that he did not spend supervising the running of his estate. It is obvious from his large output that literary composition was for Xenophon an essential natural function, and also perhaps a manifestation of a strong desire to instruct and to project his personality. But the writing of the *Anabasis*, which was probably the main work to occupy him in this period, had an ulterior purpose, to tell his side of a controversial story. As one of the commanders he had had to maintain discipline and mete out punishment, and there were no doubt some who disputed his right to the share of the spoils which he received and were eager to accuse him of greed for power. While at Kerasous on the Black Sea, after the worst dangers were over, he had formed the idea of founding a Greek city, but this had proved unpopular and made some suspicious of him afterwards. In particular, the idea of an Athenian founding a new Euxine colony may have offended certain Spartans. This would explain the fullness of Xenophon's account of his refusal of the command of the army when it was offered to him on the first occasion. Much of the story in the last two books is taken up with disputes over the command, negotiations over provisions and, perhaps most important, booty and payment for the soldiers who were, after all, mercenaries whose original paymaster, Kyros, was no longer in a position to provide for them. The feeling of many of the mercenaries, especially the Arkadian contingent which had formed the nucleus of Kyros' personal bodyguard, was that they should cut their losses and return home as quickly as possible. Suspicions lingered that Xenophon wanted, for reasons of personal glory and gain, to stay in Asia with the army. He is therefore careful in his account to show that he was not responsible for the slow disbandment of the army, whose proximity the Spartan governors of the Hellespontine cities found embarrassing. Finally, he makes a special point of telling his readers that he had been forced to sell his horse to pay for his homeward passage, and that it was only a windfall of booty in the last raid that left him in pocket.

Xenophon's estate in Skillous was near enough to many of the cities of Arkadia and Akhaia for some of his fellow-officers, now in retirement like himself, to have been neighbours. It is certain that other versions of the story were published, one of which was by an Arkadian, Sophainetos of Stymphalos. Xenophon's position was by no means secure: it was highly desirable for him, as an Athenian living under Spartan protection on Peloponnesian soil, to convince his neighbours that he had earned his comfortable retirement fairly. Unfortunately for him it was probably his Spartan connexion that ended his long sojourn at Skillous. When Spartan arms were broken by the Theban phalanx at the Battle of Leuktra (371 B.C.), she was no longer able to protect her Athenian friend, and Xenophon had to leave his estate, expelled by Sparta's enemies, the men of Elis.

We do not know for certain where he settled after this. Corinth is named by one source as both his destination after leaving Skillous and his final resting-place. But there is also a tradition that the Athenians rescinded his exile. Again, no authority says that he

returned to his native city, but we hear that his sons fought in the
Athenian cavalry at Mantineia (362 B.C.), and Gryllos was killed.
A story preserved by several ancient writers tells that the news of
Gryllos' death was brought to Xenophon while he was conducting a
sacrifice. On hearing the news, he removed his sacrificial crown,
but continued the sacrifice. When the messenger added that Gryllos
had died fighting bravely, Xenophon restored the crown to his head,
and testified to the gods that he felt greater joy at his son's
bravery than bitterness at his death. Unfortunately none of our
sources tells us where Xenophon was when he received this news, so
we are forced to rely upon the later testimony of Diogenes Laertius
(2nd century A.D.) that Xenophon resided at Corinth for most of
his remaining years. The decree of Euboulos by which his exile was
rescinded may have been as early as 387/6 B.C.; he may, therefore,
have been free to return to Athens some sixteen years before he was
expelled from Skillous; but he seems to have chosen not to do so. On
the other hand, Athens was still the literary centre of the Greek
world, and most of what he wrote must have been intended primarily
for Athenian readers. In particular, the Sokratic works - *Memorabilia*, *Apology* and *Symposium* were written with the purpose of mod-
ifying current views of the philospher's teaching and character.
The *Cavalry Commander*, in particular, was a manual based on Athenian
practice; and the *Revenues* (if that treatise is by Xenophon) had as
its subject the economic problems of Athens and their solution. It
therefore seems very likely that he visited his native city on a
number of occasions after his exile was rescinded, perhaps to introduce his latest writings and to accompany his sons to their enroll-
ment in the cavalry. The latest historical references in his writings
establish that he was still alive in 356/5 B.C. An isolated source
includes him in a list of famous men who attained ninety years. This
would mean that, if our dating of his birth is correct, Xenophon
died some time around 339 to 337 B.C. That Xenophon enjoyed a long
old age is not impossible, but this single testimony does not inspire
confidence. The question of the date of Xenophon's death must remain
open.

2. *Xenophon's Character and Talent.*

One of the most attractive personalities to come down to us
from the Classical World, Xenophon, in spite of his admiration for
Sparta, was in many ways a typical Athenian of the sort idealized
by ancient writers: fond of activity, keen to assume responsibility,
sensitive to the mood of those around him, versatile and resourceful,
he also found time to think about some of the problems affecting the
human condition. It is characteristic of the man that his main con-
clusions were optimistic, in spite of his own mixed experiences of
life. His optimism, based on conventional unquestioning piety -
there is no reason to believe that his frequent recourse to sacrifices in the *Anabasis* was not sincere - is matched only by his desire
to communicate it to others, both in the course of his adventures
and in his writings. A didactic thread runs through his work. He
was interested in the problem of ideal leadership, and after his own

military aspirations had run their course, he sublimated them in his
writings by trying to find and analyse the qualities of leadership
in others. His obituary tribute to Kyros should be read as part of
a developing theory to which Xenophon added in his later writings.
Self-discipline, example to others, honesty and fair-dealing are
the essential qualities of a leader who wishes to have the willing
obedience of those under his command, whether in an army or a state.
Compulsion should be necessary only with miscreants and occasionally
in times of emergency. A general must provide for his troops and
be ever on the watch for an advantage over the enemy. Xenophon ap-
plies these principles of generalship to political leadership, and
his exemplars are both kings and generals: Agesilaos, whom he accompanied on his campaigns, is the subject of one of his monographs
(*Agesilaos*); and the elder Kyros, who founded the Persian empire
and was by Xenophon's time a semi-mythical figure, is treated at
much greater length in an historical romance in eight books, the
Cyropaedia. They reappear in his dialogue *Hiero*, in which the poet
Simonides advises the Sicilian tyrant of that name how he may render
his rule more tolerable both to himself and his subjects. All his
writings are based on his practical experience of life to some degree, none more so than his treatise *On Horsemanship*.

The range of subject-matter covered in Xenophon's Sokratic
works is also determined by his practical and empirical outlook.
There is a story which tells how Xenophon became a pupil of Sokrates. The old philosopher met the handsome youth in a narrow passage, and stretched out his staff to bar his way. He then inquired
where every kind of commodity could be obtained, and upon receiving
an answer to each of his questions, finally asked: 'And where do
men acquire virtue?' Xenophon was puzzled, and Sokrates said: 'Then
follow me and learn'. But this story must not be allowed to deceive
us; what Sokrates offered and what Xenophon derived from his teaching need not have been the same. From Xenophon's pages Sokrates
emerges as a sound, if prosaic moralist teaching not 'virtue' in the
absolute sense but the practical virtues of self-sufficiency, self-
control, frugality and respect for the laws and authorities which
uphold them. Most of Book 3 of the *Memorabilia* is devoted to the
qualities and duties of an army officer, a subject dear to Xenophon
but not associated by other writers with Sokrates. This should
make us approach the Sokratic writings with reservations. Again,
Sokrates is made to say on more than one occasion that it is point-
less to carry studies beyond the needs of practical utility. If
this was Sokrates' philosophical position, it was close to that of
the Sophists, who confused goodness with efficiency. Since we know
that Sokrates attacked certain aspects of Sophistic teaching, we
must deduce that Xenophon's account of Sokrates is incomplete, and
perhaps even misleading, being limited by his own tastes and his
intellectual capacity. On this showing, and with Plato and Arist-
otle for comparison, we should not include Xenophon among the great
Greek philosophers, as Cicero and some of his Roman contemporaries
did. He was concerned with moral improvement rather than the cultivation of the mind. It is perhaps because of these rather limited

aims that the *Memorabilia* are for the most part less interesting
than those of Xenophon's writings which describe his moral precepts
in practice. His best Sokratic work is the *Oikonomikos*, a dialogue
on estate management based on his own experience, which incidentally
contains a delightful and piquant description of the wife's role. He
also wrote a *Symposium* and an *Apology*. But the *Anabasis* is his
freshest and liveliest work: all the important virtues and vices are
there displayed, all the worst dangers and pitfalls overcome by attention to them; and the author's part is cleverly woven into the
fabric of the narrative, never too obtrusive but always present. By
the time we reach the end we are in no doubt that it was Xenophon's
Anabasis, Xenophon's achievement. This is how the story affected
early readers. Arrian, who wrote the fullest extant account of Alexander's expedition and was himself a field officer with experience
of war against barbarians, styled himself 'the second Xenophon'. The
Anabasis was read by other Greek and Roman historians and its unique
mixture of forward-moving narrative and descriptive detail was in-
fluential. Finally, ancient literary critics, admiring the effort-
less facility and sweetness of his style, called him 'the Attic bee'.
Honey aids the digestion, and Xenophon's Greek seems to have similar
congenial properties.

3. *Greece and Persia.*

    The Persians were called 'barbarians' by the Greeks, in common
with all other peoples who did not speak Greek but spoke gibberish -
barbaros (βάρβαρος) being an onomatopoeic word to describe inartic-
ulate speech. Relations between the two civilizations could at no
point in history be defined in terms of universal friendship or hostility. Even during the great Persian War (480 - 79 B.C.) some
mainland Greek states, and most of those of Ionian Greece, fought
on the Persian side, while on a personal level Themistokles of Athens, the man who carried the greatest single responsibility for the
defeat of the Persians at the Battle of Salamis (480 B.C.), subsequently found refuge in the Persian court from the attacks of his political enemies. The Persians compensated for their naval and military shortcomings by consummate diplomatic skill. After the Persian
Wars their policy was, as Xenophon himself was fully aware, to maintain all Greek cities, as far as lay in their power, in a state of
weakness, encouraging them with promises of aid to fight one another,
and if necessary adding to the strength of the weaker in order that
it should fight on more equal terms with the stronger. During the
concluding years of the Peloponnesian War they helped Sparta build
a fleet to match that of Athens. After the war, as they saw Sparta
supreme and threatening to overrun the western satrapies, they
helped the Athenians rebuild their fleet.

    The greatest empire up to its time, and one of the greatest of
the ancient world, the Achaemenid kingdom was formed from the older
empires of Persia and Media by Kyros the Great in 559 B.C. He ruled
it for thirty years until his death, and built his capital city at
Sousa. This city was not only the King's seat but also the hub of

a complex system of roads which stretched to the corners of the empire. Satraps ruled with wide powers in twenty provinces, but each
owed allegiance to the King, who supervised them vicariously through
his agents, each known as 'the King's eye'. There was also a communication system employing riders spaced at stages with fresh horses.
But the King, remote from events as he was from his people, who regarded him as a demigod, was usually in a poor position to make informed decisions; while on a practical level the efficiency with
which an empire can be defended depends upon the speed with which
armed troops can be mobilised and brought to a trouble-spot. In
peace-time the satraps did not maintain large mobile armies, only
garrisons at strategic points, and these could be by-passed. The
sheer extent of the empire - Sousa was three months' march from the
Aegean coast - made it vulnerable to swift incursions. But the
special danger of Kyros' march lay in the fact that he was himself
a satrap, whose activities could not be clearly seen for what they
were until he transgressed his eastern boundaries. By then he was
some way towards his objective, in spite of the vigilance of
Tissaphernes.

4. *Greek Mercenary Armies.*

        Military service was as integral a part of Greek as of Roman
life. In Sparta it was compulsory and unpaid for all full citizens
[*Spartiatai* (Σπαρτιᾶται)]. Elsewhere in Greece, but especially in
Arkadia, Akhaia and Aitolia, conflict of some kind was for much of
the time either imminent or actual, so that pay was necessary to
enable those who were thus continuously involved to obtain a liveli-
hood. Again, in particular states power was sought by individuals
who, when successful, were called 'tyrants'. These usurpers needed
to employ the services of seasoned soldiers both to acquire and to
maintain their dominion. The tyrants were the first historical em-
ployers of mercenaries; but after every war there were always men
who had enjoyed the experience, or whose homes and family life had
been ruined in the course of it. It was natural that such men
should feel less tied to their cities, and should seek service for
pay with their recent enemy after the Persian Wars. We find Arkadian mercenary hoplites in regular service on the staffs of Persian
satraps during the period 480 - 430 B.C.; and Kyros, some four years
before he raised the Ten Thousand (i.e. in 405 B.C.), had an Arkadian bodyguard of 300 hoplites under Xenias. He and his agents already had contacts in Greece through these and through the Greek
officers whom he employed to command the garrisons in his satrapy.
Xenophon's account of the recruitment of the army shows that it was
done in a piecemeal way, producing a composite force of nine contingents under nine different leaders. This was inevitable for two
reasons. Even at such a favourable time as 401 B.C., soon after
a great war, numbers of mercenaries available in any single area
were not great; and Kyros required a larger mercenary force than had
previously been assembled in the Aegean area. He was one of the few
generals who could find the money to pay so many.

Even after assembly at Kelainai, the Ten Thousand regarded themselves as separate armies under different leaders. Some were serving
under officers who had commanded them during the Peloponnesian War
and had kept in touch with them. The attraction to such men of an
expedition under Kyros was obvious. He had supplied the Spartans
with large amounts of money in the closing years of the war, and
there was a widespread belief, confirmed by those already in his
service, that there was more to be had from that source. It was
money, in the end, rather than release, that they demanded when
they heard that the expedition was to be against the Great King
himself instead of the Pisidians, as they had been given to understand. Kyros, as paymaster, was acknowledged as commander-in-chief
in battle, but each contingent marched under the orders of its own
commander. There was rivalry and sometimes even conflict among
them. Xenophon also recounts many instances of indiscipline, including insolence, disobedience, assault on an officer, desertion
and mutiny. But such was the professional training of both officers and men that the imminence of battle imposed an automatic discipline, and they fought at Kounaxa with far greater cohesion than
the King's army.

5. *Xenophon and the Hoplite Army.*

The superiority of the Greek *hoplite* (lit. 'shield-carrier')
over his various barbarian counterparts is to be explained in both
military and political terms. Heavily-armed infantry arose in the
Greek *polis* as a citizen militia. It was drawn from those wealthy
enough to provide their own armour and weapons, but with insuffic-
ient means to equip a horse and serve with the highest class of
citizens in the cavalry. For various reasons, mainly economic,
cavalry played a relatively insignificant part in Greek warfare
up to the fourth century. Hoplites, on the other hand, decided
all major land battles. They combined the concept of self-sufficiency with that of co-operation to a remarkable degree in the manner of fighting that they adopted. They moved as a unit, close
together, with shields providing massive protection and spears held
horizontally for the charge as well as cast. The old Greek hoplite
army was a group of free men acting as one in battle for the common
good. No barbarian force fought with the same unity of purpose,
and the cavalry, archers and lightly-armed skirmishers which the
Persians found so effective against native tribes could not pierce
the hoplites' defences or stem their relentless progress when battle
was joined on open ground. The historian Herodotus noted the individual bravery of the Persians at the Battle of Plataia (479 B.C.)
and its futility against the Spartan line of bronze shields.

But Xenophon and his companions on the return march to the sea
had to cross terrain which was unfavourable to traditional hoplite
fighting. One of the main reasons why the *Anabasis* and its author
have always been admired by military historians is because Xenophon
appears to have devised original tactics to meet the peculiar difficulties which the Ten Thousand encountered. The two which he

employed to greatest effect were the occupation of heights above pas-
ses before the main force passed through and the dynamic use of a
mobile rearguard. In the latter the army's small contingent of
cavalry was deployed with great skill, and Xenophon's own part in
the manoeuvres was prominent. There are many examples of resource-
fulness and improvisation to add colour to the story and excite
our admiration. A typical example comes during an attack by the
Kardoukhoi, who discharged outsize arrows at them from large bows.
The Greeks collected these, fitted them with throwing straps or
thongs, and returned them as javelins. But it is in deliberation
perhaps more than in action that Xenophon's story constantly reminds
us that, although his subject is war, it is conducted through the
processes of city-state politics - by consultation among officers,
harangue and persuasion of the assembly, and open decision freely
reached and agreed. Xenophon's dream of founding a new city in such
a company is very understandable.

6. *Language and Style.*

     Before Xenophon's departure from Athens in 401, the development
of her literary dialect was mainly in the hands of the dramatic
poets. It was during the years of his sojourn in Asia and the Peloponnese that an Attic prose dialect became distinguished and reg-
ularised in the writings of Lysias, Isokrates and Plato. The con-
cepts of 'Attic purity' and 'normal Attic usage' took root in the
minds of resident Athenian authors, but Xenophon, absent from the
city at the critical time when his literary style was being formed,
remained largely impervious to their influence. Hence his style,
though basically Attic, shows many deviations from the pure dialect
of Plato and the Attic Orators. The most important are the following:

1. The widespread use of ὡς and ὡς ἄν where Attic prose writers
use ὅπως and ὅπως ἄν, introducing purpose clauses and clauses dependent on verbs of caring, striving and precaution. In the latter
type of clause he even uses ὡς with the future indicative instead
of the regular Attic ὅπως.

2. A marked partiality for the optative after ὡς ἄν and ὅπως ἄν
even in primary sequence, influenced perhaps by its 'potential'
force. Indeed, his partiality for the optative makes him much less
inclined than other prose writers to employ the subjunctive for
'vivid' effect in historic sequence.

3. Occasional use of ὡς for ὥστε + infinitive or indicative in a
consecutive (result) clause.

4. Several prepositional usages: σύν + dative (Attic usually μετά +
genitive); ἀνά and ἀμφί, rarely found in Attic authors; ἐκ, παρά and
πρός + genitive (Attic usually ὑπό + genitive) with passive verbs.
When found in Attic Greek these are mainly fifth century usages.

5. Most pervasive of all, many words which are not found in Attic

prose authors. In all his writings there are 99 words which belong to the Ionic and 62 to the Doric dialect, as well as over 300 found elsewhere only in poetry.

Xenophon achieved the liveliness and natural flow of his style which ancient critics admired by readily identifiable means. He tended to avoid the clausal complexity of the periodic style, generally preferring the running sequence of simple sentences and parallel, co-ordinate clauses. Most noticeable is his use of tense variation, with the historic present frequently employed to give immediacy and to provide high points in swiftly-moving narratives. His word-order also adds greatly to the liveliness of his style: in particular, he frequently promotes finite verbs to early positions in their clauses, thus increasing the prominence given to the action. In descriptive passages, on the other hand, verbal forms are often kept to a minimum, and their occasional omission (*ellipsis*) contributes to the informal tone of the writing.

Xenophon is not one of the more rhetorical of Greek prose writers. His favourite figure of speech is *anaphora*, beginning parallel clauses with the same word. He also achieves emphasis by disturbing the natural collocation of words (*hyperbaton*) by, for example, separating nouns from their adjectives. He also uses *asyndeton*, the omission of connecting particles and conjunctions in order to increase the speed of the narrative or the thought. Prominent among his favourite particles are δή, καί ... δή, τε καί, and μέντοι with sharp internal contrast, all of which typify the style of a demonstrative raconteur telling his story with animation and enthusiasm. Only by reading his story in the original Greek can we fully appreciate these and other felicities of his style.

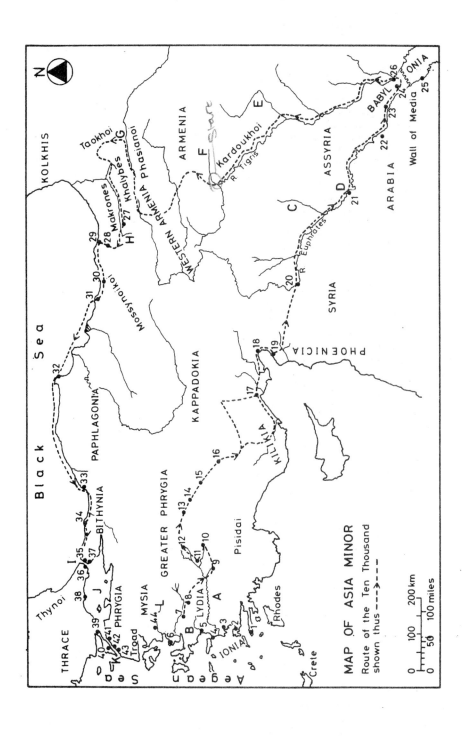

MAP OF ASIA MINOR

Route of the Ten Thousand
shown thus ---->---

PLACES AND TRIBES

The names in this list are given first in the form in which they appear in this volume (mostly directly transliterated from the Greek). The forms given in brackets by several entries are Latinized or Anglicized versions which may well be found in other works and in Classical Atlases.

Map Reference

Abydos (*Abydus*), Greek city in the Troad.   42
Aegean Sea, between Greece and Asia.
Aigospotamoi (*Aegospotami*), site of battle, in the   40
    Thracian Chersonese.
Aitolia (*Aetolia*), land in west Greece.
Akhaia (*Achaea*), land in northern Peloponnesos.
Akhaia Phthiotis, district in Thessaly.
Akragas, Greek city in Sicily.
Amphipolis, city in Makedonia.
Amprakia (*Ambracia*), city in Epeiros.
Apollonia, town in Mysia south of Propontis.
Arabia, land south of Syria and Assyria.
Araxes, tributary of Euphrates in Syria (*cf.* Phasis).   C
Arkadia (*Arcadia*), land in central Peloponnesos.
Armenia, satrapy in western Asia.
Asia, area roughly equivalent to modern Turkey.
Asine, town in Messenia.
Assyria, satrapy from the Euphrates to beyond the
    Tigris.
Athens, chief city of Attica.
Attica, land in east Greece.

Babylon, chief city in Babylonia, seat of royal   25
    power.
Babylonia, satrapy between the Euphrates and the
    Tigris.
Bithynia, satrapy in northern Asia.
Black Sea, north of Asia.
Boiotia (*Boeotia*), land in east Greece, north of
    Attika.
Bosporos (*Bosphorus*), strait connecting Propontis   I
    with the Black Sea.
Byzantion (*Byzantium*), Greek city west of Bosporos   36
    (modern Istanbul).

C-, see K-.
Chersonese, Thracian, peninsula north of Hellespont.
Corinth, city in north-eastern Peloponnesos.
Crete, island south of Aegean Sea.

Map Reference

Dardanos (*Dardanus*), Greek city in the Troad.   43
Delphoi (*Delphi*), city in Phokis.

Egypt, former Persian satrapy.
Elis, land in western Peloponnesos.
Ephesos (*Ephesus*), Greek city in Ionia.   5
Eretria, city in Euboia.
Erkheia (*Erchia*), district in Attica.
Euphrates, longest river of western Persian
   Empire.
Euxine Sea (see Black Sea).

Gambrion, town in Mysia.
Gryneion (*Grynium*), town in Mysia.
Gymnias, city in north of western Armenia.   27

Halikarnassos (*Halicarnassus*), Greek city in   2
   south-west Asia.
Halisarna, town in Mysia.
Harpasos, river in north of western Armenia.   H
Hellespont, strait connecting Aegean Sea with   K
   Propontis.
Herakleia (*Heraclea*), Greek city in Bithynia.   33
Hymettos (*Hymettus*), mountain in Attica.
Hyrkania (*Hyrcania*), satrapy south-east of Casp-
   ian Sea.

Ikonion (*Iconium*), town in Greater Phrygia.   16
Ionia, land on west coast of Asia.
Issoi (*Issus*), town in Kilikia.   18
Isthmus of Corinth, between northern Greece and
   Peloponnesos.

Kaïkos (*Caïcus*), river in Mysia.   L
Kalkhedon (*Chalcedon*), Greek city east of Bosporos.   37
Kalkhedonia, district around Kalkhedon.
Kalpes Limen (Harbour of Kalpe), town in Bithynia.   34
Kappadokia (*Cappadocia*), satrapy in central Asia.
Kardoukhoi (*Carduchians*), tribe between Assyria and
   Armenia (modern Kurdestan).
Karkasos (*Carcasus*), river in Mysia.
Kastolos (*Castolus*), town in Lydia.   8
Kaÿstros (*Caÿster*), river in western Asia.   B
Kaÿstrou Pedion (Kaÿstros Plain), town in Greater   13
   Phrygia.
Kelainai (*Celaenae*), city in Phrygia.   10
Kentrites (*Centrites*), tributary of the Tigris, in   F

Map Reference

south of Armenia.

Keramon Agora (Potters' Market), town in Greater Phrygia.   12

Kerasous (*Cerasus*), city in north-eastern Asia.   30

Khalybes (*Chalybes*), tribe in north of Armenia.

Kharmande, city in Arabia.   22

Khrysopolis, (*Chrysopolis*) Greek city east of Bosporos.   35

Kilikia (*Cilicia*), satrapy in south Asia.

Knidos (*Cnidus*), Greek city in south-western Asia.   1

Kolkhis (*Colchis*), land south-east of Black Sea.

Kolkhoi, inhabitants of Kolkhis.

Kolossai (*Colossae*), city in Greater Phrygia.   9

Komania, place in Mysia, near Pergamos.

Koroneia (*Coronea*), town in Boiotia, site of battle.

Korsote, town in Assyria.   21

Kotyora, Greek city in north-eastern Asia.   31

Kounaxa (*Cunaxa*), village in Babylonia, site of battle.   24

Laconia, land in southern Peloponnesos.

Lakedaimon (*Lacedaemon*), see Sparta.

Lampsakos (*Lampsacus*), Greek city in the Troad.   41

Leontinoi (*Leontini*), Greek city in Sicily.

Leuktra (*Leuctra*), site of battle in Boiotia.

Lousoi or -ia, city in Arkadia.

Lydia, satrapy in western Asia.

Maiandros (*Maeander*), a river in western Asia.   A

Makedonia (*Macedon*), land in north-east of mainland Greece.

Makrones, tribe near Trapezous.

Mantineia (*Mantinea*), city in Arkadia.

Marathon, site of battle in north-east Attica.

Marsyas, tributary of the Maiandros in Greater Phrygia.

Maskas, 'loop' of the Euphrates, in Assyria.   D

Media, satrapy west of the Tigris.

Media, Wall of, near Babylon between the Euphrates and Tigris.

Megara, city on the Isthmus of Corinth.

Messenia, land in south-western Peloponnesos.

Methydrion (*Methydrium*), town in Arkadia.

Miletos (*Miletus*), Greek city in Ionia.   3

Mossynoikoi, tribe near Kerasous.

Mykale (*Mycale*), promontary in Lydia, site of battle.   4

Myriandros, Phoenician city in Syria.   19

Myrina, town in Mysia, north of Phokaia.

Mysia, satrapy in north-west Asia.

Olympia, town in Elis
Orkhomenos (*Orchomenus*), city in Arkadia.

Palaigambrion, town in Mysia.
Paphlagonia, satrapy in northern Asia.
Parnassos, mountain in Phokis.
Parrhasia, district in Arkadia.
Parthenion, town in Mysia.
Peloponnesos (*Peloponnese*), southern peninsula
  of Greece.
Peltai (*Peltae*), city in Greater Phrygia.   11
Pentelikos (*Pentelicus*), mountain in Attica.
Pergamos (*Pergamum*), Greek city in Mysia.   44
Perinthos, Greek city north of Propontis.   38
Persia, land north of Persian Gulf.
Persian Empire, 20 satrapies from Asia to the
  Indus river (modern Pakistan) and north to
  Skythia (the Caucasus).
Phasianoi, tribe near river Phasis.   G
Phasis, river in Armenia (called Araxes by other
  writers).
Phoenicia, land on east coast of Mediteranean Sea.
Phokaia (*Phocaea*), Greek city in Ionia.   6
Phokis (*Phocis*), land north of Gulf of Corinth.
Pholoë, mountain between Arkadia and Elis.
Phrygia, Greater, satrapy in central Asia.
Phrygia, Lesser (Hellespontine), land in north-
  western Asia.
Pisidai, tribes in southern Asia.
Plataia (*Plataea*), city in Boiotia, site of
  battle.
Propontis, sea between Aegean and Black Sea.   J
Pylai, border fort between Arabia and Babylonia.   23

Rhodes, island off south-western Asia.

Sacred Mount, at base of Thracian Chersonese.   39
Salamis, island west of Attica, site of battle.
Sardis, capital of Lydia.   7
Selinous (*Selinus*), river in Ephesos; river at
  Skillous.
Sinope, Greek city in Paphlagonia.   32
Sittake, city in Babylonia.   26
Skillous (*Scillus*), town in Triphylia, Elis.
Sousa (*Susa*), administrative centre of Persian
  Empire.
Sparta, chief city of Laconia.
Stymphalos (*Stymphalus*), city in Arkadia.
Syracuse, Greek city in Sicily.

Map Reference

Syria, satrapy between Arabia, Phoenicia and
  Assyria.

Taokhoi, tribe in north of Armenia.
Tarsoi (*Tarsus*), chief town in Kilikia (hellen-   17
  ized).
Teuthrania, town in Mysia, west of Pergamos.
Thapsakos (*Thapsacus*), city in Syria.   20
Thasos, island in north Aegean Sea.
Thebai (*Thebes*), chief city in Boiotia.
Thessaly, land in northern Greece.
Thekhes, mountain near Trapezous.   28
Thrace, land north-east of Aegean Sea.
Thymbrion, city in Greater Phrygia.   14
Thynoi, tribe in Thrace.
Tigris, major river east of the Euphrates.
Trapezous (*Trapezus*), Greek city in north-eastern   29
  Asia.
Triphylia, district in Elis.
Troad (Trojan Plain), district in north-west Asia
  (around Troy).
Tyriaion, city in Greater Phrygia.   15

Zapatas, tributary of the Euphrates in Assyria   E
  (modern Zab).

BOOK 1

1:1 Δαρείου καὶ Παρυσάτιδος γίγνονται παῖδες δύο,
πρεσβύτερος μὲν Ἀρταξέρξης, νεώτερος δὲ Κῦρος. ἐπεὶ
δὲ ἠσθένει Δαρεῖος καὶ ὑπώπτευε τελευτὴν τοῦ βίου,
1:2 ἐβούλετο τὼ παῖδε ἀμφοτέρω παρεῖναι. ὁ μὲν οὖν πρεσβύτερος παρὼν ἐτύγχανε· Κῦρον δὲ μεταπέμπεται ἀπὸ
τῆς ἀρχῆς ἧς αὐτὸν σατράπην ἐποίησε, καὶ στρατηγὸν
δὲ αὐτὸν ἀπέδειξε πάντων ὅσοι εἰς Καστωλοῦ πεδίον
ἀθροίζονται. ἀναβαίνει οὖν ὁ Κῦρος λαβὼν Τισσαφέρνη

1:1 Δαρείου καὶ Παρυσάτιδος γίγνονται: 'Dareios and Parysatis had';
pres. tense for lively narrative as the story begins; Dareios
II, King of Persia from 424 B.C., great-grandson of Dareios I
who had invaded Greece in 490 B.C.; Parysatis was his half-sis-
ter; there had been 13 sons altogether. * τελευτήν: i.e. that
it was near. * τοῦ βίου: 'of his life'; the definite article
may often be translated as a possessive adjective. * τὼ παῖδε
ἀμφοτέρω: acc. dual.

1:2 μεταπέμπεται: '(Dareios) sent for', historic pres., used for vividness; see Introduction 6. * σατράπην: Kyros, as satrap,
ruled Lydia, Greater Phrygia and Kappadokia, i.e. most of Western Asia Minor. * ἐποίησε: 'had made'; aor. in subordinate
clause may often be translated as a pluperf. This had been in
408, when Kyros was only seventeen. * καὶ στρατηγὸν δὲ: 'and
also ... commander-in-chief'; δέ forms the connexion with the
previous sentence, and καί emphasises the following word(s);
this sentence, though grammatically independent, is parallel
in sense with the preceding relative clause.
πάντων ὅσοι ... : 'of all (those troops) who muster in the plain
of Kastolos'; Kastolos was about 30 miles east of Sardis, capital of Lydia; a plain was essential for the annual assembly
and inspection of all the satrapy's troops by the King or his
agent. Greek states had been weakening the Persian Empire's
unity in the west by playing off one satrap against another;
Dareios hoped to stop this by giving Kyros this exceptionally
large command, despite his youth.
ἀναβαίνει: 'went up', 'went inland' to Sousa, one of the Empire's
administrative centres, probably from Sardis via the Royal Road
(up to a month's journey by carriage, cf. Herodotus 5.52 - 53).
* λαβὼν Τισσαφέρνη ... : 'taking Tissaphernes (with him),
(regarding him) as a friend'; Kyros had taken over Lydia from
Tissaphernes, who had been satrap of Lydia and Ionia, and seems
not to have noticed any resentment felt by Tissaphernes.

ὡς φίλον, καὶ τῶν Ἑλλήνων δὲ ἔχων ὁπλίτας ἀνέβη
1:3 τριακοσίους, ἄρχοντα δὲ αὐτῶν Ξενίαν Παρράσιον. ἐπεὶ
δὲ ἐτελεύτησε Δαρεῖος καὶ κατέστη εἰς τὴν βασιλείαν
Ἀρταξέρξης, Τισσαφέρνης διαβάλλει τὸν Κῦρον πρὸς τὸν
ἀδελφὸν ὡς ἐπιβουλεύοι αὐτῷ. ὁ δὲ πείθεταί τε καὶ
συλλαμβάνει Κῦρον ὡς ἀποκτενῶν· ἡ δὲ μήτηρ ἐξαιτησα-
1:4 αμένη αὐτὸν ἀποπέμπει πάλιν ἐπὶ τὴν ἀρχήν. ὁ δ' ὡς
ἀπῆλθε κινδυνεύσας καὶ ἀτιμασθείς, βουλεύεται ὅπως
μήποτε ἔτι ἔσται ἐπὶ τῷ ἀδελφῷ, ἀλλ', ἢν δύνηται,
βασιλεύσει ἀντ' ἐκείνου. Παρύσατις μὲν δὴ ἡ μήτηρ
ὑπῆρχε τῷ Κύρῳ, φιλοῦσα αὐτὸν μᾶλλον ἢ τὸν βασιλεύ-
1:5 οντα Ἀρταξέρξην. ὅστις δ' ἀφικνοῖτο τῶν παρὰ βασιλέως πρὸς αὐτόν, πάντας οὕτω διατιθεὶς ἀπεπέμπετο

* τῶν Ἑλλήνων: partitive gen. Many Greeks, unemployed or exiled after the Peloponnesian War, went abroad as mercenary soldiers (see Introduction 4). * ἔχων: 'having' may often be
translated as 'with'. * ὁπλίτας: the regular heavy-armed infantry of Greek warfare; here used as a bodyguard, and paid a
special bonus.

1:3 ἐτελεύτησε: 'had died'; κατέστη: 'had been established'; see on
ἐποίησε, 1:2 above. κατέστη, strong aor. (intrans.) of καθ-
ίστημι. * διαβάλλει ... ὡς ἐπιβουλεύοι: lit. 'slanders ...
(saying) that he was plotting', i.e. 'falsely accused him ...
of plotting'; opt. in indir. statement as if after a historic
main verb (historic pres.). Xenophon accepts the falsity of
the accusation.
ὁ δὲ πείθεται: 'the (King) believed (him)', the definite article
used as a pronoun with δέ, indicating a change of grammatical
subject. * ὡς + fut. part., expressing purpose.
ἐξαιτησαμένη: 'secured his release and ... '; part. + main verb
may often be translated by two main verbs joined by 'and'.

1:4 ὁ δ' ὡς: 'when he'. * βουλεύεται ὅπως ... ἔσται: lit. 'he
considers (historic pres.) how ... he will (would) be'; ὅπως
+ fut. indic. after verb of precaution. * ἢν = ἐάν.

1:5 ὅστις δ' ἀφικνοῖτο: 'whoever came', opt., indefinite, dependent
on historic main verb. τῶν παρὰ βασιλέως: lit. 'of those from
King'; βασιλεύς, with no article, always means the King of Persia. Kyros' visitors included inspectors who visited the satrapies annually and reported any irregularity to the King. δια-
τιθείς: pres. part. of διατίθημι.

ὥστε αὐτῷ μᾶλλον φίλους εἶναι ἢ βασιλεῖ. καὶ τῶν
παρ' ἐαυτῷ δὲ βαρβάρων ἐπεμελεῖτο ὡς πολεμεῖν τε
1:6 ἱκανοὶ εἶησαν καὶ εὐνοϊκῶς ἔχοιεν αὐτῷ. τὴν δὲ ʽΕλλ-
ηνικὴν δύναμιν ἤθροιζεν ὡς μάλιστα ἐδύνατο ἐπικρυπτόμενος, ὅπως ὅτι ἀπαρασκευότατον λάβοι βασιλέα. ὧδε
οὖν ἐποιεῖτο τὴν συλλογήν. ὁπόσας εἶχε φυλακὰς ἐν
ταῖς πόλεσι παρήγγειλε τοῖς φρουράρχοις ἑκάστοις
λαμβάνειν ἄνδρας Πελοποννησίους ὅτι πλείστους καὶ
βελτίστους, ὡς ἐπιβουλεύοντος Τισσαφέρνους ταῖς πόλεσι. καὶ γὰρ ἦσαν αἱ Ἰωνικαὶ πόλεις Τισσαφέρνους τὸ
ἀρχαῖον ἐκ βασιλέως δεδομέναι, τότε δ' ἀφειστήκεσαν

καὶ τῶν παρ' ἐαυτῷ ... : 'he would also take care that his native following ... '; the subject of the subordinate clause is
often anticipated in the main sentence, here gen. with ἐπεμελεῖτο; phrases like οἱ παρ' ἐαυτῷ, οἱ σὺν ἐαυτῷ, τὸ καθ' ἐαυτούς
are best translated by collective nouns such as 'staff', 'train',
'section'; for καὶ ... δέ, see on 1:2 above. * εἶησαν = εἶεν,
opt. of εἰμί 'be'; this and ἔχοιεν are opt. in a historic purpose clause; for Xenophon's use of ὡς, see Introduction 6.1.

1:6 ἤθροιζεν: 'proceeded (began) to collect', imperf. for a continuing activity. * ὡς μάλιστα ἐδύνατο ἐπικρυπτόμενος: 'as secretly as possible'; the verb δύναμαι is often omitted from this
type of phrase, so that ὡς + superlative = 'as ... as possible'.
* ὅτι ἀπαρασκευότατον: ὅτι + superlative, as ὡς. * λάβοι:
opt. in historic purpose clause.
ὧδε οὖν ἐποιεῖτο ... : 'so he set about recruiting his forces as
follows'; ὧδε and ὅδε often refer to what immediately follows.
ὁπόσας εἶχε ... : lit. 'as many as he had garrisons in the cities
he sent orders to the garrison commanders each' i.e. 'he sent
orders to each and every commander of all the garrisons he had
in the Greek cities'; relative clauses may be placed early in
Greek for emphasis, where English puts them later. * φυλακάς: from φυλακή. There were about a dozen Greek cities on the
Ionian coast; the satrap stationed troops on their citadels to
guard them.
Πελοποννησίους: the best hoplites; Arkadians had served as mercenaries on both sides of the war between Athens and Sparta
(Thucydides 3.34; 7.57 - 58). Their commander here was to be
Xenias. * ὡς ἐπιβουλεύοντος Τισσαφέρνους: 'on the pretext
that Tissaphernes was plotting', gen. absolute. καὶ γὰρ ἦσαν
... : lit. 'and (this was plausible) for the Ionian cities did
belong to Tissaphernes (gen.)'; ἦσαν is in the emphatic position
('they were in fact'). * ἐκ βασιλέως: 'by the King' (i.e.
Dareios); a usage (ἐκ = ὑπό) found in the Ionic dialect, older
Attic prose, and poetry.   (cont.)

1:7 πρὸς Κῦρον πᾶσαι πλὴν Μιλήτου· ἐν Μιλήτῳ δὲ Τισσαφ-
ἐρνης προαισθόμενος τὰ αὐτὰ ταῦτα βουλευομένους,
τοὺς μὲν ἀπέκτεινε τοὺς δ᾽ ἐξέβαλεν. ὁ δὲ Κῦρος
ὑπολαβὼν τοὺς φεύγοντας συλλέξας στράτευμα ἐπολιόρκει Μίλητον καὶ κατὰ γῆν καὶ κατὰ θάλατταν καὶ
ἐπειρᾶτο κατάγειν τοὺς ἐκπεπτωκότας. καὶ αὕτη αὖ
1:8 ἄλλη πρόφασις ἦν αὐτῷ τοῦ ἀθροίζειν στράτευμα. πρὸς
δὲ βασιλέα πέμπων ἠξίου ἀδελφὸς ὢν αὐτοῦ δοθῆναι οἷ
ταύτας τὰς πόλεις μᾶλλον ἢ Τισσαφέρνη ἄρχειν αὐτῶν,
καὶ ἡ μήτηρ συνέπραττεν αὐτῷ ταῦτα, ὥστε βασιλεὺς
τὴν μὲν πρὸς ἑαυτὸν ἐπιβουλὴν οὐκ ἠσθάνετο, Τισσαφέρνει δὲ ἐνόμιζε πολεμοῦντα αὐτὸν ἀμφὶ τὰ στρατ-
εύματα δαπανᾶν· ὥστε οὐδὲν ἤχθετο αὐτῶν πολεμούντων.
καὶ γὰρ ὁ Κῦρος ἀπέπεμπε τοὺς γιγνομένους δασμοὺς

* δεδομέναι: perf. part. pass. of δίδωμι. * ἀφειστήκεσαν:
'had gone over'; pluperf. (intrans.) of ἀφίστημι.] Tissaphernes
had now lost virtually all Ionia, as well as Lydia.

1:7 τὰ αὐτὰ ταῦτα ... : 'that they were planning (to do) the same'.

* τοὺς μὲν ... τοὺς δ(έ): 'some ... others', a usage of the
article as pronoun. Tissaphernes' fort at Miletos would have
helped him keep control.
ἐπολιόρκει: imperf.; see on ἤθροιζεν, 1:6 above. Kyros led the
land forces; the naval commander was Tamos, an Egyptian.
αὕτη αὖ ἄλλη ... : 'this again was another pretext ... for recruiting'; οὗτος and οὕτως often refer to what immediately
precedes; τό + inf. = verbal noun ('recruiting').

1:8 πέμπων sc. ἄγγελον: 'sending word'. * ἠξίου: imperf. for an
unresolved situation. * ἀδελφὸς ὢν αὐτοῦ: 'as he was his
brother', causal part. * δοθῆναι: aor. inf. pass. of δίδωμι.
* οἷ: dat. of reflexive pronoun (acc. ἕ, gen. οὗ) used in
subordinate clauses in indir. speech to refer to subject of
main verb. * μᾶλλον ἢ Τισσαφέρνη: 'rather than that Tissaphernes ... ' (acc. + inf.). * ἀμφὶ = περί of regular Attic
prose.
αὐτῶν πολεμούντων: causal part., either gen. after ἤχθετο or
gen. absolute.
καὶ γὰρ ὁ Κῦρος ... : 'especially as (καὶ γάρ) Kyros continued
to send off the tribute accruing to the King'. * δασμός: a
payment (usually annual) made by a subject nation to the ruling
power. The King allowed his satraps a measure of independence,
trusting that his inspectors or informers would report any ab-
use of it.

βασιλεῖ ἐκ τῶν πόλεων ὧν Τισσαφέρνους ἐτύγχανεν ἔχων.
1:9 ἄλλο δὲ στράτευμα αὐτῷ συνελέγετο ἐν Χερρονήσῳ τῇ
κατ' ἀντιπέρας Ἀβύδου τόνδε τὸν τρόπον. Κλέαρχος
Λακεδαιμόνιος φυγὰς ἦν· τούτῳ συγγενόμενος ὁ Κῦρος
ἠγάσθη τε αὐτὸν καὶ δίδωσιν αὐτῷ μυρίους δαρεικούς.
ὁ δὲ λαβὼν τὸ χρυσίον στράτευμα συνέλεξεν ἀπὸ τούτων
τῶν χρημάτων καὶ ἐπολέμει ἐκ Χερρονήσου ὁρμώμενος
τοῖς Θρᾳξὶ τοῖς ὑπὲρ Ἑλληιυπόντου οἰκοῦσι καὶ ὠφέλει
τοὺς Ἕλληνας· ὥστε καὶ χρήματα συνεβάλλοντο αὐτῷ
εἰς τὴν τροφὴν τῶν στρατιωτῶν αἱ Ἑλλησποντιακαὶ
πόλεις ἑκοῦσαι. τοῦτο δ' αὖ οὕτω τρεφόμενον ἐλάν-
1:10 θανεν αὐτῷ τὸ στράτευμα. Ἀρίστιππος δὲ ὁ Θετταλὸς
ξένος ὢν ἐτύγχανεν αὐτῷ, καὶ πιεζόμενος ὑπὸ τῶν οἴκοι

* τῶν πόλεων ὧν Τισσαφέρνους: 'the cities of Tissaphernes
which', relative pronoun attracted from acc. (object of ἔχων)
into case of antecedent πόλεων.

1:9 Χερρονήσῳ τῇ κατ' ἀντιπέρας Ἀβύδου: the Thracian Chersonese as
opposed to (e.g.) the Tauric one (on the Black Sea). * τόνδε
τὸν τρόπον: 'in the following way', adverbial acc.
ἠγάσθη: 'was struck with admiration', inceptive aor., indicating
the onset of a feeling. δίδωσιν: 3rd pers. s. pres. of δίδωμι.
* δαρεικούς (sc. στατῆρας): 'darics', gold coins (worth 25 - 26 Athenian drakhmai) introduced as a standard currency throughout the
empire by Dareios I. Kyros was paying his common soldiers one daric a month (about the same wage as a skilled craftsman), half of
which was spent on food; a captain (λοχαγός, commanding a λόχος,
'company' of up to 100 infantry) received twice this sum; a general
(στρατηγός) four times; booty would be a bonus.
ἀπὸ: 'with', 'using'. * ὑπὲρ ... : 'beyond the Hellespont',
i.e. from the Persian viewpoint. οἰκοῦσι: dat. pres. part.
of οἰκέω. * τοὺς Ἕλληνας: the half-dozen or so Greek cities
there were liable to be attacked by native Thracians.
καὶ χρήματα συνεβάλλοντο: 'were also contributing money'.
* ἑκοῦσαι: 'willingly', predicative, with an adverbial force.
τοῦτο δ' αὖ ... : τοῦτο (emphatic position) with τὸ στράτευμα
(the subject); τρεφόμενον ἐλάνθανε, lit. 'being maintained',
was escaping notice'; 'so here again was an army being secretly
maintained for him'.

1:10 ξένος: 'guest-friend'; ξενία was a traditional tie of hospitality
between families, cities, or individuals and foreign states;
guest and host were considered to be protected by Zeus Xenios.
                                                    (cont.)

ἀντιστασιωτῶν ἔρχεται πρὸς τὸν Κῦρον καὶ αἰτεῖται
αὐτὸν εἰς δισχιλίους ξένους καὶ τριῶν μηνῶν μισθόν,
ὡς οὕτως περιγενόμενος ἂν τῶν ἀντιστασιωτῶν. ὁ δὲ
Κῦρος δίδωσιν αὐτῷ εἰς τετρακισχιλίους καὶ ἓξ μηνῶν
μισθόν, καὶ δεῖται αὐτοῦ μὴ πρόσθεν καταλῦσαι πρὸς
τοὺς ἀντιστασιώτας πρὶν ἂν αὐτῷ συμβουλεύσηται.
οὕτω δὲ αὖ τὸ ἐν Θετταλίᾳ ἐλάνθανεν αὐτῷ τρεφόμενον
1:11 στράτευμα. Πρόξενον δὲ τὸν Βοιώτιον ξένον ὄντα αὐτῷ
ἐκέλευσε λαβόντα ἄνδρας ὅτι πλείστους παραγενέσθαι,
ὡς εἰς Πισίδας βουλόμενος στρατεύεσθαι, ὡς πράγματα
παρεχόντων τῶν Πισιδῶν τῇ ἑαυτοῦ χώρᾳ. Σοφαίνετον
δὲ τὸν Στυμφάλιον καὶ Σωκράτη τὸν Ἀχαιόν, ξένους

The Thessalians had aided the Persian King Xerxes I (486 - 465)
when he invaded Greece, and the connexion between the countries
probably began then. * πιεζόμενος ... : 'as his political opponents at home were making things hard for him', lit. 'being
hard pressed by ... '; feelings often ran high in Greek politics, and violence was common, sometimes, as here, leading to
military activity and foreign intervention; such conflict was
called στάσις.] * εἰς δισχιλίους ξένους ... : 'about two thousand mercenaries and three months' pay'; ξένος, after meaning
'guest-friend', meant any stranger or foreigner, especially
referring to mercenary soldiers serving abroad (μισθοφόροι).
Aristippos asked for 6000 darics and received 24,000; the commander of his troops was Menon. * ὡς οὕτως περιγενόμενος ἂν:
'as this would enable him to overcome'; ὡς + part., alleged
reason; this represents the dir. περιγενοίμην ἂν 'I would overcome', potential; sc. remote fut. condition 'if you were to
give me money', implied by οὕτως.
μὴ πρόσθεν καταλῦσαι ... : sc. τὸν πόλεμον, 'cease hostilities',
'come to terms'; μὴ πρόσθεν ... πρὶν, 'not ... before (or un-
till)'; πρὶν ἂν + subjunctive, indefinite; αὐτῷ refers back to
subject of main verb.

1:11 λαβόντα ... παραγενέσθαι: 'to get ... and join (him)'; see on
ἐξαιτησαμένη, 1:3 above. * ὅτι πλείστους: see on ὅτι, 1:6
above. * ὡς εἰς Πισίδας ... : ὡς + part., 'on the pretext of';
εἰς Πισίδας, 'into (the territory of the) Pisidians', a usage
of the Ionic dialect. * πράγματα παρεχόντων τῶν Πισιδῶν ... :
gen. absolute. Kyros had in fact previously campaigned against
the fiercely independent Pisidian hill-tribes, who tended to
flout the Phrygian satrap's authority.
Σωκράτην: no connexion with the Athenian philosopher of the same
name. * σύν + dat.: usually poetic, but regularly used by
Xenophon, = μετά + gen.; see Introduction 6.4.

ὄντας καὶ τούτους, ἐκέλευσεν ἄνδρας λαβόντας ἐλθεῖν
ὅτι πλείστους, ὡς πολεμήσων Τισσαφέρνει σὺν τοῖς
φυγάσι τῶν Μιλησίων. καὶ ἐποίουν οὕτως οὗτοι.

Silver *tetradrachmon*
showing portrait of
Tissaphernes; coin
minted *ca.* 400 B.C.

καὶ ἐποίουν οὕτως οὗτοι: οὗτος and ὅδε etc. are often used as
'paragraphing' devices for the listener (Greek literature was
written to be read aloud and listened to).

*It was remarkable that Kyros managed to keep his plans secret
from the King. Artaxerxes, however, was not suspicious but inclined to trust Kyros after the rejection of Tissaphernes' earlier
accusations (Parysatis helped here), and he considered the conflict between Kyros and Tissaphernes normal and acceptable; the
system of inspectors, spies and informers ensured that he would
learn of any attempt at revolt - or so he thought. The secret had
to be kept from the Greeks too: Kyros knew that they would never
willingly march so far inland with him, as this meant leaving fam-
iliar territory for months on end (cf. Herodotus 5.49 - 50). The
most important factor in Kyros' success was the loyalty of those
few who knew his plans.*

2:1   *Kyros' agents raised their contingents. Aristippos the*
to   *Thessalian, prompted by Kyros, settled his differences with*
4:19 *his political opponents; and Xenias the Arkadian, commanded*
      by Kyros to collect all troops not required for garrison work
      in his satrapy brought them to Sardis. Exiles from Tissaph-
      ernes' satrapy were also invited to assemble there, and this
      force was soon joined by further contingents from Greece with
      their commanders. Time was not on Kyros' side once Tissaph-
      ernes deduced from the size of the gathering army his true
      purpose and rode east to warn the King.

      Kyros marched for three days through Lydia to the Maian-
      dros river, and crossed the pontoon bridge which spanned it.
      A day later he reached Kolossai, where he stayed for seven
      days and was joined by Menon the Thessalian with 1000 hoplites
      and 500 peltasts, the contingent raised by Aristippos. His
      army reached its full strength when Klearkhos the Spartan,
      Sosis the Syracusan and Sophainetos the Stymphalian (Arkadian)
      caught up with him at the city of Kelainai on the Marsyas
      river, the site of one of the King's provincial palaces.

      The whole army at this stage was composed as follows:

Commander	Hoplites	Others
Xenias	4,000	
Klearkhos	1,000	800 peltasts
		200 archers
Proxenos	1,500	500 light infantry
Menon	1,000	500 peltasts
Sokrates (Akhaian)	500	
Pasion (Megarian)	300	300 peltasts
Sophainetos	1,000	
Sosis	300	

      Kheirisophos the Spartan joined the army in Kilikia with
      700 hoplites; and 400 Greek mercenaries deserted from the army
      of Abrokomas, satrap of Phoenicia. This gave Kyros a total
      of 10,700 hoplites and 2,300 lightly-armed infantry; but he
      had to supply such cavalry as he needed from native levies.

      In 25 days, of which 14 were spent on the march, the
      army reached the easternmost city of Phrygia, Ikonion. The
      distance covered was 350 miles.

      For the other 11 days the men had rested in the cities
      of Peltai, Keramon Agora, Thymbrion, Kaÿstrou Pedion and Tiri-
      aion, where Kyros staged a parade and a mock battle-charge in
      honour of Epyaxa, queen of Kilikia, who had supplied him with
      money to pay his army. After crossing the frontier into
      Kilikia they came to that country's capital city in 13 march-
      ing days from Ikonion, passing through Kappadokia, a distance

of 320 miles. Syennesis, king of Kilikia, who had originally intended to give Kyros' army a hostile reception, was
persuaded by his wife, and also perhaps by the prospect of
the widespread plundering of his kingdom, to supply Kyros with
the next instalment of his mercenaries' pay in return for
their peaceful passage out of his territory.

But for twenty days the Greeks refused to march. Klearkhos the Spartan now emerged as the foremost Greek leader.
He succeeded temporarily in allaying the men's suspicion that
they were marching against the King, and secured for them a
pay increase of fifty per cent. They reflected that they had
already gone too far to turn back; for without Kyros' good
will and practical help they would have found the return journey exceedingly hazardous.

The march was resumed. In 5 days they reached Issoi,
120 miles from Tarsoi, and in a further 21 days travelled
300 miles to Thapsakos, with a rest of 7 at Myriandros, a
Phoenician city. Two of the Greek mercenary commanders, Xenias and Pasion, jealous of the increasing influence of Klearkhos not only over Kyros but also over their own men, boarded
a ship at Myriandros and deserted.

On arrival at Thapsakos on the Euphrates, Kyros at last
revealed to the Greek generals that the purpose of the expedition
was to attack his brother, Artaxerxes the Great King.
Klearkhos probably knew Kyros' intention already, and the soldiers accused him of this; they also accused the other commanders, though probably with less justice. But the debate,
as recorded by Xenophon, was surprisingly short; the soldiers
merely demanded more money, and on receiving a promise of this,
agreed to continue the march. Menon the Thessalian, by being
the first to lead his men across the Euphrates, earned Kyros'
special praise. After a journey of 9 days and 200 miles
through Syria along the north bank of the Euphrates they
reached the river Araxes at a point where there were many
villages well supplied with corn and wine. Here they stayed
3 days and provided themselves with food.

5:1   ἐντεῦθεν ἐξελαύνει διὰ τῆς Ἀραβίας τὸν Εὐφράτην
       ποταμὸν ἐν δεξιᾷ ἔχων σταθμοὺς ἐρήμους πέντε παρα-
       σάγγας τριάκοντα καὶ πέντε. ἐν τούτῳ δὲ τῷ τόπῳ ἦν
       μὲν ἡ γῆ πεδίον ἅπαν ὁμαλὲς ὥσπερ θάλαττα, ἀψινθίου
       δὲ πλῆρες· εἰ δέ τι καὶ ἄλλο ἐνῆν ὕλης ἢ καλάμου,
5:2   ἅπαντα ἦσαν εὐώδη ὥσπερ ἀρώματα· δένδρον δ᾽ οὐδὲν
       ἐνῆν, θηρία δὲ παντοῖα, πλεῖστοι μὲν ὄνοι ἄγριοι,
       πολλαὶ δὲ στρουθοὶ αἱ μεγάλαι· ἐνῆσαν δὲ καὶ ὠτίδες
       καὶ δορκάδες· ταῦτα δὲ τὰ θηρία οἱ ἱππεῖς ἐνίοτε
       ἐδίωκον. καὶ οἱ μὲν ὄνοι, ἐπεί τις διώκοι, προ-

5:1 ἐξελαύνει: 'advanced', historic pres.; ἐλαύνω and its compounds
     mean 'ride' or 'drive' horses; only the richer hoplites (in-
     cluding Xenophon) could afford them. Kyros' cavalry (i.e.
     men who *fought* on horseback) consisted almost entirely of nat-
     ive troops, although Klearkhos commanded more than 40 horse-
     men, mostly Thracians. Kyros himself travelled in a chariot.
     * σταθμοὺς ἐρήμους πέντε: 'five days' march through the des-
     ert'; σταθμός means 'stopping place' and hence the interval
     between nightly halts; there were established stations along
     the major roads, but not in the desert. The Greeks were un-
     used to days of continuous travel without reaching a destinat-
     ion. * παρασάγγας: 'parasangs', a Persian unit denoting two
     hours' travel, averaging 3 miles, depending on the terrain, and
     based on the Babylonian division of the whole day into 12
     'double hours'. In Book 1 an average day's journey was 5.7
     parasangs, after that a little more. Xenophon may have obtain-
     ed these figures from a *History of Persia* written by Ktesias
     of Knidos, the King's Greek doctor.
     ὥσπερ θάλαττα: 'like a (or the) sea'; throughout the following
     description Xenophon compares unfamiliar experiences with ones
     familiar to his Greek audience.
     εἰ δέ τι καὶ ἄλλο ... : 'whatever else grew there (in the way)
     of brushwood or reed(s)'; ὕλη was the nearest Greek equivalent
     for desert scrub; κάλαμος (sing. for the species) grew by the
     river. * ἅπαντα ἦσαν εὐώδη: neuter plur. subject + plur. verb;
     occasionally found in Xenophon and in this case irregular but
     perhaps influenced by ὕλη and κάλαμος.

5:2 στρουθοὶ αἱ μεγάλαι: 'ostriches'; the στρουθός itself was a spar-
     row-like bird.
     ἐδίωκον: hunting was a favourite occupation of Xenophon; these
     were impromptu expeditions, more for sport than necessity.
     διώκοι: opt., historic indefinite temporal clause (also πλησιά-
        ζοιεν).

δραμόντες ἔστασαν· πολὺ γὰρ τῶν ἵππων ἔτρεχον θᾶτ-
τον· καὶ πάλιν, ἐπεὶ πλησιάζοιεν οἱ ἵπποι, ταὐτὸν
ἐποίουν, καὶ οὐκ ἦν λαβεῖν, εἰ μὴ διαστάντες οἱ
ἱππεῖς θηρῷεν διαδεχόμενοι. τὰ δὲ κρέα τῶν ἁλισκο-
μένων ἦν παραπλήσια τοῖς ἐλαφείοις, ἁπαλώτερα δέ.

5:3 στρουθὸν δὲ οὐδεὶς ἔλαβεν· οἱ δὲ διώξαντες τῶν
ἱππέων ταχὺ ἐπαύοντο· πολὺ γὰρ ἀπέσπα φεύγουσα,
τοῖς μὲν ποσὶ δρόμῳ, ταῖς δὲ πτέρυξιν ἄρασα ὥσπερ
ἱστίῳ χρωμένη. τὰς δὲ ὠτίδας ἄν τις ταχὺ ἀνιστῇ,
ἔστι λαμβάνειν, πέτονταί τε γὰρ βραχὺ ὥσπερ οἱ πέρ-
δικες καὶ ταχὺ ἀπαγορεύουσι. τὰ δὲ κρέα αὐτῶν
5:4 ἥδιστα ἦν. πορευόμενοι δὲ διὰ ταύτης τῆς χώρας
ἀφικνοῦνται ἐπὶ τὸν Μάσκαν ποταμόν, τὸ εὖρος πλεθριαῖον.

* προδράμοντες ἔστασαν: 'used to run ahead and then stop';
see on ἐξαιτησαμένη, 1:3 above. ἔστασαν, pluperf. (intrans.)
of ἵστημι. * ταὐτὸν = τὸ αὐτὸν; the blending of words ending and beginning with vowels is called *crasis*. * οὐκ ἦν:
'it was impossible'; ἔστι, used impersonally = ἔξεστι.
* λαβεῖν: 'to get (them)', i.e. get a javelin-shot at them;
hounds and nets were not being used. * εἰ μὴ διαστάντες ... :
lit. 'if ever the horsemen having set themselves apart (δια-)
did not hunt receiving in succession (δια-)' i.e. 'except by
the horsemen placing themselves at intervals and hunting them
in relays'; διαστάντες, strong aor. part. (intrans.) of διίστημι; θηρῷεν, opt., indefinite.

5:3 οἱ δὲ διώξαντες ... : 'any horseman who chased one'.
πολὺ ... ἀπέσπα φεύγουσα: 'it drew them a long way away in its
flight'. * τοῖς μὲν ποσὶ ... : lit. 'using (a) its feet (or
legs) by running, (b) its wings, raising (them), just as (using) a sail' i.e. 'using its feet to run, and also its wings
raising them like a sail'. The flightless ostrich raises its
wings when running to assist balance; from behind it perhaps
resembled a Greek ship with single mast and sail.
ἄν τις ταχὺ ἀνιστῇ: 'if one puts them up (or flushes them)
quickly'; ἄν = ἐάν; ἀνιστῇ, pres. subjunctive of ἀνίστημι.
ἔστι: see on οὐκ ἦν, 5:2 above; pres. for general truth (also
πέτονται and ἀπαγορεύουσι). * βραχὺ: '(only) a short distance';
the hunter rushed into a flock of bustards sitting on the
ground, reluctant to rise until it was too late.

5:4 πλεθριαῖον: a πλέθρον measured about 100 feet.

ἐνταῦθα ἦν πόλις ἐρήμη, μεγάλη, ὄνομα δ' αὐτῇ Κορ-
σωτή· περιερρεῖτο δ' αὕτη ὑπὸ τοῦ Μάσκα κύκλῳ.
5:5 ἐνταῦθ' ἔμειναν ἡμέρας τρεῖς καὶ ἐπεσιτίσαντο. ἐντεῦθεν ἐξελαύνει σταθμοὺς ἐρήμους τρεῖς καὶ δέκα
παρασάγγας ἐνενήκοντα τὸν Εὐφράτην ποταμὸν ἐν δεξ-
ίᾳ ἔχων, καὶ ἀφικνεῖται ἐπὶ Πύλας. ἐν τούτοις τοῖς
σταθμοῖς πολλὰ τῶν ὑποζυγίων ἀπώλετο ὑπὸ λιμοῦ· οὐ
γὰρ ἦν χόρτος οὐδὲ ἄλλο οὐδὲν δένδρον, ἀλλὰ ψιλὴ ἦν
ἅπασα ἡ χώρα· οἱ δὲ ἐνοικοῦντες ὄνους ἀλέτας παρὰ
τὸν ποταμὸν ὀρύττοντες καὶ ποιοῦντες εἰς Βαβυλῶνα
ἦγον καὶ ἐπώλουν καὶ ἀνταγοράζοντες σῖτον ἔζων.
5:6 τὸ δὲ στράτευμα ὁ σῖτος ἐπέλιπε, καὶ πρίασθαι οὐκ
ἦν εἰ μὴ ἐν τῇ Λυδίᾳ ἀγορᾷ ἐν τῷ Κύρου βαρβαρικῷ,

πόλις ἐρήμη: 'a ghost town', as opposed to the inhabited (οἰκ-
ουμένη) and often prosperous (εὐδαίμων) towns previously visited. * ὄνομα δ' αὐτῇ: sc. ἦν, 'its name was'.
περιερρεῖτο ... κύκλῳ: 'was surrounded', but not necessarily completely. * Μάσκα: gen. in Doric dialect, spoken by many of
the Greeks in the army, including the Spartans.

5:5 Πύλας: lit. 'Gates' i.e. 'border pass', here the Gates of Babylonia, at the Euphrates.
ἐν: 'during', 'in the course of'. * ὑποζυγίων: draught or pack
animals, oxen and mules.
οὐδὲ ἄλλο οὐδὲν δένδρον: 'nor any tree besides (ἄλλο)' or 'and
no trees either'. No wonder the King had not expected Kyros to
use this route.
ὄνους ἀλέτας ... : lit. 'digging "grinding-donkeys" beside the
river and making (them)' i.e. 'quarried and manufactured mill-
stones (or grinders) by the river, ... '; the ὄνος, lit. 'donkey', was properly the upper stone of a quern (hand-mill) which
was moved to and fro over a concave lower stone (μύλη); see
Oxford Classical Dictionary, 'Mills'.

5:6 οὐκ ἦν: see on 5:2 above.
εἰ μὴ ἐν τῇ Λυδίᾳ ... : lit. 'if not in the Lydian market in
Kyros' native (army)', sc. στρατῷ, i.e. 'except from the Lydian traders attached to Kyros' native army'; soldiers had to
obtain food individually; they could not live off the land, so
Kyros had to arrange for a market, either with local inhabitants or with traders accompanying the army for this purpose;
in the desert these traders had a monopoly.

τὴν καπίθην ἀλεύρων ἢ ἀλφίτων τεττάρων σίγλων.
ὁ δὲ σίγλος δύναται ἑπτὰ ὀβολοὺς καὶ ἡμιωβέλιον
Ἀττικούς· ἡ δὲ καπίθη δύο χοίνικας Ἀττικὰς ἐχώρει.
5:7 κρέα οὖν ἐσθίοντες οἱ στρατιῶται διεγίγνοντο. ἦν
δὲ τούτων τῶν σταθμῶν οὓς πάνυ μακροὺς ἤλαυνεν,
ὁπότε ἢ πρὸς ὕδωρ βούλοιτο διατελέσαι ἢ πρὸς χιλόν.
καὶ δή ποτε στενοχωρίας καὶ πηλοῦ φανέντος ταῖς ἁμ-
άξαις δυσπορεύτου ἐπέστη ὁ Κῦρος σὺν τοῖς περὶ αὐτὸν
ἀρίστοις καὶ εὐδαιμονεστάτοις καὶ ἔταξε Γλοῦν καὶ

* τὴν καπίθην ... :'per kapithe of wheat-flour or barley meal'.
* τεττάρων σίγλων: 'for four sigloi', gen. of price; a σίγλος
was a Persian silver coin. * δύναται ἑπτὰ ὀβολοὺς ... : 'is
worth 7½ Attic (i.e. Athenian) oboloi'; 6 ὀβολοί = 1 δραχμή -
both silver. Attica (ἡ Ἀττικὴ sc. γῆ) was the area of which
Athens (Ἀθῆναι) was the capital.
δύο ... ἐχώρει: 'contained (lit. made way for) 2 Attic khoinikes';
a χοῖνιξ measured about 1½ pints, and this amount of corn (about 1 lb.) was a soldier's daily ration; it provided a large
proportion of his energy requirements. The Lydians took advantage of the shortage and their monopoly by charging 5 times
the normal price. The prices were so high that it was not
worth distinguishing between wheat and barley: the latter,
which can grow on poorer soil, would normally be cheaper (horses were fed barley as well as grass).
κρέα ... ἐσθίοντες: game and perhaps dried meat. The main in-
gredients of the Greeks' largely vegetarian diet were bread
(wheat or barley; or gruel when bread was not available),
sour wine, olive oil, vegetables (especially peas and beans),
fish and fruit: meat was rarely eaten except on festive occasions (after a sacrifice), so that this unfamiliar diet,
lower in roughage and calorific value, caused tiredness and
constipation (but cf. Thucydides 4.16.1).

5:7 ἦν δὲ τούτων ... : 'some of these marches he made (lit. 'he rode')
very long'; ἦν ... οὕς, from ἔστιν οἵ, 'there are some who',
'some', a set phrase with a singular verb. * βούλοιτο: opt.,
indefinite temporal clause. Xenophon does not dwell on the
physical hardships of the desert march; he takes the heat for
granted, and thirst was less of a problem owing to the river.
καὶ δή ποτε: 'on one particular occasion'. * στενοχωρίας καὶ
πηλοῦ φανέντος: 'when a narrow, muddy pass presented itself',
gen. absolute. * ἐπέστη: strong. aor. (intrans.) of ἐφίστημι.
τοῖς περὶ αὐτὸν ... : 'the wealthiest nobles in his train'; Glous
was the son of Tamos (see on ἐπολιόρκει, 1:7 above) and Pigres
was Kyros' interpreter.

Πίγρητα λαβόντας τοῦ βαρβαρικοῦ στρατοῦ συνεκβιβάζ-
5:8 ειν τὰς ἁμάξας. ἐπεὶ δ᾽ ἐδόκουν αὐτῷ σχολαίως ποιεῖν, ὥσπερ ὀργῇ ἐκέλευσε τοὺς περὶ αὐτὸν Πέρσας
τοὺς κρατίστους συνεπισπεῦσαι τὰς ἁμάξας. ἔνθα δὴ
μέρος τι τῆς εὐταξίας ἦν θεάσασθαι. ῥίψαντες γὰρ
τοὺς πορφυροῦς κάνδυς ὅπου ἔτυχεν ἕκαστος ἑστηκώς,
ἵεντο ὥσπερ ἂν δράμοι τις περὶ νίκης καὶ μάλα κατὰ
πρανοῦς γηλόφου, ἔχοντες τούτους τε τοὺς πολυτελεῖς
χιτῶνας καὶ τὰς ποικίλας ἀναξυρίδας, ἔνιοι δὲ καὶ
στρεπτοὺς περὶ τοῖς τραχήλοις καὶ ψέλια περὶ ταῖς
χερσίν. εὐθὺς δὲ σὺν τούτοις εἰσπηδήσαντες εἰς τὸν
πηλὸν θᾶττον ἢ ὥς τις ἂν ᾤετο μετεώρους ἐξεκόμισαν
5:9 τὰς ἁμάξας. τὸ δὲ σύμπαν δῆλος ἦν Κῦρος ὡς σπεύδων

---

* τοῦ βαρβαρικοῦ στρατοῦ: 'some of the native troops', partitive gen.

5:8 ὥσπερ ὀργῇ: 'as if in anger'; he put on a show of anger while
remaining inwardly cool.
ἔνθα δὴ μέρος ... : lit. 'then indeed it was possible to watch
a sample of (their) discipline'; ἔνθα δή indicates a turning
point.
τοὺς πορφυροῦς κάνδυς: the κάνδυς was a long-sleeved Persian robe
or caftan. Persian nobles wore purple as a sign of wealth and
luxury; the glittering reddish-purple dye, obtained from the
murex (πορφύρα), was very expensive.
ἔτυχεν ... ἑστηκώς: 'happened to be standing'; ἑστηκώς, perf.
part. (intrans.) of ἵστημι. * ἵεντο ὥσπερ ἂν ... : lit.
'they rushed just as one would run for victory' i.e. ' ... as
if it were a race'; ἵεντο, imperf. mid. of ἵημι; ἂν δράμοι,
opt. + ἄν, potential. * ἔχοντες τούτους, etc.: 'wearing
those costly tunics (of theirs) and their multicoloured trousers'; ἀναξυρίδες, a Persian word for an un-Greek item of
clothing. * ἔνιοι δὲ καὶ στρεπτοὺς: 'and some even (or also)
(wearing) torques'; στρεπτός sc. κύκλος, a collar of twisted
(cf. στρέφω) or linked metal. To the Greeks, this clothing
and jewellery were signs of exotic luxury.
θᾶττον ἢ ὥς ... : lit. 'quicker than how anyone would have
thought' i.e. 'quicker than one would have thought possible'.
* μετεώρους ἐξεκόμισαν τὰς ἁμάξας: lit. 'brought out the
carts lifted up' i.e. 'lifted the carts up and brought them
to safety'.

5:9 δῆλος ἦν Κῦρος ... : lit. 'Kyros was clear as hurrying' i.e. 'Kyros was clearly hurrying', an idiom normally found without ὡς.

πᾶσαν τὴν ὁδὸν καὶ οὐ διατρίβων ὅπου μὴ ἐπισιτισμοῦ
ἕνεκα ἤ τινος ἄλλου ἀναγκαίου ἐκαθέζετο, νομίζων,
ὅσῳ μὲν θᾶττον ἔλθοι, τοσούτῳ ἀπαρασκευοτέρῳ βασιλεῖ μαχεῖσθαι, ὅσῳ δὲ σχολαίτερον, τοσούτῳ πλέον
συναγείρεσθαι βασιλεῖ στράτευμα. καὶ συνιδεῖν δ᾽ ἦν
τῷ προσέχοντι τὸν νοῦν ἡ βασιλέως ἀρχὴ πλήθει μὲν
χώρας καὶ ἀνθρώπων ἰσχυρὰ οὖσα, τοῖς δὲ μήκεσι τῶν
ὁδῶν καὶ τῷ διεσπάσθαι τὰς δυνάμεις ἀσθενής, εἴ τις
διὰ ταχέων τὸν πόλεμον ποιοῖτο.

---

* ὅπου μὴ ... ἐκαθέζετο: lit. 'where he was not halting' i.e.
'except where he halted'; μὴ suggests 'unless'. * νομίζων,
ὅσῳ θᾶττον ... : lit. 'thinking that, by how much faster he
went, he would fight the King by that much less prepared' i.e.
'thinking that the faster he went, the less prepared the King
would be when he fought him'; the correlatives ὅσῳ + comparative
... τοσούτῳ + comparative = 'the more ... the more ... '; ἔλθοι,
opt. in historic indir. statement. * ὅσῳ δὲ σχολαίτερον ... :
'whereas the slower (he went), the greater the army that was being (i.e. would by then have been) collected for the King'.
καὶ συνιδεῖν δ᾽ ἦν ... : lit. 'also the King's empire was for
the man who applied his mind to see ... ' i.e. 'the intelligent
observer would conclude that the King's empire ... '; συνιδεῖν
... τῷ προσέχοντι, explanatory inf. and dat. of person judging.
* πλήθει μὲν χώρας ... : 'in terms of the amount of territory
and population (was) strong'. * τοῖς δὲ μήκεσι ... : lit.
'but by the lengths of its journeys' i.e. 'but owing to the
distances involved in travelling across it'. * τῷ διεσπάσθαι
τὰς δυνάμεις: lit. 'by the (fact of) its forces being dispersed'
i.e. '(owing to) the dispersal of its forces'; τό + inf. (here
perf. inf. pass. of διασπάω), verbal noun, with τὰς δυνάμεις
as acc. subject (acc. and inf. construction). ἀσθενής: sc.
οὖσα. * εἴ τις διὰ ταχέων ... :'if one was quick in mounting
one's offensive'; εἰ + opt. stands for a fut. condition of dir.
speech (ἐάν + subjunctive). Xenophon stresses that in war rapid
and efficient communications are just as important as territory
and manpower.

5:10   *On the opposite side of the Euphrates was the city of*
to   *Kharmande. The soliders purchased provisions there, cross-*
5:17   *ing the river on skins stuffed with hay. A quarrel arose*
between the contingents of Klearkhos and Menon, and Proxenos
became involved after attempting to mediate. Finally Kyros
rode into the midst of the Greeks. After he had roundly ad-
monished them for their rash disregard for the safety of the
expedition, Klearkhos, who was extremely angry at being stoned
by Menon's men, calmed down and order was restored.

6:1   ἐντεῦθεν προϊόντων ἐφαίνετο ἴχνη ἴππων καὶ κόπ-
ρος· ἡκάζετο δ᾽ εἶναι ὁ στίβος ὡς δισχιλίων ἱππέων.
οὗτοι προϊόντες ἔκαιον καὶ χιλὸν καὶ εἴ τι ἄλλο
χρήσιμον ἦν. Ὀρόντας δὲ Πέρσης ἀνὴρ γένει τε προσ-
ήκων βασιλεῖ καὶ τὰ πολέμια λεγόμενος ἐν τοῖς ἀρίστοις Περσῶν ἐπιβουλεύει Κύρῳ καὶ πρόσθεν πολεμήσας,
6:2   καταλλαγεὶς δέ. οὗτος Κύρῳ εἶπεν, εἰ αὐτῷ δοίη
ἱππέας χιλίους, ὅτι τοὺς προκατακαίοντας ἱππέας ἢ
κατακάνοι ἂν ἐνεδρεύσας ἢ ζῶντας πολλοὺς αὐτῶν ἂν
ἔλοι καὶ κωλύσειε τοῦ καίειν ἐπιόντας, καὶ ποιήσειεν
ὥστε μήποτε δύνασθαι αὐτοὺς ἰδόντας τὸ Κύρου στράτευμα βασιλεῖ διαγγεῖλαι. τῷ δὲ Κύρῳ ἀκούσαντι ταῦτα

6:1 προιόντων *sc.* αὐτῶν: 'as they advanced', gen. absolute; pres.
part. of πρόειμι (εἶμι 'go').
εἴ τι ἄλλο: 'whatever else'. * τὰ πολέμια: 'in military matters', acc. of respect. * καὶ πρόσθεν πολεμήσας: lit. 'having made war previously also';'he had also been at war with
him·on a previous occasion'.

6:2 εἰ αὐτῷ δοίη ... : 'that if he gave him ... , he would either ...
kill ... or capture ... and prevent (them) ... and make sure ...';
ὅτι is delayed until after the εἰ clause; αὐτῷ, i.e. Orontas -
Xenophon does not always use reflexive pronouns; δοίη, aor.
opt. of δίδωμι, remote fut. condition; κατακάνοι ἂν, ἂν ἔλοι,
opt., apodosis of remote fut. condition; κατακάνοι, a form not
found in 'pure' Attic prose (see Introduction 6.5); κωλύσειε,
ποιήσειεν, opt., indir. statement (historic sequence). * τοῦ
καίειν: verbal noun (τό + inf.) in gen. after κωλύσειε.
* ὥστε μήποτε δύνασθαι ... : 'that they could never get word
... that they had seen'; αὐτούς, subject of δύνασθαι (acc. and
inf. construction with ὥστε).

ἐδόκει ὠφέλιμα εἶναι, καὶ ἐκέλευεν αὐτὸν λαμβάνειν
6:3 μέρος παρ' ἑκάστου τῶν ἡγεμόνων. ὁ δ' Ὀρόντας νομίσας ἑτοίμους εἶναι αὐτῷ τοὺς ἱππέας γράφει ἐπιστολὴν παρὰ βασιλέα ὅτι ἥξοι ἔχων ἱππέας ὡς ἂν δύνηται
πλείστους· ἀλλὰ φράσαι τοῖς αὐτοῦ ἱππεῦσιν ἐκέλευεν
ὡς φίλιον αὐτὸν ὑποδέχεσθαι. ἐνῆν δὲ ἐν τῇ ἐπιστολῇ
καὶ τῆς πρόσθεν φιλίας ὑπομνήματα καὶ πίστεως. ταύτην τὴν ἐπιστολὴν δίδωσι πιστῷ ἀνδρί, ὡς ᾤετο· ὁ δὲ
6:4 λαβὼν Κύρῳ δίδωσιν. ἀναγνοὺς δὲ αὐτὴν ὁ Κῦρος συλλαμβάνει Ὀρόνταν, καὶ συγκαλεῖ εἰς τὴν ἑαυτοῦ σκηνὴν
Πέρσας τοὺς ἀρίστους τῶν περὶ αὐτὸν ἑπτά, καὶ τοὺς
τῶν Ἑλλήνων στρατηγοὺς ἐκέλευεν ὁπλίτας ἀγαγεῖν,
τούτους δὲ θέσθαι τὰ ὅπλα περὶ τὴν αὐτοῦ σκηνήν. οἱ
δὲ ταῦτα ἐποίησαν, ἀγαγόντες ὡς τρισχιλίους ὁπλίτας.
6:5 Κλέαρχον δὲ καὶ εἴσω παρεκάλεσε σύμβουλον, ὅς γε καὶ

6:3 αὐτῷ = ἑαυτῷ. * ὅτι ἥξοι: '(saying) that he would be there'
    fut. opt. in indir. statement after γράφει (historic pres.).
    ἔχων ἱππέας ... : 'with as many horsemen as possible', see on
    ἔχων, 1:2 and on ὡς μάλιστα ..., 1:6 above; ἂν δύνηται, sub-
    junctive, indefinite.
    ἀλλὰ φράσαι ... ἐκέλευεν: i.e. the letter read 'but tell ... '.
    * ὡς φίλιον: lit. 'as friendly' i.e. 'as a friend'.
    πιστῷ ἀνδρί, ὡς ᾤετο: 'to a trustworthy man - or so (lit. as) he
    believed'.

6:4 σκηνήν: perhaps a large 'pavilion', in keeping with Kyros' pos-
    ition. * ἑπτά: oriental sacred number (there were seven Roy-
    al Judges; see on τὴν κρίσιν, 6:5 below). * τούτους δὲ θέσθαι
    τὰ ὅπλα: 'and that these should rest arms'; θέσθαι, aor. inf.
    mid. of τίθημι; τίθεμαι τὰ ὅπλα, lit. 'put down one's arms',
    keeping them within easy reach while standing by in readiness.
    * αὐτοῦ = ἑαυτοῦ.
    ὡς τρισχιλίους: 'nearly three thousand'; Kyros did not know how
    widespread support for Orontas was among his native troops,
    and was taking no chances.

6:5 Κλέαρχον δὲ καί: 'Klearkhos also'. * σύμβουλον: '(as) an advis-
    er'. * ὅς γε καὶ αὐτῷ ... : lit. 'who at any rate both to him-
    self and the others seemed to have been most preferred in honour
    of the Greeks' i.e. 'since both Kyros and the other Persians
                                                  (cont.)

αὐτῷ καὶ τοῖς ἄλλοις ἐδόκει προτιμηθῆναι μάλιστα τῶν
'Ελλήνων. ἐπεὶ δ' ἐξῆλθεν, ἐξήγγειλε τοῖς φίλοις
τὴν κρίσιν τοῦ 'Ορόντα ὡς ἐγένετο· οὐ γὰρ ἀπόρρητον
6:6 ἦν. ἔφη δὲ Κῦρον ἄρχειν τοῦ λόγου ὧδε. Παρεκάλεσα
ὑμᾶς, ἄνδρες φίλοι, ὅπως σὺν ὑμῖν βουλευόμενος ὅ τι
δίκαιόν ἐστι καὶ πρὸς θεῶν καὶ πρὸς ἀνθρώπων, τοῦτο
πράξω περὶ 'Ορόντα τουτουΐ. τοῦτον γὰρ πρῶτον μὲν ὁ
ἐμὸς πατὴρ ἔδωκεν ὑπήκοον εἶναι ἐμοί· ἐπεὶ δὲ ταχ-
θείς, ὡς ἔφη αὐτός, ὑπὸ τοῦ ἐμοῦ ἀδελφοῦ οὗτος ἐπολ-
έμησεν ἐμοὶ ἔχων τὴν ἐν Σάρδεσιν ἀκρόπολιν καὶ ἐγὼ
αὐτὸν προσπολεμῶν ἐποίησα ὥστε δόξαι τούτῳ τοῦ πρὸς
ἐμὲ πολέμου παύσασθαι καὶ δεξιὰν ἔλαβον καὶ ἔδωκα.
6:7 μετὰ ταῦτα, ἔφη, ὦ 'Ορόντα, ἔστιν ὅ τι σε ἠδίκησα;

thought that of the Greeks he was held in the greatest honour';
Klearkhos' seniority was by now well-established.]
τὴν κρίσιν ... : 'how Orontas' trial had gone'; τὴν κρίσιν anti-
cipates the indir. question (see on καὶ τῶν παρ' ἑαυτῷ, 1:5 above); Ὀρόντα, Doric gen. (see on Μάσκα, 1:4 above). For official
Persian justice (the Royal Judges), cf. Herodotus 3.31, 5.25 and
7.194.

6:6 ἔφη: 3rd pers. sing. imperf. of φημί.
τοῦ λόγου: 'his speech'; or 'the conference', i.e. 'the proceedings'; Kyros would have spoken through an interpreter.
ὅπως ... ὅ τι δίκαιόν ἐστι ... τοῦτο πράξω: 'in order that ...
I may do what is just'; when a relative clause is placed early,
the relative pronoun is often 'picked up' by the antecedent
οὗτος. * Ὀρόντα τουτουΐ: 'Orontas here'; -ί, when added to
οὗτος, 'points' to someone or something nearby; a colloquial
usage of Attic Greek, common in dialogue and oratory.
ὑπήκοον εἶναι ἐμοί: 'to be my subject', inf. of purpose after
ἔδωκεν (aor. of δίδωμι).
ἀκρόπολιν: 'citadel', hill-top stronghold (that of Athens was
the most famous, being known as the Acropolis). * προσπολεμῶν: lit. 'fighting (back)' i.e. 'taking up the challenge'.
* ἐποίησα ὥστε δόξαι τούτῳ: 'I made him decide' (δοκεῖ + dat.).
* δεξιὰν ἔλαβον καὶ ἔδωκα: lit. 'I took and gave a right (hand)'
i.e. 'we shook hands', to mark the cessation of hostilities.

6:7 μετὰ ταῦτα: indicating the end of the ἐπεί clause. Kyros now
turned to address Orontas. * ἔστιν ὅ τι ... : lit. 'is there
(anything) which I have injured you?' i.e. 'have I done you
any injury?'; ὅ τι, internal (adverbial) acc.

ἀπεκρίνατο ὅτι οὔ. πάλιν δὲ ὁ Κῦρος ἠρώτα, Οὐκοῦν
ὕστερον, ὡς αὐτὸς σὺ ὁμολογεῖς, οὐδὲν ὑπ' ἐμοῦ ἀδικούμενος ἀποστὰς εἰς Μυσοὺς κακῶς ἐποίεις τὴν ἐμὴν
χώραν ὅ τι ἐδύνω; ἔφη ὁ Ὀρόντας. Οὐκοῦν, ἔφη ὁ
Κῦρος, ὁπότ' αὖ ἔγνως τὴν σεαυτοῦ δύναμιν, ἐλθὼν
ἐπὶ τὸν τῆς Ἀρτέμιδος βωμὸν μεταμέλειν τέ σοι ἔφησθα καὶ πείσας ἐμὲ πιστὰ πάλιν ἔδωκάς μοι καὶ ἔλαβες
6:8 παρ' ἐμοῦ; καὶ ταῦθ' ὡμολόγει ὁ Ὀρόντας. Τί οὖν,
ἔφη ὁ Κῦρος, ἀδικηθεὶς ὑπ' ἐμοῦ νῦν τὸ τρίτον ἐπιβουλεύων μοι φανερὸς γέγονας; εἰπόντος δὲ τοῦ Ὀρόντα ὅτι οὐδὲν ἀδικηθεὶς ἠρώτησεν ὁ Κῦρος αὐτόν·

ἀπεκρίνατο ὅτι οὔ: 'he answered that (he had) not'.
πάλιν ... ἠρώτα: lit. 'was asking again' i.e.'continued with
another question'. * Οὐκοῦν: 'is it not true that' (accent
on -οῦν), introducing a leading question inviting the answer
'Yes'. * οὐδὲν ... ἀδικούμενος: 'although you received no
injury', concessive part.
ἀποστὰς εἰς Μυσοὺς: 'did you go over to (the) Mysians and ... ',
see on ἐξαιτησαμένη, 1:3 above; ἀποστάς, strong aor. part.
(intrans.) of ἀφίστημι. Kyros refers to the hill-tribes who
had been troubling the usually unwarlike plain-dwellers of
Mysia (see on the Pisidians, 1:11 above). * κακῶς ἐποίεις
... : 'did you do my territory all the harm you could'.
ἔφη: 'said "Yes"' (to say 'No' is οὔ φημι); taking a previous
offence into consideration was an important point of Persian
law (cf. Herodotus 1.137).
ὁπότ' αὖ ἔγνως ... : 'when once again you had learned (the extent of) your own power', i.e., ironically, how little
it was   *   Ἀρτέμιδος: i.e. the Great Goddess worshipped in Asia Minor, often identified with the Greek Artemis:
her most famous temple was in the Ionian city of Ephesos.
* μεταμέλειν ... σοι ἔφησθα:'did you say that you were sorry';
μεταμέλει + dat., impersonal; ἔφησθα, 2nd pers. sing. imperf.
of φημί.
πιστὰ ... ἔδωκάς μοι, etc.: 'did you and I exchange pledges?';
see on δεξιὰν ... , 6:6 above.

6:8 Τί ... ἀδικηθεὶς ὑπ' ἐμοῦ: lit. 'having been injured what by
me ... ' i.e. 'what injury have I done you that you ... ';
Τί, internal (adverbial) acc.; also οὐδὲν below. * ἐπιβουλεύων ... φανερὸς γέγονας: 'you have been caught plotting';
see on δῆλος ... , 5:9 above.   (cont.)

'Ομολογεῖς οὖν περὶ ἐμὲ ἄδικος γεγενῆσθαι; ῏Η γὰρ
ἀνάγκη, ἔφη ὁ 'Ορόντας. ἐκ τούτου πάλιν ἠρώτησεν ὁ
Κῦρος· ῎Ετι οὖν ἂν γένοιο τῷ ἐμῷ ἀδελφῷ πολέμιος,
ἐμοὶ δὲ φίλος καὶ πιστός; ὁ δὲ ἀπεκρίνατο ὅτι Οὐδ'
εἰ γενοίμην, ὦ Κῦρε, σοι γ' ἂν ποτε ἔτι δόξαιμι.

6:9 πρὸς ταῦτα Κῦρος εἶπε τοῖς παροῦσιν· 'Ο μὲν ἀνὴρ
τοιαῦτα μὲν πεποίηκε, τοιαῦτα δὲ λέγει· ὑμῶν δὲ σὺ
πρῶτος, ὦ Κλέαρχε, ἀπόφηναι γνώμην ὅ τι σοι δοκεῖ.
Κλέαρχος δὲ εἶπε τάδε. Συμβουλεύω ἐγὼ τὸν ἄνδρα
τοῦτον ἐκποδὼν ποιεῖσθαι ὡς τάχιστα, ὡς μηκέτι δέῃ
τοῦτον φυλάττεσθαι, ἀλλὰ σχολὴ ᾖ ἡμῖν τὸ κατὰ τοῦτον εἶναι τοὺς ἐθελοντὰς φίλους, τούτους εὖ ποιεῖν.

εἰπόντος δὲ τοῦ 'Ορόντα: gen. absolute. * οὐδὲν ἀδικηθείς sc.
ἐπιβουλεύων φανερὸς γέγονεν: translate according to Kyros'
question.]
περὶ ἐμὲ ἄδικος γεγενῆσθαι: lit. 'that you have become unjust
concerning me' i.e. 'that you have been injuring me'.
* ῏Η γὰρ ἀνάγκη sc. ἐστι: lit. '(Yes) for indeed (there is)
necessity' i.e. 'Yes, I certainly must'.
ἐκ τούτου: 'at this', 'then'. * ἔτι ... ἂν γένοιο ... πολέμιος:
'would you be an enemy ... in future'; ἂν γένοιο, potential opt.
ἀπεκρίνατο ὅτι ... : 'he replied: "Even if I were to become (his
enemy) ... you would never believe it now."'; ὅτι sometimes introduces dir. speech; γενοίμην, ἂν δόξαιμι, opt. in remote fut.
condition.

6:9 πρὸς ταῦτα: 'at this', 'in response'. * 'Ο μὲν ἀνὴρ ... : the
first μέν is answered by δέ in the next sentence.
ὑμῶν δὲ σὺ ... : lit. 'of you (plur.) you first, O Klearkhos,
declare judgement, what seems good to you'; δοκεῖ μοι and
ἀποφαίνω γνώμην (no article), in the context of a trial, mean
'reach a verdict' and 'deliver the verdict'; γνώμην and the ὅ
τι clause (indir. question) both follow ἀποφῆναι.
ἐκποδὼν ποιεῖσθαι sc. ἡμᾶς: 'that we get this man out of the way'
* ὡς + superlative: see on ὡς μάλιστα ... 1:6 above.
* ὡς μηκέτι δέῃ: for purpose clause introduced by ὡς, see
Introduction 6.1; δέῃ, subjunctive of δεῖ.
ἀλλὰ σχολὴ ... : 'but (we) may be free, at least as far as this
man in concerned, to benefit our willing allies'; σχολή, lit.
'leisure'; ᾖ, subjunctive of εἰμί 'be'; τὸ κατὰ τοῦτον εἶναι,
lit. 'as far as it being according to this man'; τό + phrase,
adverbial acc.; εἶναι, explanatory inf.; ἐθελοντάς, from ἐθελοντής 'volunteer', here used as adjective.

6:10 ταύτῃ δὲ τῇ γνώμῃ ἔφη καὶ τοὺς ἄλλους πορσθέσθαι.
μετὰ ταῦτα κελεύοντος Κύρου ἔλαβον τῆς ζώνης τὸν
'Ορόνταν ἐπὶ θανάτῳ ἅπαντες ἀναστάντες καὶ οἱ συγ-
γενεῖς· εἶτα δὲ ἐξῆγον αὐτὸν οἷς προσετάχθη. ἐπεὶ
δὲ εἶδον αὐτὸν οἵπερ πρόσθεν προσεκύνουν, καὶ τότε
προσεκύνησαν, καίπερ εἰδότες ὅτι ἐπὶ θάνατον ἄγοιτο.

6:11 ἐπεὶ δὲ εἰς τὴν 'Αρταπάτα σκηνὴν εἰσήχθη τοῦ πιστοτ-
άτου τῶν Κύρου σκηπτούχων, μετὰ ταῦτα οὔτε ζῶντα
'Ορόνταν οὔτε τεθνηκότα οὐδεὶς εἶδε πώποτε οὐδὲ ὅπως
ἀπέθανεν οὐδεὶς εἰδὼς ἔλεγεν· ἤκαζον δὲ ἄλλοι ἄλλως·
τάφος δὲ οὐδεὶς πώποτε αὐτοῦ ἐφάνη.

6:10 ἔφη καὶ ...: '(Klearkhos) said that the others also agreed';
προσθέσθαι, aor. inf. mid. of προστίθημι.
κελεύοντος Κύρου: gen. absolute. * τῆς ζώνης ...: 'by the
belt, to signify the death penalty (ἐπὶ θανάτῳ)', a Persian
custom. * ἀναστάντες: strong aor. part. (intrans.) of ἀνίστημι.
καὶ οἱ συγγενεῖς: 'including the members of his family'; both
Orontas and some of the Persians present were related to Kyros,
and members of the royal family.
οἷς προσετάχθη: 'those who were given the duty', lit. 'to whom
it was ordered'.
οἵπερ: 'the very people who', more emphatic than οἵ. * προσεκύνουν: 'used to make obeisance to him'; προσκύνησις was the
oriental custom of prostrating oneself (literally grovelling)
before a superior; the Greeks hated the idea of bowing down to
a mortal (cf. Herodotus 1.134 and 7.136). * εἰδότες ὅτι:
although a verb of knowing, οἶδα is regularly followed by ὅτι
(rather than part. construction) when the fact known is emphasized. * ἄγοιτο: opt., indir. statement (hist. sequence).

6:11 'Αρταπάτα: see on 'Ορόντα, 6:5 above. * σκηπτούχων: 'sceptre-
bearers'; these officials carried sceptres as a sign of authority; the King's bodyguards were also σκηπτοῦχοι. * οὐδὲ
ὅπως ἀπέθανεν ...: 'nor (in fact) could anyone say from actual knowledge how he died.
ἤκαζον δὲ ἄλλοι ἄλλως: lit. 'some people guessed in one way (others in another)' i.e. 'people made various guesses', a common
idiom with ἄλλος and related words. Some may have recalled the
Persian custom of burying victims alive (cf. Herodotus 7.114).

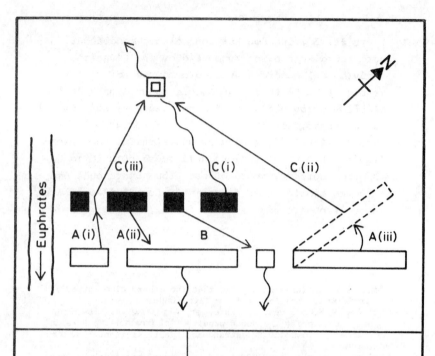

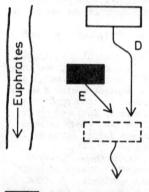

BATTLE OF KOUNAXA –

Diagrammatic view

A (i) Tissaphernes charges through Greek peltasts; (ii) Greek hoplites rout enemy opposite them; (iii) Artaxerxes wheels his right wing to encircle Greeks.

B Kyros attacks Artaxerxes, routing his bodyguard, but is killed.

C (i) Ariaios flees; (ii) Artaxerxes and (iii) Tissaphernes plunder Greek camp.

D Persians return from Greek camp, by-pass Greeks, and form up S.E. of them.

E Greeks rout Persians.

■ Kyros's forces

□ Artaxerxes's forces

. 7:1   Having thus disposed of the traitor Orontas, Kyros marched
to   fifty miles into Babylonia and held a review of his army,
7:20   thinking that the King would soon give battle. Deserters from
          Artaxerxes' army gave alarming accounts of its size: 1,200,000
          infantry divided among four commanders, 200 chariots fitted
          with scythes and 6,000 cavalry. But Kyros knew the fighting
          qualities of his army, and assured his Greek commanders that
          he was undismayed. The odds of 100 to 1 suggested by these
          reported figures had little meaning when it came to actual
          fighting between drilled units of co-ordinated hoplites and
          disorganised throngs of raw, untrained light infantry. The
          failure of the King's large cavalry contingent to harass and
          disrupt, with almost no effective opposition, the Greek pos-
          itions both before and during the Battle of Kounaxa, seems
          inexplicable in purely military terms. It appears that the
          function of the Persian cavalry was to act as the King's
          bodyguard. Kyros therefore had nothing to fear from it un-
          til he confronted his brother on the field of battle three
          days later.

8:1   καὶ ἤδη τε ἦν ἀμφὶ ἀγορὰν πλήθουσαν καὶ πλησίον
        ἦν ὁ σταθμὸς ἔνθα ἔμελλε καταλύσειν, ἡνίκα Πατηγύας
        ἀνὴρ Πέρσης τῶν ἀμφὶ Κῦρον πιστῶν προφαίνεται ἐλαύν-
        ων ἀνὰ κράτος ἱδρῶντι τῷ ἵππῳ, καὶ εὐθὺς πᾶσιν οἷς
        ἐνετύγχανεν ἐβόα καὶ βαρβαρικῶς καὶ ἑλληνικῶς ὅτι
        βασιλεὺς σὺν στρατεύματι πολλῷ προσέρχεται ὡς εἰς
        μάχην παρεσκευασμένος. ἔνθα δὴ πολὺς τάραχος ἐγένετο·

8:1 ἀγορὰν πλήθουσαν: '(the time of) a full market-place' in a town,
     i.e. mid-morning; set phrases such as this were used to indic-
     ate certain times of day. * σταθμός: see on 5:1 above.
     * ἔμελλε: i.e. Kyros. * καταλύσειν sc. τὴν ὁδόν: 'halt'.
     προφαίνεται: 'appeared in the distance', lit. ' ... ahead'; he
     was a mounted scout sent ahead to watch for the enemy.
     * ἀνὰ κράτος: 'at full speed'; normal Attic κατὰ κράτος.
     * τῷ ἵππῳ: 'with his horse', dat. of manner or attendant cir-
     cumstances; it would be typical for Xenophon, a keen horseman,
     to notice this detail. * καὶ βαρβαρικῶς: 'both in Persian ... '.
     * ὡς εἰς μάχην παρεσκευασμένος: 'ready for battle'.

Greek heavy-armed soldier (hoplite) in action wearing an elaborately decorated bronze helmet, greaves and breast-plate, with shield, spear and short sword (see on 8:3 opposite).

Based on a drawing of Greeks fighting Amazons on a mid-fifth century B.C. Attic wine-bowl (*krater*) of the red-figure style by the so-called 'Niobid painter', in the Palermo Museum, Sicily. (The curve of the spear and the shortness of his right arm result from the curvature of the vase.)

8:2 αὐτίκα γὰρ ἐδόκουν οἱ ῞Ελληνες καὶ πάντες δὲ ἀτάκ-
8:3 τοις σφίσιν ἐπιπεσεῖσθαι· Κῦρός τε καταπηδήσας
    ἀπὸ τοῦ ἅρματος τὸν θώρακα ἐνέδυ καὶ ἀναβὰς ἐπὶ
    τὸν ἵππον τὰ παλτὰ εἰς τὰς χεῖρας ἔλαβε, τοῖς τε
    ἄλλοις πᾶσι παρήγγελλεν ἐξοπλίζεσθαι καὶ καθίστ-
8:4 ασθαι εἰς τὴν ἑαυτοῦ τάξιν ἕκαστον. ἔνθα δὴ σὺν
    πολλῇ σπουδῇ καθίσταντο, Κλέαρχος μὲν τὰ δεξιὰ τοῦ
    κέρατος ἔχων πρὸς τῷ Εὐφράτῃ ποταμῷ, Πρόξενος δὲ

8:2 ἔνθα δή: see on 5:8 above. * καὶ πάντες δὲ: 'and in fact ev-
    eryone'; see on καὶ στρατηγὸν δὲ, 1:2 above. * αὐτίκα ...
    ἀτάκτοις σφίσιν ἐπιπεσεῖσθαι sc. αὐτὸν: 'that he would be upon
    them at any moment, before they could form up'; αὐτίκα, placed
    first for emphasis; σφίσιν, dat. plur. of reflexive pronoun
    σφεῖς, referring to subject of main verb.

8:3 ἅρματος: the ἅρμα was a two-wheeled vehicle with a wooden plat-
    form (δίφρος) for the driver to stand on, and rails to the
    front and sides; Kyros' chariot was fitted with a seat.
    * θώρακα: 'corslet', 'cuirass', of bronze or leather plated
    with bronze, protecting chest, stomach, and back, often worn
    over a leather jerkin (σπολάς) to prevent chafing. * παλτά:
    'javelins', light spears for throwing or thrusting. * ἐξ-
    οπλίζεσθαι: hoplite armour consisted of: a cuirass; bronze
    greaves (κνημῖδες); a bronze helmet (κράνος) with nose- and
    cheek-pieces and a plume; a circular or oval wooden shield
    three feet across (ἀσπις or ὅπλον), reinforced with bronze and
    painted with a device, and kept in a cover when not in use; an
    iron-tipped spear 7 - 8 feet long (δόρυ), with a spiked butt
    (στύραξ), whereby the spear could be rested upright; and a
    short iron two-edged sword (ξίφος). The whole suit (πανοπ-
    λία 'panoply') might weigh 70 - 75 lbs., and on the march was
    carried with the baggage or by the hoplite's slave (ὑπασπιστής
    'armour-bearer'); this equipment was privately owned by the
    hoplite, and only the better off could afford it; we know
    little about its maintenance and repair in the field.
    * καθίστασθαι εἰς τὴν ... : 'to fall in, each to his own line';
    καθίστασθαι, pres. inf. mid. of καθίστημι; τάξιν, hoplite form-
    ation, with each soldier in the line protecting the man on his
    left with his shield.

8:4 καθίσταντο: 'they proceeded to fall in', imperf. mid. of καθ-
    ίστημι.

ἐχόμενος, οἱ δ' ἄλλοι μετὰ τοῦτον, Μένων δὲ τὸ εὐώ-
8:5 νυμον κέρας ἔσχε τοῦ Ἑλληνικοῦ. τοῦ δὲ βαρβαρικοῦ
ἱππεῖς μὲν Παφλαγόνες εἰς χιλίους παρὰ Κλέαρχον
ἔστησαν ἐν τῷ δεξιῷ καὶ τὸ Ἑλληνικὸν πελταστικόν,
ἐν δὲ τῷ εὐωνύμῳ Ἀριαῖός τε ὁ Κύρου ἵππαρχος καὶ τὸ
8:6 ἄλλο βαρβαρικόν. Κῦρος δὲ καὶ οἱ ἱππεῖς τούτου
ὅσον ἑξακόσιοι ὡπλισμένοι θώραξι μὲν αὐτοὶ καὶ
παραμηριδίοις καὶ κράνεσι πάντες πλὴν Κύρου (Κῦρος

ἐχόμενος: 'coming next'. The lines of Kyros' army faced south-
east, at right angles to the Euphrates (on their right). They
comprised the centre (non-Greeks), the left (non-Greeks), and
the right (Greeks); the right was the most important position,
where the best troops were drawn up. Kyros hoped that his
right wing was wide enough for the Greek hoplites to charge the
King, who was expected to occupy a central position in his own
army. The Greek commanders were, from right to left, Klearkhos,
Proxenos, six more generals, and finally Menon. The battle
took place, according to Plutarch, near a village called Kounaxa, some 60 miles from Babylon; the exact site is disputed.
εὐώνυμον: lit. 'well-named', 'lucky' i.e. 'left'; a Greek soothsayer (μάντις) faced north when observing signs, such as the
flight of birds (οἰωνοί), from which he prophesied the future;
those coming from the west (i.e. his left) were considered unlucky, so that the left side always had unlucky associations.
To counteract this, euphemisms such as εὐώνυμος (and ἀριστερός)
were used.   * For plan of battle see p. 44.

8:5 ἱππεῖς ... Παφλάγονες: 'Paphlagonian cavalry'; a number of Greeks
were horsemen, but the cavalry units were mostly non-Greek.
* ἔστησαν: 'were positioned', strong aor. (intrans.) of
ἵστημι. * πελταστικόν: the peltasts (πελτασταί) were light-
armed troops with crescent-shaped wicker shields (πέλται),
covered with goat- or sheep-skin, and bronze-tipped javelins;
they did not fight in formation. The term peltasts is used
loosely here to include all the light-armed non-hoplite infantry, i.e. archers (τοξόται), javelin-throwers (ἀκοντισταί),
and slingers (σφενδονῆται). * ἐν δὲ τῷ εὐωνύμῳ: i.e. of
Kyros' entire army. * τὸ ἄλλο βαρβαρικόν: 'the rest of the
native forces'.

8:6 ὅσον + numeral: 'about ... '. * ὡπλισμένοι: sc. ἦσαν. * παραμηριδίοις: 'cuisses', protecting the thighs - important for a
mounted soldier (μηρός 'thigh').

δὲ ψιλὴν ἔχων τὴν κεφαλὴν εἰς τὴν μάχην καθίστατο).

8:7 οἱ δ' ἵπποι πάντες οἱ μετὰ Κύρου εἶχον καὶ προμετωπίδια καὶ προστερνίδια· εἶχον δὲ καὶ μαχαίρας οἱ ἱππ-
8:8 εῖς Ἑλληνικάς. καὶ ἤδη τε ἦν μέσον ἡμέρας καὶ οὔπω
καταφανεῖς ἦσαν οἱ πολέμιοι· ἡνίκα δὲ δείλη ἐγίγνετο,
ἐφάνη κονιορτὸς ὥσπερ νεφέλη λευκή, χρόνῳ δὲ συχνῷ
ὕστερον ὥσπερ μελανία τις ἐν τῷ πεδίῳ ἐπὶ πολύ.
ὅτε δὲ ἐγγύτερον ἐγίγνοντο, τάχα δὴ καὶ χαλκός τις
ἤστραπτε καὶ αἱ λόγχαι καὶ αἱ τάξεις καταφανεῖς
8:9 ἐγίγνοντο. καὶ ἦσαν ἱππεῖς μὲν λευκοθώρακες ἐπὶ
τοῦ εὐωνύμου τῶν πολεμίων (Τισσαφέρνης ἐλέγετο τούτων ἄρχειν), ἐχόμενοι δὲ τούτων γερροφόροι, ἐχόμενοι
δὲ ὁπλῖται σὺν ποδήρεσι ξυλίναις ἀσπίσιν (Αἰγύπτιοι

* ψιλὴν: 'unprotected'; Kyros probably wore a tall Persian
headdress (τιάρα). * εἰς τὴν μάχην καθίστατο: lit. 'was
falling in for the battle' i.e. 'went into battle'; Kyros had
ignored unanimous advice to station himself in the rear; and
now he spurned adequate personal protection. To him, the main
issue was to be resolved by personal combat with his brother;
but such bravado in a commander-in-chief must hold serious dangers for his army.

8:7 προμετωπίδια: 'frontlets', protecting the head (μέτωπον 'fore-
head'). * προστερνίδια: 'chest armour' (στέρνον 'chest').
μαχαίρας: 'sabres', curved short swords.

8:8 κονιορτός: 'dust (stirred up)', 'a dustcloud'. * χρόνῳ ...
συχνῷ: dat. of measure of difference, with comparative ὕστερον.
* ὥσπερ μελανία ... : lit. 'just as a certain blackness on the
plain over a long (distance)'; the white cloud did not turn
black but gave way to the dark mass of the army as it came
over the horizon. * τάχα δὴ ... : 'suddenly there were flash-
es of bronze'.

8:9 λευκοθώρακες: 'in white cuirasses', i.e. made of several folds
of linen - a material more suitable than bronze for a hot
climate, though providing less protection. * ἐχόμενοι sc.
ἦσαν: 'next (came)'.
γερροφόροι: 'troops with wicker shields'; the γέρρον was a large
oblong wicker shield covered with ox-hide. * ποδήρεσι ξυλίναις ἀσπίσιν: much larger than the Greek hoplites' shields.

δ' οὗτοι ἐλέγοντο εἶναι), ἄλλοι δ' ἱππεῖς, ἄλλοι
τοξόται. πάντες δ' οὗτοι κατὰ ἔθνη ἐν πλαισίῳ πλή-
8:10 ρει ἀνθρώπων ἕκαστον τὸ ἔθνος ἐπορεύετο. πρὸ δὲ
αὐτῶν ἅρματα διαλείποντα συχνὸν ἀπ' ἀλλήλων, τὰ δὴ
δρεπανηφόρα καλούμενα· εἶχον δὲ τὰ δρέπανα ἐκ τῶν
ἀξόνων εἰς πλάγιον ἀποτεταμένα καὶ ὑπὸ τοῖς δίφροις
εἰς γῆν βλέποντα, ὡς διακόπτειν ὅτῳ ἐντυγχάνοιεν.
ἡ δὲ γνώμη ἦν ὡς εἰς τὰς τάξεις τῶν Ἑλλήνων ἐλών-
8:11 των καὶ διακοψόντων. ὁ μέντοι Κῦρος εἶπεν ὅτε καλ-
έσας παρεκελεύετο τοῖς Ἕλλησι τὴν κραυγὴν τῶν βαρβάρων ἀνέχεσθαι, ἐψεύσθη τοῦτο· οὐ γὰρ κραυγῇ, ἀλλὰ

* ἐλέγετο ... ἐλέγοντο: Xenophon uses this kind of expression to indicate that he was not an eyewitness, or when he has
not checked his facts, or to maintain the appearance of impartiality. Kyros the Elder, founder of the Persian Empire, had ann-
exed Egypt, and deported a number of Egyptians to N. W. Asia Minor
in the 6th century (cf. Cyropaedia 7.1.45). * ἄλλοι:'more'.

8:10 ἅρματα διαλείποντα ... : 'at considerable intervals, the dreaded
(δή) scythed chariots, as they are called'; according to Xenophon there were 150 of them, as against Kyros' 20. He describes
them elsewhere as follows: ' ... war chariots were constructed
with strong wheels, so that they could not easily get smashed
up, and with long axles: wide vehicles are less likely to over-
turn. The driver's platform was of strong wood, built up like
a turret; it was elbow height, to enable the horses to be controlled over the front. The drivers were entirely covered with
armour except for their eyes. In addition, iron scythes about
three feet long were attached to the axles on either side of
the wheels, with others beneath the axle pointing towards the
ground. The chariots were designed to be hurled into the enemy
lines.' (Cyropaedia, 6.1.29 - 30). In Greek armies chariots
were used for transport, not fighting (see on 8:3 above).
ὡς + inf. = ὥστε: see Introduction 6.3. ὅτῳ, from ὅστις.
* ἐντυγχάνοιεν: opt., indefinite relative clause.
ἡ δὲ γνώμη sc. αὐτῶν ... : 'the idea of them was that they should
... '; ὡς + fut. participles (ἐλώντων and διακοψόντων) expressing purpose; τῶν Ἑλλήνων, used by Xenophon to denote 'his side',
even though it contained non-Greeks.

8:11 ὁ μέντοι Κῦρος εἶπεν ... ἐψεύσθη τοῦτο: 'but Kyros was wrong in
what he (had) said ... '; ὅ (from ὅς) 'as for what', and τοῦτο
                                                           (cont.)

σιγῇ ὡς ἀνυστὸν καὶ ἡσυχῇ ἐν ἴσῳ καὶ βραδέως προσ-
8:12 ῆσαν. καὶ ἐν τούτῳ Κῦρος παρελαύνων αὐτὸς σὺν Πίγ-
ρητι τῷ ἑρμηνεῖ καὶ ἄλλοις τρισὶν ἢ τέτταρσι τῷ
Κλεάρχῳ ἐβόα ἄγειν τὸ στράτευμα κατὰ μέσον τὸ τῶν
πολεμίων, ὅτι ἐκεῖ βασιλεὺς εἴη· Κἂν τοῦτ', ἔφη,
8:13 νικῶμεν, πάνθ' ἡμῖν πεποίηται. ὁρῶν δὲ ὁ Κλέαρχος
τὸ μέσον στῖφος καὶ ἀκούων Κύρου ἔξω ὄντα τοῦ εὐωνύμου βασιλέα (τοσοῦτον γὰρ πλῆθει περιῆν βασιλεὺς
ὥστε μέσον τὸ ἑαυτοῦ ἔχων τοῦ Κύρου εὐωνύμου ἔξω
ἦν), ἀλλ' ὅμως ὁ Κλέαρχος οὐκ ἤθελεν ἀποσπάσαι ἀπὸ
τοῦ ποταμοῦ τὸ δεξιὸν κέρας, φοβούμενος μὴ κυκλω-
θείη ἑκατέρωθεν, τῷ δὲ Κύρῳ ἀπεκρίνατο ὅτι αὐτῷ

'in this', acc. of respect. He had said this when addressing
the generals and captains early that morning; sustained yelling
(and other loud noises) can have a profound psychological effect in battle; cf. Herodotus 9.60 (Plataia) and Thucydides 4.34
(Sphakteria).]
σιγῇ ὡς ἀνυστὸν ... : 'as quietly and calmly as could be, slowly
(marching) in step'; the shock of this eerie and menacing silence could be just as effective as that caused by noise.
* προσῇσαν: imperf. of πρόσειμι (εἶμι'go').

8:12 ἐν τούτῳ sc. τῷ χρόνῳ: 'meanwhile'. * παρελαύνων ... τῷ Κλεάρχῳ
ἐβόα ... : 'rode along the lines ... shouting to Klearkhos to
lead his forces against the centre'; σὺν + dat., see on 1:11 above; Pigres appeared in 5:7 and Klearkhos, who was in charge
of all the Greeks in 6:5 and 8:4 above.   * ὅτι ἐκεῖ: 'because that was where'; ὅτι, causal. * εἴη: opt. of εἰμί 'be',
indirect statement after historic verb.
Κἂν τουτ', ἔφη ... : lit. '"And if this," he said, "we defeat,
everything has been done by us."' i.e. '"If we win there," he
said, "we've won everywhere."' Κἂν = καὶ ἐάν (crasis, see on 5:
2 above).

8:13 τὸ μέσον στῖφος: 'the dense mass in the centre'. * Κύρου: 'from
Kyros'. * τοσοῦτον: 'to such an extent', adverbial acc.; πλήθει: 'in numbers'. * μέσον ... ἔχων: 'although he occupied the
centre', concessive part.; Kyros' aim of having the Greeks opposite the King (8:4 above) had failed: the King was well to their
left, though perhaps not as far as Xenophon says; to fulfil the
order Klearkhos would have had to move obliquely across the front
of Kyros' centre and left (Ariaios' troops), so that Xenophon may
well be exaggerating. * ἀλλ' ὅμως: ἀλλά and δέ are sometimes
used after concessive participles, although strictly redundant.

8:14 μέλει ὅπως καλῶς ἔχοι. καὶ ἐν τούτῳ τῷ καιρῷ τὸ
μὲν βαρβαρικὸν στράτευμα ὁμαλῶς προῄει, τὸ δὲ ᾽Ελλη-
νικὸν ἔτι ἐν τῷ αὐτῷ μένον συνετάττετο ἐκ τῶν ἔτι
προσιόντων. καὶ ὁ Κῦρος παρελαύνων οὐ πάνυ πρὸς
αὐτῷ τῷ στρατεύματι κατεθεᾶτο ἑκατέρωσε ἀποβλέπων
8:15 εἴς τε τοὺς πολεμίους καὶ τοὺς φιλίους. ἰδὼν δὲ
αὐτὸν ἀπὸ τοῦ ᾽Ελληνικοῦ Ξενοφῶν Ἀθηναῖος, ὑπελάσας
ὡς συναντῆσαι ἤρετο εἴ τι παραγγέλλοι· ὁ δ᾽ ἐπιστήσας εἶπε καὶ λέγειν ἐκέλευε πᾶσιν ὅτι καὶ τὰ ἱερὰ

* ὅτι αὐτῷ μέλει ... : 'that he was taking care that all was
well', an evasive reply; adverb + ἔχω = 'be in ... condition'
(here impersonal).

8:14 τὸ μὲν βαρβαρικὸν στράτευμα ... τὸ δὲ ᾽Ελληνικὸν: i.e. the King's
and Kyros' respectively; this shows Xenophon's typically Greek
attitude to the whole campaign (see on τῶν ᾽Ελλήνων, 8:10 above);
contrast Kyros' own viewpoint (see on 8:6 above).   * προῄει: imperf. of πρόειμι (εἶμι 'go'). * ἐν τῷ αὐτῷ μένον ... : lit.
'staying in the same (place) it was being drawn up from those
still approaching' i.e. 'stayed where it was, as men kept arriv-
ing to fill up the lines'; προσιόντων, part. of πρόσειμι (εἶμι 'go').
οὐ πάνυ πρὸς + dat.: 'quite a long way from'; Kyros was still worried
about who would confront whom.

8:15 Ξενοφῶν: the author's first mention of himself, in the third person (unlike Herodotus; but following the practice of Thucydides,
who also participated in the events he described). * ὑπελάσας ὡς συναντῆσαι: lit. 'having ridden up so as to meet';
ὡς = ὥστε, see Introduction 6.3. * εἴ τι παραγγέλλοι: 'if
he had any orders'; opt., indir. question after historic verb.
ἐπιστήσας (sc. τὸν ἵππον): weak aor. part. of ἐφίστημι.
* εἶπε καὶ λέγειν ἐκέλευε: 'told (him) to tell'. * καὶ τὰ
ἱερὰ καλὰ sc. ἐστι ... : 'the omens were favourable and the victims were favourable'. Before any important enterprise, the
Greeks offered sacrifice to one or more gods, to ascertain and
'buy' their support; they liked to 'begin with the gods' (ἀπὸ
τῶν θεῶν ἄρχεσθαι). A priest (ἱερεύς) sacrificed (θύω) an un-
blemished animal by cutting its throat (σφάττω), and burnt its
body on an altar (βωμός), which could be a simple mound of turf
or an elaborately carved stone structure. For the omens (τὰ
ἱερά) to be favourable, every detail of the ritual had to go
smoothly, and the animal must not have tried to resist; also a
μάντις (8:4 above) examined the animal's internal organs (cont.)

8:16 καλὰ καὶ τὰ σφάγια καλά. ταῦτα δὲ λέγων θορύβου
ἤκουσε διὰ τῶν τάξεων ἰόντος, καὶ ἤρετο τίς ὁ θόρυβος εἴη. ὁ δὲ Κλέαρχος εἶπεν ὅτι σύνθημα παρέρχεται δεύτερον ἤδη. καὶ ὃς ἐθαύμασε τίς παραγγέλλει
καὶ ἤρετο ὅ τι καὶ εἴη τὸ σύνθημα. ὁ δ' ἀπεκρίνατο·
8:17 Ζεὺς σωτὴρ καὶ νίκη. ὁ δὲ Κῦρος ἀκούσας· Ἀλλὰ δέχομαί τε, ἔφη, καὶ τοῦτο ἔστω. ταῦτα δ' εἰπὼν εἰς
τὴν αὐτοῦ χώραν ἀπήλαυνε· καὶ οὐκέτι τρία ἢ τέτταρα
στάδια διειχέτην τὼ φάλαγγε ἀπ' ἀλλήλων ἡνίκα ἐπαιά-

(σπλάγχνα), especially the liver, to make sure there were no
strange markings or deformities; the victim (ἱερεῖον or σφάγια n. pl.) was then burnt on the altar, either just the in-
edible parts (the edible parts were roasted and distributed
to be eaten), or whole. Sacrifices were taken very seriously
and had an important effect on morale.]

8:16 θορύβου: gen. with ἤκουσε (the acc. is usual for a thing).
  * εἴη: opt., indir. question (historic).
  σύνθημα παρέρχεται δεύτερον ἤδη: 'a war-cry was being passed along
  for the second time'; the commander normally decided on and issued the war-cry, which was then passed along the lines and
  back (δεύτερον) as a double check; it provided the troops with
  a single word or phrase to concentrate on and shout when going
  into battle. At night a σύνθημα was the password which sen-
  tries demanded from anyone trying to enter the camp.
  καὶ ὅς: 'and he', ὅς as demonstrative pronoun. Kyros was fore-
  stalled in issuing it - presumably by Klearkhos.
  Ζεὺς σωτὴρ καὶ νίκη: the Greeks personified Victory as a goddess;
  the auspicious phrase used here was typical.

8:17 Ἀλλὰ δέχομαί τε ... : 'well, I accept (it); so be it.'; ἔστω
  3rd pers. sing. imperative of εἰμί 'be'; Kyros had little
  choice but to accept it; but it was an appropriate phrase since
  Kyros would have equated Zeus with Ahura-Mazda, the God of Light
  of Zoroastrianism (the Persian religion), whose embodiment on
  earth he hoped soon to be - as King; cf. Herodotus 1.131.
  οὐκέτι τρία ... : 'the two battle-lines were hardly three or four
  stadia apart' (about half a mile); διειχέτην, 3rd pers. dual
  imperf. of διέχω; τὼ φάλαγγε, nom. dual of φάλαγξ 'hoplite
  battle-line', normally eight deep, but perhaps four deep here,
  to give the Greeks a wider front. * ἐπαιάνιζον: 'began to
  sing the paean'; the παιάν was a choral hymn sung to a god,
  originally to Apollo Paian (the Healer); Greek soldiers sang the
  paean before battle to enlist the god's help and assist esprit
  de corps.

νιζόν τε οἱ ῞Ελληνες καὶ ἤρχοντο ἀντίοι ἱέναι τοῖς
8:18 πολεμίοις. ὡς δὲ πορευομένων ἐξεκύμαινέ τι τῆς φάλαγγος, τὸ ὑπολειπόμενον ἤρξατο δρόμῳ θεῖν· καὶ ἅμα
ἐφθέγξαντο πάντες οἷόνπερ τῷ ᾽Ενυαλίῳ ἐλελίζουσι,
καὶ πάντες δὲ ἔθεον· λέγουσι δέ τινες ὡς καὶ ταῖς
ἀσπίσι πρὸς τὰ δόρατα ἐδούπησαν φόβον ποιοῦντες
8:19 τοῖς ἵπποις. πρὶν δὲ τόξευμα ἐξικνεῖσθαι ἐγκλίν-
ουσιν οἱ βάρβαροι καὶ φεύγουσι. καὶ ἐνταῦθα δὴ
ἐδίωκον μὲν κατὰ κράτος οἱ ῞Ελληνες, ἐβόων δὲ ἀλλ-
8:20 ήλοις μὴ θεῖν δρόμῳ, ἀλλ᾽ ἐν τάξει ἔπεσθαι. τὰ
δ᾽ ἅρματα ἐφέροντο τὰ μὲν δι᾽ αὐτῶν τῶν πολεμίων,

* ἱέναι: inf. of εἶμι 'go'; the signal to advance was given
on the trumpet (σάλπιγξ). When Greek armies fought there was
first an exchange of missiles from the archers, javelin-throwers,
and slingers; this was to 'soften up' the enemy and find weak
points; mounted soldiers added to the harrassment. Finally the
two hoplite lines threw their spears and then clashed, each trying to press the other back, until one side broke and its troops
either fled or engaged in single combat with sword and shield;
this clash of hoplites normally decided the issue; cf. 8:3 above and Thucydides 6.67 - 71.

8:18 ὡς: 'when'. * πορευομένων sc. αὐτῶν: gen. absolute. * ἐξεκύμαινέ τι τῆς φάλαγγος: 'part of the line billowed out' i.e.
' ... surged forward', a metaphor from the sea. The hoplites
were losing their co-ordination and not keeping in line: each
man should have been shielding the man on his left (see on 8:3
above). * δρόμῳ θεῖν: 'to advance at the double', 'to run'.
* οἷόνπερ: 'the very kind of (war-cry) that' (see on οἷπερ,
6:10 above). * ᾽Ενυαλίῳ: Enyalios ('Warlike') was a title of
Ares, god of war. * ἐλελίζουσι: lit. utter the war-whoop ἐλ-
ελεῦ or ἐλελελεῦ.
καὶ ταῖς ἀσπίσι ... : lit. 'they made a noise also with the shields
against the spears' i.e. 'they also banged their spears on their
shields'; see on 8:11 above.

8:19 πρὶν δὲ τόξευμα ἐξικνεῖσθαι sc. πρὸς αὐτούς: 'before an arrow
reached (them)' i.e. 'before they came within bowshot'; they
never came closer than 200 yards. * κατὰ κράτος: see on ἀνὰ
κράτος, 8:1 above.

8:20 τὰ δ᾽ ἅρματα ... τὰ μὲν ... τὰ δὲ: 'as for the chariots, some ...
while others', all nom. (the King would have done better to
concentrate his chariots on his left, to confront the Greek
hoplites; this might well have stayed their flight). (cont.)

τὰ δὲ καὶ διὰ τῶν Ἑλλήνων κενὰ ἡνιόχων. οἱ δ'
ἐπεὶ προΐδοιεν, διίσταντο· ἔστι δ' ὅστις καὶ κατελήφθη ὥσπερ ἐν ἱπποδρόμῳ ἐκπλαγείς· καὶ οὐδὲν μέντοι οὐδὲ τοῦτον παθεῖν ἔφασαν, οὐδ' ἄλλος δὲ τῶν
Ἑλλήνων ἐν ταύτῃ τῇ μάχῃ ἔπαθεν οὐδεὶς οὐδέν,
8:21 πλὴν ἐπὶ τῷ εὐωνύμῳ τοξευθῆναί τις ἐλέγετο. Κῦρος
δ' ὁρῶν τοὺς Ἕλληνας νικῶντας τὸ καθ' αὐτοὺς καὶ
διώκοντας, ἡδόμενος καὶ προσκυνούμενος ἤδη ὡς βασιλεὺς ὑπὸ τῶν ἀμφ' αὐτόν, οὐδ' ὡς ἐξήχθη διώκειν,
ἀλλὰ συνεσπειραμένην ἔχων τὴν τῶν σὺν ἑαυτῷ ἑξα-
κοσίων ἱππέων τάξιν ἐπεμελεῖτο ὅ τι ποιήσει βασι-
λεύς· καὶ γὰρ ᾔδει αὐτὸν ὅτι μέσον ἔχοι τοῦ Περ-
8:22 σικοῦ στρατεύματος. καὶ πάντες δ' οἱ τῶν βαρβάρων

---

* ἐφέροντο: plur. verb after neuter plur. subject, irregular;
   see on ἅπαντα ... , 5:1 above.]
προΐδοιεν: aor. opt. of προοράω, indefinite temporal clause.
* διίσταντο: imperf. mid. of διίστημι.
ἔστι δ' ὅστις καὶ κατελήφθη ... : 'one man was in fact caught
like (someone) ... paralysed with fright'; ἐν ἱπποδρόμῳ:
Xenophon refers to a racing-chariot driver who had fallen out
and was too panic-stricken to take evasive action before on-
coming chariots.
καὶ οὐδὲν μέντοι ... : 'actually, however, even he was not at all
hurt, it was said; nor for that matter was any other Greek hurt -
not one'; ἔφασαν, imperf. of φημί; note the build-up of negatives;
οὐδὲ ... δέ = negative of καὶ ... δέ (see on 1:2 above).
* πλήν: 'except that', introducing a clause.

8:21 τὸ καθ' αὐτούς: 'the (section) opposite them'; αὐτοὺς = ἑαυτούς.
      * ἡδόμενος καὶ προσκυνούμενος ... : 'although he was pleased
      and was already being bowed down to as King', concessive part-
      iciples; if προσκυνούμενος is meant literally, the horsemen
      must have dismounted (for προσκύνησις, see on 6:10 above).
      * οὐδ' ὥς: 'even so ... not'; ὥς (with accent), 'thus'.
      * συνεσπειραμένην ἔχων ... : 'keeping his own troop of six
      hundred horsemen in close order'; these formed his bodyguard
      and were not a cavalry unit as such.   * ἐπεμελεῖτο ὅ τι:
      'watched (to see) what'.
      ᾔδει αὐτὸν ὅτι: 'he knew that he'; ᾔδει, imperf. of οἶδα; ὅτι,
      see on εἰδότες ὅτι, 6:10 above; αὐτόν, subject of indir. state-
      ment anticipated (for this construction, see on καὶ τῶν παρ'
      ἑαυτῷ, 1:5 above).

ἄρχοντες μέσον ἔχοντες τὸ αὐτῶν ἡγοῦνται, νομίζοντες οὕτω καὶ ἐν ἀσφαλεστάτῳ εἶναι, ἢν ᾖ ἡ ἰσχὺς
αὐτῶν ἐκατέρωθεν, καὶ εἴ τι παραγγεῖλαι χρῄζοιεν,
8:23 ἡμίσει ἂν χρόνῳ αἰσθάνεσθαι τὸ στράτευμα. καὶ
βασιλεὺς δὴ τότε μέσον ἔχων τῆς αὐτοῦ στρατιᾶς
ὅμως ἔξω ἐγένετο τοῦ Κύρου εὐωνύμου κέρατος. ἐπεὶ
δὲ οὐδεὶς αὐτῷ ἐμάχετο ἐκ τοῦ ἀντίου οὐδὲ τοῖς
αὐτοῦ τεταγμένοις ἔμπροσθεν, ἐπέκαμπτεν ὡς εἰς κύκ-
8:24 λωσιν. ἔνθα δὴ Κῦρος δείσας μὴ ὄπισθεν γενόμενος
κατακόψῃ τὸ Ἑλληνικὸν ἐλαύνει ἀντίος· καὶ ἐμβαλὼν
σὺν τοῖς ἐξακοσίοις νικᾷ τοὺς πρὸ βασιλέως τεταγ-
μένους καὶ εἰς φυγὴν ἔτρεψε τοὺς ἐξακισχιλίους, καὶ
ἀποκτεῖναι λέγεται αὐτὸς τῇ ἑαυτοῦ χειρὶ Ἀρταγέρσην
8:25 τὸν ἄρχοντα αὐτῶν. ὡς δ' ἡ τροπὴ ἐγένετο, διασπείρ-
ονται καὶ οἱ Κύρου ἐξακόσιοι εἰς τὸ διώκειν ὁρμήσ-

8:22 οὕτω: 'in this position' or 'in this way'. * καὶ ἐν ἀσφαλεσ-
      τάτῳ: 'both in the safest (place)'. * ἢν = ἐάν.
      εἴ τι παραγγεῖλαι ... : 'the army would hear any orders they
      needed to issue in half the time'; χρῄζοιεν, opt., and ἂν ...
      αἰσθάνεσθαι (= αἰσθάνοιτο of dir. speech), remote fut. condit-
      ion; ἡμίσει χρόνῳ = ἐν ἡμίσει χρόνῳ (a rare omission).

8:23 καὶ ... δὴ τότε: 'and so ... on this occasion'. * ἔχων: 'while
      he occupied', concessive, made clear by the following ὅμως.
      * ἔξω ἐγένετο ... : once again Xenophon insists on this; see
      on μέσον ... ἔχων, 8:13 above.
      τοῖς αὐτοῦ τεταγμένοις ἔμπροσθεν: 'the troops drawn up in front
      of him', i.e. the bodyguard of 6000 horsemen mentioned earlier,
      similar to Kyros' 600; τοῖς ... τεταγμένοις, dat. after ἐμάχ-
      ετο; αὐτοῦ, with ἔμπροσθεν. * ἐπέκαμπτεν ὡς εἰς κύκλωσιν:
      'he began to wheel round, intending to encircle (or outflank)
      (Kyros)'.

8:24 μὴ ὄπισθεν γενόμενος ... : 'that he might get behind the Greek
      (lines) and cut them to pieces'.
      εἰς φυγὴν ἔτρεψε: 'routed', 'put to flight', i.e. made them turn
      (τρέπομαι) and run away (φεύγω). * αὐτὸς τῇ ἑαυτοῦ χειρὶ:
      'with his own hand'.

8:25 ὡς: 'when'. * καὶ οἱ ... ἐξακόσιοι: 'the six hundred ...
      also'. * εἰς τὸ διώκειν ὁρμήσαντες: 'in their rush to pur-
      sue (the enemy).

αντες, πλὴν πάνυ ὀλίγοι ἀμφ' αὐτὸν κατελείφθησαν,
8:26 σχεδὸν οἱ ὁμοτράπεζοι καλούμενοι. σὺν τούτοις δὲ
ὧν καθορᾷ βασιλέα καὶ τὸ ἀμφ' ἐκεῖνον στῖφος· καὶ
εὐθὺς οὐκ ἠνέσχετο, ἀλλ' εἰπών· Τὸν ἄνδρα ὁρῶ, ἵετο
ἐπ' αὐτὸν καὶ παίει κατὰ τὸ στέρνον καὶ τιτρώσκει
διὰ τοῦ θώρακος, ὥς φησι Κτησίας ὁ ἰατρὸς καὶ ἰάσ-
8:27 ασθαι αὐτὸς τὸ τραῦμά φησι. παίοντα δ' αὐτὸν ἀκον-
τίζει τις παλτῷ ὑπὸ τὸν ὀφθαλμὸν βιαίως· καὶ ἐνταῦθα
μαχόμενοι καὶ βασιλεὺς καὶ Κῦρος καὶ οἱ ἀμφ' αὐτοὺς
ὑπὲρ ἑκατέρου, ὁπόσοι μὲν τῶν ἀμφὶ βασιλέα ἀπέθανον
Κτησίας λέγει· παρ' ἐκείνῳ γὰρ ἦν· Κῦρος δὲ αὐτός

* πάνυ ὀλίγοι: 'a very small number'. * ὁμοτράπεζοι: 'table-
companions', 'mess-mates', a select group who shared his table
as a mark of honour and friendship (ὁμός 'common', τράπεζα
'table'); as personal friends they would have strong feelings
of loyalty to Kyros and to each other; and feelings of shame
would prevent cowardice in times of danger. The King also had
table-companions, described as ὁμότιμοι 'equals in honour'.

8:26 οὐκ ἠνέσχετο: 'he could not contain himself' (from ἀν-έχομαι,
with the normal double augment). Again, Kyros' single-minded-
ness is emphasised as in 8:6 and 8:12 above. * Τὸν ἄνδρα
ὁρῶ: 'there he is!', 'that's him!' * ἵετο: imperf. mid. of
ἵημι. * παίει κατὰ τὸ στέρνον: 'struck (him) in the chest',
with one of his javelins (see on παλτά, 8:3 above); παίει,
mostly poetic (Introduction 6.5). It seems very strange that
Kyros could have got so close, considering the ratio of the
King's bodyguard to his own. φησι: 3rd pers. s. of φημί.
* Κτησίας: see on παρασάγγας, 5:1 above; as well as a History
of Persia, he also wrote a geographical treatise and the first
book specifically about India; only fragments of his works have
survived, quoted in other authors. * ἰάσασθαι αὐτός: 'that he
himself treated', pres. inf. with perf. meaning.

8:27 παίοντα δ' αὐτόν: 'Kyros in the act of striking'.
μαχόμενοι καὶ βασιλεύς ... : 'in the fighting between the King ...
the nom. part. is not followed by the expected main verb but
left 'in the air' (in sense it belongs inside the ὁπόσοι clause),
and the main verb is λέγει: the construction is called nominativus pendens. * ὁπόσοι μὲν τῶν ἀμφὶ ... : 'the number of
dead on the King's side is given by Ktesias, who accompanied
him'; according to Ktesias (quoted by Plutarch) the King's forces
totalled 400,000.

τε ἀπέθανε καὶ ὀκτὼ οἱ ἄριστοι τῶν περὶ αὐτὸν ἔκειντο

8:28   ἐπ' αὐτῷ. Ἀρταπάτης δ' ὁ πιστότατος αὐτῷ τῶν σκηπτούχων λέγεται, ἐπειδὴ πεπτωκότα εἶδε Κῦρον, κατα-

8:29   πηδήσας ἀπὸ τοῦ ἵππου περιπεσεῖν αὐτῷ. καὶ οἱ μὲν
φασι βασιλέα κελεῦσαί τινα ἐπισφάξαι αὐτὸν Κύρῳ, οἱ
δὲ αὐτὸν ἐπισφάξασθαι σπασάμενον τὸν ἀκινάκην· εἶχε
γὰρ χρυσοῦν, καὶ στρεπτὸν δ' ἐφόρει καὶ ψέλια καὶ
τἆλλα ὥσπερ οἱ ἄριστοι Περσῶν· ἐτετίμητο γὰρ ὑπὸ
Κύρου δι' εὔνοιάν τε καὶ πιστότητα.

ὀκτὼ οἱ ἄριστοι ... : 'the eight best (or noblest) men on his
staff lay (dead) upon him'; they had defended him to the last.

8:28   σκηπτούχων: see on 6:11 above. * περιπεσεῖν: lit. 'to have
fallen around' i.e. 'to have thrown himself down and flung his
arms around'.

8:29   φασι: 3rd pers. pl. of φημί. * βασιλέα κελεῦσαί τινα ... : 'that
the King ordered someone to slaughter him over Kyros' body'; ἐπι-
σφάττω, like σφάττω, properly refers to cutting a sacrificial
victim's throat (see on καὶ τὰ ἱερά ... , 8:15 above) and hence
to any slaughter. * αὐτὸν .(= ἑαυτὸν) ἐπισφάξασθαι ... : 'that
he drew his dagger and cut his own throat'; the mid. verb ἐπισφάξασθαι emphasizes the self-infliction of the blow; σπάομαι,
mostly poetic (see Introduction 6.5); ἀκινάκης, the short straight
Persian sword.
χρυσοῦν: 'one made of gold', and therefore, according to Persian
custom, a gift suitable to be given only by the King. * τἆλλα
= τὰ ἄλλα (crasis, see on ταὐτόν, 5:2 above).
δι' εὔνοιάν τε καὶ πιστότητα: 'for loyal support'.

*The mention of Artapates paves the way for an account of Kyros'
life and character, which interrupts the account of the battle.
This character sketch, along with those in Book 2, marked the beginning of an interest in biographical writing and they became mod-
els for later biographers; Xenophon later wrote biography on a ful-
ler scale in his Agesilaos and Cyropaedia (see Introduction 2);
contrast the emphasis on narrative interest in Herodotus (e.g.
his treatment of the life of Dareios I, Books 1 - 7, and his
death 7.4 - 5) and political interest in Thucydides (e.g. the
career of Perikles, 2.65); the idea of describing a person who
had just died was a natural extension of the funeral speech (ἐπι-
τάφιος) where a dead man's character and exploits were praised.*

9:1 Κῦρος μὲν οὖν οὕτως ἐτελεύτησεν, ἀνὴρ ὢν Περσῶν
τῶν μετὰ Κῦρον τὸν ἀρχαῖον γενομένων βασιλικώτατός
τε καὶ ἄρχειν ἀξιώτατος, ὡς παρὰ πάντων ὁμολογεῖται

9:2 τῶν Κύρου δοκούντων ἐν πείρᾳ γενέσθαι. πρῶτον μὲν
γὰρ ἔτι παῖς ὢν ὅτ' ἐπαιδεύετο καὶ σὺν τῷ ἀδελφῷ
καὶ σὺν τοῖς ἄλλοις παισί, πάντων πάντα κράτιστος

9:3 ἐνομίζετο. πάντες γὰρ οἱ τῶν ἀρίστων Περσῶν παῖδες
ἐπὶ ταῖς βασιλέως θύραις παιδεύονται· ἔνθα πολλὴν
μὲν σωφροσύνην καταμάθοι ἄν τις, αἰσχρὸν δ' οὐδὲν

9:4 οὔτ' ἀκοῦσαι οὔτ' ἰδεῖν ἔστι. θεῶνται δ' οἱ παῖδες
καὶ τιμωμένους ὑπὸ βασιλέως καὶ ἀκούουσι, καὶ ἄλλους ἀτιμαζομένους, ὥστε εὐθὺς παῖδες ὄντες μανθάν-

9:5 ουσιν ἄρχειν τε καὶ ἄρχεσθαι. ἔνθα Κῦρος αἰδημονέστατος μὲν πρῶτον τῶν ἡλικιωτῶν ἐδόκει εἶναι, τοῖς

9:1 μὲν οὖν: 'anyway', resuming the narrative. * Κῦρον τὸν ἀρχαῖον:
'Kyros the Elder'; Kyros II made a great impression on the
Greeks, including Xenophon, who wrote the semi-fictional *Cyropaedia* ('Education of Kyros') about him. * παρά: see Introduction 6.4. * τῶν Κύρου δοκούντων ... : lit. 'those seeming
to have been in experience of Kyros' i.e. 'those reputed to
have known him personally'.

9:2 πάντα: 'in every way', adverbial acc.

9:3 ἐπὶ ταῖς βασιλέως θύραις: lit. 'at the King's doors', i.e. in his
palace, 'at Court'; an oriental idiom (*cf.* 'the alien within
your gates', *Exodus* 20.10); eastern monarchs lived in far more
seclusion than leaders in Greece, where political life was conducted publicly, out of doors.
πολλὴν μὲν: 'in great measure', emphatic position. * σωφροσύνην: 'good behaviour', 'good manners', including tact and
self-control; Kyros' upbringing in general fitted him for a
life of diplomacy and physical hardship. * καταμάθοι ἄν τις:
'one would learn'. potential opt. * ἔστι: 'it is possible'.

9:4 θεῶνται: 'see for themselves', emphatic position. * εὐθὺς παῖδες ὄντες: 'right from childhood'.

9:5 αἰδημονέστατος μὲν πρῶτον: πρῶτον delayed to emphasise αἰδημονέστατος. * τῶν ἡλικιωτῶν: 'boys of his own age'. (*cont.*)

τε πρεσβυτέροις καὶ τῶν ἑαυτοῦ ὑποδεεστέρων μᾶλλον
πείθεσθαι, ἔπειτα δὲ φιλιππότατος καὶ τοῖς ἵπποις
ἄριστα χρῆσθαι· ἔκρινον δ᾿ αὐτὸν καὶ τῶν εἰς τὸν
πόλεμον ἔργων, τοξικῆς τε καὶ ἀκοντίσεως, φιλομαθ-
9:6 έστατον εἶναι καὶ μελετηρότατον. ἐπεὶ δὲ τῇ ἡλικίᾳ
ἔπρεπε, καὶ φιλοθηρότατος ἦν καὶ πρὸς τὰ θηρία μέντοι φιλοκινδυνότατος. καὶ ἄρκτον ποτὲ ἐπιφερομένην
οὐκ ἔτρεσεν, ἀλλὰ συμπεσὼν κατεσπάσθη ἀπὸ τοῦ ἵππου,
καὶ τὰ μὲν ἔπαθεν, ὧν καὶ τὰς ὠτειλὰς εἶχεν, τέλος
δὲ κατέκανε· καὶ τὸν πρῶτον μέντοι βοηθήσαντα πολλ-
οῖς μακαριστὸν ἐποίησεν.

* ἐδόκει εἶναι: 'had a reputation for being'.] * καὶ τῶν ἑαυτοῦ ... : 'being more obedient than even his own inferiors';
royal princes might be expected to demonstrate their superiority
over the nobles' sons. * ἔπειτα δὲ: 'secondly', following πρῶτον μέν. * φιλιππότατος sc. ἐδόκει εἶναι: adjectives beginning
φιλ(ο)- often occur in character descriptions.
καὶ τῶν εἰς τὸν πόλεμον ... : 'also the most eager to learn and
the most diligent in practising military skills'; τῶν εἰς τὸν
πόλεμον ἔργων, lit. 'activities for war'.

9:6 τῇ ἡλικίᾳ ἔπρεπε: lit. 'it suited (his) age' i.e. 'he was old
enough'. * καὶ φιλοθηρότατος ... : lit. 'both (the) keenest
on hunting and moreover towards the (wild) animals (the) fond-
est of danger' i.e. 'not only the keenest hunter but also the
boldest when facing the wild animals'; θηρία are animals which
are hunted.
καὶ ἄρκτον: καὶ, 'in fact'; ἄρκτος, f. * ἔτρεσεν: τρέω is rare
in prose (see Introduction 6.5). * τὰ μὲν ἔπαθεν: lit. 'suffered some things' i.e. 'received injuries'. * ὧν καὶ τὰς ...:
lit. 'of which he had the scars also' i.e. 'and bore the scars
from them too'. * κατέκανε: see on 6:2 above.
τὸν ... πρῶτον ... βοηθήσαντα ... : 'he made the first man to come
and help him an object of general envy', lit. ' ... enviable
to many', i.e. richly rewarded him, so that all would see and
take note; it was expected that good behaviour should be rewarded publicly (μακαρίζω 'bless', 'congratulate'). Kyros certainly
showed himself φιλοκίνδυνος in the battle; Xenophon himself shared his interest in horsemanship and hunting. For a Persian's upbringing, cf. Herodotus 1.136.

9:11   φανερὸς δ' ἦν, καὶ εἴ τίς τι ἀγαθὸν ἢ κακὸν ποι-
        ήσειεν αὐτόν, νικᾶν πειρώμενος, καὶ εὐχὴν δέ τινες
        αὐτοῦ ἐξέφερον ὡς εὔχοιτο τοσοῦτον χρόνον ζῆν ἔστε
        νικῴη καὶ τοὺς εὖ καὶ τοὺς κακῶς ποιοῦντας ἀλεξό-
9:12   μενος. καὶ γὰρ οὖν πλεῖστοι δὴ αὐτῷ ἐνί γε ἀνδρὶ
        τῶν ἐφ' ἡμῶν ἐπεθύμησαν καὶ χρήματα καὶ πόλεις καὶ
9:13   τὰ ἑαυτῶν σώματα προέσθαι. οὐ μὲν δὴ οὐδὲ τοῦτ'
        ἄν τις εἴποι ὡς τοὺς κακούργους καὶ ἀδίκους εἴα
        καταγελᾶν, ἀλλ' ἀφειδέστατα πάντων ἐτιμωρεῖτο.

9:11 **φανερὸς δ' ἦν καὶ** + part.: 'he was also well known for'; or 'it
      was also evident that he', 'he evidently also' (see on δῆλος,
      5:9 above). * **ἀγαθὸν ἢ κακὸν** ... : **ἀγαθὸν** and **κακὸν** (n. acc.)
      ποιέω also take acc. of the person; **ποιήσειεν**, opt., indefinite.
      * **νικᾶν**: 'to outdo', 'to surpass'.
      εὐχὴν αὐτοῦ ... **ὡς εὔχοιτο** ... **ζῆν**: 'a prayer of his that he might
      live'; **εὔχοιτο**, opt., indir. statement (historic sequence).
      * **ἔστε νικῴη** ... : 'until he had outdone both those who bene-
      fited and those who harmed (him)'; **νικῴη**, opt., indefinite.
      * **ἀλεξόμενος**: 'in giving like for like'; rewarding one's friends
      and taking revenge on one's enemies (as conspicuously as poss-
      ible) was considered to be correct behaviour; indeed, Kyros felt
      his honour satisfied only if he went one better.

9:12 **καὶ γὰρ οὖν**: 'consequently', 'as a result'. * **πλεῖστοι δὴ αὐτῷ**
      ... : lit. 'very many indeed ... to him, one man at any rate
      of those in our time' i.e. 'far more ... to him than to any
      other individual of our time'; **εἷς** is often used in this way
      with a superlative. * **καὶ χρήματα**: 'both money'; the Helles-
      pontine cities did not know they were financing Kyros' expedit-
      ion (see 1:9 above), so unless Xenophon is being careless, per-
      haps he is referring to the Ionians (**πόλεις**) or the Milesian
      exiles (see 1:6 - 7 above). * **τὰ ἑαυτῶν σώματα**: 'their own
      persons'. * **προέσθαι**: aor. inf. mid. of **προίημι**.

9:13 **οὐ μὲν δὴ οὐδὲ** ... : lit. 'nor indeed would one say this' i.e.
      'it could certainly not be said either'; **εἴποι ἄν**, potential
      opt. * **τοὺς κακούργους καὶ ἀδίκους**: 'criminals and lawbreak-
      ers'; at Athens, **κακοῦργος** often meant 'robber', 'thief'; ἄ-
      δικος, 'unjust' referred to anything illegal; however, the
      verbs **κακουργέω** and **ἀδικέω** are often found together with no dis-
      tinction in meaning. * **εἴα** (εἴ-α-ε): imperf. of **ἐάω**. * **κατα-
      γελᾶν**: lit. 'to laugh scornfully' i.e. 'to mock his authority'.
      * **ἀλλά**: 'on the contrary'. * **ἀφειδέστατα πάντων**: lit. 'most
      unsparingly of all' i.e. 'more ruthlessly than any'.

πολλάκις δ' ἦν ἰδεῖν παρὰ τὰς στειβομένας ὁδοὺς
καὶ ποδῶν καὶ χειρῶν καὶ ὀφθαλμῶν στερομένους ἀνθρ-
ώπους· ὥστ' ἐν τῇ Κύρου ἀρχῇ ἐγένετο καὶ Ἕλληνι καὶ
βαρβάρῳ μηδὲν ἀδικοῦντι ἀδεῶς πορεύεσθαι ὅποι τις
9:14 ἤθελεν, ἔχοντι ὅ τι προχωροίη. τούς γε μέντοι ἀγαθοὺς εἰς πόλεμον ὡμολόγητο διαφερόντως τιμᾶν. καὶ
πρῶτον μὲν ἦν αὐτῷ πόλεμος πρὸς Πισίδας καὶ Μυσούς·
στρατευόμενος οὖν καὶ αὐτὸς εἰς ταύτας τὰς χώρας
οὓς ἑώρα ἐθέλοντας κινδυνεύειν, τούτους καὶ ἄρχοντας ἐποίει ἧς κατεστρέφετο χώρας, ἔπειτα δὲ καὶ

ἦν: 'it was possible'. παρὰ τὰς στειβομένας ὁδοὺς: perhaps as
beggars. * καὶ ποδῶν καὶ ... καὶ: 'feet or ... or', probably
not all at once.
ἐγένετο: 'it was possible'. * μηδὲν ἀδικοῦντι: 'if he was law-
abiding'; μη- (as opposed to οὐ-) indicates a conditional or
indefinite participle. * ἔχοντι ὅ τι προχωροίη: lit. 'holding
whatever went well (or was convenient)' i.e. 'carrying whatever
suited him'; προχωροίη, opt., indefinite. If people were punished 'πολλάκις', the deterrent effect may have been weaker
than Xenophon implies.

9:14 τούς ... ἀγαθοὺς εἰς πόλεμον: lit. 'those good (or brave) in war'.
* ὡμολόγητο ... τιμᾶν: lit. 'he had been agreed to honour'
i.e. 'it was agreed that he honoured'.
καὶ πρῶτον μὲν ... : 'the first example of this was when he was
fighting (the) Pisidians and Mysians'; a new governor toured
the borders of his province cleaning up potential trouble-spots;
for these tribes, see on 1:11 and 6:7 above.
στρατευόμενος οὖν ... : lit. 'so going on expeditions even himself into these territories' i.e. 'so he personally led expeditions into these territories and ... '. * οὓς ... τούτους:
see on ὅ τι ... τοῦτο, 6:6 above. * ἑώρα (ἐ-ώρα-ε): imperf.
of ὁράω. * καὶ ἄρχοντας: 'the actual rulers', 'rulers as
well', i.e. besides being his army commanders. * ἧς κατεστρέφετο χώρας: 'of an area he was subduing', relative clause
placed early (see on ὁπόσας εἶχε, 1:6 above), with relative
pronoun attracted from acc. into case of antecedent χώρας
(see on τῶν πόλεων ὦν, 1:8 above). Kyros had promised the
Greek officers on the morning of the battle that, if they were
victorious, he would put his friends in charge of the satrapies
hitherto ruled by his brother's appointees. * ἔπειτα δὲ: i.e.
'after these campaigns', following πρῶτον μέν.

9:15 ἄλλοις δώροις ἐτίμα ὥστε φαίνεσθαι τοὺς μὲν ἀγαθοὺς εὐδαιμονεστάτους, τοὺς δὲ κακοὺς δούλους τούτων
ἀξιοῦσθαι εἶναι. τοιγαροῦν πολλὴ ἦν ἀφθονία αὐτῷ
τῶν ἐθελόντων κινδυνεύειν, ὅπου τις οἴοιτο Κῦρον
9:16 αἰσθήσεσθαι. εἰς γε μὴν δικαιοσύνην εἴ τις αὐτῷ
φανερὸς γένοιτο ἐπιδείκνυσθαι βουλόμενος, περὶ παντὸς ἐποιεῖτο τούτους πλουσιωτέρους ποιεῖν τῶν ἐκ
9:17 τοῦ ἀδίκου φιλοκερδούντων. καὶ γὰρ οὖν ἄλλα τε
πολλὰ δικαίως αὐτῷ διεχειρίζετο καὶ στρατεύματι ἀλ-
ηθινῷ ἐχρήσατο. καὶ γὰρ στρατηγοὶ καὶ λοχαγοί, οἳ
χρημάτων ἕνεκα πρὸς ἐκεῖνον ἔπλευσαν, ἔγνωσαν

9:15 ὥστε φαίνεσθαι τοὺς μὲν ἀγαθοὺς sc. ὄντας: 'so that the brave
were shown (to be)'; τοὺς ... ἀγαθοὺς, subject of φαίνεσθαι,
acc. and inf. construction after ὥστε. * τοὺς δὲ κακοὺς ...
ἀξιοῦσθαι: 'while cowards were thought worthy'.
πολλὴ ἦν ἀφθονία ... : 'he had a plentiful supply of men willing
... '. * ὅπου τις οἴοιτο: lit. 'wherever one thought', i.e.
'wherever it was thought', opt., indefinite; the brave made sure
they were seen to be brave.

9:16 εἰς γε μὴν δικαιοσύνην: 'as for justice'. * φανερὸς γένοιτο:
see on δῆλος, 5:9 and on φανερὸς, 9:11 above; opt., indefinite.
* ἐπιδείκνυσθαι: sc. δικαιοσύνην.
περὶ παντὸς ἐποιεῖτο: 'he considered it all-important'.
* τῶν ... φιλοκερδούντων: gen. of comparison (κέρδος 'gain',
'profit', 'advantage'); ἐκ τοῦ ἀδίκου: 'by unjust means'.

9:17 καὶ γὰρ οὖν: see on 9:12 above. * ἄλλα τε πολλὰ ... δικαίως ... :
lit. 'both many other things were being managed justly for him
and ... ' i.e. 'his administration in general was conducted
fairly; in particular (owing to his fairness) he had the services of a genuine army'; ἄλλοι τε ... καί (and similar phrases),
'all (others) ... and especially'. Kyros avoided what other
oriental commanders had permitted, the swelling of his ranks
by incompetent soldiers through nepotism, corruption, or the
desire to keep up appearances; for Kyros' sense of justice, see
also 6:5 and 6:7 above.
λοχαγοί: there were at least 130 of them. For officers' pay, see
on δαρεικούς, 1:9 above. * χρημάτων ἕνεκα ... : lit. 'sailed
to him for the sake of money' i.e. 'came from overseas to serve
him as mercenaries'.
ἔγνωσαν κερδαλεώτερον ... : lit. 'knew (it) to be more profitable
for Kyros to command well than (their) monthly profit' i.e.
'knew that service under Kyros' able command brought in more
(cont.)

κερδαλεώτερον εἶναι Κύρῳ καλῶς ἄρχειν ἢ τὸ κατὰ μῆνα
κέρδος.

9:22   δῶρα δὲ πλεῖστα μὲν οἶμαι εἷς γε ἀνὴρ ἐλάμβανε
διὰ πολλά· ταῦτα δὲ πάντων δὴ μάλιστα τοῖς φίλοις
διεδίδου, πρὸς τοὺς τρόπους ἑκάστου σκοπῶν καὶ ὅτου
9:23   μάλιστα ὁρῴη ἕκαστον δεόμενον. καὶ ὅσα τῷ σώματι
αὐτοῦ κόσμον πέμποι τις ἢ ὡς εἰς πόλεμον ἢ ὡς εἰς
καλλωπισμόν, καὶ περὶ τούτων λέγειν αὐτὸν ἔφασαν
ὅτι τὸ μὲν ἑαυτοῦ σῶμα οὐκ ἂν δύναιτο τούτοις πᾶσι
κοσμηθῆναι, φίλους δὲ καλῶς κεκοσμημένους μέγιστον

than their basic monthly pay'; ἔγνωσαν, although a verb of knowing, is here followed by the inf. (as opposed to part.) construction. The extra booty and special rewards they expected ensured
their loyalty; for Kyros' promises before the battle, see on ἧς
κατεστρέφετο χώρας, 9:14 above.]

9:22   δῶρα δὲ πλεῖστα ... : lit. 'he, one man at any rate, I believe,
received (the) most gifts' i.e. 'as for gifts, I believe he received more than any other individual'; δῶρα, emphatic position;
πλεῖστα ... εἷς: see on πλεῖστοι, 9:12 above; οἶμαι, parenthetic.
* διὰ πολλά: 'for many reasons'.
πάντων δὴ μάλιστα: lit. 'most of all indeed' i.e. 'more than anyone else at all'. * διεδίδου: 3rd pers. sing. imperf. of δια-
δίδωμι. * ὅτου μάλιστα ὁρῴη ... : lit. 'of whatever most he
saw each man being in need' i.e. 'whatever he saw each man needed most'; ὅτου, gen. (of ὅστις) with δεόμενον (part. construction
after verb of perceiving); ὁρῴη, opt., indefinite.

9:23   ὅσα τῷ σώματι ... : lit. 'as many (things) as anyone sent (as) adornment for his body ... concerning these too ... ' i.e. 'as for all
those gifts he was sent to adorn his person ... about them also
...'; ὅσα ... τούτων, see on ὅ τι ... τοῦτο, 6:6 above; ὅσος (ὅσοι) often means 'all that (those) which'; πέμποι, opt., indefinite.
* ὡς: indicates the sender's intention; πόλεμον ... καλλωπισμόν:
i.e. armour, clothing, jewels.
τὸ μὲν ἑαυτοῦ ... : lit. 'be adorned as to his own body' i.e.
'have himself adorned'; τὸ ... σῶμα, acc. object of κοσμέω,
'retained' with pass. inf., or acc. of respect. * οὐκ ἂν
δύναιτο: 'he could not', potential opt. * φίλους δὲ ... νομίζοι sc. εἶναι: 'but that he thought that friends ... (were)';
νομίζοι, opt., continuation of indir. speech after λέγειν ...
ὅτι; φίλους (εἶναι), acc. and inf. with νομίζοι.

9:24 κόσμον ἀνδρὶ νομίζοι. καὶ τὸ μὲν τὰ μεγάλα νικᾶν
τοὺς φίλους εὖ ποιοῦντα οὐδὲν θαυμαστόν, ἐπειδή γε
καὶ δυνατώτερος ἦν· τὸ δὲ τῇ ἐπιμελείᾳ περιεῖναι τῶν
φιλῶν καὶ τῷ προθυμεῖσθαι χαρίζεσθαι, ταῦτα ἔμοιγε
9:25 μᾶλλον δοκεῖ ἀγαστὰ εἶναι. Κῦρος γὰρ ἔπεμπε βίκους
οἴνου ἡμιδεεῖς πολλάκις ὁπότε πάνυ ἡδὺν λάβοι,
λέγων ὅτι οὔπω δὴ πολλοῦ χρόνου τούτου ἡδίονι οἴνῳ
ἐπιτύχοι· Τοῦτον οὖν σοὶ ἔπεμψε καὶ δεῖταί σου τήμ-
9:26 ερον τοῦτον ἐκπιεῖν σὺν οἷς μάλιστα φιλεῖς. πολλάκις δὲ χῆνας ἡμιβρώτους ἔπεμπε καὶ ἄρτων ἡμίσεα καὶ
ἄλλα τοιαῦτα, ἐπιλέγειν κελεύων τὸν φέροντα· Τούτοις ἥσθη Κῦρος· βούλεται οὖν καὶ σὲ τούτων γεύσασθαι.

9:24 τὸ μὲν τὰ μεγάλα ... : lit. 'the (fact that he) outdid (his)
friends in respect of the great things when benefiting (is)
nothing surprising' (sc. ἐστι), i.e. 'the fact that he outdid
his friends in conferring great benefits is not at all surprising'; τὸ ... νικᾶν, verbal noun, subject of sentence; τὰ
μεγάλα, acc. of respect; εὖ ποιοῦντα sc. αὐτόν, subject of
νικᾶν. * γε: 'at any rate', 'after all'; καί, 'also' i.e. besides conferring the benefits.
τὸ δὲ ... περιεῖναι + gen.: 'but the (fact that he) surpassed
... '. * τῇ ἐπιμελείᾳ: 'in his care' i.e. ' ... consideration'.
* τῷ προθυμεῖσθαι + inf.: 'in his eagerness to'.
ταῦτα: pl., referring to ἡ ἐπιμελεία and τὸ προθυμεῖσθαι; ταῦτα
is the subject of δόκει, so strictly τὸ ... περιεῖναι is acc.
of respect, 'as for the fact that ... '.

9:25 βίκους: a rare word, used by Herodotus to refer to Babylonian
wine-casks, possibly made of wood. * πάνυ ἡδὺν λάβοι: 'he
(had) received (some that was) very good', lit. ' ... sweet';
opt., indefinite. * οὔπω δὴ πολλοῦ χρόνου τούτου: lit. 'not
yet indeed within this long time' i.e. 'certainly not ... for
a long time now'. * ἐπιτύχοι + dat.: 'he had ... come across',
opt., indir. statement (historic sequence).
Τοῦτον οὖν σοὶ ἔπεμψε: change to dir. speech, with Kyros speaking
in the 3rd pers. * σου: gen. after δεῖται.
σὺν οἷς μάλιστα φιλεῖς: lit. 'with (those) whom you most love'
i.e.'with your best friends'; relative pronoun attracted from
acc. (object of φιλεῖς) to case of antecedent (not expressed)
dat. after σύν: this is regularly found with a preposition and
relative clause (see on τῶν πόλεων ὧν, 1:8 above). For Persian
fondness for wine, cf. Herodotus 1.133.

9:27 ὅπου δὲ χιλὸς σπάνιος πάνυ εἴη, αὐτὸς δ᾽ ἐδύνατο
παρασκευάσασθαι διὰ τὸ πολλοὺς ἔχειν ὑπηρέτας
καὶ διὰ τὴν ἐπιμέλειαν, διαπέμπων ἐκέλευε τοὺς
φίλους τοῖς τὰ ἑαυτῶν σώματα ἄγουσιν ἵπποις ἐμβάλ-
λειν τοῦτον τὸν χιλόν, ὡς μὴ πεινῶντες τοὺς ἑαυτοῦ
9:28 φίλους ἄγωσιν. εἰ δὲ δή ποτε πορεύοιτο καὶ πλεῖστοι
μέλλοιεν ὄψεσθαι, προσκαλῶν τοὺς φίλους ἐσπουδαιο-
λογεῖτο, ὡς δηλοίη οὓς τιμᾷ. ὥστε ἔγωγε ἐξ ὧν ἀκούω
οὐδένα κρίνω ὑπὸ πλειόνων πεφιλῆσθαι οὔτε Ἑλλήνων
9:29 οὔτε βαρβάρων. τεκμήριον δὲ τούτου καὶ τόδε· παρὰ
μὲν Κύρου δούλου ὄντος οὐδεὶς ἀπῄει πρὸς βασιλέα,

9:27 εἴη: opt., indefinite. * διὰ τὸ ... ἔχειν: 'owing to his having'.
* διαπέμπων ἐκέλευε τοὺς φίλους: 'he used to distribute it
among his friends and tell them' (see on ἐξαιτησαμένη, 1:3
above).
τοῖς τὰ ἑαυτῶν ... : 'to the horses that carried their persons'.
ὡς + subj.; purpose (see Introduction 6.1); πεινῶντες ... ἄγωσιν:
'be hungry when carrying'.

9:28 δή: the end of the list; almost 'finally'. * πορεύοιτο ... μέλλοιεν: opt., indefinite (εἰ ... ποτε virtually = ὁπότε 'whenever'). * ὄψεσθαι sc. αὐτόν. * ὡς δηλοίη: opt., purpose.
* οὓς: οὕστινας (from ὅστις) would be more usual in an indir.
question.
ἐξ ὧν ἀκούω: see on σὺν οἷς μάλιστα φιλεῖς, 9:25 above.
* πεφιλῆσθαι: perf. inf. pass. of φιλέω.

9:29 τεκμήριον ... καὶ τόδε sc. ἐστι: 'here (is) further proof'; ἐστι
is often omitted with τεκμήριον.
δούλου ὄντος: 'although he was a slave' (concessive part.), i.e.
of the King, an absolute monarch whose subjects were often referred to thus by the Greeks, with their different political
system. According to Xenophon, when Kyros addressed the Greek
officers before the battle, he expressed his envy of Greek
political freedom, which was considered to be the source of
their self-confidence and resilience, and hence of their military superiority: 'Freedom is what I should choose in prefer-
ence to all I possess and many times more'; cf. Euripides,
Helen 276 (referring to the Egyptians): 'Barbarians are all
slaves but one'. * ἀπῄει: imperf. of ἄπειμι (εἶμι 'go'),
'left' i.e. 'deserted' (also ἀπῆλθον). * δή: 'of course',
'as you know'.

πλὴν 'Ορόντας ἐπεχείρησε (καὶ οὗτος δὴ ὃν ᾠετο πιστόν οἱ εἶναι ταχὺ αὐτὸν ηὗρε Κύρῳ φιλαίτερον ἢ
ἑαυτῷ), παρὰ δὲ βασιλέως πολλοὶ πρὸς Κῦρον ἀπῆλθον,
ἐπεὶ πολέμιοι ἀλλήλοις ἐγένοντο, καὶ οὗτοι μέντοι
οἱ μάλιστα αὐτοὺς ἀγάμενοι, νομίζοντες παρὰ Κύρῳ
ὄντες ἀγαθοὶ ἀξιωτέρας ἂν τιμῆς τυγχάνειν ἢ παρὰ
9:30 βασιλεῖ. μέγα δὲ τεκμήριον καὶ τὸ ἐν τῇ τελευτῇ
τοῦ βίου αὐτῷ γενόμενον ὅτι καὶ αὐτὸς ἦν ἀγαθὸς καὶ
κρίνειν ὀρθῶς ἐδύνατο τοὺς πιστοὺς καὶ εὔνους καὶ
9:31 βεβαίους. ἀποθνῄσκοντος γὰρ αὐτοῦ πάντες οἱ περὶ
αὐτὸν φίλοι καὶ συντράπεζοι ἀπέθανον μαχόμενοι ὑπὲρ
Κύρου πλὴν Ἀριαίου· οὗτος δὲ τεταγμένος ἐτύγχανεν
ἐπὶ τῷ εὐωνύμῳ τοῦ ἱππικοῦ ἄρχων· ὡς δ' ἤσθετο
Κῦρον πεπτωκότα, ἔφυγεν ἔχων καὶ τὸ στράτευμα πᾶν
οὗ ἡγεῖτο.

πιστόν οἱ: 'loyal to him'; for οἱ (= οἷ, reflexive), see on
1:8 above. * καὶ οὗτοι μέντοι : 'and these moreover'.
ὄντες ἀγαθοὶ ... ἂν τυγχάνειν: 'if they conducted themselves honourably ... they would get', part. and inf. standing for opt.
of dir. speech, in remote fut. condition; τιμῆς: gen. with
τυγχάνειν.

9:30 μέγα δὲ τεκμήριον ... : 'what happened ... (is) also strong (or
clear) evidence' (sc. ἐστι). * ὅτι καὶ αὐτὸς ἦν ... : lit.
'that both he himself was brave (or noble) and was able to pick
out correctly the loyal and well-disposed and reliable' i.e.
'both of his own courage (or nobility) and of his ability to
select unerringly men whose loyal support he could rely on'.
To be a good judge of character was vital in a world of
treachery.

9:31 συντράπεζοι: see on ὁμοτράπεζοι, 8:25 above.
Κῦρον πεπτωκότα: indir. statement (acc. and part.) with verb of
perceiving.
ἔχων καὶ: 'taking with him'; Ariaios was rather a crucial except-
ion, as Kyros' second-in-command, in charge of all his native
cavalry; the 40 horsemen under Klearkhos (see on ἐξελαύνει,
5:1 above) also deserted shortly after.

With the mention of Kyros' death and Araios' behaviour, we return from the character of Kyros to the battle.

10:1   ἐνταῦθα δὴ Κύρου ἀποτέμνεται ἡ κεφαλὴ καὶ ἡ χεὶρ
        ἡ δεξιά. βασιλεὺς δὲ καὶ οἱ σὺν αὐτῷ διώκων εἰσπίπ-
        τει εἰς τὸ Κύρειον στρατόπεδον· καὶ οἱ μὲν μετὰ Ἀρι-
        αίου οὐκέτι ἵστανται, ἀλλὰ φεύγουσι διὰ τοῦ αὐτῶν
        στρατοπέδου εἰς τὸν σταθμὸν ἔνθεν ὡρμῶντο· τέτταρες
10:2   δ' ἐλέγοντο παρασάγγαι εἶναι τῆς ὁδοῦ. βασιλεὺς δὲ καὶ
        οἱ σὺν αὐτῷ τά τε ἄλλα πολλὰ διαρπάζουσι καὶ τὴν Φωκ-
        καΐδα τὴν Κύρου παλλακίδα τὴν σοφὴν καὶ καλὴν λεγομέ-
10:3   νην εἶναι λαμβάνει. ἡ δὲ Μιλησία ἡ νεωτέρα ληφθεῖσα
        ὑπὸ τῶν ἀμφὶ βασιλέα ἐκφεύγει γυμνὴ πρὸς τῶν Ἑλλήν-
        νων οἳ ἔτυχον ἐν τοῖς σκευοφόροις ὅπλα ἔχοντες, καὶ

10:1   ἐνταῦθα δὴ: 'and then', resuming the narrative. * ἀποτέμνεται
        ἡ κεφαλὴ ... : to be impaled and displayed as a deterrent to
        other potential traitors; impaling was a customary dishonour-
        able punishment in Persia (cf. Herodotus 3.132 and 159, 7.238).
        βασιλεὺς δὲ διώκων: Xenophon's account differs from that of
        Ktesias (quoted by Plutarch), according to whom the King, after
        being wounded, retreated to a nearby hill and rested.
        * στρατόπεδον: simply the collection of baggage, camp-follow-
        ers etc.; there would have been no time to erect tents or fort-
        ifications.
        ἵστανται: pres. mid. of ἵστημι. * αὐτῶν: 'their own', = ἑαυτῶν.
        τέτταρες δ' ἐλέγοντο ... : lit. 'there were said to be four para-
        sangs of the journey' i.e. 'it was said to be a journey of 16
        miles'.

10:2   τά τε ἄλλα ... : 'indulged in widespread looting, and in partic-
        ular (the King) received (or captured)' (see on ἄλλα τε πολλά,
        9:17 above). * παλλακίδα: the presence of non-combatants
        (camp-followers, slaves, etc.) is taken for granted by Xeno-
        phon (cf. the Lydian traders, 5:6 above). * τὴν σοφὴν ... :
        'who was said to be clever and beautiful'; women were kept in
        seclusion, so Xenophon had probably not seen her; see on ἐλέ-
        γετο ... , 8:9 above.

10:3   ἡ δὲ Μιλησία: Miletos - an Ionian city (also Phokaia, 10:2 above);
        mercenaries were evidently not all that Kyros 'picked up' in
        Ionia. For Persians' concubines, cf. Herodotus, 1:135.
        * γυμνή: 'not fully dressed', i.e. with no outdoor cloak (ἱμ-
        άτιον) over her tunic (χιτών, ankle length, possibly sleeved);
        cf. ψιλός, 8:5 above. * πρὸς τῶν Ἑλλήνων sc. τούτους.
        * ὅπλα ἔχοντες: 'under arms', standing guard.

ἀντιταχθέντες πολλοὺς μὲν τῶν ἁρπαζόντων ἀπέκτειναν,
οἱ δὲ καὶ αὐτῶν ἀπέθανον· οὐ μὴν ἔφυγόν γε, ἀλλὰ καὶ
καὶ ταύτην ἔσωσαν καὶ τἆλλα ὁπόσα ἐντὸς αὐτῶν καὶ
10:4 χρήματα καὶ ἄνθρωποι ἐγένοντο πάντα ἔσωσαν. ἐνταῦθα
διέσχον ἀλλήλων βασιλεύς τε καὶ οἱ Ἕλληνες ὡς τριάκοντα στάδια, οἱ μὲν διώκοντες τοὺς καθ' αὐτοὺς ὡς
πάντας νικῶντες, οἱ δ' ἁρπάζοντες ὡς ἤδη πάντες νικ-
10:5 ῶντες. ἐπεὶ δ' ᾔσθοντο οἱ μὲν Ἕλληνες ὅτι βασιλεὺς
σὺν τῷ στρατεύματι ἐν τοῖς σκευοφόροις εἴη, βασιλεὺς
δ' αὖ ἤκουσε Τισσαφέρνους ὅτι οἱ Ἕλληνες νικῷεν τὸ
καθ' αὐτοὺς καὶ εἰς τὸ πρόσθεν οἴχοιντο διώκοντες,
ἐνταῦθα δὴ βασιλεὺς μὲν ἀθροίζει τε τοὺς ἑαυτοῦ καὶ
συντάττεται, ὁ δὲ Κλέαρχος ἐβουλεύετο Πρόξενον καλ-
έσας (πλησιαίτατος γὰρ ἦν) εἰ πέμποιέν τινας ἢ πάν-
10:6 τες ἴοιεν ἐπὶ τὸ στρατόπεδον ἀρήξοντες. ἐν τούτῳ

ἀντιταχθέντες πολλοὺς ... : 'formed up to fight the looters and
killed several of them, though some of their own number were
also killed'.
οὐ μὴν ... γε: 'however ... not'.
τἆλλα ὁπόσα ... : 'everything else that was inside their lines
(or camp), both matériel (i.e. things) and personnel - they
saved it all'; τἆλλα = τὰ ἄλλα (crasis, see on 5:2 above).

10:4 ἐνταῦθα: 'at this point'. * ὡς τριάκοντα στάδια: 3 - 4 miles.
* οἱ μὲν διώκοντες ... οἱ δ' ἁρπάζοντες: Kyros' and the King's
men respectively. * ὡς πάντας νικῶντες: 'thinking they had
beaten all the enemy'; ὡς ἤδη πάντες νικῶντες: 'thinking they
were already victorious on all fronts'.

10:5 ᾔσθοντο ... ὅτι ... ἤκουσε ... ὅτι: see on εἰδότες ὅτι, 6:10 above. * οἱ μὲν Ἕλληνες: ᾔσθοντο belongs inside the μὲν
'clause', and is placed early for emphasis. * εἴη ... νικῷεν:
opt., indir. statement (historic sequence). * τὸ καθ' αὐτούς:
see on 8:21 above. * εἰς τὸ πρόσθεν ... : 'had left and gone
ahead in pursuit'. * πλησιαίτατος i.e. the nearest commander
(2nd from the right; see on ἐχόμενος, 8:4 above). * πέμποιεν
... ἢ ... ἴοιεν: 'they were to send ... or ... go', opt. indir.
deliberative question (historic sequence) with εἰ (whether),
standing for subjunctive of dir. speech. * τινας ... πάντες:
'a detachment ... in full force'. * ἀρήξοντες: fut. part.,
purpose.

καὶ βασιλεὺς δῆλος ἦν προσιὼν πάλιν, ὡς ἐδόκει,
ὅπισθεν. καὶ οἱ μὲν Ἕλληνες στραφέντες παρεσκευάζοντο ὡς ταύτῃ προσιόντος καὶ δεξόμενοι, ὁ δὲ βασιλεὺς ταύτῃ μὲν οὐκ ἦγεν, ᾗ δὲ παρῆλθεν ἔξω τοῦ εὐωνύμου κέρατος, ταύτῃ καὶ ἀπῆγεν, ἀναλαβὼν καὶ τοὺς
ἐν τῇ μάχῃ πρὸς τοὺς Ἕλληνας αὐτομολήσαντας καὶ
10:7 Τισσαφέρνη καὶ τοὺς σὺν αὐτῷ. ὁ γὰρ Τισσαφέρνης ἐν
τῇ πρώτῃ συνόδῳ οὐκ ἔφυγεν, ἀλλὰ διήλασε παρὰ τὸν
ποταμὸν κατὰ τοὺς Ἕλληνας πελταστάς· διελαύνων δὲ
κατέκανε μὲν οὐδένα, διαστάντες δ' οἱ Ἕλληνες
ἔπαιον καὶ ἠκόντιζον αὐτούς· Ἐπισθένης δὲ Ἀμφιπολίτης ἦρχε τῶν πελταστῶν καὶ ἐλέγετο φρόνιμος γενέσ-
10:8 θαι. ὁ δ' οὖν Τισσαφέρνης ὡς μεῖον ἔχων ἀπηλλάγη,
πάλιν μὲν οὐκ ἀναστρέφει, εἰς δὲ τὸ στρατόπεδον

10:6 ἐν τούτῳ: see on 8:12 above.]
στραφέντες παρεσκευάζοντο: 'turned about and began to get ready'.
* ὡς ταύτῃ προσιόντος καὶ δεξόμενοι: ὡς + fut. part. indicating the Greeks' assumptions; προσιόντος sc. αὐτοῦ, gen. absolute. * ὁ δὲ βασιλεὺς ... ἦγεν (sc. τὸν στρατόν) ... : lit.
'but the King was not leading (his army) by that (route), but
by which (route) he passed ... by that he also led (it) away'
i.e. 'but that was not the direction the King took; instead he
marched back using the same route as when he passed ... '; ᾗ
and ταύτῃ are correlatives (see on ὅ τι ... τοῦτο, 6:6 above).

10:7 οὐκ ἔφυγεν ... : 'had not fled, but had ridden (-ήλασε) along the
river and charged (κατά) through (δι-) the Greek peltasts';
Ἕλληνας πελταστάς, two nouns = noun + adjective; for peltasts
see on πελταστικόν, 8:5 above.
διαστάντες: strong aor. part. (intrans.) of διίστημι. * κατέκανε: see on 6:2 above. * ἔπαιον καὶ ἠκόντιζον αὐτούς: 'kept
striking them with sword and javelin'; ἔπαιον, see on παίει,
8:26 above.

10:8 ὁ δ' οὖν Τισσαφέρνης ... : 'anyway, when Tissaphernes came out
of it the loser, he ... '; δ' οὖν, resuming the narrative after digression; μεῖον ἔχω, 'have the worst of it'. When a subordinate clause has the same subject as the main sentence, the
subject is generally placed first in Greek, outside the subordinate clause; but in English it often comes inside the clause,
to be 'picked up' by a pronoun.

ἀφικόμενος τὸ τῶν Ἑλλήνων ἐκεῖ συντυγχάνει βασιλεῖ,
10:9 καὶ ὁμοῦ δὴ πάλιν συνταξάμενοι ἐπορεύοντο. ἐπεὶ δ'
ἦσαν κατὰ τὸ εὐώνυμον τῶν Ἑλλήνων κέρας, ἔδεισαν
οἱ Ἕλληνες μὴ προσάγοιεν πρὸς τὸ κέρας καὶ περιπτύξαντες ἀμφοτέρωθεν αὐτοὺς κατακόψειαν· καὶ ἐδόκει
αὐτοῖς ἀναπτύσσειν τὸ κέρας καὶ ποιήσασθαι ὄπισθεν
10:10 τὸν ποταμόν. ἐν ᾧ δὲ ταῦτα ἐβουλεύοντο, καὶ δὴ βασιλεὺς παραμειψάμενος εἰς τὸ αὐτὸ σχῆμα κατέστησεν
ἀντίαν τὴν φάλαγγα ὥσπερ τὸ πρῶτον μαχούμενος συνῄει. ὡς δὲ εἶδον οἱ Ἕλληνες ἐγγὺς τε ὄντας καὶ
παρατεταγμένους, αὖθις παιανίσαντες ἐπῇσαν πολὺ ἔτι
10:11 προθυμότερον ἢ τὸ πρόσθεν. οἱ δ' αὖ βάρβαροι οὐκ
ἐδέχοντο, ἀλλ' ἐκ πλέονος ἢ τὸ πρόσθεν ἔφευγον· οἱ

'* καὶ ... δή: 'and so', concluding the episode (see on δή,
9:28 above).

10:9 τὸ εὐώνυμον: i.e. their original left wing (Menon's division),
now on the right. * προσάγοιεν ... κατακόψειαν: opt., fear
clause with μή ('lest'). * πρὸς τὸ κέρας: 'towards that
wing', i.e. towards its rear. * περιπτύξαντες: lit. 'having
enfolded' i.e. 'after outflanking them'. * ἀμφοτέρωθεν: i.e.
front and rear. * ἀναπτύσσειν: lit. 'to unfold' i.e. 'to deploy', 'to extend (the front of)', by bringing the rear lines
forward and to the right, to counter the enemy's encircling
movement. * ποιήσασθαι ὄπισθεν τὸν ποταμόν: 'get the river
in their rear'.

10:10 καὶ δή: 'already'; almost 'suddenly'. * παραμειψάμενος: 'by-
passed them and ... ', i.e. changed position (ἀμείβομαι) and
marched past (παρ-). * κατέστησεν: weak aor. (trans.) of
καθίστημι. * ὥσπερ ... μαχούμενος συνῄει: 'just as when he
had advanced to join battle'; the verb after ὥσπερ is usually
omitted, but not here; μαχούμενος, fut. part., purpose; συνῄει,
imperf. of σύνειμι (εἶμι 'go'). * παιανίσαντες, see on ἐπαιάνιζον, 8:17 above.
παρατεταγμένους: 'in battle order', i.e. hoplite formation, side
by side (παρα-); see on καθίστασθαι, 8:3 above. * ἐπῇσαν:
'advanced to attack', imperf. of ἔπειμι (εἶμι 'go').

10:11 βάρβαροι; see 8:14 and 8:19 above; but since Ariaios' flight it
now really was 'Greeks versus barbarians'.
οὐκ ἐδέχοντο ... ἔφευγον: 'did not wait for ... started running';
(cont.)

δ' ἐπεδίωκον μέχρι κώμης τινός· ἐνταῦθα δ' ἔστησαν
10:12 οἱ Ἕλληνες· ὑπὲρ γὰρ τῆς κώμης γήλοφος ἦν, ἐφ' οὗ
ἀνεστράφησαν οἱ ἀμφὶ βασιλέα, πεζοὶ μὲν οὐκέτι, τῶν
δὲ ἱππέων ὁ λόφος ἐνεπλήσθη, ὥστε τὸ ποιούμενον μὴ
γιγνώσκειν. καὶ τὸ βασίλειον σημεῖον ὁρᾶν ἔφασαν,
10:13 ἀετόν τινα χρυσοῦν ἐπὶ πέλτης ἀνατεταμένον. ἐπεὶ
δὲ καὶ ἐνταῦθ' ἐχώρουν οἱ Ἕλληνες, λείπουσι δὴ
καὶ τὸν λόφον οἱ ἱππεῖς, οὐ μὴν ἔτι ἀθρόοι, ἀλλ'
ἄλλοι ἄλλοθεν· ἐψιλοῦτο δ' ὁ λόφος τῶν ἱππέων· τέλος
10:14 δὲ καὶ πάντες ἀπεχώρησαν. ὁ οὖν Κλέαρχος οὐκ ἀνεβίβαζεν ἐπὶ τὸν λόφον, ἀλλ' ὑπ' αὐτὸν στήσας τὸ

---

imperf., i.e. 'did not even begin to ... '. * ἐκ πλέονος:
lit. 'from a greater (distance)' i.e. 'when they were further
away'.] * ἔστησαν: strong aor. (intrans.) of ἵστημι.

10:12 πεζοὶ μὲν οὐκέτι: i.e. ' ... were no longer with them', but in
full flight; the expected verb is forgotten and the subject
changes to λόφος. * ὥστε τὸ ποιούμενον μὴ γιγνώσκειν sc.
τοὺς Ἕλληνας: 'so that they (i.e. the Greeks) could not learn
what was going on' or ' ... what they (the Persians) were doing'.
σημεῖον: the standard was an important point of orientation for
the troops in the turmoil of battle, and was also a visible
symbol of the army's might; in retreat it was a rallying point.
* ὁρᾶν ἔφασαν: 'they said that they saw'. * πέλτης: see on
πελταστικόν, 8:5 above. * ἀνατεταμένον: 'with outstretched
wings'; the spread eagle is a favourite motif, symbolizing
majesty and strength. (The hill mentioned here may be that
referred to by Ktesias; see on βασιλεὺς δὲ διώκων, 10:1 above.

10:13 δή: 'of course', 'actually', emphasising λείπουσι; almost 'at
once'. * καὶ τὸν λόφον: 'even ... the hill-top'; they abandoned even this advantageous and easily defended position.
* οὐ μὴν: 'not at all'.
ἄλλοι ἄλλοθεν: lit. 'some from one side (of the hill) (others
from another)' i.e. 'in all directions'; see on ἄλλοι ἄλλως,
6:11 above.

10:14 οὐκ ἀνεβίβαζεν ἐπὶ τὸν λόφον sc. τὸ στράτευμα: 'did not march up
the hill'. * ὑπ' αὐτὸν στήσας: 'halted ... at the foot and
... '; στήσας, weak aor. part. (trans.) of ἵστημι.

στράτευμα πέμπει Λύκιον τὸν Συρακόσιον καὶ ἄλλον
ἐπὶ τὸν λόφον καὶ κελεύει κατιδόντας τὰ ὑπὲρ τοῦ
10:15 λόφου τί ἐστιν ἀπαγγεῖλαι. καὶ ὁ Λύκιος ἤλασέ τε
καὶ ἰδὼν ἀπαγγέλλει ὅτι φεύγουσιν ἀνὰ κράτος. σχεδὸν δ᾽ ὅτε ταῦτα ἦν καὶ ἥλιος ἐδύετο.

κατιδόντας τὰ ὑπὲρ ... : lit. 'having looked down at the (things)
beyond the hill-top to report back what it was' i.e. 'to have
a look at things on the other side of the hill and report back
what was happening' (τί ἐστιν, indir. question); ἀνὰ κράτος,
see on 8:1 above.

10:15 σχεδὸν δ᾽ ὅτε ... : lit. 'almost when these things were, (the)
sun was also setting' i.e. 'at about this time the sun began
to set'; no article with ἥλιος; so also sometimes σελήνη 'the
moon', γῆ 'the earth', and θάλαττα 'the sea' (see on ὥσπερ
θάλαττα, 5:1 above).

* * * * * *

Greek hoplite (centre right) and cavalryman (extreme right) fighting
Persians in typical caps and trousers (ἀναξυρίδες, see on 1:5:8 above),
   Based on a marble relief from the so-called 'Alexander sarcophagus'
of the late fourth century B.C., found at Sidon and now in the Arch-
aeological museum, Istanbul. [The horseman (extreme left) is thought
to be Alexander the Great.]

74

BOOK 2

1:2
to
5:26

*The Greeks heard of Kyros' death the morning after the
battle, when heralds came from Artaxerxes to inform them
that the King, having killed Kyros, claimed the victory and
demanded that they surrender their arms. The Greeks, who
regarded themselves as victors, refused and joined Ariaios,
who had been Kyros' second-in-command. The King sent a
second delegation, this time to arrange a truce prior to
the negotiation of a treaty. The satrap Tissaphernes, whom
the King had entrusted with full powers to deal with the
Greeks, offered to escort them out of the King's land. The
Greeks, reflecting that their original contract had not included marching against Artaxerxes, accepted the offer, and
after a delay of 20 days, during which the seeds of suspicion were sown on both sides, the march north along the banks
of the Tigris began. 3 days' marching brought them to the
Wall of Media near Babylon, and a further 2 to Sittake.
Continuing their northerly journey along the east bank of
the Tigris, they reached its confluence with its greatest
tributary, the Zapatas, after a further 14 days, and encamped
on its banks for 3 days. They had marched over 250 miles
since the treaty. Klearkhos and Tissaphernes now exchanged
assurances that it was in neither side's interest to violate
the terms of the safe conduct, and agreed to hold a meeting
at which they would each name those who had informed them of
the other side's intended treachery. Xenophon stresses that
in fact nothing overtly suspicious had been done by either
side.*

5:27   τῇ δὲ ὑστεραίᾳ ὁ Κλέαρχος ἐλθὼν ἐπὶ τὸ στρατόπεδον δῆλός τ' ἦν πάνυ φιλικῶς οἰόμενος διακεῖσθαι

5:27   ὁ Κλέαρχος ἐλθὼν ἐπὶ τὸ στρατόπεδον: 'Klearkhos, on returning to
his camp'; the definite article (τὸ) is often translated as a
possessive adjective. Klearkhos, the Spartan general who had
become the leader of the Greeks, was returning to camp after
dinner and overnight stay with Tissaphernes. * δῆλός τ' ἦν ... :
'made it clear that he thought he was on very friendly terms
with ... '; δῆλός εἰμι + part., 'I clearly', 'I make it clear
that I'; φιλικῶς ... διακεῖσθαι + dat., lit. 'that he felt ...
friendly towards', inf. construction after οἰόμενος.

τῷ Τισσαφέρνει καὶ ἃ ἔλεγεν ἐκεῖνος ἀπήγγελλεν, ἔφη
τε χρῆναι ἰέναι παρὰ Τισσαφέρνη οὓς ἐκέλευσε, καὶ
οἳ ἂν ἐξελεγχθῶσι διαβάλλοντες τῶν Ἑλλήνων, ὡς
προδότας αὐτοὺς καὶ κακόνους τοῖς Ἕλλησιν ὄντας
5:28 τιμωρηθῆναι. ὑπώπτευε δὲ εἶναι τὸν διαβάλλοντα
Μένωνα, εἰδὼς αὐτὸν καὶ συγγεγενημένον Τισσαφέρνει
μετ' Ἀριαίου καὶ στασιάζοντα αὐτῷ καὶ ἐπιβουλεύοντα,
ὅπως τὸ στράτευμα ἅπαν πρὸς αὐτὸν λαβὼν φίλος ᾖ
5:29 Τισσαφέρνει. ἐβούλετο δὲ καὶ ὁ Κλέαρχος ἅπαν τὸ
στράτευμα πρὸς ἑαυτὸν ἔχειν τὴν γνώμην καὶ τοὺς
παραλυποῦντας ἐκποδὼν εἶναι. τῶν δὲ στρατιωτῶν

* ἃ ἔλεγεν ἐκεῖνος ἀπήγγελλεν sc. ταῦτα: 'was reporting what
Tissaphernes had been (imperf.) saying'; relative clauses are often placed early in Greek, but later in English. * ἔφη τε ... :
'and he said that (those) whom Tissaphernes had invited must
go to him ... ', i.e. all the Greek officers; χρῆναι, inf. (of
impersonal χρή) construction after ἔφη; ἰέναι, inf. of εἶμι 'go',
after χρῆναι. * καὶ οἳ ἂν ... : 'and that whoever among the
Greeks was found guilty of making false accusations ... '; ἂν
+ subj., indefinite; τῶν Ἑλλήνων, partitive gen., sc. τούτους,
acc. subject of τιμωρηθῆναι (acc. and inf. after χρῆναι).
* ὡς ... αὐτοὺς ... ὄντας: 'for being ... themselves', thus
exonerating Klearkhos from guilt; ὡς + part., alleged reason.

5:28 τὸν διαβάλλοντα: 'the one making the accusations'. * Μένωνα:
Menon, a Thessalian general, originally commanded the Greeks'
right wing (the most important position); Kyros had promoted
Klearkhos to this position and Menon resented his authority;
they had already had one serious row. Like many Thessalian
aristocrats, he was a guest-friend of the Persian King (see on
ξένος 1:1:10 above), and this may have increased Klearkhos'
suspicion. * αὐτὸν καὶ ... : 'both that he had been having
dealings with Tissaphernes (while) with Ariaios and that he
was stirring up trouble against him', lit. 'revolting and plotting against him'; συγγεγενημένον, στασιάζοντα, ἐπιβουλεύοντα,
part. construction after εἰδὼς: αὐτῷ = ἑαυτῷ. * ὅπως τὸ στράτευμα ... : 'in order to win over ... and (thereby) gain Tissaphernes' friendship'; αὐτὸν = ἑαυτόν.

5:29 καὶ Κλέαρχος: 'Klearkhos too'. * πρὸς ἑαυτὸν ... : lit. 'to have
(their) inclination towards himself' i.e. 'to side with him'.
* τοὺς παραλυποῦντας ἐκποδὼν εἶναι: lit. 'those causing extra
(παρα-) trouble to be out of the way', i.e. 'to be rid of the
trouble-makers'.

ἀντέλεγόν τινες αὐτῷ μὴ ἰέναι πάντας τοὺς λοχαγοὺς
5:30 καὶ στρατηγοὺς μηδὲ πιστεύειν Τισσαφέρνει. ὁ δὲ
Κλέαρχος ἰσχυρῶς κατέτεινεν, ἔστε διεπράξατο πέντε
μὲν στρατηγοὺς ἰέναι, εἴκοσι δὲ λοχαγούς· συνηκολούθησαν δὲ ὡς εἰς ἀγορὰν καὶ τῶν ἄλλων στρατιωτῶν
ὡς διακόσιοι
5:31   ἐπεὶ δὲ ἦσαν ἐπὶ θύραις ταῖς Τισσαφέρνους, οἱ
μὲν στρατηγοὶ παρεκλήθησαν εἴσω, Πρόξενος Βοιώτιος,
Μένων Θετταλός, Ἀγίας Ἀρκάς, Κλέαρχος Λάκων, Σω-
5:32 κράτης Ἀχαιός· οἱ δὲ λοχαγοὶ ἐπὶ θύραις ἔμενον.
οὐ πολλῷ δὲ ὕστερον ἀπὸ τοῦ αὐτοῦ σημείου οἵ τ'
ἔνδον συνελαμβάνοντο καὶ οἱ ἔξω κατεκόπησαν. μετὰ

ἀντέλεγον ... μὴ ἰέναι ... μηδὲ πιστεύειν: 'began to object to ...
going ... and trusting'; imperf. for unresolved situation; μὴ +
inf. construction after verbs of preventing and denying.
* λοχαγοὺς καὶ στρατηγούς: there were now nine generals and
100 - 150 captains (each commanding a λόχος 'company' of up to
100 infantry).

5:30 κατέτεινεν ἔστε ... : 'kept insisting, until he got them to agree
to five generals ... going'; διεπράξατο, lit. 'achieved', 'got
his way'.
συνηκολούθησαν δὲ ... : 'about two hundred of the other soldiers
also accompanied (them), intending to go to market', i.e. to
buy provisions from the local inhabitants (see on εἰ μὴ ἐν τῇ
Λυδίᾳ 1:5:6 above). Possibly Klearkhos took them in case of
trouble (which itself might have added fuel to Menon's accusations); but they were not armed. [Xenophon's account differs
from that of Ktesias (see on παρασάγγος, 1:5:1 and
on Κτησίας 1:8:26 above), who says that Klearkhos was forced
by the others to go and face a trial, just as Orontas had been
tried by Kyros after his defection (1:6:1 - 11).]

5:31 ἐπὶ θύραις ταῖς Τισσαφέρνους: 'at the entrance to Tissaphernes'
tent'. * Σωκράτης: no connexion with the Athenian philosopher
of the same name.

5:32 πολλῷ ... : 'long afer', dat. of measure of difference, with
comparative ὕστερον. * ἀπό: 'at'; σημείου, according to the
historian Diodorus Siculus, a red (or purple) flag was raised;
perhaps it was an alarm signal when 35 men were seen instead
of 25. * συνελαμβάνοντο: imperf., implying 'they were arrest-
ed and while they were being held ...'.

δὲ ταῦτα τῶν βαρβάρων τινες ἱππέων διὰ τοῦ πεδίου
ἐλαύνοντες ᾧτινι ἐντυγχάνοιεν ῞Ελληνι ἢ δούλῳ ἢ
5:33 ἐλευθέρῳ πάντας ἔκτεινον. οἱ δὲ ῞Ελληνες τήν τε
ἱππασίαν ἐθαύμαζον ἐκ τοῦ στρατοπέδου ὁρῶντες καὶ
ὅ τι ἐποίουν ἠμφεγνόουν, πρὶν Νίκαρχος Ἀρκὰς ἧκε
φεύγων τετρωμένος εἰς τὴν γαστέρα καὶ τὰ ἔντερα ἐν
ταῖς χερσὶν ἔχων, καὶ εἶπε πάντα τὰ γεγενημένα.
5:34 ἐκ τούτου δὴ οἱ ῞Ελληνες ἔθεον ἐπὶ τὰ ὅπλα πάντες
ἐκπεπληγμένοι καὶ νομίζοντες αὐτίκα ἥξειν αὐτοὺς
5:35 ἐπὶ τὸ στρατόπεδον. οἱ δὲ πάντες μὲν οὐκ ἦλθον,
Ἀριαῖος δὲ καὶ Ἀρτάοζος καὶ Μιθραδάτης, οἳ ἦσαν
Κύρῳ πιστότατοι· ὁ δὲ τῶν Ἑλλήνων ἑρμηνεὺς ἔφη καὶ
τὸν Τισσαφέρνους ἀδελφὸν σὺν αὐτοῖς ὁρᾶν καὶ γιγνώσκειν. συνηκολούθουν δὲ καὶ ἄλλοι Περσῶν τεθωρ-

μετὰ δὲ ταῦτα: 'then', 'next'. * πεδίου: the Zapatas basin.
* ἐτυγχάνοιεν: opt., indefinite. * ἢ δούλῳ ἢ ἐλευθέρῳ:
'slave or free', see on παλλακίδα, 1:10:2 above. * πάντας:
plur. antecedent to ᾧτινι, according to its sense; for position
of relative clause, see on ἃ ἔλεγεν ... , 5:27 above.

5:33 τὴν ... ἱππασίαν: 'this riding about', 'this display of horsemanship'. * ὅ τι ἐποίουν: 'as to what they had been doing', indir. question. * ἠμφεγνόουν: from ἀμφι-γνοέω, with the normal
double augment. * εἶπε πάντα τὰ γεγενημένα: 'told (them) all
that had happened'.

5:34 ἐκ τούτου δὴ: 'at this', 'then', δὴ emphasising a turning point
in the narrative. * ἔθεον: imperf., 'began to run'. * τὰ
ὅπλα: these would have been stacked together in the middle of the
camp. * ἐκπεπληγμένοι καὶ νομίζοντες ... : 'in panic, thinking that they (i.e. the Persians) would be in (lit. 'have come
to') the camp at any moment'; αὐτίκα, emphatic position.

5:35 οἱ δὲ: subject, the article as pronoun + δέ, indicating a change
of grammatical subject. * ἦσαν: 'had been', when Kyros was
alive.
ἔφη καὶ τὸν Τισσαφέρνους ... : lit. 'said that he saw and recognised Tissaphernes' brother also with them' i.e. ' ... could
see someone else he recognised with them, Tissaphernes' brother';
σύν + dat. = μετά + gen., poetic, but regularly used by Xenophon.
καὶ ἄλλοι Περσῶν: 'other Persians also'. [* εἰς: 'as many as',
'about', with numbers.

5:36 ακισμένοι εἰς τριακοσίους. οὗτοι ἐπεὶ ἐγγὺς ἦσαν,
προελθεῖν ἐκέλευον εἴ τις εἴη τῶν Ἑλλήνων ἢ στρατηγὸς ἢ λοχαγός, ἵνα ἀπαγγείλωσι τὰ παρὰ βασιλέως.

5:37 μετὰ ταῦτα ἐξῆλθον φυλαττόμενοι τῶν Ἑλλήνων στρατηγοὶ μὲν Κλεάνωρ Ὀρχομένιος καὶ Σοφαίνετος Στυμφάλιος,
σὺν αὐτοῖς δὲ Ξενοφῶν Ἀθηναῖος, ὅπως μάθοι τὰ περὶ
Προξένου· Χειρίσοφος δ᾽ ἐτύγχανεν ἀπὼν ἐν κώμῃ τινὶ

5:38 σὺν ἄλλοις ἐπισιτιζόμενος. ἐπειδὴ δὲ ἔστησαν εἰς
ἐπήκοον, εἶπεν Ἀριαῖος τάδε. Κλέαρχος μέν, ὦ ἄνδρες
Ἕλληνες, ἐπεὶ ἐπιορκῶν τε ἐφάνη καὶ τὰς σπονδὰς

5:36 ἐγγύς: i.e. within shouting distance.
προελθεῖν ἐκέλευον ... : lit. 'if there was any general ... of
the Greeks, they were ordering (him) to come forward' i.e.
'they said that any of the Greek generals ... should come forward'; imperf. for unresolved situation; εἴη, opt., indir.
speech (historic sequence). * ἀπαγγείλωσι τὰ παρὰ βασιλέως:
lit. 'they might report the (things) from King' i.e. 'the King's
message'; ἀπαγγείλωσι, subj. with ἵνα (purpose); βασιλέως, see
on τῶν παρὰ βασιλέως, 1:1:5 above.

5:37 φυλαττόμενοι: 'on their guard', 'cautiously'. * Κλεάνωρ: the
oldest general, who had said that he would rather die than surrender. * Ξενοφῶν: this is the author's third brief reference
to himself (see on 1:8:15 above). * τὰ περὶ Προξένου: 'news
of Proxenos'; we learn of Xenophon's friendship with him in
Book 3.
Χειρίσοφος: a Spartan noble and general commanding 700 hoplites –
by now in a pre-eminent position, though Xenophon does not mention this. Sparta alone of Greek states contributed officially
to Kyros' army, giving Kheirisophos special permission to travel abroad (his hoplites may well have been non-Spartans). He
would have been keen to learn his fellow-countryman's fate.

5:38 ἔστησαν εἰς ἐπήκοον: lit. 'had taken up their positions (having
come) into earshot' i.e. 'had come within earshot and stopped';
ἔστησαν, strong aor. (intrans.) of ἵστημι. * τάδε: 'as follows'; ὅδε and ὧδε often refer to what follows.
Κλέαρχος μέν ... : 'Greeks, since Klearkhos has evidently been
violating his oath ... '; μέν is followed by two δέ sentences;
φαίνομαι + part., 'be evidently', see on δῆλος, 5:27 above.
In return for Tissaphernes' protection he had sworn not to
plunder the districts they passed through. Xenophon records
no violations on Klearkhos' part.

λύων, ἔχει τὴν δίκην καὶ τέθνηκε, Πρόξενος δὲ καὶ
Μένων, ὅτι κατήγγειλαν αὐτοῦ τὴν ἐπιβουλήν, ἐν μεγ-
άλῃ τιμῇ εἰσιν. ὑμᾶς δὲ βασιλεὺς τὰ ὅπλα ἀπαιτεῖ·
αὐτοῦ γὰρ εἶναί φησιν ἐπείπερ Κύρου ἦσαν τοῦ ἐκεί-
5:39 νου δούλου. πρὸς ταῦτα ἀπεκρίναντο οἱ ῞Ελληνες, ἔλε-
γε δὲ Κλεάνωρ δ' Ὀρχομένιος· ῏Ω κάκιστε ἀνθρώπων Ἀρι-
αῖε καὶ οἱ ἄλλοι ὅσοι ἦτε Κύρου φίλοι, οὐκ αἰσχύνεσθε οὔτε θεοὺς οὔτ᾽ ἀνθρώπους, οἵτινες ὀμόσαντες ἡμῖν
τοὺς αὐτοὺς φίλους καὶ ἐχθροὺς νομιεῖν, προδόντες
ἡμᾶς σὺν Τισσαφέρνει τῷ ἀθεωτάτῳ τε καὶ πανουργ-
οτάτῳ τούς τε ἄνδρας αὐτοὺς οἷς ὤμνυτε ἀπολωλέκατε

ἔχει τὴν δίκην: 'he has received his punishment', pres. with perf.
meaning. * εἰσιν: 'are (held)'. Xenophon does not dwell on
the part played by his friend Proxenos, who, according to Ktesias, had been deceived by Menon.
ὑμᾶς δὲ ... : 'and as for you, the King demands his arms'; ὑμᾶς
(emphatic position) and τὰ ὅπλα, both acc. with ἀπαιτεῖ, lit.
'asks for them back', as explained in the next sentence.
αὐτοῦ γὰρ ... : 'for he says they are his', 'as he says they belong to him'; εἶναί sc. αὐτά, acc. and inf. with φησιν, 3rd
pers. sing. of φημί. * ἐπείπερ Κύρου ... : 'seeing that they
used to belong to Kyros (who was) his slave', ἦσαν, plur. verb
with neut. plur. subject (irregular); ἐκείνου, not normally
put between article and noun; δούλου, see on 1:9:29 above.

5:39 οἱ ἄλλοι ὅσοι ἦτε: 'all you others who used to be'; ὅσος (ὅσοι)
often means 'all that which', 'all those who'. * οὐκ αἰσχύνεσθε: a rhetorical question (i.e. expecting no answer), implying strong condemnation. * οἵτινες ὀμόσαντες ... προδόντες ...:
'you swore ... but betrayed ... and ...'; 'despite your oath ...
you betrayed ...'; the Greek continues with a relative clause
and participles, but English prefers several main verbs (joined
by 'and' or 'but'); this complex or 'periodic' type of sentence
is a feature of set speeches, and figures less in narrative or
conversation; ἡμῖν goes equally with ὀμόσαντες and τοὺς αὐτούς;
τοὺς αὐτούς ... νομιεῖν: lit. 'that you would consider the same
men (as) friends and enemies' i.e. 'that you would make an offensive and defensive alliance with us', a set phrase. * σὺν
Τισσαφέρνει ... : 'in collaboration with that godless criminal
Tissaphernes' * τοὺς ... ἄνδρας αὐτοὺς 'the very men'.
* ὤμνυτε: imperf. (ὄμνυμι) for a continuing situation, 'you
were under oath', 'you had sworn'. * ἀπολωλέκατε (and ἔρχεσθε
over): main verbs.

καὶ τοὺς ἄλλους ἡμᾶς προδεδωκότες σὺν τοῖς πολεμ-
5:40 ίοις ἐφ' ἡμᾶς ἔρχεσθε; ὁ δὲ Ἀριαῖος εἶπε· Κλέαρχος
γὰρ πρόσθεν ἐπιβουλεύων φανερὸς ἐγένετο Τισσαφέρνει
τε καὶ Ὀρόντᾳ, καὶ πᾶσιν ἡμῖν τοῖς σὺν τούτοις. ἐπὶ
5:41 τούτοις Ξενοφῶν τάδε εἶπε. Κλέαρχος μὲν τοίνυν εἰ
παρὰ τοὺς ὅρκους ἔλυε τὰς σπονδάς, τὴν δίκην ἔχει·
δίκαιον γὰρ ἀπόλλυσθαι τοὺς ἐπιορκοῦντας· Πρόξενος
δὲ καὶ Μένων ἐπείπερ εἰσὶν ὑμέτεροί τε εὐεργέται,
ἡμέτεροί τε στρατηγοί, πέμψατε αὐτοὺς δεῦρο· δῆλον
γὰρ ὅτι φίλοι γε ὄντες ἀμφοτέροις πειράσονται καὶ
5:42 ὑμῖν καὶ ἡμῖν τὰ βέλτιστα συμβουλεύειν. πρὸς ταῦτα
οἱ βάρβαροι πολὺν χρόνον διαλεχθέντες ἀλλήλοις ἀπῆλθον οὐδὲν ἀποκρινάμενοι.

* τοὺς ἄλλους ἡμᾶς: 'the rest of us'; προδεδωκότες: perf. part.
of προδίδωμι.

5:40 γάρ: used when explaining what has just been said; in replies it
means 'yes, for' or 'no, for'; here, either acknowledging the
facts, 'yes, (we have joined the Persians) for ... ', or denying the alleged motive, 'no, (we are not traitors) for'.
* φανερὸς ἐγένετο + part.: see on φαίνομαι, 5:38 above.
* Τισσαφέρνει: dat. with ἐπιβουλεύων. * πᾶσιν ἡμῖν ... : 'all
of us who were with them'.
ἐπὶ τούτοις: lit. 'in succession to these things' i.e. 'next'.

5:41 Κλέαρχος ... εἰ: 'if Klearkhos' or 'as for Klearkhos, if ... '.
* ὅρκους: plur. often used for a single oath. * ἔλυε: 'was
in violation of', 'had broken', imperf. for continuing state.
δίκαιον sc. ἐστι. * ἀπόλλυσθαι τοὺς ἐπιορκοῦντας: 'that those
who break their oaths (should) perish (or be destroyed)'; ἀπόλλυσθαι, inf. mid. or pass. of ἀπόλλυμι. * Πρόξενος δὲ ... :
sentence begins with Proxenos and Menon as subject, but construction alters half way, making them object of main verb πέμψατε - a natural shift in hurried, excited speech; grammatically,
they are the subjects of the ἐπείπερ clause.
δῆλον ... ὅτι: ἐστι is normally omitted from this phrase, which
virtually becomes an adverbial expression, 'obviously'.
* φίλοι γε ὄντες: i.e. 'since they are, as you say, friends';
part. + γε, causal. * τὰ βέλτιστα συμβουλεύειν: 'to give the
best advice'.

5:42 πρὸς ταῦτα: 'in response to this', with ἀποκρινάμενοι. * πολὺν
χρόνον διαλεχθέντες: 'had a long discussion and ... '.

6:1   οἱ μὲν δὴ στρατηγοὶ οὕτω ληφθέντες ἀνήχθησαν ὡς
       βασιλέα καὶ ἀποτμηθέντες τὰς κεφαλὰς ἐτελεύτησαν,
       εἷς μὲν αὐτῶν Κλέαρχος ὁμολογουμένως ἐκ πάντων τῶν
       ἐμπείρως αὐτοῦ ἐχόντων δόξας γενέσθαι ἀνὴρ καὶ
6:2   πολεμικὸς καὶ φιλοπόλεμος ἐσχάτως. καὶ γὰρ δὴ ἕως
       μὲν πόλεμος ἦν τοῖς Λακεδαιμονίοις πρὸς τοὺς Ἀθην-
       αίους παρέμενεν, ἐπειδὴ δὲ εἰρήνη ἐγένετο, πείσας
       τὴν αὐτοῦ πόλιν ὡς οἱ Θρᾷκες ἀδικοῦσι τοὺς Ἕλληνας

6:1   μὲν: not followed immediately by δέ, as the character description
       intervenes. * δή: 'and so', indicating a climax.
       οὕτω: 'as I have described'; οὗτος and οὕτω(ς) often refer to what
       precedes (as opposed to ὅδε and ὧδε referring to what follows).
       * ἀνήχθησαν: i.e. into the interior, to Babylon.
       * ὡς + acc.: 'to' a person. * ἀποτμηθέντες τὰς κεφαλὰς ἐτελ-
       εύτησαν: lit. 'having been cut off as to (their) heads they
       died' i.e. 'they were put to death by being beheaded'; the act-
       ive form of this would be ἀπέτεμε τὰς κεφαλὰς αὐτοῖς 'he cut off
       their heads'; in the pass., the indir. object (dat. of person
       affected) becomes the subject (nom.), and the dir. object is re-
       tained in the acc. Kyros had already suffered this treatment
       (1:10:1). Ktesias says that they were put on show in Babylon
       before being executed, and that he had tried to alleviate Klear-
       khos' conditions; Parysatis (the queen mother, who had favoured
       Kyros above Artaxerxes) wanted Klearkhos to be spared; but the
       King's wife Stateira insisted on his death. * εἷς ... δόξας:
       lit. 'one ... having seemed', sing. in apposition to plur. sub-
       ject; translate as separate sentence, with 'seemed' as main verb.
       * ἐκ: 'by' (after ὁμολογουμένως), a poetic usage; see Introduction
       6.4. * τῶν ἐμπείρως αὐτοῦ ἐχόντων: 'those who knew him personally';
       adverb + ἔχω, 'be in ... condition'. * καὶ πολεμικὸς ... : 'ex-
       tremely good at and keen on war'; 'a born soldier and dedicated';
       adjectives in -ικός denote ability or talent; adjectives beginn-
       ing φιλο- often occur in character descriptions (1:9:5 - 6); ἐσ-
       χάτως (emphatic position) qualifies both adjectives.

6:2   καὶ γὰρ δή: 'a good indication is that ... '. * πόλεμος ἦν ... :
       'the Spartans were at war with ... '; for the Peloponnesian War,
       431 - 404, see Introduction 1. * παρέμενεν sc. τοῖς Λακεδαι-
       μονίοις: 'stayed with them' i.e. obediently; not literally - he
       had been sent on missions to Byzantion, Kalkhedon, and elsewhere.
       * ὡς: 'that'. * τοὺς Ἕλληνας: the half-dozen or so Greek cit-
       ies in the Thracian Chersonese, which were liable to be attacked
       by native Thracians; see on Χερρόνησῳ ... , 1:1:9 above. * ὡς
       ἐδύνατο: 'as (best) he could'. The Spartans' foreign policy was
       unadventurous, partly owing to their constant fear of uprisings
                                                              (cont.)

καὶ διαπραξάμενος ὡς ἐδύνατο παρὰ τῶν ἐφόρων ἐξέπλει
ὡς πολεμήσων τοῖς ὑπὲρ Χερρονήσου καὶ Περίνθου Θρᾳ-
6:3 ξίν. ἐπεὶ δὲ μεταγνόντες πως οἱ ἔφοροι ἤδη ἔξω ὄντος ἀποστρέφειν αὐτὸν ἐπειρῶντο ἐξ Ἰσθμοῦ, ἐνταῦθα
οὐκέτι πείθεται, ἀλλ᾽ ᾤχετο πλέων εἰς Ἑλλήσποντον.
6:4 ἐκ τούτου καὶ ἐθανατώθη ὑπὸ τῶν ἐν Σπάρτῃ τελῶν ὡς
ἀπειθῶν. ἤδη δὲ φυγὰς ὢν ἔρχεται πρὸς Κῦρον, καὶ
ὁποίοις μὲν λόγοις ἔπεισε Κῦρον ἀλλαχοῦ γέγραπται,
6:5 δίδωσι δὲ αὐτῷ Κῦρος μυρίους δαρεικούς· ὁ δὲ λαβὼν

among their serfs (called Εἵλωτες 'Helots'); the government was
suspicious of independent-minded individuals, so that the frustrated Klearkhos used whatever means he could to persuade them.]
* τῶν ἐφόρων: 'the *ephors*', the five ruling officials, elected
annually by the citizens, who controlled foreign policy (lit.
'overseers', ἐπί + ὁράω). * ἐξέπλει: 'set sail', 'began his
voyage', imperf. for uncompleted action. * ὡς + fut. part.: 'intending to'. * ὑπὲρ Χερρονήσου: i.e. 'to the north of the Chersonese' from the Greek viewpoint.

6:3 πως: 'for some reason'; perhaps their instinctive caution; or their
suspicion of Klearkhos' aims and methods. * ἔξω: 'outside'
Spartan territory (i.e. the Peloponnese) and therefore beyond
direct Spartan control. * ὄντος sc. αὐτοῦ: gen. absolute, irregular since αὐτόν follows. * Ἰσθμοῦ: i.e. of Corinth: no
article with this, the best known Isthmus; see on βασιλεύς for
the King, 1:1:5 above. * οὐκέτι πείθεται sc. αὐτοῖς: 'he refused to obey them any longer', historic present, often used for vividness (also ἔρχεται, 6:4 below). * ᾤχετο πλέων: lit. 'had de-
parted sailing' i.e. 'sailed off'.

6:4 ἐκ τούτου: 'as a result'. * τῶν ... τελῶν: i.e. the council of
28 elders (γερουσία). * ὡς ἀπειθῶν: 'for disobeying orders',
ὡς + part., alleged reason.
ὁποίοις ... λόγοις: 'the argument(s) he used to ... ', indir.
question. * ἔπεισε: i.e. to finance his war, which was now a
private enterprise; translate 'gained his support', as Kyros did
not need persuading - Klearkhos' plans fitted in with his plans
to usurp the throne. * ἀλλαχοῦ γέγραπται: in 1:1:9 Xenophon
did not mention these arguments; nor are they found elsewhere in
his work. Perhaps he wrote these obituaries before Book 1, and
forgot to include the arguments there; or perhaps he refers to
another author's work, now lost. * δαρεικούς: see on 1:1:9 above.

6:5 ὁ δὲ λαβών: 'when he had received (it)'.

οὐκ ἐπὶ ῥᾳθυμίαν ἐτράπετο, ἀλλ' ἀπὸ τούτων τῶν χρημάτων συλλέξας στράτευμα ἐπολέμει τοῖς Θρᾳξί, καὶ
μάχῃ τε ἐνίκησε καὶ ἀπὸ τούτου δὴ ἔφερε καὶ ἦγεν
αὐτοὺς καὶ πολεμῶν διεγένετο μέχρι Κῦρος ἐδεήθη τοῦ
στρατεύματος· τότε δὲ ἀπῆλθεν ὡς σὺν ἐκείνῳ αὖ πολ-
6:6 εμήσων. ταῦτα οὖν φιλοπολέμου μοι δοκεῖ ἀνδρὸς
ἔργα εἶναι, ὅστις ἐξὸν μὲν εἰρήνην ἄγειν ἄνευ αἰσχύνης καὶ βλάβης αἱρεῖται πολεμεῖν, ἐξὸν δὲ ῥᾳθυμεῖν
βούλεται πονεῖν ὥστε πολεμεῖν, ἐξὸν δὲ χρήματα ἔχειν
ἀκινδύνως αἱρεῖται πολεμῶν μείονα ταῦτα ποιεῖν· ἐκεῖνος δὲ ὥσπερ εἰς παιδικὰ ἢ εἰς ἄλλην τινὰ ἡδονὴν
6:7 ἤθελε δαπανᾶν εἰς πόλεμον. οὕτω μὲν φιλοπόλεμος ἦν·

* οὐκ ἐπὶ ῥᾳθυμίαν ἐτράπετο: 'he did not sink into (lit. turn
to) idleness'. * ἀπὸ: 'with', 'using'.
ἀπὸ τούτου ... : 'from that time on, of course, he kept plundering
and fighting them continuously until Kyros wanted his army', i.e.
for his own expedition against the King; δὴ indicates the important point in the story; ἄγω καὶ φέρω (the usual order) 'lead
(cattle) and carry (goods)', a set phrase for 'plunder'; δια-
γίγνομαι + part., 'do (something) continuously'.

6:6 ταῦτα: i.e. 'the above account'; see on οὕτω, 6:1 above.
* φιλοπολέμου: qualifies ἀνδρός; emphatic position. * ὅστις
... αἱρεῖται ... : '(the kind of man) who ... chooses ... ',
pres. tense for general truths. * ἐξὸν: lit. 'it being permitted' i.e. 'when he can', acc. n. s. part of ἔξεστι, ('it is
possible') accusative absolute, used in the case of impersonal
verbs instead of gen. absolute. * ἄνευ αἰσχύνης: 'without
(incurring) shame', by deserting an ally in need; καὶ βλάβης:
'or harm', from an aggressor. * πόνειν ὥστε πολεμεῖν: lit. 'to
work so as to fight' i.e. 'to work hard if it means fighting'; ὥστε sometimes implies 'on condition that' (= ἐφ' ᾧτε). * πολεμῶν:
'by fighting', pres. part. * μείονα ταῦτα ποιεῖν: lit. 'make
these things less' i.e. 'diminish his funds'; hoplites bought their
own equipment, which was expensive (see on ἐξοπλίζεσθαι, 1:8:3 above).
ἐκεῖνος: Klearkhos. * παιδικά: 'a boy-friend', neuter plur.; a
sexual relationship with a younger man was considered normal among most Greeks.

6:7 οὕτω μὲν φιλοπόλεμος ἦν: 'such was his enjoyment of war'; οὗτος
and ὅδε are often used as 'paragraphing' devices for the listener; see on 1:1:11 above.

πολεμικὸς δὲ αὖ ταύτῃ ἐδόκει εἶναι ὅτι φιλοκίνδυνός
τε ἦν καὶ ἡμέρας καὶ νυκτὸς ἄγων ἐπὶ τοὺς πολεμίους
καὶ ἐν τοῖς δεινοῖς φρόνιμος, ὡς οἱ παρόντες παντα-
6:8 χοῦ πάντες ὡμολόγουν. καὶ ἀρχικὸς δ' ἐλέγετο εἶναι
ὡς δυνατὸν ἐκ τοῦ τοιούτου τρόπου οἷον κἀκεῖνος
εἶχεν. ἱκανὸς μὲν γὰρ ὡς τις καὶ ἄλλος φροντίζειν
ἦν ὅπως ἔχοι ἡ στρατιὰ αὐτῷ τὰ ἐπιτήδεια καὶ παρα-
σκευάζειν ταῦτα, ἱκανὸς δὲ καὶ ἐμποιῆσαι τοῖς παρ-
6:9 οῦσιν ὡς πειστέον εἴη Κλεάρχῳ. τοῦτο δ' ἐποίει ἐκ

πολεμικὸς δ' αὖ ... : 'his abilities as a soldier, on the other
hand, were shown in that ... '; ταύτῃ ... ὅτι: 'by virtue of the
fact that'. * φιλοκίνδυνός ... : 'he not only courted danger,
leading (his men) against the enemy by night as well as by day,
but also kept his head in (those) dangers'. Commanders rarely
risked a night attack since, although it might have the advantage of surprise, it was difficult to consolidate an initial victory in the darkness (cf. the Athenians' night attack on Epipolai
in the Peloponnesian War, Thucydides 7.43 - 44).
* πανταχοῦ: 'everywhere', 'on every campaign'.

6:8 ὡς δυνατὸν sc. ἦν: 'as far as possible'. * ἐκ τοῦ τοιούτου ... :
lit. 'from the character of such a kind as he also had', i.e.
'considering the actual nature of his character'; κἀκεῖνος = καὶ
ἐκεῖνος; the blending of words ending and beginning with vowels
is called crasis; καὶ emphasises the whole clause, 'as well as
his other (good) qualities'.
ἱκανὸς μὲν γὰρ ... : lit. 'for on the one hand he was able as anyone else also to consider how the army might have the supplies
for him and to provide these things' i.e. 'for example, he was
as capable as anyone of thinking of ways in which his army could
get its supplies, and of (actually) providing them'; ὅπως ἔχοι,
opt., purpose, after φροντίζειν (although ὅπως + fut. indic. is
normal after a verb of precaution); αὐτῷ, dat. of person interested ('ethic' dat.), indicating Klearkhos' personal concern.
* ἱκανὸς δὲ καὶ ... : lit. 'on the other hand (he was) able also to produce in those present (the idea) that ... ' i.e. 'capable also of impressing on those with him that ... '. * πειστέον εἴη Κλεάρχῳ: 'Klearkhos must be obeyed'; πειστέον (ἐστι)
'one must obey', neuter verbal adjective from πείθομαι, expressing obligation; εἴη, opt., indir. statement after ἐμποιῆσαι.
Κλεάρχῳ: the mention of his name emphasises the idea, as if it
were his motto.

6:9 τοῦτο δ' ἐποίει ... : 'he achieved this (result) by ⌊being stern';
χαλεπὸς agrees with the subject (Klearkhos).

τοῦ χαλεπὸς εἶναι· καὶ γὰρ ὁρᾶν στυγνὸς ἦν καὶ τῇ
φωνῇ τραχύς, ἐκόλαζέ τε ἰσχυρῶς, καὶ ὀργῇ ἐνίοτε,
6:10 ὡς καὶ αὐτῷ μεταμέλειν ἔσθ' ὅτε. καὶ γνώμῃ δ'
ἐκόλαζεν· ἀκολάστου γὰρ στρατεύματος οὐδὲν ἡγεῖτο
ὄφελος εἶναι, ἀλλὰ καὶ λέγειν αὐτὸν ἔφασαν ὡς δέοι
τὸν στρατιώτην φοβεῖσθαι μᾶλλον τὸν ἄρχοντα ἢ τοὺς
πολεμίους, εἰ μέλλοι ἢ φυλακὰς φυλάξειν ἢ φίλων
ἀφέξεσθαι ἢ ἀπροφασίστως ἰέναι πρὸς τοὺς πολεμί-
6:11 ους. ἐν μὲν οὖν τοῖς δεινοῖς ἤθελον αὐτοῦ ἀκούειν
σφόδρα καὶ οὐκ ἄλλον ἡροῦντο οἱ στρατιῶται· καὶ
γὰρ τὸ στυγνὸν τότε φαιδρὸν αὐτοῦ ἐν τοῖς ἄλλοις

καὶ γάρ, etc.: lit. 'for indeed he was gloomy to look at and harsh
  in (his) voice' i.e. 'in fact he had a gloomy appearance and a
  harsh voice'; ὁρᾶν, explanatory inf., limiting the sense of
  στυγνός. * ὡς = ὥστε; see Introduction 6.3. * καὶ αὐτῷ
  μεταμέλειν: 'even he was sorry' for being so severe. * ἔσθ'
  (= ἔστι) ὅτε: lit. 'there is (a time) when' i.e. 'at times'.

6:10 καὶ γνώμῃ δέ: lit. 'but ... deliberately also' i.e. 'on principle',
  in contrast to ὀργῇ; for καὶ ... δέ, see on 1:1:2 above.
  ἀκολάστου γὰρ ... : lit. 'for he thought that there was no help
  of an unpunished army' i.e. ' ... an undisciplined army was no
  use'. * ἀλλὰ καὶ ... ἔφασαν: 'but they said that he even said';
  ἔφασαν, 3rd pers. plur. imperf. of φημί; Xenophon uses this kind
  of expression either to indicate that he was not an eyewitness,
  or when he has not checked his facts, or to maintain the appearance of impartiality. * ὡς δέοι ... εἰ μέλλοι: opt., in indir.
  speech after λέγειν; εἰ μέλλοι + fut. inf.: 'if he were to ... '.
  * φίλων ἀφέξεσθαι: lit. 'keep off friends' i.e. 'refrain from
  plundering allies'. * ἀπροφασίστως: lit. 'without making excuses' (πρόφασις 'excuse').

6:11 ἐν μὲν οὖν ... : οὖν 'therefore'; μέν, followed by ὅτε δ(έ) ἔξω ...,
  6:12 below. * αὐτοῦ ἀκούειν σφόδρα: 'listen to (i.e. obey) him
  implicitly'. * οὐκ ἄλλον sc. ἄρχοντα.
  καὶ γάρ: 'in fact', introducing another reason. * τὸ στυγνὸν ...
  φαιδρὸν αὐτοῦ ... ἔφασαν φαίνεσθαι sc. εἶναι: 'they said that
  his gloominess appeared (to be) cheerfulness'; τὸ στυγνὸν, φαιδ-
  ρόν, τὸ χαλεπὸν 'sternness', ἐρρωμένον 'strength', σωτήριον 'sal-
  vation', and χαλεπόν, all neuter adjectives used as abstract
  nouns, those without the article being predicates. * ἐν τοῖς
  ἄλλοις προσώποις: 'in contrast with the faces of the others',
                                                          (cont.)

προσώποις ἔφασαν φαίνεσθαι καὶ τὸ χαλεπὸν ἐρρωμένον
πρὸς τοὺς πολεμίους ἐδόκει εἶναι, ὥστε σωτήριον,
6:12 οὐκέτι χαλεπὸν ἐφαίνετο· ὅτε δ' ἔξω τοῦ δεινοῦ γένοιντο καὶ ἐξείη πρὸς ἄλλους ἀρξομένους ἀπιέναι,
πολλοὶ αὐτὸν ἀπέλειπον· τὸ γὰρ ἐπίχαρι οὐκ εἶχεν,
ἀλλ' ἀεὶ χαλεπὸς ἦν καὶ ὠμός· ὥστε διέκειντο πρὸς
αὐτὸν οἱ στρατιῶται ὥσπερ παῖδες πρὸς διδάσκαλον.
6:13 καὶ γὰρ οὖν φιλίᾳ μὲν καὶ εὐνοίᾳ ἐπομένους οὐδέποτε
εἶχεν· οἵτινες δὲ ἢ ὑπὸ πόλεως τεταγμένοι ἢ ὑπὸ τοῦ
δεῖσθαι ἢ ἄλλῃ τινὶ ἀνάγκῃ κατεχόμενοι παρείησαν

which were even gloomier, not from habit but from fear.]
* πρὸς τοὺς πολεμίους: 'in the face of the enemy', when his
sternness, however disagreeable at other times, was to their advantage.

6:12 ὅτε δ(έ) ... : 'but when the danger had passed'; γένοιντο (and ἐξείη), opt., indefinite. * ἐξείη (sc. αὐτούς) πρὸς ἄλλους ... :
lit. 'it was permitted (for them) to go away to others about to
be commanded' i.e. 'they could go off and serve other commanders';
ἔξεστι + acc. and inf. (less common than dat. and inf.); ἀρξομένους, fut. part. mid. with pass. meaning, indicating purpose
and agreeing with (αὐτούς), not ἄλλους. * ἀπέλειπον: 'used to
leave'.
τὸ ἐπίχαρι: 'attractiveness','pleasantness of manner', another
neuter adjective used as an abstract noun.
διέκειντο ... ὥσπερ: 'had the same feelings ... as'.

6:13 καὶ γὰρ οὖν: 'for as a matter of fact', 'for this reason also',
giving the result (οὖν) and explaining it (γάρ) further (καί).
* φιλίᾳ καὶ εὐνοίᾳ: 'out of friendship and goodwill', emphatic
position. * ἐπομένους: '(men) following (him)'.
οἵτινες ... παρείησαν αὐτῷ: lit. 'whoever was near him' i.e. 'anyone who served with him'; παρείησαν (= πάρειεν), opt., indefinite.
* ὑπὸ πόλεως τεταγμένοι: 'officially assigned to him', by Sparta
or an allied (or subject) city, such as Byzantion or Kalkhedon
(see on παρέμενεν, 6:2 above). * ὑπὸ τοῦ δεῖσθαι: 'through poverty'; ὑπό is sometimes used with things, especially if destructive; τό + inf., verbal noun. There was virtually no public wel-
fare system, so that many Greeks, unemployed and landless after
the Peloponnesian War, served as mercenary soldiers for pay and
booty (see on τῶν Ἑλλήνων, 1:1:2 above and Introduction 4).
* ἄλλῃ τινὶ ἀνάγκῃ κατεχόμενοι: 'compelled for any other reason'.
* [σφόδρα πειθομένοις ἐχρῆτο: 'he found very obedient'; for
σφόδρα, see on 6:11 above.

6:14 αὐτῷ, σφόδρα πειθομένοις ἐχρῆτο. ἐπεὶ δὲ ἄρξαιντο
νικᾶν σὺν αὐτῷ τοὺς πολεμίους, ἤδη μεγάλα ἦν τὰ
χρησίμους ποιοῦντα εἶναι τοὺς σὺν αὐτῷ στρατιώτας·
τό τε γὰρ πρὸς τοὺς πολεμίους θαρραλέως ἔχειν παρῆν
καὶ τὸ τὴν παρ' ἐκείνου τιμωρίαν φοβεῖσθαι αὐτοὺς
6:15 εὐτάκτους ἐποίει. τοιοῦτος μὲν δὴ ἄρχων ἦν· ἄρχεσθαι δὲ ὑπὸ ἄλλων οὐ μάλα ἐθέλειν ἐλέγετο. ἦν δὲ ὅτε
ἐτελεύτα ἀμφὶ τὰ πεντήκοντα ἔτη.

6:16 Πρόξενος δὲ ὁ Βοιώτιος εὐθὺς μὲν μειράκιον ὢν
ἐπεθύμει γενέσθαι ἀνὴρ τὰ μεγάλα πράττειν ἱκανός·
καὶ διὰ ταύτην τὴν ἐπιθυμίαν ἔδωκε Γοργίᾳ ἀργύριον

6:14 ἄρξαιντο: opt., indefinite. * ἤδη μεγάλα ... : lit. 'now great
were the (things) making the soldiers with him useful' i.e. 'immediately there were powerful influences ensuring his fellow-sol-
diers' efficiency'; μεγάλα, emphatic position.
τό ... θαρραλέως ἔχειν παρῆν sc. αὐτοῖς: 'they had confidence';
τό ... ἔχειν, verbal noun as subject; adverb + ἔχω, see on τῶν
ἐμπείρως ἐχόντων, 6:1 above; πρός: 'in the face of'. * τὸ τὴν
παρ' ἐκείνου ... : 'their fear of the punishment (they would
get) from him (for disobeying) ensured their good behaviour',
verbal noun as subject of ἐποίει.

6:15 τοιοῦτος μὲν ... : 'so this was his character when in command'.
ἄρχεσθαι δὲ ... : lit. 'but to be commanded by others he was said
to be not very willing' i.e. 'but as for being under the command
of others, he was said rather to resent it'; ἄρχεσθαι, inf. with
ἐθέλειν, emphatic position; οὐ μάλα, understatement, = 'not at
all'; ἐλέγετο: see on ἔφασαν, 6:10 above.
ὅτε ἐτελεύτα: 'at the time of his death', imperf. for a continuing
state. * ἀμφὶ τὰ πεντήκοντα ἔτη: 'about fifty years old'; the
article is regularly used with round numbers.

*For Klearkhos' character, note also his row with Menon (1:5:11),
and his actions at Kounaxa (1:8:13 and 8:16). Compare Kyros' character (1:5:8, 8:26, 9:1 - 30). For similar obituaries, cf. Thucydides on Themistokles (1.138) and Perikles (2.65).*

6:16 εὐθὺς ... μειράκιον ὢν: 'right from early youth', i.e. early teens.
* τὰ μεγάλα πράττειν: 'to do great things'.
ἔδωκε Γοργίᾳ ἀργύριον: i.e. became one of his (fee-paying) students;
ἔδωκε, aor. of δίδωμι. Gorgias of Leontinoi in Sicily taught the
new art of public speaking (ἡ ῥητορική) at Athens and elsewhere;
ambitious politicians paid considerable sums for lessons, (cont.)

6:17 τῷ Λεοντίνῳ. ἐπεὶ δὲ συνεγένετο ἐκείνῳ, ἱκανὸς
νομίσας ἤδη εἶναι καὶ ἄρχειν καὶ φίλος ὢν τοῖς
πρώτοις μὴ ἡττᾶσθαι εὐεργετῶν, ἦλθεν εἰς ταύτας τὰς
σὺν Κύρῳ πράξεις· καὶ ᾤετο κτήσεσθαι ἐκ τούτων ὄνομα
6:18 μέγα καὶ δύναμιν μεγάλην καὶ χρήματα πολλά· τούτων
δ᾽ ἐπιθυμῶν σφόδρα ἔνδηλον αὖ καὶ τοῦτο εἶχεν ὅτι
τούτων οὐδὲν ἂν ἐθέλοι κτᾶσθαι μετὰ ἀδικίας, ἀλλὰ
σὺν τῷ δικαίῳ καὶ καλῷ ᾤετο δεῖν τούτων τυγχάνειν,
6:19 ἄνευ δὲ τούτων μή. ἄρχειν δὲ καλῶν μὲν κἀγαθῶν

since, in democratic cities, their power depended not on birth
or wealth but on their ability to persuade their fellow-citizens;
most teachers of rhetoric charged 300 - 500 drakhmai for a course
of lessons; Gorgias' fee was 100,000 drakhmai. In 427 B.C., during the Peloponnesian War, he had led a diplomatic mission to
Athens to enlist her help against Syracuse. Menon may also have
been his pupil; and his elaborate style also influenced the historian Thucydides.]

6:17 συνεγένετο ἐκείνῳ: lit. 'was with him', i.e. 'had attended his lec-
tures'. * ἱκανὸς νομίσας ... : lit. 'having considered that he
was now able both to rule (or command) and, being friendly with
the chief men, not to be inferior while benefiting' i.e.
'and considered himself capable both of assuming authority (or
a command) and, in his friendships with other leading figures,
of holding his own in conferring benefits'. * ἦλθεν εἰς ...
πράξεις: 'he embarked upon these actions', i.e. the expedition
and the activities leading up to it.
τούτων: sc. τῶν πράξεων. * ὄνομα: i.e. reputation.

6:18 τούτων δ᾽ ἐπιθυμῶν ... : lit. 'but desiring these things on the
other hand he had this (quality) too (as) very evident, (namely)
that ... ' i.e. 'despite these ambitions, he made it abundantly
clear that it was also a principle of his ... '; τούτων, n. gen.
with ἐπιθυμῶν, concessive part. * ἐθέλοι: opt., potential, sc.
remote fut. condition implied by μετὰ ἀδικίας 'unjustly'.
* σὺν τῷ δικαίῳ ... : 'in accordance with justice and honour'.
* δεῖν sc. ἑαυτόν: inf. in indir. statement after ᾤετο.
* τούτων: i.e. reputation etc.; gen. with τυγχάνειν.

6:19 καλῶν μὲν κἀγαθῶν (= καὶ ἀγαθῶν, crasis see on κἀκεῖνος, 6:8 above):
'men of quality', 'decent men', contrasted (μέν) with οἱ ἄδικοι
below; gen. with ἄρχειν; καλὸς κἀγαθός is a set phrase, lit.
'handsome and brave', i.e. 'a true gentleman'.

ἱκανὸς ἦν· οὐ μέντοι οὔτ' αἰδῶ τοῖς στρατιώταις αὐτοῦ οὔτε φόβον ἱκανὸς ἐμποιῆσαι, ἀλλὰ καὶ ἠσχύνετο
μᾶλλον τοὺς στρατιώτας ἢ οἱ ἀρχόμενοι ἐκεῖνον· καὶ
φοβούμενος μᾶλλον ἦν φανερὸς τὸ ἀπεχθάνεσθαι τοῖς
6:20 στρατιώταις ἢ οἱ στρατιῶται τὸ ἀπιστεῖν ἐκείνῳ. ᾤετο
δὲ ἀρκεῖν πρὸς τὸ ἀρχικὸν εἶναι καὶ δοκεῖν τὸν μὲν
καλῶς ποιοῦντα ἐπαινεῖν, τὸν δὲ ἀδικοῦντα μὴ ἐπαινεῖν. τοιγαροῦν αὐτῷ οἱ μὲν καλοί τε κἀγαθοὶ τῶν
συνόντων εὔνοι ἦσαν, οἱ δὲ ἄδικοι ἐπεβούλευον ὡς
εὐμεταχειρίστῳ ὄντι. ὅτε δὲ ἀπέθνῃσκεν ἦν ἐτῶν ὡς
τριάκοντα.

οὐ μέντοι ... : 'however, he was not able to inspire his soldiers
with either respect for or fear of himself'; αἰδῶ, acc. of αἰδώς
'shame' or 'respect' for a commander; αὐτοῦ (= ἑαυτοῦ), objective
gen. with αἰδῶ and φόβον: ἱκανὸς sc. ἦν; + inf., see on 6:8 above.
* καὶ ἠσχύνετο ... : 'he was actually more inhibited in front
of the soldiers than those under his command were in front of
him'; ἠσχύνετο, lit. 'felt ashamed before', 'felt embarrassed';
οἱ ἀρχόμενοι ἐκεῖνον sc. ἠσχύνοντο; for the importance of shame
as a motivating factor, see on οὐκ αἰσχύνεσθε, 5:39 and ἄνευ αἰσχύνης, 6:6 above.
φοβούμενος ... ἦν φανερός: see on δῆλος, 5:27 above. * τὸ ἀπεχθάνεσθαι + dat.: 'being unpopular with', 'unpopularity with',
verbal noun - object of φοβούμενος. * τὸ ἀπιστεῖν ἐκείνῳ
(sc. φοβούμενοι ἦσαν φανεροί): 'disobeying his orders'; ἀπιστέω
'disobey', poetic meaning (usually = 'distrust').

6:20 ἀρκεῖν: inf. in indir. statement after ᾤετο (for dir. ἀρκεῖ, impersonal). * πρὸς τὸ ... εἶναι καὶ δοκεῖν sc. εἶναι: 'for the
purpose of being and appearing (to be) able to command' i.e.
'in order to be - and be seen to be - an able commander'.
* τὸν μὲν καλῶς ποιοῦντα: 'the man who did right' (cf. τὸν δὲ
ἀδικοῦντα: 'the one who did wrong'). * ἐπαινεῖν ... μὴ ἐπαινεῖν: both inf. after ἀρκεῖν.
αὐτῷ οἱ μέν ... : 'the decent men among his associates supported
him, while the nasty characters (ἄδικοι) ... '. * ὡς εὐμεταχειρίστῳ ὄντι sc. αὐτῷ: 'as they thought he was easily manipul-
ated'; ὡς + part., alleged reason.
ἐτῶν: 'years of age', gen. of measure. 30 was young to be a general; Xenophon was about the same age; ὡς: 'about', with numbers.

6:21 Μένων δὲ ὁ Θετταλὸς δῆλος ἦν ἐπιθυμῶν μὲν πλούτου
ἰσχυρῶς, ἐπιθυμῶν δὲ ἄρχειν, ὅπως πλείω λαμβάνοι,
ἐπιθυμῶν δὲ τιμᾶσθαι, ἵνα πλείω κερδαίνοι· φίλος τε
ἐβούλετο εἶναι τοῖς μέγιστον δυναμένοις, ἵνα ἀδικῶν
6:22 μὴ διδοίη δίκην. ἐπὶ δὲ τὸ κατεργάζεσθαι ὧν ἐπιθυμοίη συντομωτάτην ᾤετο ὁδὸν εἶναι διὰ τοῦ ἐπιορκεῖν τε καὶ ψεύδεσθαι καὶ ἐξαπατᾶν, τὸ δ᾽ ἁπλοῦν καὶ
6:23 ἀληθὲς ἐνόμιζε τὸ αὐτὸ τῷ ἠλιθίῳ εἶναι. στέργων δὲ
φανερὸς μὲν ἦν οὐδένα, ὅτῳ δὲ φαίη φίλος εἶναι,
τούτῳ ἔνδηλος ἐγίγνετο ἐπιβουλεύων. καὶ πολεμίου
μὲν οὐδενὸς κατεγέλα, τῶν δὲ συνόντων πάντων ὡς κατα-

6:21 δῆλος + part.: see on 5:27 above. * ἐπιθυμῶν ... ἰσχυρῶς + gen.:
'had an enormous desire for ... '; also + inf. (ἄρχειν and τιμᾶσθαι). * πλείω: 'more (money)', n. acc. plur.; λαμβάνοι: opt.,
purpose with ὅπως (also πλείω κερδαίνοι with ἵνα, 'make (still)
more money').
τοῖς μέγιστον δυναμένοις: 'the most powerful'.
ἵνα ἀδικῶν ... : 'in order to do wrong without paying the penalty';
διδοίη, opt. of δίδωμι, purpose with ἵνα.

6:22 τὸ κατεργάζεσθαι ὧν ἐπιθυμοίη: 'achieving (or the achievement of -
verbal noun) whatever he desired', sc. ταῦτα as object of κατεργάζεσθαι; ἐπιθυμοίη, opt., indefinite. * ἐπὶ ... συντομωτάτην
... ὁδὸν ... διὰ: metaphor from travelling (σύντομος ὁδός 'short
cut'); ὁδὸν εἶναι, acc. and inf. after ᾤετο. * τοῦ ἐπιορκεῖν
... : 'perjury, lies, and deception'. * τὸ δ᾽ ἁπλοῦν καὶ ἀληθὲς:
'sincerity and truthfulness'. * τὸ αὐτὸ τῷ ἠλιθίῳ: 'the same
thing as (dat.) simple-mindedness'.

6:23 στέργων δὲ φανερός: see on 5:40 and on δῆλος 5:27 above (also ἔν-
δηλος) * ὅτῳ δὲ φαίη ... : lit. 'but towards whoever he said
that he was friendly, against him he used to become evident plotting' i.e. 'but if he said he was anyone's friend, it would become obvious that he was ... '; ὅτῳ dat. of ὅστις, with φίλος;
φαίη, opt. of φημί, indefinite; εἶναι, inf. after φαίη; τούτῳ
dat. with ἐπιβουλεύων; when a relative clause comes early, the
relative pronoun is often 'picked up' by οὗτος as antecedent.
τῶν ... συνόντων: 'his associates', gen. with καταγελῶν. * ὡς
καταγελῶν ἀεὶ διελέγετο: 'in conversation he gave the impression
that he was mocking ... '; ὡς + part., 'as if'.

6:24 γελῶν ἀεὶ διελέγετο. καὶ τοῖς μὲν τῶν πολεμίων κτήμ-
ασιν οὐκ ἐπεβούλευε· χαλεπὸν γὰρ ᾤετο εἶναι τὰ τῶν
φυλαττομένων λαμβάνειν; τὰ δὲ τῶν φίλων μόνος ᾤετο
6:25 εἰδέναι ὅτι ῥᾷστον ἀφύλακτα λαμβάνειν. καὶ ὅσους
μὲν αἰσθάνοιτο ἐπιόρκους καὶ ἀδίκους ὡς εὖ ὡπλισμένους ἐφοβεῖτο, τοῖς δ' ὁσίοις καὶ ἀλήθειαν ἀσκοῦσιν
6.26 ὡς ἀνάνδροις ἐπειρᾶτο χρῆσθαι. ὥσπερ δέ τις ἀγάλλεται ἐπὶ θεοσεβείᾳ καὶ ἀληθείᾳ καὶ δικαιότητι, οὕτω
Μένων ἠγάλλετο τῷ ἐξαπατᾶν δύνασθαι, τῷ πλάσασθαι
ψευδῆ, τῷ φίλους διαγελᾶν· τὸν δὲ μὴ πανοῦργον τῶν

6:24 χαλεπὸν ... εἶναι: 'that it was difficult', inf. construction with
     ᾤετο (also εἰδέναι).
     τὰ τῶν φυλαττομένων sc. κτήματα: 'the (property) of men on their
     guard' (also τὰ ... τῶν φίλων). * μόνος ... εἰδέναι lit. 'that
     he alone knew'. * ῥᾷστον sc. ὄν: 'that (it was) easiest (or
     very easy)'. * ἀφύλακτα: '(things left) unguarded'.

6:25 ὅσους ... αἰσθάνοιτο sc. ὄντας: 'all those he saw (or noticed)',
     opt., indefinate; see on οἱ ἄλλοι ὅσοι ... , 5:39 above.
     * ἐπιόρκους καὶ ἀδίκους sc. ὄντας: 'who had broken their oaths
     and behaved unjustly', 'were liars and criminals'. * ἐφοβεῖτο:
     sc. τούτους, antecedent of ὅσους. * ὡς εὖ ὡπλισμένους: 'as (he
     considered them) well armed', i.e. as well as himself; the meta-
     phor from combat (used ironically) is continued by ἀσκοῦσιν and
     ἀνάνδροις. * τοῖς δ' ὁσίοις ... : 'but those (who were) pious
     and practiced truthfulness', whose religious scruples would make
     them abide by oaths; ἀσκοῦσιν, dat. plur. of pres. part. of ἀσ-
     κέω, properly referring to athletic training; all dat. with
     χρῆσθαι. * ὡς ἀνάνδροις ... : lit. 'he tried to treat as un-
     manly'; ἄνανδρος, 'no true man', 'cowardly'.

6:26 τις: 'one', indefinite. * ἀγάλλεται ἐπὶ θεοσεβείᾳ ... : 'takes
     pride in being godfearing, truthful and just'. * τῷ ἐξαπατᾶν
     ... ; 'being able to deceive (people), fabricating his lies, and
     laughing at friends'; ἐξαπατᾶν inf. with δύνασθαι; πλάσασθαι
     and διαγελᾶν, parallel to δύνασθαι; πλάττω, lit. 'mould' (clay
     etc.), hence 'form', 'fabricate' - here mid., denoting self-advan-
     tage; ψευδῆ, neuter plur. of ψευδής, used as a noun.
     μὴ sc. ὄντα: 'who (was) not', 'if (he was) not'; μὴ + part. has
     conditional meaning.

ἀπαιδεύτων ἀεὶ ἐνόμιζεν εἶναι. καὶ παρ' οἷς μὲν
ἐπεχείρει πρωτεύειν φιλίᾳ, διαβάλλων τοὺς πρώτους
6:27 τούτῳ ᾤετο δεῖν κτήσασθαι. τὸ δὲ πειθομένους τοὺς
στρατιώτας παρέχεσθαι ἐκ τοῦ συναδικεῖν αὐτοῖς
ἐμηχανᾶτο. τιμᾶσθαι δὲ καὶ θεραπεύεσθαι ἠξίου ἐπι-
δεικνύμενος ὅτι πλεῖστα δύναιτο καὶ ἐθέλοι ἂν ἀδικ-
εῖν. εὐεργεσίαν δὲ κατέλεγεν, ὁπότε τις αὐτοῦ ἀφ-
ίσταιτο, ὅτι χρώμενος αὐτῷ οὐκ ἀπώλεσεν αὐτόν.

* τῶν ἀπαιδεύτων: '(one) of the uneducated' i.e. 'uneducated'.
καὶ παρ' οἷς ... : 'and with whom on the one hand he was trying
to be first in friendship, falsely accusing the first (men), by
this he thought (it) to be necessary to gain (friendship)' i.e.
'also, when he was trying to become someone's best friend, he
thought he had to achieve this by slandering those who were already his best friends'; παρ' οἷς = παρὰ τούτοις ὧν παρ' οἷς;
μὲν: this sentence refers to Menon's equals, the next (τὸ δὲ
πειθομένους) to his inferiors; τούτῳ, i.e. τῷ διαβάλλειν etc.;
κτήσασθαι sc. τὴν φιλίαν.

6:27 τὸ δὲ πειθομένους ... : lit. 'on the other hand, he devised the
rendering of the soldiers obedient for himself by joining in
wrongdoing with them' i.e. 'on the other hand, he contrived to
obtain his soldiers' obedience by joining in their crimes';
παρέχεσθαι, mid. denoting self-advantage.
θεραπεύεσθαι: 'to receive men's attentions'; θεραπεύω, lit. 'be a
servant (θεράπων)', 'serve', hence 'pay one's attentions to',
'flatter'. * ἠξίου: 'expected', as if it were his right; ἀξιόω,
lit. 'think oneself worthy (ἄξιος)' of something, hence 'claim'
or 'expect' it.
πλεῖστα δύναιτο ... : 'he was able and would be willing to commit
most crimes'; δύναιτο, opt., indir. statement (historic sequence);
ἐθέλοι, potential opt. People flattered him in case he used his
abilities against them.
εὐεργεσίαν δὲ κατέλεγεν ... ὅτι: 'he used to reckon (it) a kindness
... that'. * χρώμενος αὐτῷ: 'in his dealings with him'; χράομαι
usually implies friendly dealings. * οὐκ ἀπώλεσεν: 'he had not
destroyed'.

6:28 καὶ τὰ μὲν δὴ ἀφανῆ ἔξεστι περὶ αὐτοῦ ψεύδεσθαι, ἃ
δὲ πάντες ἴσασι τάδ᾽ ἐστί. παρὰ Ἀριστίππου μὲν ἔτι
ὡραῖος ὢν στρατηγεῖν διεπράξατο τῶν ξένων, Ἀριαίῳ
δὲ βαρβάρῳ ὄντι, ὅτι μειρακίοις καλοῖς ἥδετο, οἰκειότατος ἔτι ὡραῖος ὢν ἐγένετο, αὐτὸς δὲ παιδικὰ
6:29 εἶχε Θαρύπαν ἀγένειος ὢν γενειῶντα. ἀποθνῃσκόντων

6:28 τὰ μὲν δὴ ἀφανῆ: lit. 'in respect of the unseen things indeed on
the one hand' i.e. 'of course (δή), concerning his secret life',
acc. of respect; a deliberately vague phrase. * ψεύδεσθαι:
'be untruthful' or 'be mistaken'. It may be that ἀφανῆ refers
to his private motives, and Xenophon wishes to appear fair by
giving him the benefit of the doubt. * ἃ δὲ πάντες ... : 'but
the following facts are common knowledge'; τάδ(ε), see on 5:38
above.
παρὰ Ἀριστίππου ... στρατηγεῖν ... : lit. 'from Aristippos he managed to get (himself) to be general'. * ἔτι ὡραῖος ὤν: 'while
he was still in the bloom of youth', i.e. in his teens and at
his most attractive to an older man; but rather young for military command. Xenophon does not imply that the homosexual relationship was in itself disgraceful (see on παιδικά, 6:6 above),
but that a private sexual relationship should not have been the
basis of a military arrangement.
ξένων: 'mercenaries' (see on ξένος, 1:1:10 above); genitive after
στρατηγεῖν. Aristippos, a Thessalian noble, had recruited mercenaries in his fight against political opponents; Kyros had given
him 24,000 drakhmai (six months' pay for 4000 soldiers), on the
understanding that he would subsequently send them to join the
army Kyros was secretly collecting for his own expedition (see
on 1:1:10 above); in fact Menon brought 1000 hoplites and 500
peltasts (light-armed troops). * Ἀριαίῳ: dat. with οἰκειότατος;
βαρβάρῳ ὄντι: 'who was not Greek'; this made the relationship
especially disgraceful. * ὅτι: 'because', causal. * παιδικὰ
εἶχε ... : lit. 'and he himself being beardless had a boy-friend
Tharypas having a beard' i.e. ' ... while in his early teens he
had a boy-friend called Tharypas who was an adult'; παιδικά normally means the younger person in the relationship; Menon's pre-
cocious behaviour is emphasized, and the growth of beard refers
not to fashion but to maturity.

6:29 ἀποθνῃσκόντων δὲ ... : 'when his fellow-generals were put to death
because they had joined Kyros' expedition (or had served with
(cont.)

δὲ τῶν συστρατήγων ὅτι ἐστράτευσαν ἐπὶ βασιλέα σὺν
Κύρῳ, ταύτὰ πεποιηκὼς οὐκ ἀπέθανε, μετὰ δὲ τὸν τῶν
ἄλλων θάνατον στρατηγῶν τιμωρηθεὶς ὑπὸ βασιλέως ἀπέθανεν, οὐχ ὥσπερ Κλέαρχος καὶ οἱ ἄλλοι στρατηγοὶ
ἀποτμηθέντες τὰς κεφαλάς, ὅσπερ τάχιστος θάνατος
δοκεῖ εἶναι, ἀλλὰ ζῶν αἰκισθεὶς ἐνιαυτὸν ὡς πονηρὸς
λέγεται τῆς τελευτῆς τυχεῖν.

6:30   Ἀγίας δὲ ὁ Ἀρκὰς καὶ Σωκράτης ὁ Ἀχαιὸς καὶ τούτω
ἀπεθανέτην. τούτων δὲ οὔθ᾽ ὡς ἐν πολέμῳ κακῶν οὐδεὶς κατεγέλα οὔτ᾽ εἰς φιλίαν αὐτοὺς ἐμέμφετο. ἤστην δὲ ἄμφω ἀμφὶ τὰ πέντε καὶ τριάκοντα ἔτη ἀπὸ
γενεᾶς.

Kyros in his campaign) against the King, although he had done
the same, he was not put to death'; ἀποθνήσκω is often treated
as a pass. verb (the corresponding act. verb being ἀποκτείνω);
βασιλέα (and βασιλέως), see on 1:1:5 above; ταύτὰ = τὰ αὐτά
(crasis; see on κἀκεῖνος, 6:8 above). * μετὰ δὲ ... : 'but
(it was only) after ... (that) ... ', emphatic position.
τιμωρηθεὶς ... ἀπέθανεν: 'he suffered punishment and death at
the hands of the King'. * ἀποτμηθέντες τὰς κεφαλάς, see on
6:1 above. * ὅσπερ τάχιστος ... : 'which is reputed to be the
quickest death'.
ζῶν αἰκισθεὶς: 'by being kept alive and tortured' until he died;
such treatment of one's enemies was uncommon among the Greeks
(but cf. Herodotus 9.120, Thucydides 7.86 and 87, Xenophon Hellenika 2.1.31 - 32). * ὡς πονηρὸς ... : lit. 'is said to have
met a death as a villain' i.e. ' ... a criminal's death'; Xenophon gives no more details, but suggests the brutality and trea-
cherous ingratitude of the King. Perhaps the execution was delayed as a reward for luring the other generals into the trap;
and the King's mother Parysatis (who had favoured Kyros) may
have brought about his torture and death.

6:30   καὶ τούτω ἀπεθανέτην: lit. 'died, these two also' i.e. 'were put
to death with the others'; τούτω, nom. dual; ἀπεθανέτην, 3rd
pers. dual aor. of ἀποθνήσκω. * τούτων: gen. with κατεγέλα.
* ὡς ... κακῶν sc. ὄντων: 'for being cowards'. * εἰς: 'in
the matter of'. * ἤστην: 3rd pers. dual imperf. of εἰμί 'be'.
ἀμφὶ τὰ ... : for ἀμφὶ with article and number, see on 6:15 above;
ἀπὸ γενεᾶς: (years) 'of age'.

* * * * * *

BOOK 3

1:2　　*Still deep in the heart of the King's land, but now also*
to　　*leaderless and deserted by Ariaios, the Greeks were close to*
1:3　　*despair; or at least, most of them were. But one man who,*
　　　like his comrades, was unable to sleep through the long night,
　　　turned his thoughts to some purpose.

1:4　　ἦν δέ τις ἐν τῇ στρατιᾷ Ξενοφῶν Ἀθηναῖος, ὃς
　　　οὔτε στρατηγὸς οὔτε λοχαγὸς οὔτε στρατιώτης ὢν συν-
　　　ηκολούθει, ἀλλὰ Πρόξενος αὐτὸν μετεπέμψατο οἴκοθεν
　　　ξένος ὢν ἀρχαῖος· ὑπισχνεῖτο δὲ αὐτῷ εἰ ἔλθοι, φί-
　　　λον αὐτὸν Κύρῳ ποιήσειν, ὃν αὐτὸς ἔφη κρείττω ἑαυτῷ

1:4　　ἦν δέ τις ... : Xenophon has mentioned himself briefly four times
　　　(1:8:15; 2:4:15, 5:37 and 5:41); now he introduces himself (mod-
　　　estly - τις) as a major participant in the events. * οὔτε στρα-
　　　τηγὸς ... : 'was accompanying (them) neither (as) a general, nor
　　　a captain, nor a private' or 'though he was neither ... ', con-
　　　cessive part. * ἀλλὰ Πρόξενος ... : 'but (because) Proxenos,
　　　an old guest-friend, (had) invited him over from Athens'; μετε-
　　　πέμψατο, best translated as pluperf. since this action precedes
　　　the main narrative; for ξένος, see on 1:1:10 above; a friend from
　　　abroad was automatically a guest-friend. Proxenos of Thebai
　　　(Thebes) in Boiotia had also been a guest-friend of Kyros (1:1:
　　　11) in whose expedition he commanded 1500 heavy-armed and 500
　　　light-armed troops; among the Greek generals he had been second
　　　only to the Spartan Klearkhos. For his character and death see
　　　2:5:31 - 32 and 2:6:16 - 20 above.
　　　ὑπισχνεῖτο: 'he had promised', imperf. for unresolved situation.
　　　* εἰ ἔλθοι: 'if he went', opt., fut. condition in indir. speech,
　　　dependent on historic verb (= dir. ἐὰν ἔλθῃς). * φίλον αὐτὸν
　　　Κύρῳ ποιήσειν: 'to make him a friend of Kyros', 'to introduce him
　　　to Kyros', fut. inf., indir. statement after verb of promising.
　　　* ὃν αὐτὸς ... : lit. 'whom he said that he himself thought bet-
　　　ter for himself than (his) native land' i.e. 'and he said he per-
　　　sonally thought he would do better with Kyros than at home', and
　　　so Xenophon should join him too; an added incentive besides the

　　　　　　　　　　　　　　　　　　　　　　　　　　　　　　(*cont.*)

1:5 νομίζειν τῆς πατρίδος. ὁ μέντοι Ξενοφῶν ἀναγνοὺς τὴν
     ἐπιστολὴν ἀνακοινοῦται Σωκράτει τῷ Ἀθηναίῳ περὶ τῆς
     πορείας. καὶ ὁ Σωκράτης ὑποπτεύσας μή τι πρὸς τῆς
     πόλεως ὑπαίτιον εἴη Κύρῳ φίλον γενέσθαι, ὅτι ἐδόκει
     ὁ Κῦρος προθύμως τοῖς Λακεδαιμονίοις ἐπὶ τὰς Ἀθήνας

chance to fight, and the hope of pay and booty; *cf.* Kyros' promise to the Greeks of rich rewards on the eve of the battle of
Kounaxa: 'I think I shall cause many to choose life with me instead of life at home'. For Proxenos' political ambitions, see
2:6:16 - 17 above.]

1:5 ἀνακοινοῦται Σωκράτει τῷ Ἀθηναίῳ: lit. 'communicates (its contents)
     for himself with Sokrates the (well-known) Athenian' i.e. 'told
     Sokrates and asked his opinion'; ἀνακοινοῦται, historic present,
     often used for vividness; mid. denoting self-interest. This Sok-
     rates was the famous Athenian philosopher; one of his beliefs,
     according to Plato (*Kriton,* 49), was that taking vengeance was
     wrong no matter what the provocation; Xenophon was a follower of
     his, and, since foreign travel was not undertaken lightly in
     those days (particularly if fighting was involved), he sought
     the advice of his old teacher. For Xenophon's writings about
     Sokrates, see Introduction 2.
     ὑποπτεύσας μή τι ... : 'suspecting that to become a friend of Kyros
     might be something reprehensible in the eyes of the state, be-
     cause Kyros seemed to have enthusiastically supported the Spartans
     in the war against Athens'; ὑποπτεύσας ... συμβουλεύει, 'he sus-
     pected ... and advised', part. + main verb often translated by
     two main verbs joined by 'and'; εἴη, opt. in fear clause with μή.
     Λακεδαιμονίοις, Lakedaimon was an alternative name for Sparta,
     the most powerful state in the Peloponnese. At the end of the
     Peloponnesian War, Kyros provided Sparta with enough money to
     tilt the balance against Athens; in return, Sparta had given Kyros
     military assistance - the only Greek state to do so officially.
     (See on Χειρίσοφος, 2:5:37 above.) The Athenians would already
     have been suspicious of Xenophon: firstly, he admired the Spartan
     way of life, with its emphasis on strict obedience and military
     prowess; secondly, he came from the wealthy class which had mostly
     supported 'the Thirty', an undemocratic and brutal régime set
     up after Athens' defeat in 404; so Xenophon probably felt uneasy
     living in Athens after democracy was restored in 403. (Sokrates
     himself had friends among the Thirty, and this may have been one
     reason why he was condemned to death in 399 on a charge of 'be-
     lieving in strange gods' and 'corrupting the young'.)

συμπολεμῆσαι, συμβουλεύει τῷ Ξενοφῶντι ἐλθόντα εἰς
1:6 Δελφοὺς ἀνακοινῶσαι τῷ θεῷ περὶ τῆς πορείας. ἐλθὼν
δ' ὁ Ξενοφῶν ἐπήρετο τὸν Ἀπόλλω τίνι ἂν θεῶν θύων
καὶ εὐχόμενος κάλλιστα καὶ ἄριστα ἔλθοι τὴν ὁδὸν ἥν
ἐπινοεῖ καὶ καλῶς πράξας σωθείη. καὶ ἀνεῖλεν αὐτῷ
1:7 ὁ Ἀπόλλων θεοῖς οἷς ἔδει θύειν. ἐπεὶ δὲ πάλιν ἦλθε,

* ἐλθόντα ... ἀνακοινῶσαι sc. αὐτόν: 'to go ... and communicate
(his concern)'; despite the preceding dat., the construction
continues as a regular indir. command (acc. and inf.). * Δελφοὺς: at Delphoi (Delphi), high on Mt. Parnassos in Phokis (the
supposed centre of the world), was the most famous shrine of
Apollo, god of prophecy. People came from all over the Greek
world and beyond to consult the oracle with questions ranging
from the personal (as here) to matters of national importance.
A priestess called the Pythia (ἡ Πυθία) went into a frenzied
trance and uttered oracular responses in verse which were often
ambiguous (see e.g. Herodotus 1.84 - 91; Aeschylus, Eumenides
1 - 33; Euripides, Ion). It was always considered important for
the gods to support a venture, and support from the god of Delphoi could be particularly useful in the face of a hostile Athenian public (cf. Plato, Apology 20e - 21a).

1:6 ἐλθὼν ... ἐπήρετο: see on ὑποπτεύσας ... συμβουλεύει, 1:5 above.
   * τίνι ἂν ... : lit. 'sacrificing and praying to whom of gods
   would he most honourably and best go the way which he was intending and having done well would be saved' i.e. 'to which god he
   should sacrifice and pray in order that he might go on his intended journey in the best possible way, make a success of it, and
   come home safely'; ἂν ... ἔλθοι ... σωθείη, opt., potential; θύων and εὐχόμενος have conditional force; κάλλιστα and ἄριστα mean
   virtually the same - to use both is emphatic (cf. καλὸς κἀγαθός
   2:6:19); τὴν ὁδόν, internal (adverbial) acc.; σῴζω is often equivalent to a verb of motion ('bring safely', pass. 'come safely').
   For sacrifice before an important enterprise, see on καὶ τὰ ἱερὰ
   καλά, 1:8:15 above). The prayer would include a vow to be fulfilled after the successful outcome of the enterprise.
ἀνεῖλεν ... θεοῖς οἷς ἔδει θύειν: lit. 'answered with gods to whom
   he had to sacrifice' i.e. 'in his response said which gods he
   had to sacrifice to'; θεοῖς, either attracted from acc. (object
   of ἀνεῖλεν) to dat. by οἷς, or instrumental dat.; the gods named
   were Zeus the King (as we learn in Book 4) and perhaps Hermes
   (god of travellers) and Herakles (protector from evil and travellers' guide).

λέγει τὴν μαντείαν τῷ Σωκράτει. ὁ δ' ἀκούσας ἠτιᾶτο
αὐτὸν ὅτι οὐ τοῦτο πρῶτον ἠρώτα πότερον λῷον εἴη αὐτῷ πορεύεσθαι ἢ μένειν, ἀλλ' αὐτὸς κρίνας ἰτέον εἶναι τοῦτ' ἐπυνθάνετο ὅπως ἂν κάλλιστα πορευθείη. Ἐπεὶ
μέντοι οὕτως ἤρου, ταῦτ', ἔφη, χρὴ ποιεῖν ὅσα ὁ θεὸς
1:8 ἐκέλευσεν. ὁ μὲν δὴ Ξενοφῶν οὕτω θυσάμενος οἷς ἀν-
εἷλεν ὁ θεὸς ἐξέπλει, καὶ καταλαμβάνει ἐν Σάρδεσι
Πρόξενον καὶ Κῦρον μέλλοντας ἤδη ὁρμᾶν τὴν ἄνω ὁδόν,
1:9 καὶ συνεστάθη Κύρῳ. προθυμουμένου δὲ τοῦ Προξένου

1:7 πάλιν ἦλθε: from Delphoi to Athens.]
ὁ δ' ἀκούσας: 'when he heard (it), he ... ', a use of the definite
article (with δέ) as pronoun, indicating a change of grammatical
subject. * ἠτιᾶτο: imperf. as he did not press his point.
* τοῦτο ... τοῦτ(ο): explained by indir. questions which follow;
omit in translation. * εἴη: opt., indir. question dependent on
historic verb. * ἰτέον εἶναι: 'that he must go', indir. version
of ἰτέον (ἐστι) 'one must go', neuter verbal adjective from εἶμι
'go', expressing obligation (cf. πειστέον 2:6:8). * ἐπυνθάνετο
ὅπως ... : 'he had enquired (imperf.) how his journey could be
accomplished most successfully'; ὅπως 'how', introducing indir.
question; ἂν ... πορευθείη, opt., potential; Xenophon had 'begged
the question' as to whether to go at all.
Ἐπεὶ μέντοι ... : 'however', he said, 'since that is how you put
your question, you must do all that the god commanded'; ταῦτ(α),
object of ποιεῖν; ἔφη (3rd pers. sing. imperf. of φημί) often
interrupts the sentence; ὅσος (ὅσοι) often means 'all that which',
'all those who'.

1:8 ὁ μὲν δὴ ... : 'so, of course, after sacrificing (to the gods)
whom Apollo had ordained, Xenophon set sail', landing at Ephesos
(where he made further enquiry of the gods); οὕτω, explained by
the relative clause, may be omitted in translation; θυσάμενος,
mid., since the actual sacrifice was performed by a priest;
οἷς = τοῖς θεοῖς οἷς, case of the relative pronoun being attracted from the acc. (object of ἀνεῖλεν); ἐξέπλει, imperf. for uncompleted action, 'began his voyage'. * Σάρδεσι: Sardis was the
capital of Lydia and the administrative centre of Kyros' satrapy
(province); see Introduction 3. * τὴν ἄνω ὁδόν: 'on their journey inland', internal (adverbial) acc. * συνεστάθη: aor. pass.
of συνίστημι.

καὶ ὁ Κῦρος συμπρουθυμεῖτο μεῖναι αὐτόν· εἶπε δὲ ὅτι
ἐπειδὰν τάχιστα ἡ στρατεία λήξῃ, εὐθὺς ἀποπέμψει
1:10 αὐτόν. ἐλέγετο δὲ ὁ στόλος εἶναι εἰς Πισίδας. ἐστρατεύετο μὲν δὴ οὕτως ἐξαπατηθεὶς οὐχ ὑπὸ Προξένου (οὐ
γὰρ ᾖδει τὴν ἐπὶ βασιλέα ὁρμὴν οὐδὲ ἄλλος οὐδεὶς τῶν
'Ελλήνων πλὴν Κλεάρχου)· ἐπεὶ μέντοι εἰς Κιλικίαν
ἦλθον, σαφὲς πᾶσιν ἤδη ἐδόκει εἶναι ὅτι ὁ στόλος εἴη
ἐπὶ βασιλέα. φοβούμενοι δὲ τὴν ὁδὸν καὶ ἄκοντες ὅμως οἱ πολλοὶ δι' αἰσχύνην καὶ ἀλλήλων καὶ Κύρου συν-
1:11 ηκολούθησαν· ὧν εἷς καὶ Ξενοφῶν ἦν. ἐπεὶ δὲ ἀπορία

1:9 προθυμουμένου δὲ ... : lit. 'with Proxenos being eager Kyros also
was equally eager for him to stay' i.e. 'Proxenos was eager that
he should stay with them - an eagerness shared by Kyros, who
said ... '; προθυμουμένου ... τοῦ Προξένου, gen. absolute;⟧
αὐτόν, subject of μεῖναι.
ἐπειδὰν τάχιστα + subjunctive: 'as soon as', indefinite temporal
clause. * ἀποπέμψαι αὐτόν:'he would send him home'.
εἰς Πισίδας: 'into (the territory of the) Pisidians', see on 1:1:11
above.

1:10 ἐστρατεύετο μὲν ... : 'in this way, then, Xenophon was deceived into joining the expedition'; οὗτος and οὕτως often refer to what
immediately precedes. * οὐ γὰρ ᾖδει ... : 'he (i.e. Proxenos)
did not know about the (planned) attack on the King; nor did anyone else among the Greeks ... '; βασιλέα, see on 1:1:5 above;
for the reason for the deception, see on 1:1:11 above. * Κλεάρχου: for his career and feud with the Thessalian general Menon,
see Book 1; for his harsh character, his denunciation by Proxenos
and Menon, and his execution by Tissaphernes, see Book 2.
εἰς Κιλικίαν: beyond Pisidian territory. * εἴη: opt., indir.
statement dependent on historic verb. * φοβούμενοι: 'although
they were apprehensive about ... ', part. with concessive force.
* ἄκοντες: 'unwillingly'; this adjective is often used adverbially. * δι' αἰσχύνην ... : lit. 'because of shame both of each
other and of Kyros' i.e. 'for fear of losing both each other's
and Kyros' respect', by appearing cowardly and ungrateful; ἀλλήλων and Κύρου, objective gen.; for shame as a motivating factor,
see on 1:8:25 and 2:6:19 above.
ὧν: 'of these', connecting relative, not often used except to sum
up what precedes. * καὶ Ξενοφῶν: omit 'also' in translation.

1:11 ἐπεὶ δὲ ἀπορία ἦν: 'since it was a difficult situation' or 'when
the difficulty arose'; the narrative is resumed at the point
(cont.)

ἦν, ἐλυπεῖτο μὲν σὺν τοῖς ἄλλοις καὶ οὐκ ἐδύνατο
καθεύδειν· μικρὸν δ᾽ ὕπνου λαχὼν εἶδεν ὄναρ. ἔδοξεν
αὐτῷ βροντῆς γενομένης σκηπτὸς πεσεῖν εἰς τὴν πατρῴαν
1:12 οἰκίαν, καὶ ἐκ τούτου λάμπεσθαι πᾶσα. περίφοβος δ᾽
εὐθὺς ἀνηγέρθη, καὶ τὸ ὄναρ τῇ μὲν ἔκρινεν ἀγαθόν,
ὅτι ἐν πόνοις ὢν καὶ κινδύνοις φῶς μέγα ἐκ Διὸς ἰδεῖν
ἔδοξε· τῇ δὲ καὶ ἐφοβεῖτο, ὅτι ἀπὸ Διὸς μὲν βασιλέως
τὸ ὄναρ ἐδόκει αὐτῷ εἶναι, κύκλῳ δὲ ἐδόκει λάμπεσθαι
τὸ πῦρ, μὴ οὐ δύναιτο ἐκ τῆς χώρας ἐξελθεῖν τῆς βασιλέως, ἀλλ᾽ εἴργοιτο πάντοθεν ὑπό τινων ἀποριῶν.

where five leading Greek generals have been killed and a number
of Greek troops massacred (see 2:5:27 - 32).   * σὺν + dat.,
poetic but regularly used by Xenophon (= μετά + gen.); see Introduction 6.4.]
μικρὸν ... ὕπνου: either acc. object of λαχών + partitive gen. or
adverbial acc. and partitive gen. with λαχών.   * εἶδεν ὄναρ:
'had a dream'.
ἔδοξεν αὐτῷ ... : 'it seemed to him that there was a clap of thunder, and a flash of lightning struck his paternal house, and this
made it all shine'; σκηπτός is subject of ἔδοξεν but English prefers the impersonal; note the lack of connecting particle (asyndeton); πατρῴαν, 'inherited from his father' (Gryllos) - it was
near Athens (see Introduction 1); ἐκ, 'as a result of'; λάμπεσθαι emphasises the light rather than the (destructive) flames,
in accordance with the first interpretation of the dream; πᾶσα,
adverbial, emphatic position, sc. οἰκία, 2nd. subject of ἔδοξεν.

1:12 τῇ μὲν ... τῇ δὲ: 'in one way ... in another way'.   * ἀγαθόν:
'(as) auspicious', predicative.   * ἐν πόνοις ὢν ... : '(when)
in the midst of ... '.   * φῶς μέγα ἐκ Διὸς: i.e. a sign of good
fortune from the god responsible for thunder and lightning.
* ἰδεῖν ἔδοξε: 'he thought he had seen'; ἰδεῖν, indir. statement.
καὶ ἐφοβεῖτο ... μή: 'he was also afraid ... that'.   * Διὸς ...
βασιλέως: 'Zeus the King' i.e. in his character as king of gods
and men, and protector of kings; for Xenophon's sacrifice to this
god, see on 1:6 above.   * δύναιτο ... εἴργοιτο: opt., fear clause
with μή (negative οὐ) dependent on historic verb.   * βασιλέως:
i.e. Artaxerxes, who did in fact claim to be the embodiment on
earth of Ahura-Mazda, the Persian equivalent of Zeus; see on 1:
8:17 above.   * τινων: 'various'; they were stranded over 1000
miles from home, with no guide, no friendly market in which to
buy provisions, and surrounded by the enemy.   Dreams were believed to come from the gods; their interpretation (oneiromancy) was an
(cont.)

1:13 ὁποῖόν τι μὲν δή ἐστι τὸ τοιοῦτον ὄναρ ἰδεῖν ἔξεστι
σκοπεῖν ἐκ τῶν συμβάντων μετὰ τὸ ὄναρ. γίγνεται γὰρ
τάδε. εὐθὺς ἐπειδὴ ἀνηγέρθη πρῶτον μὲν ἔννοια αὐτῷ
ἐμπίπτει· Τί κατάκειμαι; ἡ δὲ νὺξ προβαίνει· ἅμα δὲ
τῇ ἡμέρᾳ εἰκὸς τοὺς πολεμίους ἥξειν. εἰ δὲ γενησόμεθα ἐπὶ βασιλεῖ, τί ἐμποδὼν μὴ οὐχὶ πάντα μὲν τὰ
χαλεπώτατα ἐπιδόντας, πάντα δὲ τὰ δεινότατα παθόντας
1:14 ὑβριζομένους ἀποθανεῖν; ὅπως δ' ἀμυνούμεθα οὐδεὶς

early form of divination (cf. Herodotus 6:107; Aeschylus, Khoe-
phoroi 527 - 551; Euripides, Iphigeneia in Tauris 42 - 58 and
Hekabe 68 - 74; Aristophanes, Frogs 1331 - 1344); sometimes an
expert soothsayer (μάντις) interpreted the dream (see on τὰ ἱερὰ
καλά, 1:8:15 above).]

1:13 ὁποῖόν τι ... : 'what it really means to have such a dream may be
seen from subsequent events'; ὁποῖόν τι ... ἐστι, 'what kind of
thing it is', indir. question dependent on σκοπεῖν (inf. after
ἔξεστι); τὸ ... ἰδεῖν, verbal noun, subject of ἐστι; the main
verb is ἔξεστι.
γίγνεται γὰρ τάδε: 'this is what did happen'; γίγνεται, historic
pres. (also ἐμπίπτει); ὅδε and ὧδε often refer to what immediately follows.
εὐθὺς ἐπειδὴ ... : 'firstly, the moment he woke up ... '; another
example of asyndeton (see on ἔδοξεν αὐτῷ, 1:11 above).
εἰκὸς (sc. ἐστι) τοὺς πολεμίους ἥξειν: '(it is) likely that the enemy will be here'.
εἰ δὲ γενησόμεθα ... : 'if we fall into the hands of the King, what
will prevent us from witnessing all the most painful sights, ex-
periencing all the most terrible sufferings, and being (shame-
fully)tortured to death?'; εἰ ... γενήσομεθα, fut. indic. (rather than ἐάν + subjunctive) for a vivid warning; τί ἐμποδὼν sc.
ἐστι, lit. 'what (is) in the way', treated as a verb of prevention
with inf. sometimes preceded by μή (or τοῦ or both); if the verb
of prevention is itself negative (or, as here, virtually negative:
τί ἐμποδὼν = οὐδὲν ἐμποδών), it is followed by μὴ οὐ + inf.;
ἐπιδόντας ... παθόντας ... ἀποθανεῖν sc. ἡμᾶς; ὕβρις (and ὑβρίζω)
refers to the worst physical ill-treatment, involving the humil-
iation or shame of the victim (see on δι' αἰσχύνην, 1:10 above);
as an Athenian legal term it meant 'grievous bodily harm' (cf.
Kyros' use of blinding and mutilation, 1:9:13; his own death, 1:
10:1; and the year-long torture of Menon, 2:6:29 above).

1:14 ὅπως δ' ἀμυνούμεθα ... : 'as for defending ourselves, no-one is
preparing for this or paying any attention to it'; ὅπως + fut.
(cont.)

παρασκευάζεται ούδὲ ἐπιμελεῖται, ἀλλὰ κατακείμεθα
ὥσπερ ἐξὸν ἡσυχίαν ἄγειν. ἐγὼ οὖν τὸν ἐκ ποίας πόλεως στρατηγὸν προσδοκῶ ταῦτα πράξειν; ποίαν δ' ἡλικίαν ἐμαυτῷ ἐλθεῖν ἀναμένω; οὐ γὰρ ἔγωγ' ἔτι πρεσβύτερος ἔσομαι, ἐὰν τήμερον προδῶ ἐμαυτὸν τοῖς πολεμίοις.

indic., put first for emphasis, regular construction with verbs
of precaution (παρασκευάζεται and ἐπιμελεῖται).] * ὥσπερ ἐξὸν
+ inf.: 'as if (we) could'; ἐξὸν, acc. n. s. part. of ἔξεστι,
lit. 'it being possible', acc. absolute, used in the case of impersonal verbs instead of gen. absolute.
ἐγὼ οὖν ... : lit. 'therefore, I myself am expecting the general
from what city to do this?' i.e. 'what about me, then? What country am I expecting the general (to come) from to organize our defence?' (There was a good candidate, but Xenophon does not mention
him here).
ποίαν δ' ἡλικίαν ... : 'what "right age" am I waiting for before
I go myself?', lit. ' ... for myself to go'; Xenophon was about
30, the minimum age for a general in the Athenian army; Proxenos
had also been about 30, Agias and Sokrates of Akhaia (generals
also executed by Tissaphernes) 35, and Klearkhos 50; Kyros had
been only 24.
οὐ γὰρ ἔγωγ(ε) ... : lit. '(there is no point in waiting) for I at
any rate will not be any older ... ' i.e. 'I'll never be any older ... '; grim humour. * προδῶ: aor. subj. (with ἐὰν) of προ-
δίδωμι. Xenophon lacked confidence for other reasons also: firstly, he held no official position of command (see on οὔτε στρατηγὸς ... ἀλλὰ Πρόξενος, 1:4 above); secondly, he was one of the
very few Athenians present amidst mostly Spartans and other Pel-
oponnesians, former enemies of his homeland - which was ironic,
considering his sympathies (see on Λακεδαιμονίοις, 1:5 above).
But he felt that he was the natural successor to Proxenos, whose
troops he had got to know; so he decided to take the initiative,
and to stop finding excuses for inactivity.

1:15   *Xenophon assembled the captains of Proxenos' contingent*
to   *and, with characteristic optimism, pointed out that they were*
1:37   *no longer bound by their treaty; moreover, they knew from the*
        King's previous behaviour that he was afraid to face them in
        open battle. At a subsequent meeting of the surviving officers
        of the whole army, Xenophon said that the soldiers would now
        be looking to their officers for an initiative, and a new lead-
        ership. He added some practical suggestions as to what they
        should do next.

1:38   καὶ νῦν πρῶτον μὲν οἶμαι ἂν ὑμᾶς μέγα ὀνῆσαι τὸ
        στράτευμα, εἰ ἐπιμεληθείητε ὅπως ἀντὶ τῶν ἀπολωλότων
        ὡς τάχιστα στρατηγοὶ καὶ λοχαγοὶ ἀντικατασταθῶσιν.
        ἄνευ γὰρ ἀρχόντων οὐδὲν ἂν οὔτε καλὸν οὔτε ἀγαθὸν
        γένοιτο ὡς μὲν συνελόντι εἰπεῖν οὐδαμοῦ, ἐν δὲ δὴ
        τοῖς πολεμικοῖς παντάπασιν. ἡ μὲν γὰρ εὐταξία σῴζειν
1:39   δοκεῖ, ἡ δὲ ἀταξία πολλοὺς ἤδη ἀπολώλεκεν. ἐπειδὰν δὲ

1:38   **ἂν ὑμᾶς ... ὀνῆσαι ... εἰ ἐπιμεληθείητε:** 'that you would benefit
        ... if you saw to it ... ', remote fut. condition in indir.
        statement (acc. and inf.) with οἶμαι (dir. version of apodosis =
        ὀνήσαιτε ἄν, aor. opt.); ὑμᾶς, Xenophon excludes himself owing
        to his unofficial position; ἐπιμεληθείητε: aor. opt. pass. (in
        mid. sense). * ὅπως ... ἀντικατασταθῶσιν: aor. subj. pass. of
        ἀντικαθίστημι; ὅπως + subj. after ἐπιμελέομαι, indir. deliber-
        ative question or purpose clause. * τῶν ἀπολωλότων: 'those
        who have died', perf. part. (intrans.) of ἀπόλλυμι; ὡς + super-
        lative, 'as ... as possible'.
        οὐδὲν ἂν ... : 'there could be no honourable or brave action';
        ἂν ... γένοιτο, opt., potential; cf. καλὸς καγαθός, 2:6:19 above.
        * ὡς μὲν συνελόντι ... : lit. 'on the one hand nowhere as for
        (someone) having summed up to say, on the other hand in warlike
        matters altogether' i.e. 'broadly speaking, anywhere, least of
        all, of course, in war'; ὡς ... εἰπεῖν, inf. limiting the sense
        of οὐδαμοῦ.
        σῴζειν δοκεῖ: 'is known to bring safety'. * ἤδη: 'before now'.
        * ἀπολώλεκεν: perf. of ἀπόλλυμι; 'has destroyed' (and will do
        so again); Xenophon's words are the commonplaces of commanders,
        but no less effective for that.

1:39   **ἐπειδὰν δὲ καταστήσησθε:** ἂν + subj. in indefinite temporal clause;
        aor. subj. mid. of καθίστημι; δὲ, answering πρῶτον μὲν at the
        start of 1:38 above.

καταστήσησθε τοὺς ἄρχοντας ὅσους δεῖ, ἢν καὶ τοὺς
ἄλλους στρατιώτας συλλέγητε καὶ παραθαρρύνητε, οἶμαι
1:40 ἂν ὑμᾶς πάνυ ἐν καιρῷ ποιῆσαι. νῦν μὲν γὰρ ἴσως καὶ
ὑμεῖς αἰσθάνεσθε ὡς ἀθύμως μὲν ἦλθον ἐπὶ τὰ ὅπλα,
ἀθύμως δὲ πρὸς τὰς φυλακάς· ὥστε οὕτω γ' ἐχόντων οὐκ
οἶδα ὅ τι ἄν τις χρήσαιτο αὐτοῖς εἴτε νυκτὸς δέοι τι
1:41 εἴτε καὶ ἡμέρας. ἢν δέ τις αὐτῶν τρέψῃ τὰς γνώμας
ὡς μὴ τοῦτο μόνον ἐννοῶνται τί πείσονται, ἀλλὰ καὶ

* ὅσους: see on Ἐπεὶ μέντοι ... , 1:7 above.   * δεῖ: sc.
καταστήσασθαι.
ἢν καὶ ...: ἢν (= ἐάν) ... συλλέγητε ... παραθαρρύνητε, fut. condition, followed by indir. remote fut. apodosis ἂν ὑμᾶς ... ποιῆσαι
(= dir. ποιήσαιτε ἄν, aor. opt.) dependent on οἶμαι; οἶμαι ἄν ... :
lit. 'I think that you would do (it) very much in season' i.e.
' ... you'd be doing exactly the right thing'.

1:40 νῦν μὲν γὰρ ... : 'for in the present situation, you too can probably see their depressed mood, both when they came (back) to the
camp, and when they went on sentry-duty'; αἰσθάνεσθε, pres. rather than more logical past tense, since the men's depression was
continuing; τὰ ὅπλα, i.e. where they were stacked, in the middle
of the camp; φυλακάς, from φυλακή. At the time of the generals'
execution, about 200 men had gone unarmed to buy provisions in
nearby villages; when they discovered what had happened, many of
them actually spent the night away from the camp (2:5:30 and 5:37).
ὥστε οὕτω ... : lit. 'so that (these things or these men) being so,
at any rate I don't know what use one would make of them' i.e.
'and so in these circumstances (or with the men in this state),
I don't know what use they'd be' (to a commander); adverb + ἔχω,
'be in ... condition'; ἐχόντων sc. τούτων either n. or possibly
m. (despite αὐτοῖς, dat. with χρήσαιτο: for this irregular usage,
see on ὄντος, 2:6:3 above); ὅ τι, from ὅστις, internal (adverbial) acc.; ἄν ... χρήσαιτο, opt., apodosis of remote fut. condition. * εἴτε νυκτὸς ... : lit. 'whether it were necessary at
all by night or even by day' i.e. 'if they were needed tomorrow,
let alone tonight', to repulse an enemy attack; δέοι, opt., remote fut. condition; τι, internal (adverbial) acc.; it was then
about midnight, and Xenophon was suggesting that the enemy might
even attack before daybreak.

1:41 ἢν (= ἐάν) δέ τις ... : 'but if anyone turns their thought away
from an obsession with what will happen to them to what they
will actually be doing ... '; ὡς + subj., purpose (see Introduction 6.1); τοῦτο, explained by the following indir. question,
τί πείσονται - 'what (disaster) they will suffer'.

1:42 τί ποιήσουσι, πολὺ εὐθυμότεροι ἔσονται.   ἐπίστασθε
γὰρ δὴ ὅτι οὔτε πλῆθός ἐστιν οὔτε ἰσχὺς ἡ ἐν τῷ πολέμῳ τὰς νίκας ποιοῦσα, ἀλλ' ὁπότεροι ἂν σὺν τοῖς
θεοῖς ταῖς ψυχαῖς ἐρρωμενέστεροι ἴωσιν ἐπὶ τοὺς πολεμίους, τούτους ὡς ἐπὶ τὸ πολὺ οἱ ἀντίοι οὐ δέχονται.

1:43   He concluded his speech by exhorting his fellow officers
to   to set an example of courage to the men. Kheirisophos the
1:46   Spartan spoke in praise of Xenophon's speech, and urged the
              immediate election of officers to replace those who had been
              murdered.

1:47   ἐκ τούτου ἡρέθησαν ἄρχοντες ἀντὶ μὲν Κλεάρχου
          Τιμασίων Δαρδανεύς, ἀντὶ δὲ Σωκράτους Ξανθικλῆς

* εὐθυμότεροι: εὔθυμος is the opposite of ἄθυμος above.

1:42 δή: 'of course', 'I'm sure'. * οὔτε πλῆθος ... : 'it is not numbers nor (physical) strength which produces victories in war';
ἡ ... ποιοῦσα goes with both πλῆθος and ἰσχύς, but agrees with
the nearer noun. * ὁπότεροι ἄν ... : 'whichever side advances
with the gods on their side and with stouter hearts, their attack,
generally, the other side does not wait for'; ὁπότεροι ... τούτους: when relative clauses are placed early for emphasis, the
relative pronoun is often 'picked up' by οὗτος: ἐρρωμενέστεροι:
from ἐρρωμένος (perf. part. pass. of ῥώννυμι), but comparative
formed as if from adjective in -ης. Another commonplace, but
particularly apt in their situation; Xenophon recognises the importance of morale, greatly affected by a belief in the gods'
support; they had an advantage in physical toughness and superior
arms (he believed), but they must abandon negative thoughts.

1:47 ἐκ τούτου: 'at this', 'then'. * ἡρέθησαν: probably by the captains (λοχαγοί, each commanding a λόχος 'company' of about 100
men) of those divisions lacking a general; it is unclear whether
the surviving generals played any part in the elections.
* Τιμασίων Δαρδανεύς: from Dardanos on the Hellespont, where
Klearkhos had recruited troops supposedly to fight the native
Thracians (see on Χερρονήσῳ ... , 1:1:9 above).

Ἀχαιός, ἀντὶ δὲ Ἀγίου Κλεάνωρ Ἀρκάς, ἀντὶ δὲ Μένωνος
Φιλήσιος Ἀχαιός, ἀντὶ δὲ Προξένου Ξενοφῶν Ἀθηναῖος.

2:1   The new generals called a meeting of the whole army in the
to   centre of the camp and realistically explained the seriousness
2:9   of the situation to the troops. Xenophon was in the middle of
      a speech urging self-reliance when a man sneezed. This was uni-
      versally recognised as a good omen from Zeus himself, and Xeno-
      phon continued his speech on an optimistic note.

2:10   'Ετύγχανον λέγων ὅτι πολλαὶ καὶ καλαὶ ἐλπίδες ἡμῖν
       εἶεν σωτηρίας. πρῶτον μὲν γὰρ ἡμεῖς μὲν ἐμπεδοῦμεν
       τοὺς τῶν θεῶν ὅρκους, οἱ δὲ πολέμιοι ἐπιωρκήκασί τε
       καὶ τὰς σπονδὰς παρὰ τοὺς ὅρκους λελύκασιν. οὕτω δ'

Κλεάνωρ Ἀρκάς: from Orkhomenos; already mentioned as the oldest
   general, who now added Agias' division to his own (see 2:5:
   37 and 5:39 above).
Φιλήσιος Ἀχαιός: probably from Akhaia Phthiotis as Menon was Thessalian.
ἀντὶ δὲ Προξένου Ξενοφῶν: see final note on 1:14 above; Dardanos
   and the Thessalian cities had been Athens' allies in the Peloponnesian War, which may have helped Xenophon feel more at home.
   The nominations were confirmed by a general assembly next morning.

2:10   'Ετύγχανον λέγων ... : 'as I was saying, we can have very high hopes
   of a safe homecoming'; εἶεν, 3rd pers. pl. opt. of εἰμί 'be', indir. statement dependent on historic verb; ἡμῖν: Xenophon can now
   include himself (see on ὑμᾶς, 1:38 above); σωτηρίας, the word at
   which the sneeze occurred, so that they prayed to Zeus the Saviour
   (Σωτήρ), vowing their thank-offering for safety on reaching a friendly
   land (τὰ σωτήρια). For the sneeze as an omen, cf. Homer, Odyssey
   17.541.
τοὺς τῶν θεῶν ὅρκους: 'the oaths we swore to the gods'; τῶν θεῶν,
   objective gen; Ariaios had changed sides; Tissaphernes had broken
   his promise to assist the Greeks, and had insulted Zeus Xenios
   (see on ξένος, 1:1:10).
οὕτω δ' ἐχόντων: sc. τούτων, neuter.

ἐχόντων εἰκὸς τοῖς μὲν πολεμίοις ἐναντίους εἶναι τοὺς
θεούς, ἡμῖν δὲ συμμάχους, οἵπερ ἱκανοί εἰσι καὶ τοὺς
μεγάλους ταχὺ μικροὺς ποιεῖν καὶ τοὺς μικροὺς κἄν ἐν
2:11 δεινοῖς ὦσι σῴζειν εὐπετῶς, ὅταν βούλωνται. ἔπειτα
δέ, ἀναμνήσω γὰρ ὑμᾶς καὶ τοὺς τῶν προγόνων τῶν ἡμετέρων κινδύνους, ἵνα εἰδῆτε ὡς ἀγαθοῖς τε ὑμῖν προσήκει εἶναι σῴζονταί τε σὺν τοῖς θεοῖς καὶ ἐκ πάνυ
δεινῶν οἱ ἀγαθοί. ἐλθόντων μὲν γὰρ Περσῶν καὶ τῶν
σὺν αὐτοῖς παμπληθεῖ στόλῳ ὡς ἀφανιούντων τὰς Ἀθήνας,

* εἰκὸς sc. ἐστι: an argument from probability is a common rhetorical device. * καὶ τοὺς μεγάλους ... : (capable) 'of quickly
making even (or both of quickly making) the mighty weak and of
saving the weak'; for this pious hope, see on ὁπότεροι ἄν ... ,
1:42 above; military harangues often included assurances of divine
support. * κἄν = καὶ ἐάν (crasis), 'even if'. * ἐν δεινοῖς:
'in terrible danger'.

2:11 ἔπειτα δέ ... : lit. 'and then, for I shall remind you ... ' i.e.
'secondly - and let me also remind you of the dangers faced by
our ancestors'; ἀναμιμνήσκω takes the acc. of the person and of
the thing. A reference to 'our ancestors' is another common
rhetorical device, making the audience feel they must not dis-
grace them. * εἰδῆτε: subj. of οἶδα, purpose with ἵνα; after
the parenthesis which begins at ἀναμνήσω γάρ, Xenophon does not
continue with a main verb (e.g. ἴστε 'you must know'), but treats
ἀναμνήσω itself as the main verb, continuing with the subordinate
purpose clause; this change of construction in mid-stream is called anacoluthon. * ὡς ἀγαθοῖς ... : 'not only that you are expected to be brave ... '; οἶδα, although a verb of knowing (usually + part. construction), is regularly followed by ὅτι or ὡς when
the fact known is emphasized, or is a strongly held belief.
* σῴζονταί τε ... : 'but also that men are saved ... even from
the most terrible danger, (if they are) brave'; σῴζονται and οἱ
ἀγαθοί, both in emphatic positions.
ἐλθόντων μὲν ... : 'for when (the) Persians and their allies had
(actually) arrived with a massive armament, ... '; ἐλθόντων, gen.
absolute, emphatic position, contrasted with the present situation, where the Persians were on their own ground; τῶν σὺν αὐτοῖς,
e.g. Lydians; for σύν + dat., see on 1:11 above. * ὡς + fut. part.:
purpose. In 499 the Greek cities in Ionia revolted from Persian
rule, and Athens sent 20 warships to help them (Sparta refused
to help, since it would involve a three months' journey from the
sea). Dareios I (King of Persia 521 - 486 and great-great-grand-
father of Artaxerxes) suppressed the revolt in 494, and sent an
expedition of 20,000 men to punish Athens (see Herodotus, 5 and 6).

ὑποστῆναι αὐτοῖς Ἀθηναῖοι τολμήσαντες ἐνίκησαν αὐτ-

2:12   τούς. καὶ εὐξάμενοι τῇ Ἀρτέμιδι ὁπόσους ἂν κατακάνοιεν τῶν πολεμίων τοσαύτας χιμαίρας καταθύσειν τῇ
θεῷ, ἐπεὶ οὐκ εἶχον ἱκανὰς εὑρεῖν, ἔδοξεν αὐτοῖς
κατ' ἐνιαυτὸν πεντακοσίας θύειν, καὶ ἔτι καὶ νῦν

* ὑποστῆναι αὐτοῖς ... : 'the Athenians boldly held out against them and defeated them' see on ὑποπτεύσας συμβουλεύει,
1:5 above; ὑποστῆναι, strong aor. inf. (intrans.) of ὑφίστημι,
emphatic position. The Persians crossed the Aegean Sea, defeating island after island, and reached Attica in 490; Athens stood
alone, the Spartans having agreed to help but 'only after the
full moon', a delay of six days which made their offer useless.
Naturally Xenophon did not mention this to his present audience
(nor the help given to the Persians by the Thebans and Thessalians), but gave the conflict a pan-Hellenic character (ἡμετέρων
above). The Persians fought the Athenians at Marathon, outnumber-
ing them 2 to 1; for some reason they did not use their cavalry
and were defeated with the loss of 6400 men - a humiliating but
not crippling blow; the Athenians lost only 192 men, and the battle
became legendary as the miraculous event which saved Greek civilization from being absorbed into the Persian Empire - something for
Xenophon to be proud of (cf. Herodotus 6.48 - 49 and 94 - 106).

2:12   εὐξάμενοι: 'after vowing'; the annual festival of the Huntress
(Ἀγροτέρα, i.e. Artemis) had taken place a few days before the
battle, in late September; in their prayers the Athenians had included a request for help, and this vow. * ὁπόσους ἂν ... :
'that however many ... they killed, they would sacrifice to the
goddess that number of ... '; ὁπόσους ... τοσαύτας, see on ὁπότεροι ... τούτους, 1:42 above; κατακάνοιεν (a word not found in
'pure' Attic prose), opt., indefinite relative clause in indir.
speech (historic sequence), = dir. subjunctive + ἂν (in regular
Attic prose there would be no ἂν with this opt.). For sacrifices,
see on καὶ τὰ ἱερὰ καλά, 1:8:15 above; this sacrifice was not 'pre-
payment', but a thanksgiving and fulfilment of a vow - a reward
to Ἄρτεμις for her help in the battle. The vow proved to be very
expensive. * οὐκ εἶχον: 'they were not able', a fairly common
meaning of ἔχω. * ἔδοξεν αὐτοῖς: impersonal verb + dat., despite the nom. part. εὐξάμενοι, which is left 'in the air'; this
type of anacoluthon (see on ἵνα εἰδῆτε, 2:11 above) is called nominativus pendens. * κατ' ἐνιαυτὸν: at the festival of the Huntress.
ἔτι καὶ νῦν ἀποθύουσιν: ἀπο-, i.e. 'duly paying off', in instalments;
the original vow had been fulfilled by 477; by Xenophon's time
the event had become an annual victory celebration (cf. Aristophanes, Knights 660 - 662). The Athenians also issued commemorative
coins with the moon (representing Artemis) appearing behind the
usual owl of Athena.

2:13 ἀποθύουσιν. ἔπειτα ὅτε Ξέρξης ὕστερον ἀγείρας τὴν
ἀναρίθμητον στρατιὰν ἦλθεν ἐπὶ τὴν Ἑλλάδα, καὶ
τότε ἐνίκων οἱ ἡμέτεροι πρόγονοι τοὺς τούτων προ-
γόνους καὶ κατὰ γῆν καὶ κατὰ θάλατταν. ὧν ἔστι
μὲν τεκμήρια ὁρᾶν τὰ τρόπαια, μέγιστον δὲ μαρτύριον
ἡ ἐλευθερία τῶν πόλεων ἐν αἷς ὑμεῖς ἐγένεσθε καὶ
ἐτράφητε· οὐδένα γὰρ ἄνθρωπον δεσπότην ἀλλὰ τοὺς
θεοὺς προσκυνεῖτε. τοιούτων μέν ἐστε προγόνων.

2:13 ἔπειτα: asyndeton; see on ἔδοξεν αὐτῷ, 1:11 . * Ξέρξης: King of
Persia 486 - 465, son of Dareios I. * τὴν ἀναρίθμητον στρατιὰν: 'his (or those) countless troops'; perhaps 180,000 altogether
(Herodotus' total is 5 million!). * καὶ τότε: 'that was another
time when'; ὅτε and τότε are correlatives. * ἐνίκων: 'were victorious', imperf. denoting a state. * τούτων: i.e. the Persians'.
* κατὰ γῆν: Plataia 479 B.C.
κατὰ θάλατταν: Salamis 480 and Mykale 479 B.C.; but the Persians
did manage to devastate Attica and burn Athens; the magnificent
temples of the Acropolis were built to replace those destroyed
by the Persians.
ὧν ἔστι ... : lit. 'of which things it is possible on the one hand
to see the trophies (as) proofs' i.e. 'as a proof of these victories, one can see the trophies'; ὧν, connecting relative, see
on 1:10 above; ἔστι = ἔξεστι; a τρόπαιον was a monument marking
the rout (τροπή) of an enemy, set up where they turned (τρέπομαι)
and fled; the victors hung captured armour on a post or tree-trunk
as a visible symbol of their victory; later they might build a
permanent monument there or transfer the spoils (σκῦλα) to the
temple of the god believed to have assisted them; the Athenians
enlarged their treasury at Delphoi (see on τὸ ... τοῦ Ἀπόλλωνος,
5:3:5 below) to receive the spoils of Marathon; for dedications
made after Salamis, see Herodotus 8.121 - 122 and those after
Plataia, Herodotus 9:81 and Thucydides 1.132. * μαρτύριον: sc.
ἐστι. * ὑμεῖς ἐγένεσθε ... : 'you yourselves were born and
raised'.
δεσπότην: '(as) master', with unlimited power, e.g. over slaves.
* προσκυνεῖτε: see on προσεκύνουν, 1:6:10 above.
τοιούτων μέν ἐστε προγόνων: 'this is the kind of ancestor you are
descended from'; τοιούτων, gen. of origin, emphatic position;
Xenophon rounds off his reference to 'our ancestors' (2:11 above).
When the Greeks learned about the absolute monarchies of Persia,
Egypt, etc. (through men like Herodotus), they became very aware
and staunchly proud of their own independence and political freedom; however much the Greek city-states quarrelled with each other, they usually united to defend this freedom against a common
enemy; see δούλου ὄντος, 1:9:29 above. Xenophon returns to the
present situation (μέν), reminding the men of their recent suc-
cesses and saying that Ariaios' desertion was in fact to their
advantage - they were better off without him.

2:14   Xenophon reminded the soldiers of their recent victory
to   and then, with telling humour, minimized the importance of
3:5   the Persian superiority in cavalry, saying that men and not
          horses fight and win battles. Nor, he continued, need there
          be a shortage of guides; and prisoners, with their own
          lives at risk, would be more reliable for this purpose than
          Tissaphernes had been. Supplies should cause no problem,
          especially in hostile territory where they could be seized as
          the spoils of war without payment. Parts of the King's terr-
          itory could be occupied for considerable periods if the Greeks'
          passage was held up; the most serious obstacle to their safe
          return perhaps lay within themselves: like the Lotus-Eaters,
          they might find life in this pleasant land so congenial that
          they would wish to stay rather than face the arduous journey
          home. They must therefore prepare themselves for tighter
          discipline and for a drastic reduction in the amount of equip-
          ment carried.

          It was decided that the hoplites should be formed into a
          hollow square, with Kheirisophos leading, two older generals
          on the flanks, and Xenophon and Timasion in the rear. The
          next day the army was approached by Mithradates, who claimed
          to be a supporter of Kyros. But the generals decided, after
          brief negotiations with him, that no further parleys should
          be held with Persians.

3:6   μετὰ ταῦτα ἀριστήσαντες καὶ διαβάντες τὸν Ζαπάταν
         ποταμὸν ἐπορεύοντο τεταγμένοι τὰ ὑποζύγια καὶ τὸν

3:6   ἀριστήσαντες: Xenophon had addressed the men at the crack of dawn;
         breakfast was eaten straight afterwards, and consisted mainly of
         wheat gruel and bread with wine (see on κρέα ... ἐσθίοντες, 1:5:
         6 above). * διαβάντες τὸν Ζαπάταν ποταμόν: by fording it 25
         miles from where it joined the Tigris; the Persians made no att-
         empt to stop them. * ἐπορεύοντο τεταγμένοι: 'they began to
         march in formation', in the 'hollow square' (in fact oblong) pre-
         viously agreed on, with Kheirisophos commanding the van, the two
         oldest generals (Kleanor and another - perhaps Philesios or Soph-
         ainetos) on the flanks, and the youngest (Timasion and Xenophon)
         in the rear - the most dangerous position in a retreat (cf. Thucyd-
         ides 7.78, ἐν πλαισίῳ τετάχθαι). They were making for nearby vil-
         lages to get provisions. Kheirisophos had taken over from Klear-
         khos as leader of the Greeks, but Xenophon does not make this
         clear (see on ἐγὼ οὖν, 1:14 and on Χειρίσοφος, 2:5:37 above).

ὄχλον ἐν μέσῳ ἔχοντες.   οὐ πολὺ δὲ προεληλυθότων αὐτῶν ἐπιφαίνεται πάλιν ὁ Μιθραδάτης, ἱππέας ἔχων ὡς
διακοσίους καὶ τοξότας καὶ σφενδονήτας ὡς τετρακοσ-
3:7 ίους μάλα ἐλαφροὺς καὶ εὐζώνους.   καὶ προσήει μὲν
ὡς φίλος ὢν πρὸς τοὺς "Ελληνας, ἐπεὶ δ᾽ ἐγγὺς ἐγένετο, ἐξαπίνης οἱ μὲν αὐτῶν ἐτόξευον καὶ ἱππεῖς καὶ
πεζοί, οἱ δ᾽ ἐσφενδόνων καὶ ἐτίτρωσκον.   οἱ δὲ ὀπισθοφύλακες τῶν ῾Ελλήνων ἔπασχον μὲν κακῶς ἀντεποίουν
δ᾽ οὐδέν· οἵ τε γὰρ Κρῆτες βραχύτερα τῶν Περσῶν

* ἔχοντες: 'with', a common usage (also ἔχων below).
* τὰ ὑποζύγια ... : pack animals, oxen, mules and any horses
captured from the enemy; they would now have been carrying the
minimum of baggage, having burnt their carts and tents.   τὸν
ὄχλον: lit. 'the crowd', a soldier's word for the non-combatant
camp-followers (slaves, prisoners, wounded etc.) accompanying the
army (see on παλλακίδα, 1:10:2 above); the hoplites and peltasts
formed the protecting 'square' round them.
προεληλυθότων αὐτῶν: 'they were not much further ahead when ... ';
gen. absolute, perf. part. emphasizing their present position.
ἐπιφαίνεται πάλιν ὁ Μιθραδάτης: Mithradates, a former ally of Kyros,
had joined Tissaphernes immediately after the execution of the
generals (2:5:35); on the previous day he had offered to help the
Greeks, who refused his offer, realizing he was in league with
Tissaphernes.   * ὡς: 'about', with numbers.   * σφενδονήτας: the
sling (σφενδόνη) comprised a one-inch strap of leather or plaited
sinew 3 feet long, with a wider 'pocket' in the middle; one end
was held between forefinger and thumb, the other fastened to another finger of the same hand; the slinger loaded the pocket with
a missile, whirled the sling round his head or parallel to his
body, released the free end, and projected the missile at a speed
which could exceed 90 feet per second; in skilled hands it was
an extremely accurate and deadly weapon.   Missiles (see on καὶ
ταῖς μολυβδίσιν, 3:17 below) were carried in a leather bag (δίφ-
θερα).   * εὐζώνους: lit. 'well-girt', with one's tunic (χιτών)
hitched up and held in place by the belt (ζώνη), i.e. 'ready for
action'.

3:7 προσήει: imperf. of πρόσειμι (εἶμι 'go').   * ὡς φίλος ὢν: 'as if
on friendly terms'.   * οἱ μὲν ... οἱ δ(έ): 'some ... others',
a common use of the definite article as pronoun.
οἱ ... Κρῆτες βραχύτερα ... ἐτόξευον: 'the Cretan (archers) had a
shorter range'; the Cretans were famous as archers and had served
as mercenaries of Athens in the war with Sparta (Thucydides 7.57);
Klearkhos had brought 200, but their bows were shorter and (cont.)

ἐτόξευον καὶ ἄμα ψιλοὶ ὄντες εἴσω τῶν ὅπλων κατεκέκλειντο, οἵ τε ἀκοντισταὶ βραχύτερα ἠκόντιζον ἢ ὡς
3:8 ἐξικνεῖσθαι τῶν σφενδονητῶν. ἐκ τούτου Ξενοφῶντι
ἐδόκει διωκτέον εἶναι· καὶ ἐδίωκον τῶν τε ὁπλιτῶν
καὶ τῶν πελταστῶν οἳ ἔτυχον σὺν αὐτῷ ὀπισθοφυλακοῦν-
τες· διώκοντες δὲ οὐδένα κατελάμβανον τῶν πολεμίων.
3:9 οὔτε γὰρ ἱππεῖς ἦσαν τοῖς Ἕλλησιν οὔτε οἱ πεζοὶ
τοὺς πεζοὺς ἐκ πολλοῦ φεύγοντας ἐδύναντο καταλαμβάνειν

therefore less powerful than those of the Persians; the effective
range of Greek bows was probably about 200 yards. * τῶν Περσῶν:
gen. of comparison.] * ψιλοὶ ὄντες: 'because they wore no armour',
see on 1:8:6 above. * εἴσω τῶν ὅπλων κατεκέκλειντο: lit. 'had
been shut up inside the arms' i.e. 'were enclosed by the hoplite
lines', over which they had to shoot; this too decreased their
range and made aiming impossible. * οἵ τε ἀκοντισταὶ ... : lit.
'and the javelin-throwers were throwing their javelins shorter
than so as to reach the slingers' i.e. 'and the range of the
(Greek) javelin-throwers was too short to reach the (enemy)
slingers'; ὡς = ὥστε; τῶν σφενδονητῶν, gen. of object aimed at,
with ἐξικνεῖσθαι 'reach (and hit)'; the iron-tipped javelin (ἀκ-
όντιον) was 3 - 6 feet long and could be thrown at least 175
yards; a rotary motion imparted by a throwing loop (ἀγκύλη)
aided its accuracy; for the slingers' range see 3:17 below.

3:8 ἐκ τούτου: 'as a result'. * διωκτέον εἶναι: 'that they must give
chase', indir. version of διωκτέον (ἐστι) 'one must pursue',
neuter verbal adjective from διώκω, expressing obligation; see
on ἰτέον εἶναι, 1:7 and πειστέον, 2:6:8 above.
καὶ ἐδίωκον ... : 'this was done by those of the hoplites and peltasts who ... '. * ὁπλιτῶν/πελταστῶν: see on 1:8:3 and 1:8:5 above.
διώκοντες: 'in their pursuit' or 'they chased them but ... ', concessive part.

3:9 οὔτε γὰρ ἱππεῖς ... : lit. 'for neither were there horsemen to the
Greeks nor were the foot-soldiers able to overtake in a small
place the infantry fleeing from a great (distance)' i.e. 'since
the Greeks had no cavalry, and it was impossible for their infantry to overtake the enemy's infantry over a short distance, as
they would take to flight when still a long way off'; τοῖς Ἕλλησιν, possessive dat.; τοὺς πεζοὺς, emphatic position, 'even
their infantry (let alone their cavalry)'; the bringing together
of different cases of the same noun for emphasis is called polyptoton. Kyros' native cavalry had all deserted with their leader
Ariaios when Kyros was killed (1:9:31); the remaining 40 cavalry
(mostly Thracians) were in Klearkhos' division and deserted soon
(cont.)

ἐν ὀλίγῳ χωρίῳ· πολὺ γὰρ οὐχ οἶόν τε ἦν ἀπὸ τοῦ ἄλλ-
3:10 ου στρατεύματος διώκειν.   οἱ δὲ βάρβαροι ἱππεῖς καὶ
φεύγοντες ἅμα ἐτίτρωσκον εἰς τοὔπισθεν τοξεύοντες
ἀπὸ τῶν ἵππων, ὁπόσον δὲ προδιώξειαν οἱ ῞Ελληνες,
3:11 τοσοῦτον πάλιν ἐπαναχωρεῖν μαχομένους ἔδει. ὥστε
τῆς ἡμέρας ὅλης διῆλθον οὐ πλέον πέντε καὶ εἴκοσι
σταδίων, ἀλλὰ δείλης ἀφίκοντο εἰς τὰς κώμας. ἔνθα
δὴ πάλιν ἀθυμία ἦν. καὶ Χειρίσοφος καὶ οἱ πρεσβύτατοι τῶν στρατηγῶν Ξενοφῶντα ᾐτιῶντο ὅτι ἐδίωκεν ἀπὸ
τῆς φάλαγγος καὶ αὐτός τε ἐκινδύνευε καὶ τοὺς πολεμ-
3:12 ίους οὐδὲν μᾶλλον ἐδύνατο βλάπτειν. ἀκούσας δὲ Ξενοφῶν ἔλεγεν ὅτι ὀρθῶς αἰτιῷντο καὶ αὐτὸ τὸ ἔργον

after, leaving some of their horses behind; other horses were
used for travel by richer hoplites, e.g. Xenophon himself.]
οὐχ οἶόν τε ἦν ... διώκειν: 'it was impossible to continue the
pursuit'; πολὺ (emphatic position) qualifies διώκειν.

3:10 καὶ φεύγοντες ... : 'in the very act of fleeing continued to in-
flict wounds by shooting behind them' - a difficult feat, especially before the invention of stirrups; τοὔπισθεν = τὸ ὄπισθεν
(crasis). * ὁπόσον δὲ προδιώξειαν ... : 'however far the Greeks
advanced in their pursuit, they had to retreat again that distance, fighting all the way'; ὁπόσον ... τοσοῦτον, correlatives,
acc. of extent of space; προδιώξειαν, aor. opt., indefinite.

3:11 τῆς ἡμέρας ὅλης: 'during the whole day', gen. of time within which
(also δείλης). * πέντε καὶ εἴκοσι σταδίων: gen. of comparison;
under 3 miles; an unhindered day's march might cover 20 miles.
* τὰς κώμας: where they were to get provisions.
ἔνθα δὴ: 'and now', 'and of course', see on 1:5:8 above.
οἱ πρεσβύτατοι: i.e. Kleanor and the other general who commanded
the flanks, see on ἐπορεύοντο τεταγμένοι, 3:6 above.   *
ἐδίωκεν ἀπὸ τῆς φάλαγγος: 'he had left the lines to pursue the enemy'; φάλαγγος, lit. 'battle formation', here = the main body of
troops. * οὐδὲν μᾶλλον ἐδύνατο: 'had been no more able', 'for
all that, had not been able'.

3:12 ἀκούσας δὲ ... : 'on hearing (this criticism), Xenophon ... '.
* ἔλεγεν: 'began by saying', imperf. for uncompleted action.
* ὀρθῶς αἰτιῷντο: 'they were right to reproach him', opt., indir.
statement (historic). * αὐτὸ τὸ ἔργον ... : 'the event itself
gave them their evidence', 'the facts spoke for themselves'.

αὐτοῖς μαρτυροίη. Ἀλλ' ἐγώ, ἔφη, ἠναγκάσθην διώκειν,
ἐπεὶ ἑώρων ἡμᾶς ἐν τῷ μένειν κακῶς μὲν πάσχοντας,
3:13 ἀντιποιεῖν δὲ οὐδὲν δυναμένους. ἐπειδὴ δὲ ἐδιώκομεν,
ἀληθῆ, ἔφη, ὑμεῖς λέγετε· κακῶς μὲν γὰρ ποιεῖν οὐδὲν
μᾶλλον ἐδυνάμεθα τοὺς πολεμίους, ἀνεχωροῦμεν δὲ παγ-
3:14 χαλέπως. τοῖς οὖν θεοῖς χάρις ὅτι οὐ σὺν πολλῇ ῥώμῃ,
ἀλλὰ σὺν ὀλίγοις ἦλθον, ὥστε βλάψαι μὲν μὴ μεγάλα,
3:15 δηλῶσαι δὲ ὧν δεόμεθα. νῦν γὰρ οἱ μὲν πολέμιοι τοξεύ-
ουσι καὶ σφενδονῶσιν ὅσον οὔτε οἱ Κρῆτες ἀντιτοξεύειν
δύνανται οὔτε οἱ ἐκ χειρὸς βάλλοντες ἐξικνεῖσθαι· ὅταν
δὲ αὐτοὺς διώκωμεν, πολὺ μὲν οὐχ οἷόν τε χωρίον ἀπὸ

* μαρτυροίη: opt., indir. statement; a metaphor from the law-
courts.
ἔφη: see on ἐπεὶ μέντοι ... , 1:7 above. * ἡμᾶς ἐν τῷ μένειν ... :
'that all the time we waited ... '; ἡμᾶς ... πάσχοντας ... δυναμένους, acc. and part., indir. statement after verb of perceiving;
τῷ μένειν, dat. of verbal noun (τό + inf.). * οὐδὲν: both object of ἀντιποιεῖν and adverbial with δυναμένους.

3:13 ἐπειδὴ δὲ ... : 'but when we did give chase, – you're quite right';
ἀληθῆ ... λέγετε is substituted for 'I did run a risk ... '.
ἀνεχωροῦμεν: '(we) had to retreat', imperf. for repeated action.

3:14 τοῖς οὖν θεοῖς χάρις sc. ἔστω: 'so thanks be to the gods', 'so
thank the gods'; the piety is genuine; see e.g. on Xenophon's
visit to Delphoi, 1:5 – 6 above. * οὐ σὺν πολλῇ ... : 'they
didn't come with a large force but in small (enough) numbers to
do no great damage, while showing up our shortcomings'; σὺν, see
on 1:11 above; ὧν = ταῦτα ὧν, gen. with δεόμεθα. Hoplite armour
prevented severe wounds (see on ἐξοπλίζεσθαι, 1:8:3 above); later
8 ἰατροί (lit. 'doctors' i.e. 'medical orderlies') were appointed
to dress wounds.

3:15 νῦν: 'as things are'. * ὅσον οἱ Κρῆτες ... : lit. 'as far as neither the Cretans are able to shoot arrows back nor those throwing
by hand (are able) to reach' i.e. 'too far for our Cretan archers
to shoot back, or for those throwing missiles by hand to reach';
οἱ ἐκ χειρὸς βάλλοντες, i.e. javelin-throwers; for their range
and for Cretan archers, see on 3:7 above.
πολὺ μὲν ... : πολύ, with χωρίον 'distance', emphatic position,
acc. of extent of space; οἷόν τε, sc. ἦν; ἐν ὀλίγῳ sc. χωρίῳ:
'over a short distance', emphatic position, contrasted (μὲν ...
δὲ) with πολύ ... χωρίον.

τοῦ στρατεύματος διώκειν, ἐν ὀλίγῳ δὲ οὐδ᾿ εἰ ταχὺς
εἴη πεζὸς πεζὸν ἂν διώκων καταλάβοι ἐκ τόξου ῥύματος.
3:16 ἡμεῖς οὖν εἰ μέλλομεν τούτους εἴργειν ὥστε μὴ δύνασθαι βλάπτειν ἡμᾶς πορευομένους, σφενδονητῶν τε τὴν
ταχίστην δεῖ καὶ ἱππέων. ἀκούω δ᾿ εἶναι ἐν τῷ στρατεύματι ἡμῶν ῾Ροδίους, ὧν τοὺς πολλούς φασιν ἐπίστασθαι σφενδονᾶν, καὶ τὸ βέλος αὐτῶν καὶ διπλάσιον φέρ-
3:17 εσθαι τῶν Περσικῶν σφενδονῶν. ἐκεῖναι γὰρ διὰ τὸ
χειροπληθέσι τοῖς λίθοις σφενδονᾶν ἐπὶ βραχὺ ἐξικνοῦνται, οἱ δέ γε ῾Ρόδιοι καὶ ταῖς μολυβδίσιν

* εἰ ταχὺς ... : εἴη ... ἂν ... καταλάβοι, opt., unfulfilled past
condition; πεζὸς πεζὸν, polyptoton; see on τοὺς πεζοὺς, 3:9 above.
* ἐκ τόξου ῥύματος: lit. 'from a drawing of a bow' i.e. 'when he
was already out of bowshot', see ἐκ πολλοῦ, 3:9 above.

3:16 ἡμεῖς: 'as for us'; after the εἰ clause, the main verb is the impersonal δεῖ, leaving the nom. ἡμεῖς 'in the air' (nominativus
pendens, see on ἔδοξεν αὐτοῖς, 2:12 above). * τούτους εἴργειν
ὥστε μὴ + inf.: 'to prevent them from ... '; for the usual construction see on τί ἐμποδών, 1:13 above. * σφενδονητῶν ... :
gen. with δεῖ; τὴν ταχίστην sc. ὀδόν: 'as quickly as possible',
adverbial acc. * εἶναι ... ῾Ροδίους: acc. and inf., instead of
regular part. construction after verb of perceiving (ἀκούω = 'I
am told'). * ὧν τοὺς πολλούς ... : 'the majority of whom, they
say, know how to use a sling'; τοὺς πολλούς ... ἐπίστασθαι, acc.
and inf. with φασιν (also τὸ βέλος ... φέρεσθαι). Rhodes was
famous for its slingers. * τὸ βέλος ... : lit. 'their missile
is carried even twice as far compared with the Persian slingshot'
i.e. 'their missiles fly (or carry) fully twice as far as ... ';
σφενδονῶν, gen. of comparison after διπλάσιον.

3:17 ἐκεῖναι γὰρ ... : lit. 'for those (missiles), because of (their)
using the sling with the stones filling the hand' i.e. 'the
reason is that because the Persians use hand-sized stones in
their slings, their missiles ... '; ἐκεῖναι sc. αἱ σφενδόναι,
'those yonder' i.e. 'the enemy's'; τὸ ... σφενδονᾶν, verbal noun;
χειροπληθέσι 'as big as a fist', predicative, a poetic word (Introduction 6.5). * ἐπὶ βραχὺ ἐξικνοῦνται: 'have a short range'.
* καὶ ταῖς μολυβδίσιν: 'lead bullets as well', dat. with χρῆσθαι; ταῖς indicates the whole class. The egg-shaped or biconical
bullets were made of stone or clay; or of lead, cast in a mould
(sometimes inscribed e.g. with the commander's name); they normally weighed ¼ - 1¼ oz. and could be slung 450 yards. The large
Persian stones weighed about ½ lb. but had a limited range owing
to their surface area and resultant air resistance.

3:18 ἐπίστανται χρῆσθαι. ἦν οὖν αὐτῶν ἐπισκεψώμεθα τίνες
πέπανται σφενδόνας, καὶ τούτων τῷ μὲν δῶμεν αὐτῶν
ἀργύριον, τῷ δὲ ἄλλας πλέκειν ἐθέλοντι ἄλλο ἀργύριον
τελῶμεν, καὶ τῷ σφενδονᾶν ἐντεταλμένῳ ἄλλην τινὰ
ἀτέλειαν εὑρίσκωμεν, ἴσως τινὲς φανοῦνται ἱκανοὶ ἡμᾶς
3:19 ὠφελεῖν. ὁρῶ δὲ καὶ ἵππους ὄντας ἐν τῷ στρατεύματι,
τοὺς μέν τινας παρ' ἐμοί, τοὺς δὲ τῶν Κλεάρχου καταλελειμμένους, πολλοὺς δὲ καὶ ἄλλους αἰχμαλώτους
σκευοφοροῦντας. ἂν οὖν τούτους πάντας ἐκλέξαντες
σκευοφόρα μὲν ἀντιδῶμεν, τοὺς δὲ ἵππους εἰς ἱππέας
κατασκευάσωμεν, ἴσως καὶ οὗτοί τι τοὺς φεύγοντας

3:18 ἦν οὖν ... : 'so if we inspect (the troops to see) which of them
... '; ἦν = ἐάν; αὐτῶν, partitive gen; πέπανται: poetic word
(Introduction 6.5). * τούτων τῷ μὲν ... : 'give money for those
(slings) to any(lit. the one) of them -i.e. Rhodians), and pay
more money to anyone else (lit. the other) who is willing to
plait more'; τούτων sc. τῶν σφενδόνων, with ἀργύριον; δῶμεν, aor.
subjunctive of δίδωμι; ἄλλο, i.e. 'likewise'. * τῷ σφενδονᾶν
ἐντεταλμένῳ: lit. 'for the one who has been commanded to use the
sling' i.e. 'for anyone we've ordered to be a slinger'. * ἄλλην τινὰ ἀτέλειαν: 'some extra exemption (or privilege)', in addition to the payment, i.e. exemption from fatigues (duties such
as keeping watch or gathering firewood).

3:19 ἵππους ὄντας: indir. statement, part. construction after ὁρῶ.
* παρ' ἐμοί: 'in my division', his own (brought with him) plus
any captured from the enemy. * τῶν Κλεάρχου: 'belonging to
Klearkhos' men'; καταλελειμμένους: see on οὔτε γὰρ ἱππεῖς, 3:9
above.
ἐκλέξαντες σκευοφόρα μὲν ἀντιδῶμεν: 'we pick out ... and replace
them with (ordinary) pack-animals', i.e. mules or oxen (= ὑποζύγια; see on 3:6 above); ἀντιδῶμεν, aor. subjunctive of ἀντι-
δίδωμι, with ἄν (= ἐάν). * τοὺς δὲ ἵππους ... : lit. 'and
equip the horses for horsemen' i.e. 'and equip them as cavalry
horses'; each needed a saddle-cloth (ἐφίππιον or κασῆς) and har-
ness (σκευή) - reins (ἡνίαι), bridle (χαλινός), bit (στόμιον)
(stirrups and horseshoes had not yet been invented), and any armour they could improvise (see on 1:8:7 above).
* καὶ οὗτοι sc. οἱ ἵπποι or οἱ ἱππῆς 'these too will cause them
(i.e. the enemy) some annoyance when they run away'; τι, adverbial acc.

3:20 ἀνίασουσιν. ἔδοξε καὶ ταῦτα. καὶ ταύτης τῆς νυκτὸς
σφενδονῆται μὲν εἰς διακοσίους ἐγένοντο, ἵπποι δὲ καὶ
ἱππεῖς ἐδοκιμάσθησαν τῇ ὑστεραίᾳ εἰς πεντήκοντα, καὶ
σπολάδες καὶ θώρακες αὐτοῖς ἐπορίσθησαν, καὶ ἵππαρχος
ἐπεστάθη Λύκιος ὁ Πολυστράτου Ἀθηναῖος.

3:20 ἔδοξε καὶ ταῦτα: 'these proposals were also accepted'.
ταύτης τῆς νυκτός: 'during that night', gen. of time within which.
* εἰς: 'getting on for', with numbers. * ἐδοκιμάσθησαν: 'were
examined and approved as fit', 'passed muster'.   *
σπολαδές ... ἐπορίσθησαν: leather jerkins prevented the armour
from chafing the skin. Normally soldiers bought their own equipment, but in this emergency they were equipped from the common
store of booty taken from the enemy. For types of equipment,
see on ἐξοπλίζεσθαι, 1:8:3 above. * ἵππαρχος ἐπεστάθη: 'was
put in command of them'; ἐπεστάθη, aor. pass. of ἐφίστημι.
* ὁ Πολυστράτου: '(son) of Polystratos', another Athenian (see
on προδῷ, 1:14 above); a Greek's full indentification included
(a) name, (b) father's name (gen.) (husband's name for a married
woman), and (c) place of birth or residence.

*Xenophon showed his qualities as a commander both by recognizing
errors in the present tactics, and by making practical suggestions.
Realizing that the best form of defence was attack, he showed a talent for improvization in his use of packhorses for cavalry, providing the element of speed over long distances. His method of increasing the range of retaliatory fire involved a psychological as
well as practical problem. Hoplites had been the acknowledged main-
stay of Greek armies, and gained the greatest honour; only better
off, socially superior soldiers possessed hoplite armour. Light-
armed troops had a secondary, skirmishing role; slingers (whose
weapon was very cheap) had very little glory (rarely appearing in
vase-paintings, for example, unlike hoplites). During this expedition, however, hoplite tactics were often impracticable; hoplite
armour proved inadequate in defence and cumbersome in attack; skirmishers came into their own. Hunting with the sling was a national
sport in Rhodes, but Xenophon realised that special incentives were
needed to persuade Rhodian hoplites to join their lower class com-
patriots in the field. The Greeks were also learning the difference
between a rout and a tactical withdrawal. In hoplite warfare to
turn and run was a sign of defeat; to avoid pitched battle a sign
of weakness. The Persians, however, were not behaving 'like cowardly dogs' (as Xenophon put it) but adopting tactics for which they
had been carefully trained. Xenophon showed his adaptability by
playing them at their own game. This was perhaps to be expected
from an Athenian; a Spartan would have been more conservative (cf.
the lesson learnt by Demosthenes in Aitolia in 426 and applied on
Sphakteria in 425 B.C.; Thucydides 3.97 - 8 and 4.32 - 33).*

4:1   *As they marched north, the Greeks had to repel frequent*
to   *attacks by highly mobile units of cavalry, archers and peltasts*
5:18   *led by Mithradates and a large mixed force under Tissaphernes.*
             As they reached more mountainous terrain, they found it necess-
             ary to abandon their single hollow-square formation and break
             the column up into smaller units. To avoid facing attack from
             above, they sent advanced detachments of peltasts, when poss-
             ible, to occupy high ground before the main column proceeded
             through the valleys.

Greek hoplite overcoming a Persian in hand-to-hand combat. The Greek
has an Attic helmet, greaves and a shield (see on 1:8:3 above) with
Pegasos emblem; the Persian is in multi-coloured garb including trousers (ἀναξυρίδες; see on 1:5:8 above) and a Phrygian cap (see note
after 4:5:18); besides his sword he carries a bow in his left hand
(mostly obscured by the shield).
    From the inside of an early fifth century B.C. Attic wine cup (*kylix*)
of the red-figure style in the Royal Scottish Museum, Edinburgh.

BOOK 4

1:5   *As the Greeks penetrated more deeply into the mountainous*
to   *heartland of Kurdestan, the native Kardoukhoi rolled huge boul-*
5:2   *ders down on to their slowly advancing column, which could only*
      move at the speed of its baggage train. The Kardoukhoi were
      dislodged by a detachment led by Xenophon whose men were called
      upon to do much mountaineering in the pursuit of the elusive
      enemy. This sort of terrain was the natural element for arch-
      ers, and the Greeks were fortunate to have Cretan bowmen to
      use against the natives, many of whom used no other weapons
      and relied on hit-and-run tactics. The Ten Thousand were glad
      to escape from this territory.

      After fording the Kentrites river into Armenia, they were
      at first able to make good progress over the southern plain of
      that country, whose satrap Tiribazos appeared anxious only that
      they should pass through his territory with a minimum of trouble,
      and offered them food and camping facilities on this condition.
      They agreed, and obtained supplies from local villages. But
      the first heavy falls of winter snow made their quarters extreme-
      ly uncomfortable, and they also heard that Tiribazos was muster-
      ing reinforcements with the purpose of attacking them. They
      decided to strike first, and sacked his camp. Then they pressed
      on as quickly as they could, and reached the Euphrates near its
      source four days later.

5:3   ἐντεῦθεν ἐπορεύοντο διὰ χιόνος πολλῆς καὶ πεδίου
      σταθμοὺς τρεῖς παρασάγγας πεντεκαίδεκα. ὁ δὲ τρίτος
      ἐγένετο χαλεπὸς καὶ ἄνεμος βορρᾶς ἐναντίος ἔπνει

5:3   ἐντεῦθεν: near the source of the Euphrates river (eastern branch).
    * διὰ χιόνος πολλῆς καὶ πεδίου: lit. 'through deep snow and across
    a plain' i.e. 'across a plain deep in snow'. * σταθμοὺς τρεῖς
    παρασάγγας πεντεκαίδεκα: 'three days' march, (a distance of) fif-
    teen parasangs', about 45 miles, see on παρασάγγας, 1:5:1 above;
    the Greeks had to cover as much distance as possible before Tiri-
    bazos (governor of Western Armenia) could reform his army; hence
    the speed of this march.
    τρίτος: sc. σταθμός. * ἄνεμος βορρᾶς: 'a north wind', two nouns =
    adjective and noun; βορρᾶς, Attic dialect form of βορέας. * ἐν-
    αντίος: 'in their faces'.

παντάπασιν ἀποκαίων πάντα καὶ πηγνὺς τοὺς ἀνθρώπους.
5:4 ἔνθα δὴ τῶν μάντεών τις εἶπε σφαγιάσασθαι τῷ ἀνέμῳ,
καὶ σφαγιάζεται· καὶ πᾶσι δὴ περιφανῶς ἔδοξε λῆξαι
τὸ χαλεπὸν τοῦ πνεύματος. ἦν δὲ τῆς χιόνος τὸ βάθος
ὀργυιά· ὥστε καὶ τῶν ὑποζυγίων καὶ τῶν ἀνδραπόδων
5:5 πολλὰ ἀπώλετο καὶ τῶν στρατιωτῶν ὡς τριάκοντα.ʼ διεγένοντο δὲ τὴν νύκτα πῦρ καίοντες· ξύλα δ᾿ ἦν ἐν τῷ
σταθμῷ πολλά· οἱ δὲ ὀψὲ προσιόντες ξύλα οὐκ εἶχον.
οἱ οὖν πάλαι ἥκοντες καὶ τὸ πῦρ καίοντες οὐ προσίεσαν

---

* ἀποκαίων: lit. 'burning off' i.e. 'blasting'; the effects of
frostbite and scorching of the skin are identical. * πηγνὺς:
pres. part. of πήγνυμι.

5:4 ἔνθα δή: see on 1:5:8 above. * μάντεων: soothsayers accompanied
an army to ensure that it kept on good terms with the gods; they
interpreted omens (οἰωνοί) from (a) sacrifices - see on καὶ τὰ
ἱερὰ καλά, 1:8:15 above, (b) dreams - see e.g. 3:1:11 - 12
above, (c) bird behaviour (augury) - e.g. Aeschylus, *Agamemnon*
108 - 138, (d) celestial phenomena - e.g. an eclipse of the moon,
Thucydides 7.50; their advice was taken very seriously. * εἶπε
+ inf.: 'told (them) to', indir. command.
τῷ ἀνέμῳ: i.e. to the god Boreas [who was worshipped at Athens because he had helped destroy the Persian fleet at Salamis in 480
and at Mykale 479 B.C. (*cf.* Herodotus 7.189)]. * καὶ σφαγιάζε-
ται: 'which was done', passive; historic pres., often used for
vividness; see Introduction 6.
πᾶσι ... περιφανῶς: emphatic position, reinforced by δή ('indeed').
* τὸ χαλεπὸν: 'the severity'; τό + adj. = abstract noun; this
shows the psychological effect of the sacrifice.
ἦν: 'was actually', emphatic position. * ὀργυιά: six feet.
καὶ τῶν ὑποζυγίων ... : see on τὰ ὑποζύγια, 3:3:6 above; the horses
were now being used for the cavalry - 3:3:19 above; ἀνδραπόδων,
slaves captured in war (δοῦλος is the general word for slave).
* ὡς: 'about', with numbers.

5:5 διεγένοντο δὲ ... : 'they kept fires going all night'.
σταθμῷ: the stopping place, not the distance between nightly stopping places as in 5:3 above (see on σταθμοὺς ... , 1:5:1 above).
προσιόντες: pres. part of πρόσειμι (εἶμι 'go').
οἱ ... τὸ πῦρ καίοντες: 'those who ... had their fires burning';
the definite article is often translated by a possessive adjective. * προσίεσαν: imperf. of προσίημι.

πρὸς τὸ πῦρ τοὺς ὀψίζοντας, εἰ μὴ μεταδοῖεν αὐτ-
5:6 τοῖς πυροὺς ἢ ἄλλο τι εἴ τι ἔχοιεν βρωτόν. ἔνθα
δὴ μετεδίδοσαν ἀλλήλοις ὧν εἶχον ἕκαστοι. ἔνθα δὲ
τὸ πῦρ ἐκαίετο διατηκομένης τῆς χιόνος βόθροι ἐγίγνοντο μεγάλοι ἔστε ἐπὶ τὸ δάπεδον· οὗ δὴ παρῆν μετ-
5:7 ρεῖν τὸ βάθος τῆς χιόνος. ἐντεῦθεν δὲ τὴν ἐπιοῦσαν
ἡμέραν ὅλην ἐπορεύοντο διὰ χιόνος, καὶ πολλοὶ τῶν ἀνθρώπων ἐβουλιμίασαν. Ξενοφῶν δ' ὀπισθοφυλακῶν καὶ κατα-
λαμβάνων τοὺς πίπτοντας τῶν ἀνθρώπων ἠγνόει ὅ τι τὸ
5:8 πάθος εἴη. ἐπειδὴ δὲ εἶπέ τις αὐτῷ τῶν ἐμπείρων ὅτι
σαφῶς βουλιμιῶσι κἄν τι φάγωσιν ἀναστήσονται, περιιὼν

* εἰ μὴ μεταδοῖεν: 'if (ever) they did not share', aor. opt.
of μεταδίδωμι, indefinite.
ἄλλο εἴ τι ... : 'anything (or whatever) else they had to eat';
ἔχοιεν, opt., indefinite; for soldiers' food, see on κρέα ...
ἐσθίοντες, 1:5:6 above; their first instinct was self-preservat-
ion rather than mutual assistance.

5:6 μετεδίδοσαν ... ἕκαστοι: 'each group did share ... ', imperf; ὧν
= τούτων ἃ, partitive gen. after μετεδίδοσαν, attracted from
acc. (object of εἶχον); ἔνθα: 'where' (relative), a meaning
rare in prose. * διατηκομένης ... : gen. absolute. * ἔστε
ἐπί: 'right down to'; οὗ: lit. 'where' i.e. 'there', connecting
relative (see on ὧν, 3:1:10 and 2:13 above).

5:7 ἐπιοῦσαν: f. acc. s. pres. part. of ἔπειμι (εἶμι 'go'). * ἐβουλιμίασαν: 'fell ill through starvation', inceptive aor.; βουλι-
μία 'ravenous hunger', from βοῦς lit. 'ox', i.e. (in compounds)
'big', and λιμός 'hunger'; they were collapsing through hypoglycae-
mia (low blood sugar) due to an inadequate intake of calories for
the cold conditions; they did not realize that extra food was needed.
Ξενοφῶν: the author always refers to himself in the 3rd pers.; see
on 1:8:15 above; ὀπισθοφυλακῶν: from ὀπισθοφυλακέω: Xenophon was
the general in command of the rearguard, the most important position in a retreat; besides military responsibilities (e.g. ward-
ing off enemy harrassment), he had to maintain the morale of his
troops. * τοὺς πίπτοντας τῶν ἀνθρώπων: 'the men who were collapsing'. * εἴη: opt. of εἰμί 'be', indir. question after historic main verb.

5:8 τις ... τῶν ἐμπείρων: 'someone who had seen it before'. * κἄν =
καὶ ἐάν, + subj.; the blending of words ending and beginning with
a vowel is called crasis. * ἀναστήσονται: fut. mid. of ἀνίστημι.

ἐπὶ τὰ ὑποζύγια, εἴ πού τι ὁρῴη βρωτόν, διεδίδου καὶ
διέπεμπε διδόντας τοὺς δυναμένους παρατρέχειν τοῖς
5:9 βουλιμιῶσιν. ἐπειδὴ δέ τι ἐμφάγοιεν, ἀνίσταντο καὶ
ἐπορεύοντο.

5:12 ἐφείποντο δὲ τῶν πολεμίων συνειλεγμένοι τινὲς καὶ
τὰ μὴ δυνάμενα τῶν ὑποζυγίων ἥρπαζον καὶ ἀλλήλοις
ἐμάχοντο περὶ αὐτῶν. ἐλείποντο δὲ τῶν στρατιωτῶν οἵ
τε διεφθαρμένοι ὑπὸ τῆς χιόνος τοὺς ὀφθαλμοὺς οἵ τε
ὑπὸ τοῦ ψύχους τοὺς δακτύλους τῶν ποδῶν ἀποσεσηπότες.

* περιιὼν ἐπί ... : lit. 'going round to the baggage animals,
if he saw anything edible anywhere, he distributed (it) and sent
in all directions (δι-) those able to run along (the lines) giving (it) to those starving' i.e. 'he went round among the baggage
train, and whatever he saw to eat anywhere he distributed, sending out men with the strength to run up and down the lines giving
it to the sufferers'; περιιὼν, part. of περίειμι (εἶμι 'go');
περιιὼν ... διεδίδου: part. + main verb often translated by two
main verbs joined by 'and'; ὁρῴη, opt., indefinite; διεδίδου, 3rd
pers. sing. imperf. of διαδίδωμι; διδόντας, pres. part. of δίδωμι.

5:9 ἐμφάγοιεν: opt., indefinite temporal clause; ἐμφαγεῖν often = 'to
snatch a bite'. * ἀνίσταντο: imperf. mid. of ἀνίστημι, repeated
action (of several people). * ἐπορεύοντο: imperf., 'carried on
marching'.

5:12 συνειλεγμένοι: 'who had banded together'. * τὰ μὴ δυνάμενα τῶν
ὑποζυγίων: 'any disabled baggage animals'; μή + part., generic
(indefinite).
ἐλείποντο δὲ ... : 'at the same time'; emphatic position of verb,
parallel to ἐφείποντο above.
οἱ ... διεφθαρμένοι ... τοὺς ὀφθαλμούς: 'those who had lost their
eyesight'; διεφθαρμένοι: pass. agreeing with the person, although
in the act. the person affected is dat.; ὀφθαλμοὺς (also δακτύλους), acc. of part affected, limiting sense of part. ('retained'
from act. construction, where it is dir. object).
* ὑπό: sometimes used with things, especially if destructive;
the sun's ultra-violet radiation, strongly reflected by snow,
can damage the retina, sometimes permanently. * οἵ ... τοὺς
δακτύλους τῶν ποδῶν ἀποσεσηπότες: 'those whose toes had rotted
off'; severe frostbite involves σφάκελος 'gangrene' (i.e. rotting)
of the hands, feet, or face.

5:13 ἦν δὲ τοῖς μὲν ὀφθαλμοῖς ἐπικούρημα τῆς χιόνος εἴ τις
μέλαν τι ἔχων πρὸ τῶν ὀφθαλμῶν ἐπορεύετο, τῶν δὲ ποδῶν εἴ τις κινοῖτο καὶ μηδέποτε ἡσυχίαν ἔχοι καὶ εἰς
5:14 τὴν νύκτα ὑπολύοιτο· ὅσοι δὲ ὑποδεδεμένοι ἐκοιμῶντο,
εἰσεδύοντο εἰς τοὺς πόδας οἱ ἱμάντες καὶ τὰ ὑποδήματα
περιεπήγνυντο· καὶ γὰρ ἦσαν, ἐπειδὴ ἐπέλιπε τὰ ἀρχαῖα
ὑποδήματα, καρβάτιναι πεποιημέναι ἐκ τῶν νεοδάρτων
5:15 βοῶν. διὰ τὰς τοιαύτας οὖν ἀνάγκας ὑπελείποντό τινες

5:13 ἦν ... ἐπικούρημα τῆς χιόνος: 'it was a help ... against the snow'
i.e. snow-blindness; ἦν, emphatic position; χιόνος, objective
gen. * τις: 'one', indefinite. * ἔχων ... ἐπορεύετο: 'held
... while marching'; English often puts the main verb earlier;
or 'marched with', a common meaning of ἔχων. * τῶν ... ποδῶν:
'for the feet', possessive gen. after ἐπικούρημα, instead of
dat. (as τοῖς ... ὀφθαλμοῖς). * κινοῖτο ... ἔχοι ... ὑπολύοιτο:
opt., indefinite; (ἐπορεύετο is indicative since the indefinite
idea is in the part. ἔχων - Xenophon might have written ἔχοι ...
πορευόμενος). Movement helped maintain the circulation of the
blood. * ὑπολύοιτο (also ὑποδεδεμένοι and ὑποδήματα): ὑποδέω
'tie up under (the feet)', 'put on sandal', hence ὑπόδημα 'sandal'; so ὑπολύω 'untie under' i.e. 'take off sandal'; mid. for
action done to oneself; a Greek sandal comprised a leather sole
tied to the foot and ankle by two or more leather straps (ἱμάντες).

5:14 ὅσοι: '(in the case of) all those who'; ὅσος (ὅσοι) often means
'all that which', 'all those who'. εἰσεδύοντο: sc. τουτοῖς, antecedent to ὅσοι. * περιεπήγνυντο: 'froze to their feet', imperf.
pass. of περιπήγνυμι; neuter plur. verb, irregular
(see on ἅπαντα ἦσαν ... , 1:5:1 and ἦσαν, 2:5:38 above).
καὶ γὰρ ἦσαν ... πεποιημέναι sc. αὐτοῖς: 'in fact they had ... which
they had made', pluperf. pass. of ποιέω, ἦσαν in emphatic position
(= ἐπεποίηντο). * ἐπέλιπε: 'had worn out'; aor. in subordinate
clauses often translated as pluperf. * καρβάτιναι: 'raw-hide
sandals', made of undressed leather, perhaps covering the whole
foot; βοῶν, 'ox-hide'. Normally the animal's hide (δέρμα, δορά,
βύρσα) was stripped off or flayed (δέρω), and cleaned; the tanner
dressed or tanned (βυρσοδέψω) the raw hide (δέρρις) by soaking
it in tan and kneading it (δέψω); the resultant leather (διφθέρα,
σκῦτος) was used e.g. for clothing and harnesses. Here the hide
was not being tanned, so that it shrank and stiffened as it dried
out; nor were the sandals reinforced by metal studs (ἧλοι) as proper ones might be; but flaying and sandal-making itself must have
been difficult in their present situation.

5:15 διὰ τὰς τοιαύτας ... : 'because of difficulties like these, inevit-
ably ... '.

τῶν στρατιωτῶν· καὶ ἰδόντες μέλαν τι χωρίον διὰ τὸ
ἐκλελοιπέναι αὐτόθεν τὴν χιόνα ἤκαζον τετηκέναι· καὶ
ἐτετήκει διὰ κρήνην τινὰ ἥ πλησίον ἦν ἀτμίζουσα ἐν
νάπῃ. ἐνταῦθ᾽ ἐκτραπόμενοι ἐκάθηντο καὶ οὐκ ἔφασαν
5:16 πορεύεσθαι. ὁ δὲ Ξενοφῶν ἔχων τοὺς ὀπισθοφύλακας
ὡς ἤσθετο, ἐδεῖτο αὐτῶν πάσῃ τέχνῃ καὶ μηχανῇ μὴ ἀπο-
λείπεσθαι, λέγων ὅτι ἕπονται πολλοὶ πολέμιοι συνειλεγμένοι, καὶ τελευτῶν ἐχαλέπαινεν. οἱ δὲ σφάττειν
5:17 ἐκέλευον· οὐδὲ γὰρ ἂν δύνασθαι πορευθῆναι. ἐνταῦθα

μέλαν τι χωρίον ... : 'a patch of ground which was dark owing to
the disappearance of the snow ... '; τό + inf., verbal noun;
χιόνα, acc. subject of both ἐκλελοιπέναι and τετηκέναι. * τετηκέναι: 'that it had melted', indir. statement with ἤκαζον.
ἀτμίζουσα: hot springs are common in volcanic regions; the under-
ground stream had melted the snow on the surface some distance
from the spring.
οὐκ ἔφασαν πορεύεσθαι: 'said they were not going on'; οὐ φήμι +
inf. = 'say that ... not'.

5:16 ὁ δὲ Ξενοφῶν ... ὡς ἤσθετο: 'but when Xenophon noticed (them), he
... '; when the subject of a subordinate clause is the same as
that of the main sentence, English usually puts it inside the
subordinate clause, Greek outside in the main clause. * ἔχων:
'who commanded'. * ἐδεῖτο αὐτῶν ... : 'he begged them with every means at his disposal' (including force, as we learn in Book
5); αὐτῶν, gen. after ἐδεῖτο, imperf. for repeated and inconclus-
ive action. * ἕπονται, emphatic position. * τελευτῶν ἐχαλέπαινεν: lit. 'ending (part.) he grew angry' i.e. 'finally ... ',
imperf. denoting the gradual increase in his anger.
οἱ δέ: 'but they', a use of the article as pronoun (with δέ), indicating a change of grammatical subject. * σφάττειν ἐκέλευον:
'told (him) to cut (their) throats'; σφάττω properly refers to
cutting a sacrificial victim's throat (see on καὶ τὰ ἱερὰ καλά,
1:8:15 above), hence to any slaughter, though here the word seems
to convey their helplessness and vulnerability. * οὐδὲ γὰρ ...:
'the fact was, they would not be able to continue'; indir. statement after verb of saying implied by ἐκέλευον, standing for dir.
ἂν δυναίμεθα, potential opt.; οὐδὲ γάρ, negative of καὶ γάρ, 'for
in fact ... not'.

5:17 ἐνταῦθα: 'in the circumstances'; note the lack of connecting particle (asyndeton).

ἔδοξε κράτιστον εἶναι τοὺς ἑπομένους πολεμίους φοβῆσαι, εἴ τις δύναιτο, μὴ ἐπιπέσοιεν τοῖς κάμνουσι.
καὶ ἦν μὲν σκότος ἤδη, οἱ δὲ προσῆσαν πολλῷ θορύβῳ
5:18 ἀμφὶ ὧν εἶχον διαφερόμενοι. ἔνθα δὴ οἱ μὲν ὀπισθοφύλακες ἅτε ὑγιαίνοντες ἐξαναστάντες ἔδραμον εἰς τοὺς
πολεμίους· οἱ δὲ κάμνοντες ἀνακραγόντες ὅσον ἐδύναντο
μέγιστον τὰς ἀσπίδας πρὸς τὰ δόρατα ἔκρουσαν. οἱ δὲ
πολέμιοι δείσαντες ἧκαν αὐτοὺς καιὰ τῆς χιόνος εἰς
τὴν νάπην, καὶ οὐδεὶς ἔτι οὐδαμοῦ ἐφθέγξατο.

τοὺς ... πολεμίους φοβῆσαι ... μὴ ἐπιπέσοιεν: opt., fear clause in
historic sequence introduced by μή, 'to frighten the enemy... (and
deter them) from attacking'. * εἴ τις δύναιτο: lit. 'if one could'
i.e. 'if at all possible', opt., indefinite in historic sequence.
* τοῖς κάμνουσι: 'those suffering from exhaustion'.
καὶ ἦν ... : 'it was actually dark by then'; ἦν, emphatic position.
* οἱ δὲ: 'and the enemy', see on 5:16 above. * προσῆσαν: imperf. of πρόσειμι (εἶμι 'go').
ἀμφὶ ὧν εἶχον: 'over what they had got' i.e. their booty; relative
pronoun attracted from acc. (object of εἶχον) to case of antecedent (not expressed) gen. after ἀμφί; see on ὧν, 5:6 above.

5:18 ἔνθα δὴ ... : 'that was the cue for the rearguard, who had their
health and strength, to go into action and charge ... '. ἔνθα
δὴ, see on 1:5:8 above; ἅτε ὑγιαίνοντες, causal part.; ἐξαναστάντες, strong aor. part. (intrans.) of ἐξανίστημι.
ἀνακραγόντες ὅσον ἐδύναντο μέγιστον: 'having raised the loudest
shout they could'. * τὰς ἀσπίδας ... : lit. 'beat their shields
against their spears' i.e. 'beat their spears on their shields'.
ἧκαν ... : 3rd pers. plur. aor. indic. of ἵημι; αὐτοὺς = ἑαυτούς.
κατά: 'down through'. * οὐδεὶς ἔτι ... : 'not a sound was heard
from any of them afterwards', i.e. they gave no more trouble; the
pursuers thought that large numbers were attacking them; for the
psychological effect of noise in battle, see on 1:8:11 and for
the beating of spears on shields, on καὶ ταῖς ἀσπίσι, 1:8:18 above.

*Winter campaigns were avoided by Greek armies, and their clothing
did not protect head or legs from the elements; Xenophon does not
say whether caps were worn (κυνίαι, of skin; πῖλοι, πιλίδια, of felt);
the καρβάτιναι (5:14 above) were warmer than sandals, but there was
little time or material for providing anything further; moreover,
despite the unusual severity of the weather, the Greeks would not
have wanted to imitate the 'soft' orientals with their trousers
(ἀναξυρίδες), long sleeves (χειρῖδες, sometimes fur-lined), and
gloves (δακτυλῆθραι) - see on 1:5:8 above, Cyropaedia 8.8.17 and
Herodotus 5.49. Any soldiers left behind would certainly have died.*

5:19   The snow almost halted the army's progress, but the offi-
to   cers forced the men to keep moving until they reached the
6:27   shelter of a group of Armenian villages, the houses of which
         were built underground, with men and animals living together.
         Here the army was able to enjoy food and rest, a state which
         came easily to them after drinking the local barley-wine,
         which the natives sucked from bowls through reeds. The army
         moved out of these villages after seven days, taking the local
         chieftain as a guide and his son as a hostage. The chieftain
         deserted after being punished by Kheirisophos for not leading
         the army to a village, but his son stayed with the army.

         The next obstacle to their progress confronted them as
         they reached a pass before descending to the plains of north-
         ern Armenia. The pass was held against them by the Khalybes,
         Taokhoi and Phasianoi; but the Greeks, on Xenophon's suggestion,
         seized the heights of the pass by night. Next day there were
         two engagements in the mountains and the pass, and the enemy
         were put to flight.

7:1   ἐκ δὲ τούτων ἐπορεύθησαν εἰς Ταόχους σταθμοὺς πέντε
         παρασάγγας τριάκοντα· καὶ τὰ ἐπιτήδεια ἐπέλιπε· χωρία
         γὰρ ᾤκουν ἰσχυρὰ οἱ Τάοχοι, ἐν οἷς καὶ τὰ ἐπιτήδεια
7:2   ἅπαντα εἶχον ἀνακεκομισμένοι. ἐπεὶ δ᾽ ἀφίκοντο πρὸς
         χωρίον ὃ πόλιν μὲν οὐκ εἶχεν οὐδ᾽ οἰκίας (συνεληλυθ-
         ότες δ᾽ ἦσαν αὐτόσε καὶ ἄνδρες καὶ γυναῖκες καὶ κτήνη

7:1 ἐκ δὲ τούτων: 'after this' i.e. the capture of the pass. * εἰς
     Ταόχους: 'into (the territory of the) Taokhoi', a usage of the
     Ionic dialect. * σταθμοὺς πέντε παρασάγγας τριάκοντα: probably
     nearer 60 miles than the usual 90; see on 5:3 and on παρασάγγας,
     1:5:1 above.
     χωρία ... ἰσχυρά: 'strongholds', probably on hill-tops. * καὶ:
     'also', as well as their persons. * ἀνακεκομισμένοι: 'which
     they had taken away with them', perf. part. mid., denoting self-
     advantage.

7:2 ἀφίκοντο: i.e. the Greeks. * συνεληλυθότες ... ἦσαν: pluperf. of
     συνέρχομαι (= συνεληλύθεσαν).

πολλά), Χειρίσοφος μὲν οὖν πρὸς τοῦτο προσέβαλλεν
εὐθὺς ἥκων· ἐπειδὴ δὲ ἡ πρώτη τάξις ἀπέκαμνεν, ἄλλη
προσῄει καὶ αὖθις ἄλλη· οὐ γὰρ ἦν ἀθρόοις περιστῆναι,
7:3 ἀλλ᾽ ἀπότομον ἦν κύκλῳ. ἐπειδὴ δὲ Ξενοφῶν ἦλθε σὺν
τοῖς ὀπισθοφύλαξι καὶ πελτασταῖς καὶ ὁπλίταις, ἐνταῦθα
δὴ λέγει Χειρίσοφος· Εἰς καλὸν ἥκεις· τὸ γὰρ χωρίον
αἱρετέον· τῇ γὰρ στρατιᾷ οὐκ ἔστι τὰ ἐπιτήδεια, εἰ μὴ
7:4 ληψόμεθα ιὸ χωρίον. ἐνταῦθα δὴ κοινῇ ἐβουλεύοντο·
καὶ τοῦ Ξενοφῶντος ἐρωτῶντος τί τὸ κωλῦον εἴη εἰσ-

πολλά: 'in great numbers', emphatic position. * μὲν οὖν: 'anyway',
resuming after the parenthesis; strictly redundant in the middle
of the sentence.
προσέβαλλεν: 'tried to attack', imperf. for uncompleted activity;
εὐθὺς ἥκων: 'immediately he arrived'.
τάξις: 'detachment'. * ἀπέκαμνεν: 'was getting exhausted'.
* προσῄει: imperf. of πρόσειμι (εἶμι 'go').
οὐ ... ἦν: 'it was impossible', ἔστι, used impersonally, = ἔξεστι.
* ἀθρόοις περιστῆναι: 'for a continuous line to surround (it)';
περιστῆναι, strong aor. inf. (intrans.) of περιίστημι. * ἀλλ᾽
ἀπότομον ἦν κύκλῳ: lit. 'as it was sheer in a circle' i.e. 'as
it was ringed by steep cliffs'.

·3 ἐπειδὴ δὲ Ξενοφῶν ... : 'the very moment Xenophon arrived with the
peltasts and the hoplites of the rearguard, Kheirisophos said to
him'; σύν + dat., poetic, but regularly used by Xenophon, = μετά
+ gen. (Introduction 6.4); for peltasts (here including all light-
armed troops), see on πελταστικόν, 1:8:5 and for hoplites, on ὁπλίτας, 1:1:2 and ἐξοπλίζεσθαι, 1:8:3 above.

Εἰς καλόν: 'in the nick of time'. * τὸ ... χωρίον αἱρετέον sc.
ἔστι: 'the place must be captured'; αἱρετέος, pass. adjective
from αἱρέω, expressing obligation (see on πειστέον, 2:6:8, ἰτέον
... , 3:1:7 and on διωκτέον, 3:3:8, though those are used in act.
sense).
τῇ ... στρατιᾷ οὐκ ἔστι ... , εἰ μὴ ληψόμεθα: 'the army doesn't have
... (and won't have) if we don't ... '; στρατιᾷ, possessive dat.;
εἰ + fut. indic. (rather than ἐάν + subjunctive) for a forceful
warning.

7:4 ἐνταῦθα δὴ κοινῇ ἐβουλεύοντο: 'so they immediately held a council
of war'.
τοῦ Ξενοφῶντος ἐρωτῶντος: gen. absolute. * τί τὸ κωλῦον ... :
'what it was that prevented them from entering ... '; κωλῦον, n.
pres. part. of κωλύω, used as a noun with τό; εἴη, opt., in indir. question (historic).

ελθεῖν εἶπεν ὁ Χειρίσοφος· Μία αὕτη πάροδός ἐστιν ἣν
ὁρᾷς· ὅταν δέ τις ταύτῃ πειρᾶται παριέναι, κυλίνδουσι
λίθους ὑπὲρ ταύτης τῆς ὑπερεχούσης πέτρας· ὃς δ᾽ ἂν
καταληφθῇ, οὕτω διατίθεται. ἅμα δ᾽ ἔδειξε συντετριμ-
7:5 μένους ἀνθρώπους καὶ σκέλη καὶ πλευράς. Ἢν δὲ τοὺς
λίθους ἀναλώσωσιν, ἔφη ὁ Ξενοφῶν, ἄλλο τι ἢ οὐδὲν
κωλύει παριέναι; οὐ γὰρ δὴ ἐκ τοῦ ἐναντίου ὁρῶμεν
εἰ μὴ ὀλίγους τούτους ἀνθρώπους, καὶ τούτων δύο ἢ
7:6 τρεῖς ὡπλισμένους. τὸ δὲ χωρίον, ὡς καὶ σὺ ὁρᾷς,
σχεδὸν τρία ἡμίπλεθρά ἐστιν ἃ δεῖ βαλλομένους διελθ-
εῖν· τούτου δὲ ὅσον πλέθρον δασὺ πίτυσι διαλειπούσαις

Μία αὕτη ... : 'the only approach route is the one you see'; Μία,
    emphatic position; αὕτη, subject, not with πάροδος (which is pre-
    dicate without the article). * πειρᾶται: subjunctive, indefin-
    ite. * παριέναι: inf. of πάρειμι (εἶμι 'go'). * ὑπέρ: 'down
    from' (+ gen.).
ὃς δ᾽ ἂν ... : 'whoever gets hit ends up like that'; ὃς ἂν + sub-
    junctive, indefinite (ὅστις is commoner in this sense); καταληφθῇ,
    lit. 'gets caught' (see on λαβεῖν, 1:5:2 above).
ἅμα: 'as he spoke'.
συντετριμμένους ἀνθρώπους ... : 'men with legs and ribs crushed';
    σκέλη and πλευράς, acc. of part affected, limiting sense of part.
    ('retained acc.'; see on οἱ διεφθαρμένοι τοὺς ὀφθαλμούς, 5:12 above).

7:5 Ἢν = ἐάν (+ subj.). * ἄλλο τι ἢ οὐδὲν: lit. '(is it) anything
    other than nothing' i.e. 'nothing, surely'; ἄλλο τι ἢ introduces
    a question inviting the listener to agree.
    οὐ ... εἰ μή: 'nothing but'. * δή: almost 'look!' * ἐκ τοῦ ἐν-
    αντίου: 'opposing (us)'. * ὀλίγους τούτους ἀνθρώπους: those
    (men) (who are) few men'; ὀλίγους, emphatic position; τούτους,
    not qualifying ἀνθρώπους (which would need the article; see on
    Μία αὕτη πάροδος, 7:4 above). * δύο ἢ τρεῖς: '(only) two or
    three'.

7:6 χωρίον: 'space' i.e. 'distance'. * ὡς καὶ σὺ ὁρᾷς: 'as you can
    see for yourself'; καί, 'as well as I'. * τρία ἡμίπλεθρα: 50
    yards. * βαλλομένους sc. ἡμᾶς: 'under attack', 'within range
    of their missiles'.
    πλέθρον: 35 yards. * δασύ sc. ἐστι: '(is) covered'. * διαλειπ-
    ούσαις: 'with gaps between'; see on ἅρματα διαλείποντα, 1:8:10
    above.

μεγάλαις, ἀνθ' ὧν ἐστηκότες ἄνδρες τί ἂν πάσχοιεν ἢ
ὑπὸ τῶν φερομένων λίθων ἢ ὑπὸ τῶν κυλινδομένων; τὸ
λοιπὸν οὖν ἤδη γίγνεται ὡς ἡμίπλεθρον, ὃ δεῖ ὅταν
7:7 λωφήσωσιν οἱ λίθοι παραδραμεῖν. Ἀλλὰ εὐθύς, ἔφη ὁ
Χειρίσοφος, ἐπειδὰν ἀρξώμεθα εἰς τὸ ὁασὺ προσιέναι,
φέρονται οἱ λίθοι πολλοί. Αὐτὸ ἄν, ἔφη, τὸ δέον εἴη.
θᾶττον γὰρ ἀναλώσουσι τοὺς λίθους. ἀλλὰ πορευώμεθα
ἔνθεν ἡμῖν μικρόν τι παραδραμεῖν ἔσται, ἢν δυνώμεθα
καὶ ἀπελθεῖν ῥᾴδιον, ἢν βουλώμεθα.
7:8 ἐντεῦθεν ἐπορεύοντο Χειρίσοφος καὶ Ξενοφῶν καὶ
Καλλίμαχος Παρράσιος λοχαγός· τούτου γὰρ ἡ ἡγεμονία
ἦν τῶν ὀπισθοφυλάκων λοχαγῶν ἐκείνη τῇ ἡμέρᾳ· οἱ δὲ

* ἀνθ' ὧν ἐστηκότες ... : 'and if men stood behind them, what
harm would they come to?'; ἀνθ' ὧν, lit. 'opposite which' (the
use of ἀντί to indicate position is otherwise confined to early
poetry); ἐστηκότες, perf. part. (intrans.) of ἵστημι, equivalent
to remote fut. condition (εἰ + opt.); πάσχοιεν, opt., apodosis
of condition. * ὑπό: see on 5:12 above. * κυλινδομένων: κυλίνδω is a poetic form of κυλινδέω (Introduction 6.5).
ἤδη: Xenophon imagines the crossing actually being made. * γίγνεται ὡς ἡμίπλεθρον: 'comes (or is reduced) to about fifteen
yards'. * ὅταν λωφήσωσιν οἱ λίθοι: 'when the hail of stones
abates'; λωφήσωσιν, subj., indefinite temporal.

7:7 εὐθύς ... ἐπειδὰν ... : 'at the very moment we ... '. * φέρονται
... πολλοί: 'fly thick and fast'.
Αὐτὸ ἄν ... : '"That'd be exactly what we need," said Xenophon';
Αὐτὸ ... τὸ δέον (neuter pres. part. of δεῖ, see τὸ κωλῦον, 7:4
above), lit. 'the necessary thing itself'; εἴη, opt., potential
(with ἄν).
πορευώμεθα: 'let us advance', jussive subjunctive. * ἔνθεν: '(to
a point) from which', sc. ἐκεῖσε. * ἡμῖν μικρόν ... : 'we'll
have a short distance to run across'. * ἢν = ἐάν.
* ἀπελθεῖν: 'to come back'. * ῥᾴδιον: sc. ἔσται.

7:8 ἐντεῦθεν: asyndeton, see on ἐνταῦθα, 5:17 above. * ἐπορεύοντο:
'began to advance', imperf. * λοχαγός: in command of a λόχος
'company' of up to 100 men.
τούτου γάρ ... : lit. 'his was the command of the captains of the
rearguard ... ' i.e. he was the officer commanding the captains
of the rearguard ... '; they took turns at this responsible task
(see on ὀπισθοφυλάκων, 5:7 above).

ἄλλοι λοχαγοὶ ἔμενον ἐν τῷ ἀσφαλεῖ. μετὰ τοῦτο οὖν
ἀπῆλθον ὑπὸ τὰ δένδρα ἄνθρωποι εἰς τοὺς ἑβδομήκοντα,
οὐχ ἀθρόοι ἀλλὰ καθ᾽ ἕνα, ἕκαστος φυλαττόμενος ὡς

7:9 ἐδύνατο. Ἀγασίας δὲ ὁ Στυμφάλιος καὶ Ἀριστώνυμος
Μεθυδριεύς, καὶ οὗτοι τῶν ὀπισθοφυλάκων λοχαγοὶ ὄντες, καὶ ἄλλοι δέ, ἐφέστασαν ἔξω τῶν δένδρων· οὐ
γὰρ ἦν ἀσφαλῶς ἐν τοῖς δένδροις ἑστάναι πλέον ἢ τὸν

7:10 ἕνα λόχον. ἔνθα δὴ Καλλίμαχος μηχανᾶταί τι· προέτρεχεν ἀπὸ τοῦ δένδρου ὑφ᾽ ᾧ ἦν αὐτὸς δύο ἢ τρία
βήματα· ἐπεὶ δὲ οἱ λίθοι φέροιντο, ἀνεχάζετο εὐπετῶς·
ἐφ᾽ ἑκάστης δὲ προδρομῆς πλέον ἢ δέκα ἅμαξαι πετρῶν

7:11 ἀνηλίσκοντο. ὁ δὲ Ἀγασίας ὡς ὁρᾷ τὸν Καλλίμαχον ἃ
ἐποίει, καὶ τὸ στράτευμα πᾶν θεώμενον, δείσας μὴ οὐ

τῷ ἀσφαλεῖ: 'the safe (area)', 'safety'; τό + adj. = abstract noun
(see on τὸ χαλεπόν, 5:4 above).
ἀπῆλθον ὑπὸ + acc.: 'reached the shelter of'. * εἰς τούς: 'up to',
'about'; the article is regularly used with round numbers.
* φυλαττόμενος ... : 'keeping (as much) under cover as possible'.

7:9 καὶ οὗτοι ... ὄντες: 'who were also ... '. * καὶ ἄλλοι δέ: 'and
also some others'. * ἐφέστασαν: 'had taken up positions nearby',
pluperf. (intrans.) of ἐφίστημι. * ἔξω: 'outside (the cover of)'.
οὐ ... ἦν: 'it was not possible', see on 7:2 above; ἑστάναι: 'to
stand', perf. inf. (intrans.) of ἵστημι. τὸν ἕνα λόχον: acc.
(subject of ἑστάναι) rather than the more usual dat. after ἦν
(= ἔξην).

7:10 ἔνθα δή ... : 'then Kallimakhos had a clever idea'; ἔνθα δή, almost
'suddenly' (see 1:5:8 above); a dramatic sentence. * προέτρεχεν:
'he would run forward', imperf. for repeated action; the *asyndeton*
speeds the narrative. * αὐτός: 'personally'; translate 'the particular tree he was under'.
φέροιντο: opt., indefinite temporal clause. * ἀνεχάζετο: poetic
word (Introduction 6.5).
ἐφ᾽: 'at'. The use of cover was a novelty to troops trained in
hoplite tactics (see on οὐκέτι τρία, 1:8:17 above and note at
end of Book 3).

7:11 ὁ δὲ Ἀγασίας ... : 'when Agasias saw what Kallimakhos had been doing,
he ... ', see on ὁ δὲ Ξενοφῶν, 5:16 above; τὸν Καλλίμαχον: the
subject of the indir. question (ἃ ἐποίει) anticipated in the main
sentence ('anticipatory acc.', object of ὁρᾷ) - a common idiom;
ἅ, relative pronoun used as indir. interrogative (= ἅτινα).
* πᾶν θεώμενον: 'all watching', like spectators in a theatre
(θέατρον).

πρῶτος παραδράμοι εἰς τὸ χωρίον, οὔτε τὸν Ἀριστώνυμον
πλησίον ὄντα παρακαλέσας οὔτε Εὐρύλοχον τὸν Λουσιέα,
ἑταίρους ὄντας, οὐδὲ ἄλλον οὐδένα χωρεῖ αὐτός, καὶ
7:12 παρέρχεται πάντας. ὁ δὲ Καλλίμαχος ὡς ὁρᾷ αὐτὸν παρ-
ιόντα, ἐπιλαμβάνεται αὐτοῦ τῆς ἴτυος· ἐν δὲ τούτῳ
παραθεῖ αὐτοὺς Ἀριστώνυμος Μεθυδριεύς, καὶ μετὰ τοῦτον Εὐρύλοχος Λουσιεύς· πάντες γὰρ οὗτοι ἀντεποιοῦντο
ἀρετῆς καὶ διηγωνίζοντο πρὸς ἀλλήλους· καὶ οὕτως ἐρίζοντες αἱροῦσι τὸ χωρίον. ὡς γὰρ ἅπαξ εἰσέδραμον,
7:13 οὐδεὶς ἔτι πέτρος ἄνωθεν ἠνέχθη. ἐνταῦθα δὴ δεινὸν
ἦν θέαμα. αἱ γὰρ γυναῖκες ῥίπτουσαι τὰ παιδία εἶτα
καὶ ἑαυτὰς ἐπικατερρίπτουν, καὶ οἱ ἄνδρες ὡσαύτως.
ἔνθα δὴ καὶ Αἰνέας ὁ Στυμφάλιος λοχαγὸς ἰδών τινα
θέοντα/ὡς ῥίψοντα ἑαυτὸν /στολὴν ἔχοντα καλὴν/ἐπιλαμ-
7:14 βάνεται/ὡς κωλύσων./ ὁ δὲ αὐτὸν ἐπισπᾶται, καὶ ἀμφό-

---

* δείσας μὴ οὔ ... : 'fearing that he (Agasias) would not be
the first to ... '; δείσας, inceptive aorist, for the onset of
an emotion (see on ἐβουλιμίασαν, 5:7 above).] παραδράμοι: opt.,
fear clause after historic verb. * τὸ χωρίον: 'the (enemy) position'. * ὄντα ... ὄντας: 'although he was ... although they
were', concessive participles. * Εὐρύλοχον: when Xenophon's
armour-bearer (ὑπασπιστής) had deserted, taking his shield with
him, in the territory of the Kardoukhoi, Eurylokhos had saved
Xenophon from enemy missiles by protecting him with his own
shield. * οὐδὲ ἄλλον οὐδένα: 'or anyone else at all'; after
οὔτε ... οὔτε, οὐδέ is emphatic; see on οὐδὲ ἄλλο οὐδὲν δένδρον,
1:5:5 above. * αὐτός: 'by himself'.

7:12 αὐτοῦ τῆς ἴτυος: 'the rim of his shield'; αὐτοῦ, possessive gen.;
ἴτυος, gen. after ἐπιλαμβάνεται. * τούτῳ: sc. τῷ χρόνῳ.
ἀντεποιοῦντο ἀρετῆς ... : 'were rivals in valour and (always) competing with each other', imperf. for continued activity; ἀρετή,
'excellence' of any kind, especially bravery in war; for comrade-
ship see on ὁμοτράπεζοι, 1:8:25 above. * οὕτως ἐρίζοντες: 'in
this spirit of rivalry'.
ὡς ... ἅπαξ εἰσέδραμον: 'once they had charged in'; see on ἐπέλιπε,
5:14 above. * οὐδεὶς ἔτι ... : 'no more stones flew (down) ...'.

7:13 δεινόν: separated from θέαμα, emphatic.
ὡς ῥίψοντα ... ὡς κωλύσων: ὡς + fut. part., purpose.

7:14 ὁ δέ: see on οἱ δέ, 5:16 and 5:17 above.

τεροι ᾤχοντο κατὰ τῶν πετρῶν φερόμενοι καὶ ἀπέθανον.
ἐντεῦθεν ἄνθρωποι μὲν πάνυ ὀλίγοι ἐλήφθησαν, βόες δὲ
καὶ ὄνοι πολλοὶ καὶ πρόβατα.

7:15   *7 days' marching after this through the country of the*
to   *Khalybes brought some of the fiercest opposition that they*
7:18   *encountered. The Khalybes fought with knives at close quarters,*
              and yielded no provisions from their fortified villages.

7:19   ἐντεῦθεν διῆλθον σταθμοὺς τέτταρας παρασάγγας εἴκοσι πρὸς πόλιν μεγάλην καὶ εὐδαίμονα καὶ οἰκουμένην
ἣ ἐκαλεῖτο Γυμνιάς. ἐκ ταύτης τῆς χώρας ὁ ἄρχων τοῖς
῞Ελλησιν ἡγεμόνα πέμπει, ὅπως διὰ τῆς ἑαυτῶν πολεμίας
7:20 χώρας ἄγοι αὐτούς. ἐλθὼν δ᾽ ἐκεῖνος λέγει ὅτι ἄξει
αὐτοὺς πέντε ἡμερῶν εἰς χωρίον ὅθεν ὄψονται θάλατταν·

* ᾤχοντο ... φερόμενοι: 'went tumbling'.
ἐντεῦθεν: *asyndeton.* * βόες ... ὄνοι: useful to replace the baggage animals lost in the territory of the Kardoukhoi and during
the march through the snow (5:4 and 5:12 above). * πολλοί: 'in
great numbers'. For siege warfare, see *Oxford Classical Diction-*
ary, 'Siegecraft, Greek'.

7:19 ἐντεῦθεν: from the villages, 60 miles from the Harpasos river.
     * σταθμοὺς τέτταρας παρασάγγας εἴκοσι: 80 - 85 miles; see on
  σταθμοὺς τρεῖς ... , 5:3 and on παρασάγγας, 1:5:1 above.
     * οἰκουμένην: some Asiatic cities were deserted; they had al-
ready passed one (Korsote) - see on πόλις ἐρήμη, 1:5:4 above.
ἑαυτῶν πολεμίας: 'at war with his people'. * ἄγοι: opt., purpose
clause (with ὅπως) after πέμπει (historic present).

7:20 ἡμερῶν: gen. of time within which. * θάλατταν: the coast meant
     Greek cities and (they hoped) an easy voyage home (see note after
     1:1:11 above).

εἰ δὲ μή, τεθνάναι ἐπηγγείλατο. καὶ ἡγούμενος ἐπειδὴ
ἐνέβαλεν εἰς τὴν πολεμίαν, παρεκελεύετο αἴθειν καὶ
φθείρειν τὴν χώραν. ᾧ καὶ δῆλον ἐγένετο ὅτι τούτου
7:21 ἕνεκα ἔλθοι, οὐ τῆς τῶν Ἑλλήνων εὐνοίας. καὶ ἀφικνοῦνται ἐπὶ τὸ ὄρος τῇ πέμπτῃ ἡμέρᾳ· ὄνομα δὲ τῷ ὄρει
ἦν Θήχης. ἐπεὶ δὲ οἱ πρῶτοι ἐγένοντο ἐπὶ τοῦ ὄρους
7:22 καὶ κατεῖδον τὴν θάλατταν, κραυγὴ πολλὴ ἐγένετο. ἀκούσας δὲ ὁ Ξενοφῶν καὶ οἱ ὀπισθοφύλακες ᾠήθησαν καὶ
ἔμπροσθεν ἄλλους ἐπιτίθεσθαι πολεμίους· εἴποντο γὰρ
καὶ ὄπισθεν οἱ ἐκ τῆς καιομένης χώρας, καὶ αὐτῶν οἱ
ὀπισθοφύλακες ἀπέκτεινάν τέ τινας καὶ ἐζώγρησαν ἐν-
έδραν ποιησάμενοι, καὶ γέρρα ἔλαβον ⟨δ⟩ασειῶν βοῶν ὠμο-
7:23 βόεια/ἀμφὶ τὰ εἴκοσιν. ἐπειδὴ δὲ ἡ βοὴ πλείων τε

εἰ δὲ μή: 'but if (he did) not'. * τεθνάναι: 'to be put to death',
lit. 'to be dead', perf. for the state, emphasizing the promise.
ἡγούμενος: 'he led the way and ... '. * τὴν πολεμίαν sc. χώραν:
'enemy (country)'.
αἴθειν καὶ φθείρειν: lit. 'to burn and destroy' i.e. 'to ravage with
fire and sword'; αἴθω, poetic (Introduction 6.5).
ᾧ καὶ δῆλον ἐγένετο: 'so that it became quite clear'; ᾧ, lit. 'by
which', connecting relative - not a common idiom; see on οὗ, 5:6
and on ὧν, 3:1:10 and 3:2:13 above. * τούτου ἕνεκα: 'that was
why'. * ἔλθοι: opt., indir. statement after historic verb.
* τῆς τῶν Ἑλλήνων εὐνοίας: 'out of good will towards the Greeks';
Ἑλλήνων, objective gen.

7:21 τὸ ὄρος: presumably mentioned by the guide, i.e. χωρίον ὅθεν ὄψονται θάλατταν, 7:20 above.
οἱ πρῶτοι: 'the vanguard'.

7:22 καὶ ἔμπροσθεν: 'ahead also', besides those attacking in the rear.
* ἄλλους ... πολεμίους: 'yet another enemy force'; adjective
separated from noun for emphasis.
οἱ ἐκ τῆς καιομένης χώρας: 'the inhabitants of the district they
were burning', complying with the guide's request. * ἀπέκτεινάν
τέ ... : translate aor. tenses as pluperf. (see on ἐπέλιπε, 5:14
above); ἐζώγρησαν, 'taken (others) prisoner'; γέρρα, see on γερροφόροι, 1:8:9 above. * δασειῶν βοῶν ὠμοβόεια: 'of undressed
ox-hide with the hair still on', see on καρβάτιναι, 5:14 above
(ὠμός 'raw').

ἐγίγνετο καὶ ἐγγύτερον καὶ οἱ ἀεὶ ἐπιόντες ἔθεον
δρόμῳ ἐπὶ τοὺς ἀεὶ βοῶντας καὶ πολλῷ μείζων ἐγίγνετο
ἡ βοὴ ὅσῳ δὴ πλείους ἐγίγνοντο, ἐδόκει δὴ μεῖζόν τι
εἶναι τῷ Ξενοφῶντι, καὶ ἀναβὰς ἐφ' ἵππον καὶ Λύκιον
7:24 καὶ τοὺς ἱππέας ἀναλαβὼν παρεβοήθει· καὶ τάχα δὴ
ἀκούουσι βοώντων τῶν στρατιωτῶν θάλαττα θάλαττα καὶ
παρεγγυώντων. ἔνθα δὴ ἔθεον ἅπαντες καὶ οἱ ὀπισθο-
7:25 φύλακες, καὶ τὰ ὑποζύγια ἡλαύνετο καὶ οἱ ἵπποι. ἐπεὶ
δὲ ἀφίκοντο πάντες ἐπὶ τὸ ἄκρον, ἐνταῦθα δὴ περιέβαλ-
λον ἀλλήλους καὶ στρατηγοὺς καὶ λοχαγοὺς δακρύοντες.
καὶ ἐξαπίνης ὅτου δὴ παρεγγυήσαντος οἱ στρατιῶται
7:26 φέρουσι λίθους καὶ ποιοῦσι κολωνὸν μέγαν. ἐνταῦθα
ἀνετίθεσαν δερμάτων πλῆθος ὠμοβοείων καὶ βακτηρίας

7:23 οἱ ἀεὶ ... : 'as successive groups came up they ran towards those
      taking up the shout'; ἀεὶ can mean 'at any one time'. * πολλῷ
      μείζων ... : 'the shout naturally grew much louder as the number
      of men increased'; πολλῷ, dat. of measure of difference (with comp.
      μείζων), clarified by ὅσῳ ... πλείους (= πλείονες) ἐγίγνοντο, lit.
      'by as much as they were becoming more'. * μεῖζόν τι: 'something
      pretty serious', a regular meaning of the comparative.
      Λύκιον: the Athenian cavalry commander; for the cavalry, see 3:3:
      19 - 20 above. * παρεβοήθει: imperf., uncompleted action.

7:24 τάχα δὴ: 'suddenly' (see on 1:8:8 above). * στρατιωτῶν: gen. of
      source of sound, after ἀκούουσι.
      θάλαττα θάλαττα: this scene has earned the soldiers' cry a place
      in the Oxford Dictionary of Quotations. * παρεγγυώντων: like
      an order or watchword issued by the commander (see on σύνθημα ...,
      1:8:16 above).
      ἔνθα δὴ ... : 'then the entire rearguard also began to run'.
      * ὑποζύγια: see on 5:4 and 3:3:6 above.

7:25 ἐνταῦθα δὴ: 'immediately', marking the climax. * δακρύοντες:'with
      tears in their eyes', emphatic position.
      ὅτου δὴ παρεγγυήσαντος: lit. 'someone or other having issued the
      order' i.e. 'at someone's suggestion', gen. absolute; ὅτου δὴ,
      from ὅστις δὴ 'someone or other'. * κολωνόν: as a kind of altar
      or trophy (see on τρόπαιον, 3:2:13 above).

7:26 ἀνετίθεσαν: imperf. of ἀνατίθημι. * δερμάτων ... ὠμοβοείων: 'un-
      dressed ox-hides' (see on δασειῶν βοῶν ... , 7:22 and on καρβάτ-
      ιναι, 5:14 above). * βακτηρίας: used when in the mountains
                                                              (cont.)

καὶ τὰ αἰχμάλωτα γέρρα, καὶ ὁ ἡγεμὼν αὐτός τε κατέ-
7:27 τεμνε τὰ γέρρα καὶ τοῖς ἄλλοις διεκελεύετο. μετὰ
ταῦτα τὸν ἡγεμόνα οἱ Ἕλληνες ἀποπέμπουσι δῶρα δόντες ἀπὸ κοινοῦ ἵππον καὶ φιάλην ἀργυρᾶν καὶ σκευὴν
Περσικὴν καὶ δαρεικοὺς δέκα· ᾔτει δὲ μάλιστα τοὺς
δακτυλίους, καὶ ἔλαβε πολλοὺς παρὰ τῶν στρατιωτῶν.
κώμην δὲ δείξας αὐτοῖς οὗ σκηνήσουσι καὶ τὴν ὁδὸν
ἣν πορεύσονται εἰς Μάκρωνας, ἐπεὶ ἑσπέρα ἐγένετο,
ᾤχετο τῆς νυκτὸς ἀπιών.

(also a Spartan symbol of authority and means of enforcing discipline), but no longer needed; they offered these items as an im-
promptu thanksgiving to the gods they believed had brought them
to safety (a full ceremony came later, 8:25 below); they were
not home, but within sight of the sea; the worst seemed to be over.
* κατέτεμνε ... διεκελεύετο sc. τὸ αὐτὸ ποιεῖν: (imperf. for repeated action) to prevent their subsequent re-use by his enemies;
while the Greeks rejoiced, the guide was thinking of more practical matters.

7:27 δόντες: aor. part. of δίδωμι. * κοινοῦ: 'the common store' of
booty which would eventually be shared out (also referred to as
δημόσιον 'public property', to be distinguished from soldiers'
individual baggage and rations; see 5:5 and 5:8 above).
φιάλην ἀργυρᾶν: a bowl used for drinking or pouring libations
(drink offerings); ἀργυρᾶν, contracted form of ἀργυρέαν.
σκευὴν Περσικὴν: see on τοὺς πορφυροῦς κάνδυς, 1:5:8 above.
* δαρεικούς: see on 1:1:9 above; also illustration p. 172.
τοὺς δακτυλίους: 'their rings'; a silver or gold ring was the only
jewellery normally worn by a Greek man, as an ornament or (often)
as a signet-ring.
σκηνήσουσι ... πορεύσονται: fut., representing the tense used by
the guide (virtual indir. speech). * εἰς: see on εἰς Ταόχους,
7:1 above. * ᾤχετο τῆς νυκτὸς ἀπιών: 'he disappeared during the
night'; νυκτός, gen. of time within which.

8:1   *After receiving assurances that the Ten Thousand only*
to   *wished to pass through their territory in order to reach the*
8:24   *sea, the Makrones escorted them for 3 days and saw them over*
           their northern frontier into Kolkhis. In that country they
           had to fight an uphill pitched battle, which they won by an
           outflanking movement. The Kolkhians, in order to counter this,
           drew men away from their centre, and the Greeks drove through,
           dividing the enemy in two and causing them to retreat in dis-
           array. The local inhabitants kept bees, but the honey that
           they yielded caused violent illness to those Greeks who ate
           it; and it was 4 days before they could begin the final stage
           of their journey to the sea, reaching Trapezous (Trebizond) in
           two days.

           Greatly relieved after surviving their encounters with
           the rigours of the weather and the hostility of successive
           tribesmen, they rested for 30 days in the first Greek city
           they had seen for many months, on the southern shore of the
           Euxine (Black Sea).

8:25   μετὰ δὲ τοῦτο τὴν θυσίαν ἣν ηὔξαντο παρεσκευάζοντο·
        ἦλθον δ' αὐτοῖς ἱκανοὶ βόες ἀποθῦσαι τῷ Διὶ τῷ σωτῆρι
        καὶ τῷ Ἡρακλεῖ ἡγεμόσυνα καὶ τοῖς ἄλλοις δὲ θεοῖς
        ἃ ηὔξαντο. ἐποίησαν δὲ καὶ ἀγῶνα γυμνικὸν ἐν τῷ

8:25 θυσίαν: for this typical piety, see on 1:8:15 and 3:2:12 (sacrifice)
      and for religion, see on 5:4; 1:6:7 and 8:16 - 17; 2:6:25 - 26; 3:
      1:5 - 6, 1:11 - 12, 1:42, 2:10 and 3:14 above. * ηὔξαντο: 'they
      had vowed', when they began the retreat from Kounaxa; the offer-
      ing was due now that they had reached a friendly country.
      ἦλθον: 'had come', as ξένια 'gifts of hospitality' (see on ξένος, 1:
      1:10 above) from the Greeks of Trapezous and the less hostile
      Kolkhoi. * αὐτοῖς ἱκανοὶ ... ἀποθῦσαι ... ἡγεμόσυνα: 'enough
      ... for them to sacrifice (the) thank-offerings for safe-conduct';
      ἡγεμών 'Guide' was a title of Herakles; similarly thank-offerings
      for safety were called σωτήρια. * καὶ ... δὲ: 'and also', see
      on καὶ στρατηγὸν δὲ, 1:1:2 above; individuals fulfilled their own vows.
      ἐποίησαν δὲ ... : 'they also held games (or sports)'; ἀγών 'contest',
      i.e. a competitive festival (e.g. athletic, dramatic, musical),
      here γυμνικός 'sporting', i.e. including any sports for which com-
      petitors were naked (γυμνός).

ὄρει ἔνθαπερ ἐσκήνουν. εἴλοντο δὲ Δρακόντιον Σπαρτιάτην, ὃς ἔφυγε παῖς ἔτι ὢν οἴκοθεν, παῖδα ἄκων
κατακανὼν ξυήλῃ πατάξας, δρόμου τ' ἐπιμεληθῆναι καὶ
8:26 τοῦ ἀγῶνος προστατῆσαι. ἐπειδὴ δὲ ἡ θυσία ἐγένετο,
τὰ δέρματα παρέδοσαν τῷ Δρακοντίῳ, καὶ ἡγεῖσθαι ἐκέλευον ὅπου τὸν δρόμον πεποιηκὼς εἴη. ὁ δὲ δείξας

Σπαρτιάτην: the people of Laconia (ἡ Λακωνική sc. γῆ) comprised (a)
Σπαρτιᾶται or Ὁμοῖοι, 'Spartiates' or 'Equals', a ruling class
born of citizen parents and living in Sparta itself; (b) ὑπομεί-
ονες, lower-class citizens; (c) περίοικοι, inhabiting areas around
(περι-) Sparta, free but without political rights; (d) Εἵλωτες
'Helots', serfs with no rights (see on ὡς ἐδύνατο, 2:6:2 above);
(e) νεοδαμώδεις, emancipated Helots. * ἔφυγε ... οἴκοθεν: 'had
fled (or been exiled from) his home country'. * ἄκων: 'accidentally'; ἕκων 'willing' and ἄκων 'unwilling' are often used adverbially. * κατακανῶν: causal part.; a word not found in 'pure'
Attic prose. * ξυήλῃ: the Spartan curved dagger; πατάξας: 'by
stabbing (him)'. Spartan foreign policy was unadventurous (see
on ὡς ἐδύνατο, 2:6:2 above) so a Spartiate would only go abroad
for a special reason; e.g. Klearkhos (special permission, then
exiled, see on 2:6:2 - 4), and Kheirisophos (special permission:
see on 2:5:37 and on Λακεδαιμονίοις, 3:1:5 above). A man who had
killed another often went into exile to avoid the vengeance of
his victim's family; the shedder or suspected shedder of blood
was held to be ritually polluted, and this pollution or blood-
guilt (μίασμα) touched the whole community, whose laws accordingly demanded recompense for the victim's family, and a penalty
(often exile) as well. Spartan law (or the victim's family) may
not have distinguished between wilful murder and involuntary homi-
cide (as Athenian law did), even in the case of one so young as
Drakontios. * δρόμου: 'a foot-race' or '(the preparation of) a
running-track', which would also be used for the other events.
* ἐπιμεληθῆναι ... προστατῆσαι: inf. of purpose after εἴλοντο;
as προστάτης, he would e.g. announce the winners, present prizes (ἆθλα).

8:26 τὰ δέρματα: of the sacrificial victims; normally a perquisite of
the priest who made the sacrifice (and saleable as material for
e.g. clothing and armour); it is unclear whether Drakontios was
priest, or received the hides simply as a gift, or to be used as
prizes. * ἡγεῖσθαι ἐκέλευον ... : 'directed (him) to lead (them)
(to) where he had set out the course'; πεποιηκὼς εἴη (= πεποιήκοι),
perf. opt. of ποιέω, subordinate clause in indir. command after
historic verb; ideally a course was flat, covered in sand (ψάμ-
μος), about 600 feet long, with a set of wooden starting traps
(ὕσπληξ) or a rope between posts (βαλβίδες), and a stone pillar
(cont.)

οὕπερ ἐστηκότες ἐτύγχανον, Οὗτος ὁ λόφος, ἔφη, κάλλιστος τρέχειν ὅπου ἄν τις βούληται. Πῶς οὖν, ἔφασαν,
8:27 δυνήσονται παλαίειν ἐν σκληρῷ καὶ δασεῖ οὕτως; ὁ δ'
εἶπε· Μᾶλλόν τι ἀνιάσεται ὁ καταπεσών. ἠγωνίζοντο
δὲ παῖδες μὲν στάδιον τῶν αἰχμαλώτων οἱ πλεῖστοι, δόλιχον δὲ Κρῆτες πλείους ἤ ἑξήκοντα ἔθεον, πάλην δὲ καὶ
πυγμὴν καὶ παγκράτιον ἕτεροι· καὶ καλὴ θέα ἐγένετο·
πολλοὶ γὰρ κατέβησαν καὶ ἄτε θεωμένων τῶν ἑταιρῶν

(στήλη) at the far end as a goal or turning-point (καμπή); but
some improvisation would have been necessary here.
ἐστηκότες ἐτύγχανον: 'they happened to be standing' or 'they were
actually standing'; ἐστηκότες, perf. part. (intrans.) of ἵστημι.
κάλλιστος: sc. ἐστι. * τρέχειν: 'for running', explanatory (ep-
exegetic) inf. * ὅπου ἄν τις βούληται: subj. + ἄν, indefinite
(τις = 'one').
ἐν σκληρῷ ... : 'on hard, overgrown ground like this'; οὕτως, emphatic position.
Μᾶλλόν τι: 'a bit more'. * ὁ καταπεσών: 'the one who gets thrown';
πίπτω (and its compounds) used as pass. of βάλλω.

8:27 ἠγωνίζοντο: 'competing in ... were', emphatic position. * στάδιον;
for length of the 'stadium' see on ἠγεῖσθαι ἐκέλευον, 8:26 above.
* τῶν αἰχμαλώτων οἱ πλεῖστοι: 'the majority from among the prisoners', gen. of origin; there were by now few prisoners.
* δόλιχον: between 3 and 12 circuits (δίαυλοι - double lengths)
of the stadium. * πλείους = πλείονες. * Κρῆτες: for the Cretan archers, see on 3:3:7 above. * ἔθεον: strictly redundant,
as ἠγωνίζοντο is outside the μέν 'clause' and would serve as the
verb in the δέ 'clause' also.
πάλην ... : usually 3 throws were needed to win; πυγμὴν: the fists
were usually protected by leather straps (ἱμάντες), not gloves;
παγκράτιον: a combination of boxing and wrestling, in which the
twisting of limbs and strangling were permitted.
θέα: 'spectacle', 'sight', 'show'(cf. θεάομαι, θέατρον). Other events not included were the long jump (ἄλμα, performed with ἀλτ-
ῆρες lit. 'jumpers' i.e. 'weights'), throwing the discus (δίσκος)
and the javelin (ἀκοντισμός), which, together with running and
wrestling, made up the pentathlon (πεντᾶθλον). Wrestling and
boxing were thought to be a useful part of military training,
as was the race in armour (ὁπλιτοδρόμος).
πολλοὶ ... κατέβησαν: lit. 'many descended (into the stadium)'
i.e. 'there were many entries', a regular meaning of καταβαίνω,
though not strictly appropriate here, as the stadium was not in
a hollow (as was usual) but on a hill-top. * θεωμένων τῶν ἑταιρῶν: gen. absolute; causal part. with ἄτε; ἑταιρῶν, from
ἑταίρα; they were from among the prisoners.

8:28 πολλὴ φιλονικία ἐγίγνετο. ἔθεον δὲ καὶ ἵπποι καὶ
ἔδει αὐτοὺς κατὰ τοῦ πρανοῦς ἐλάσαντας ἐν τῇ θαλάττῃ
ἀναστρέψαντας πάλιν ἄνω πρὸς τὸν βωμὸν ἄγειν. καὶ
κάτω μὲν οἱ πολλοὶ ἐκαλινδοῦντο· ἄνω δὲ πρὸς τὸ ἰσχυρῶς ὄρθιον μόλις βάδην ἐπορεύοντο οἱ ἵπποι· ἔνθα
πολλὴ κραυγὴ καὶ γέλως καὶ παρακέλευσις ἐγίγνετο.

* πολλὴ φιλονικία ἐγίγνετο: 'there was keen competition'.

8:28 ἔθεον δὲ καὶ ἵπποι ... : 'there was also a horse race (or horse-
racing)'; an ἀγὼν ἱππικός, as opposed to γυμνικός (see on ἐποίησαν δὲ ... , 8:25 above); αὐτούς: the riders. * τοῦ πρανοῦς:
lit. 'the steep (ground)' i.e. 'the hillside', adj. with article
used as noun (also τὸ ὄρθιον below). * ἐλάσαντας ... ἀναστρέψαντας ... ἄγειν sc. τοὺς ἵππους: 'to ride ... , turn ... , and
come (lit. 'bring') ... '; see on περιιών ..., 5:8 above. * ἐν
τῇ θαλάττῃ ... τὸν βωμόν: in this improvised ἱππόδρομος, the altar set up for the sacrifice (8:25 above) served as a starting-
and finishing-point, and the water's edge as καμπή (see on ἡγεῖσθαι ἐκέλευον, 8:26 above).
κάτω ... ἄνω: 'on the way down ... on the way up', emphatic position. * πρὸς τὸ ἰσχυρῶς ὄρθιον: 'against the extremely steep
slope'.
μόλις βάδην ἐπορεύοντο: 'could scarcely proceed at a walk'.
ἔνθα: 'so', asyndeton.

* * * * * *

BOOK 5

1:2　　*The majority of the Ten Thousand now wished to make the*
to　　*last part of the journey by sea, which the Greeks regarded as*
2:23　*the natural element for long-distance travel. Never more than*
　　　fifty miles from it in their native land, Xenophon and his com-
　　　rades had travelled without sight of it for a greater distance
　　　than any Greek army recorded before. Now they looked to it
　　　for an easy homeward passage. But ships proved hard to come
　　　by, and while they waited for them to be collected, they were
　　　forced to plunder local tribes for provisions.

3:1　　ἐπεὶ δὲ οὔτε Χειρίσοφος ἧκεν οὔτε πλοῖα ἱκανὰ ἦν
　　　οὔτε τὰ ἐπιτήδεια ἦν λαμβάνειν ἔτι, ἐδόκει ἀπιτέον
　　　εἶναι. καὶ εἰς μὲν τὰ πλοῖα τούς τε ἀσθενοῦντας ἐν-
　　　εβίβασαν καὶ τοὺς ὑπὲρ τεττεράκοντα ἔτη καὶ παῖδας

3:1　ἐπεὶ δὲ ... : Kheirisophos had gone to borrow warships (τριήρεις)
　　and merchantmen (πλοῖα) from his friend Anaxibios, admiral (ναύ-
　　αρχος) of the Spartan fleet; rather than await his return, Xeno-
　　phon borrowed a warship from Trapezous, with which Polykrates of
　　Athens captured some Greek merchantmen; their cargoes were unload-
　　ed and put into the charge of the Akhaian generals Philesios (who
　　had replaced Menon after the execution of the generals, see on
　　ἡρέθησαν, 3:1:47 above) and Xanthikles (who had replaced Sokrates
　　of Akhaia). Anaxibios had overall command of the governors (ἁρμ-
　　οσταί 'harmosts') and their garrisons (φρουραί) which Sparta had
　　installed in the Greek islands and cities of Asia after 'liberat-
　　ing' them from Athenian domination at the end of the Peloponnesian
　　War. * οὔτε ... ἦν ... ἔτι: 'and it was no longer possible'; ἦν
　　= ἔξην.
　　ἐδόκει ἀπιτέον εἶναι: i.e. immediately, by land; ἐδόκει, imperf.,
　　as they reluctantly came to this conclusion; ἀπιτέον (ἐστι), 'one
　　must depart', n. verbal adjective from ἄπειμι (εἶμι 'go'), expres-
　　sing obligation (see on πειστέον, 2:6:8 and ἰτέον, 3:1:7 above).
　　This was the last thing they wanted to do, being (as one man said)
　　'tired of packing, walking, running, carrying arms, standing in
　　line, doing guard duty, and fighting', and wanting to reach Greece
　　by lying on their backs 'like Odysseus'; but Xenophon had private-
　　ly persuaded the coastal cities to make sure the roads to the west
　　were passable.
　　τοὺς ὑπὲρ τεττεράκοντα: for the ages of some of the generals, see
　　on ποίαν δ' ἡλικίαν, 3:1:14 above; παῖδας καὶ γυναῖκας: captured
　　during the expedition (ἀνδράποδα).

καὶ γυναῖκας καὶ τῶν σκευῶν ὅσα μὴ ἀνάγκη ἦν ἔχειν.
καὶ Φιλήσιον καὶ Σοφαίνετον τοὺς πρεσβυτάτους τῶν
στρατηγῶν εἰσβιβάσαντες τούτων ἐκέλευον ἐπιμελεῖσθαι·
3:2 οἱ δὲ ἄλλοι ἐπορεύοντο· ἡ δὲ ὁδὸς ὡδοποιημένη ἦν. καὶ
ἀφικνοῦνται πορευόμενοι εἰς Κερασοῦντα τριταῖοι πόλιν
Ἑλληνίδα ἐπὶ θαλάττῃ Σινωπέων ἄποικον ἐν τῇ Κολχίδι
3:3 χώρᾳ. ἐνταῦθα ἔμειναν ἡμέρας δέκα· καὶ ἐξέτασις σὺν
τοῖς ὅπλοις γίγνεται καὶ ἀριθμός, καὶ ἐγένοντο ὀκτακισχίλιοι καὶ ἑξακόσιοι. οὗτοι ἐσώθησαν ἐκ τῶν ἀμφὶ
τοὺς μυρίους· οἱ δὲ ἄλλοι ἀπώλοντο ὑπό τε πολεμίων

* τῶν σκευῶν ... : 'any baggage it was not essential to keep';
σκευῶν, from σκεῦος n.; ὅσος (ὅσοι) often means 'all that which',
'all those who'; μή, denoting a general (indefinite) statement.
Σοφαίνετος: a general from Stymphalos who had joined Kyros' expedition with 1000 hoplites. * πρεσβυτάτους: but in Book 2 Kleanor
is 'the eldest' (see on ἐπορεύοντο τεταγμένοι, 3:3:6 above); this
seems to be a slip by Xenophon. * εἰσβιβάσαντες ... ἐκέλευον:
'they sent ... on board with orders to ... '; ἐκέλευον: imperf.
for continuing situation. * τούτων: gen. with ἐπιμελεῖσθαι.
ἐπορεύοντο: 'resumed the march', imperf. * ὡδοποιημένη ἦν: pluperf. pass. of ὁδοποιέω (= ὡδοποίητο).

3:2 Κερασοῦντα: the city where the Greeks had first found the cherry
(κερασός).
Σινωπέων ἄποικον: colonists (ἄποικοι) from Miletos founded several
more Asian cities in the 7th century, including Abydos (1:1:9 above) and Sinope; usually colonies became independent of their
mother city and enjoyed good relations with their non-Greek neighbours; Sinope in turn founded Kotyora, Trapezous and Kerasous
(7th/6th century), and the latter two cities paid Sinope tribute
(φόρος); the native Kolkhoi remained hostile and the Ten Thousand
had to take supplies from them by force, while Trapezous provided
a market more willingly (see on ἦλθον, 4:8:25 above).

3:3 ἐνταῦθα: lack of connecting particle (asyndeton) speeds the narrative (also οὗτοι below). * ἀριθμός: 'a count', not only for cur-
iosity but to assist the distribution of booty.
ἐσώθησαν: 'were left alive', 'had come through safely'. * τῶν
ἀμφὶ τοὺς μυρίους: 'the (original number of) about ten thousand';
the article τοὺς is regularly used with round numbers.

3:4 καὶ χιόνος καὶ εἴ τις νόσῳ. ἐνταῦθα καὶ διαλαμβάν-
ουσι τὸ ἀπὸ τῶν αἰχμαλώτων ἀργύριον γενόμενον. καὶ
τὴν δεκάτην, ἣν τῷ Ἀπόλλωνι ἐξεῖλον καὶ τῇ ᾿Εφεσίᾳ
Ἀρτέμιδι, διέλαβον οἱ στρατηγοὶ τὸ μέρος ἕκαστος φυλάττειν τοῖς θεοῖς· ἀντὶ δὲ Χειρισόφου Νέων ὁ Ἀσιναῖος
3:5 ἔλαβε. Ξενοφῶν οὖν τὸ μὲν τοῦ Ἀπόλλωνος ἀνάθημα ποι-
ησάμενος ἀνατίθησιν εἰς τὸν ἐν Δελφοῖς τῶν Ἀθηναίων

χιόνος: see 4:5:3 - 18 above. * εἴ τις: lit. 'if anyone (did
so perish)' i.e. 'a few'. * νόσῳ: little medical attention was
available beyond the dressing of flesh wounds; resistance to disease had been lowered by exhaustion, extremes of climate, unusual
diet, and low morale. Originally there had been 10,700 hoplites
and 2300 light-armed troops; a rough count made when they first
encountered the Kolkhoi came to 8000 hoplites and 1800 light-
armed. No wonder the Greek cities were alarmed at the approach
of such a large 'mobile community' - roughly the size of Sparta!

3:4 καί: 'also'. * τὸ ἀπὸ τῶν ... : 'the proceeds from the sale of
their captures', including the ransoming of prisoners (λύσις)
or their sale into slavery (ἀνδραποδισμός), and the sale of booty
(ἁρπαγή) e.g. cattle (λεία) and arms (σκῦλα); αἰχμαλώτων, m. or
n. The mercenary troops had been looking forward to this distribution throughout the campaign; until now the booty had been
common property (see on κοινοῦ, 4:7:27 above).
τὴν δεκάτην: the tithe was a customary thank-offering to the gods
(see on θυσίαν, 4:8:25 above). * τῷ Ἀπόλλωνι ... : a hunter
dedicated part of his catch to Apollo and Artemis the Huntress
(Ἀγροτέρα); Apollo was associated with Greek civilization (see
on Δελφούς, 3:1:5 and 3:1:6 above), Artemis with the Persian Empire and its defeat (see on Ἀρτέμιδος, 1:6:7 above). * οἱ
στρατηγοί ... : ' ... so that each of them could look after his
share for the gods'; οἱ στρατηγοί ... ἕκαστος, nom. of whole and
part; φυλάττειν, inf. of purpose after διέλαβον; the generals included Kheirisophos, Xenophon, Philesios, Xanthikles and Sophainetos.
ἀντὶ ... Χειρισόφου ... ἔλαβε: 'received Kheirisophos' share'.
* Νέων ὁ Ἀσιναῖος: lieutenant (ὑποστράτηγος) in command of Kheirisophos' men in his absence; Asine was in Messenia, a land ruled
by Sparta, and Neon was a περίοικος (see on Σπαρτιάτην, 4:8:25
above).

3:5 τὸ ... τοῦ Ἀπόλλωνος ... : 'had his offering to Apollo made and
dedicated it at the treasury ... '; ἀνατίθησιν, 3rd pers. s.
pres. of ἀνατίθημι; for Delphoi, see on 3:1:5 above. The treasury, a small Doric temple, still stands near the remains of those
                                                         (cont.)

θησαυρὸν καὶ ἐπέγραψε τό τε αὐτοῦ ὄνομα καὶ τὸ Προξένου, ὃς σὺν Κλεάρχῳ ἀπέθανε· ξένος γὰρ ἦν αὐτοῦ.

3:6 τὸ δὲ τῆς Ἀρτέμιδος τῆς Ἐφεσίας, ὅτ' ἀπῄει σὺν
Ἀγησιλάῳ ἐκ τῆς Ἀσίας τὴν εἰς Βοιωτοὺς ὁδόν, κατα-
λείπει παρὰ Μεγαβύζῳ τῷ τῆς Ἀρτέμιδος νεωκόρῳ, ὅτι

of other states; it was built as a thank-offering to Apollo after
the expulsion of the tyrants (unconstitutional rulers) from Athens in 510 B.C. (cf. Herodotus 5.62 - 65), and enlarged after the
battle of Marathon (see on ὑποστῆναι αὐτοῖς, 3:2:11 and τρόπαιον,
3:2:13 above); cf. Plutarch, Lysander 1 and 18, for offerings
after his Thracian campaign in 404 B.C. Temples were the earli-
est financial institutions, sometimes having considerable income
from land (see 3:9 - 12 below); they served as banks, taking de-
posits from individuals and kings, and from cities, which either
had their own treasuries (e.g. the Parthenon at Athens) or used
Pan-Hellenic shrines (e.g. Olympia); by the end of the 5th century,
private bankers (τραπεζῖται) with their τράπεζαι ('tables', 'stalls')
in the market place had taken over much of the business.]
* ἐπέγραψε ... : epitaphs might contain simply a name and the
word χαῖρε 'farewell'; or a few lines of verse (e.g. Herodotus
7.228 on the Spartans who fell at Thermopylai in 480 B.C.; Thucydides 6.59 on Arkhedike, daughter of Hippias, tyrant of Athens).
* ἀπέθανε: 'had been killed'; for the generals' execution, see
2:5:31 - 32 above; for Proxenos' character, 2:6:16 - 20; and for
his relationship with Xenophon, 3:1:4 above. For Klearkhos' career, see Books 1 and 2, and for his character, 2:6:1 - 15 above.
* ξένος: see on 1:1:10.

3:6 τὸ ... τῆς Ἀρτέμιδος: sc. μέρος. * ὅτ' ἀπῄει: imperf. of ἄπειμι
(εἶμι 'go'); ὅτ' = ὅτε. * Ἀγησιλάῳ: Agesilaos, king of Sparta
399 - 390 B.C., was much admired by Xenophon who served under him
from 396 and wrote his biography (Introduction 2); he invaded
Phrygia and defeated Tissaphernes (396 - 4), but was recalled to
fight the Boiotians and their allies, including Athens; he returned overland (Xenophon, Hellenika 3.4.2 - 29, 4.1.1 - 2 and 4.3.1 -
21), and was victorious at the battle of Koroneia, 394.
* τὴν εἰς Βοιωτοὺς ὁδόν: 'to join the expedition against Boiotia';
εἰς Βοιωτοὺς, 'into (the territory of the) Boiotians', 'against
(the) Boiotians', a usage of the Ionic dialect; ὁδόν, adverbial
acc. * Μεγαβύζῳ: a Greek, despite his Persian name; Asiatic cities often had mixed cultures (cf. Herodotus' relative Panyassis
of Halikarnassos - another native name). * νεωκόρῳ: lit: 'tem-
ple-sweeper' from νεώς 'temple' and κορέω 'sweep' (cf. Euripides,
Ion 115, 121 and 795); but the 'warden' was an important official
at a major shrine, responsible for the protection and maintenance
(cont.)

αὐτὸς κινδυνεύσων ἐδόκει ἰέναι, καὶ ἐπέστειλεν, ἥν
μὲν αὐτὸς σωθῇ, αὐτῷ ἀποδοῦναι, εἰ δέ τι πάθοι,
ἀναθεῖναι ποιησάμενον τῇ Ἀρτέμιδι ὅ τι οἴοιτο χαρ-
3:7 ιεῖσθαι τῇ θεῷ. ἐπεὶ δ᾽ ἔφευγεν ὁ Ξενοφῶν, κατοικοῦντος ἤδη αὐτοῦ ἐν Σκιλλοῦντι ὑπὸ τῶν Λακεδαιμονίων
οἰκισθέντος παρὰ τὴν Ὀλυμπίαν ἀφικνεῖται Μεγάβυζος
εἰς Ὀλυμπίαν θεωρήσων καὶ ἀποδίδωσι τὴν παρακατα-
θήκην αὐτῷ. Ξενοφῶν δὲ λαβὼν χωρίον ὠνεῖται τῇ θεῷ
3:8 ὅπου ἀνεῖλεν ὁ θεός. ἔτυχε δὲ διαρρέων διὰ τοῦ χω-
ρίου ποταμὸς Σελινοῦς. καὶ ἐν Ἐφέσῳ δὲ παρὰ τὸν
τῆς Ἀρτέμιδος νεὼν Σελινοῦς ποταμὸς παραρρεῖ, καὶ

of the precinct, its physical and ritual cleanliness, and sometimes, as here, for financial matters.] * αὐτὸς κινδυνεύσων
ἐδόκει ἰέναι: 'he thought that *he* would encounter danger on his
journey', whereas Megabyzos would not.
ἥν ... σωθῇ: ἥν = ἐάν + subj.; σωθῇ, see on ἐσώθησαν, 3:3 above.
* αὐτῷ = ἑαυτῷ; ἀποδοῦναι: aor. inf. of ἀποδίδωμι, indir. command. * εἰ ... τι πάθοι: 'if anything should happen to him',
a common euphemism; remote fut. condition, unlike preceding clause.
* ἀναθεῖναι ποιησάμενον: 'he should get any offering made which
he thought ... , and dedicate it'; ἀναθεῖναι, aor. inf. of ἀνα-
τίθημι.

3:7 ἔφευγεν: 'was in exile', imperf. for continuing situation; the decree exiling Xenophon from Athens had been passed in 399 B.C. or
soon after, as a result of his pro-Spartan sympathies, and his
part in Kyros' expedition. The Ten Thousand were mostly Pelopon-
nesians; Athens was trying to get on good terms with Persia; for
Sokrates' fears about this, see on 3:1:5 above. This section
down to 3:13 refers to events subsequent to 394 B.C. (See Introduction 1.) * κατοικοῦντος ... αὐτοῦ: gen. absolute; κατοικέω
'dwell as an immigrant (or colonist)'. * Σκιλλοῦντι: Skillous
was in Triphylia, a district in Elis under Spartan control.
* παρὰ τὴν Ὀλυμπίαν: 'near Olympia', παρά + acc., expressing
motion, with οἰκισθέντος. * θεωρήσων: 'to see the games', a
Pan-Hellenic tourist attraction; fut. part., purpose; ἀποδίδωσι:
3rd pers. s. pres. of ἀποδίδωμι.
χωρίον: 'estate', already under cultivation (see on οἶνον, 3:9 below). * ἀνεῖλεν ὁ θεός: i.e. Apollo; ἀνεῖλεν, see on 3:1:6
above.

3:8 ποταμὸς Σελινοῦς: 'a river Selinous'.
νεὼν: acc. of νεώς, Attic declension; the coincidence was considered a good omen. Perhaps wild celery, σέλινον, grew by the banks
of each river, as apparently at the town Selinous in Sicily.

ἰχθύες τε ἐν ἀμφοτέροις ἕνεισι καὶ κόγχαι· ἐν δὲ τῷ
ἐν Σκιλλοῦντι χωρίῳ καὶ θῆραι πάντων ὁπόσα ἐστὶν
3:9 ἀγρευόμενα θηρία. ἐποίησε δὲ καὶ βωμὸν καὶ ναὸν
ἀπὸ τοῦ ἱεροῦ ἀργυρίου, καὶ τὸ λοιπὸν δὲ ἀεὶ δεκα-
τεύων τὰ ἐκ τοῦ ἀγροῦ ὡραῖα θυσίαν ἐποίει τῇ θεῷ.
καὶ πάντες οἱ πολῖται καὶ οἱ πρόσχωροι ἄνδρες καὶ
γυναῖκες μετεῖχον τῆς ἑορτῆς. παρεῖχε δὲ ἡ θεὸς
τοῖς σκηνοῦσιν ἄλφιτα, ἄρτους, οἶνον, τραγήματα, καὶ
τῶν θυομένων ἀπὸ τῆς ἱερᾶς νομῆς λάχος, καὶ τῶν θηρ-
3:10 ευομένων δέ. καὶ γὰρ θήραν ἐποιοῦντο εἰς τὴν ἑορτὴν

---

* ἕνεισι: 3rd pers. pl. of ἕνειμι (εἰμί 'be'). * κόγχαι:
'mussels' (also called μύες) or perhaps 'cockles'.
καὶ θῆραι (sc. ἕνεισι) ... : 'there is also hunting of every kind
of game there', a favourite pastime of Xenophon, who considered
it to be a good training for war; his Hunting Manual (Κυνηγετι-
κός) may have been written at Skillous.

3:9 ἐποίησε δὲ καὶ βωμὸν: 'he also built an altar'. * ναὸν: not the
Attic declension - unusual in Attic prose (cf. νεών, 3:8 above);
ἀεὶ: 'regularly'.
πολῖται: i.e. of Olympia. For sacrifice, see on καὶ τὰ ἱερὰ καλά, 1:
8:15 above and for tithing , on τὴν δεκάτην, 3:4 above. The whole
estate was a holy place (ἱερόν) or precinct (τέμενος); an altar was
the minimum requirement for worship (i.e. sacrifice) - Xenophon
mentions it first; sometimes, as here, a temple (ναός, ἱερόν) was
built as a house for the deity, with the altar in front; so the
god's image (ἄγαλμα) could watch the proceedings from a pedestal
in the cella or inner sanctum (ναός or ἄδυτον 'place not to be entered'), which was sometimes situated behind a front hall (πρόναος);
worshippers entered the temple as individuals, not as a congregat-
ion. A small temple might have 2 columns (κίονες) in the doorway
like the Athenian treasury at Delphoi (see on τὸ ... τοῦ Ἀπόλλωνος, 3:5 above); for larger temples, see on 3:12 below.
παρεῖχε: emphatic position, '(in return) ... provided'. * τοῖς
σκηνοῦσιν: either lit. 'those camping (there)' in tents (σκηναί)
for the festival, or 'the banqueters', taking σκηνέω as a military term, 'be in one's quarters (for a meal)'.
* ἄλφιτα: for bread. * οἶνον: vines take years to mat-
ure, so the land (χωρίον, 3:7 above) was already under cultivation. * τραγήματα: lit. 'nibbles' (from τρώγω, aor. ἔτραγον), e.g.
fresh or dried fruit. * τῶν θυομένων ... : 'a share of the animals from the sacred pasture which were sacrificed'. * καὶ ...
δέ: 'and also', see on καὶ στρατηγὸν δὲ, 1:1:2 above.

οἵ τε Ξενοφῶντος παῖδες καὶ οἱ τῶν ἄλλων πολιτῶν, οἱ
δὲ βουλόμενοι καὶ ἄνδρες συνεθήρων· καὶ ἡλίσκετο τὰ
μὲν ἐξ αὐτοῦ τοῦ ἱεροῦ χώρου, τὰ δὲ καὶ ἐκ τῆς Φολ-
3:11 όης, σύες καὶ δορκάδες καὶ ἔλαφοι; ἔστι δὲ ὁ τόπος
ᾗ ἐκ Λακεδαίμονος εἰς Ὀλυμπίαν πορεύονται ὡς εἴκοσι
στάδιοι ἀπὸ τοῦ ἐν Ὀλυμπίᾳ Διὸς ἱεροῦ. ἔνι δ' ἐν τῷ
ἱερῷ χώρῳ καὶ λειμὼν καὶ ὄρη δένδρων μεστά, ἱκανὰ
σῦς καὶ αἶγας καὶ βοῦς τρέφειν καὶ ἵππους, ὥστε καὶ
τὰ τῶν εἰς τὴν ἑορτὴν ἰόντων ὑποζύγια εὐωχεῖσθαι.
3:12 περὶ δὲ αὐτὸν τὸν ναὸν ἄλσος ἡμέρων δένδρων ἐφυτεύθη
ὅσα ἐστὶ τρωκτὰ ὡραῖα. ὁ δὲ ναὸς ὡς μικρὸς μεγάλῳ

3:10 οἱ ... Ξενοφῶντος παῖδες: we learn in Book 7 that Xenophon had no
sons when he joined Kyros' expedition; his wife was Philesia,
whom he may not have married till his return to Greece in 394;
his sons were Gryllos, named after Xenophon's father, as was
customary, and Diodoros (Introduction 1). * οἱ δὲ βουλόμενοι
... : 'and any who wanted to also joined in'.
ἡλίσκετο τὰ μὲν ... : 'some (of the game) was caught in the sacred
area itself, and some also on (Mount) Pholoë', on the borders of
Elis and Arkadia, not part of the estate; χώρου, rare in Attic
prose, but common in Xenophon. * σύες: wild boar as opposed to
domestic pigs (σῦς, 3:11 below).

3:11 ᾗ ἐκ Λακεδαίμονος ... : lit. '(on the road) by which they travel
from Sparta ... ' i.e. 'on the road from Sparta'; the Greeks
preferred to travel by sea; roads between towns were usually
narrow (cf. Sophokles, Oidipous Tyrannos 800 - 805) and in poor
condition; exceptions were those leading to the Pan-Hellenic
shrines (see also on ἀναβαίνει, 1:1:2 above for the Persian
Royal Road). * ὡς εἴκοσι στάδιοι: 2 miles; nom. in apposition
to τόπος; ὡς, 'about', with numbers. * τοῦ ἐν Ὀλυμπίᾳ ... : see
on 4:8:25.
ἔνι = ἔνεστι. * καὶ λειμὼν: 'both meadowland', watered by the
Selinous.
ἱκανὰ ... τρέφειν: 'suitable for rearing'. * ἵππους: another of
Xenophon's hobbies; for his treatise On Horsemanship, see Introduction 2; the Elean plain was good horse-rearing country.
* καὶ τὰ τῶν: καὶ, 'even' or 'also', as well as their owners.
* ὑποζύγια: oxen, mules, horses.

3:12 περὶ δὲ ... : 'immediately surrounding the temple a grove of trees
was planted'; ἡμέρων, from ἥμερος 'cultivated'. * ὅσα ἐστὶ
τρωκτὰ ὡραῖα: lit. 'as many as there are edible (fruits) in season' i.e. 'producing every kind of fruit during the year'; τρωκ-
τά, see on τραγήματα, 3:9 above; the shade and appearance of the
trees would also have been appreciated.

τῷ ἐν Ἐφέσῳ ἥκασται, καὶ τὸ ξόανον ἔοικεν ὡς κυπ-
3:13 αρίττινον χρυσῷ ὄντι τῷ ἐν Ἐφέσῳ. καὶ στήλη ἕστηκε
παρὰ τὸν ναὸν γράμματα ἔχουσα· ΙΕΡΟΣ Ο ΧΩΡΟΣ ΤΗΣ ΑΡ-
ΤΕΜΙΔΟΣ. ΤΟΝ ΕΧΟΝΤΑ ΚΑΙ ΚΑΡΠΟΥΜΕΝΟΝ ΤΗΝ ΜΕΝ ΔΕΚΑΤΗΝ
ΚΑΤΑΘΥΕΙΝ ΕΚΑΣΤΟΥ ΕΤΟΥΣ. ΕΚ ΔΕ ΤΟΥ ΠΕΡΙΤΤΟΥ ΤΟΝ ΝΑΟΝ
ΕΠΙΣΚΕΥΑΖΕΙΝ. ΑΝ ΔΕ ΤΙΣ ΜΗ ΠΟΙΗΙ ΤΑΥΤΑ ΤΗΙ ΘΕΩΙ ΜΕ-
ΛΗΣΕΙ.

ὡς μικρὸς ... : lit. 'has been made similar to the (one) in Ephesos
as a small (one) to a great (one)' i.e. 'is a small replica of
the great one at Ephesos' (cf. ὡς μικρὸν μεγάλῳ εἰκάσαι 'to compare small with great'); ἥκασται, perf. pass. of εἰκάζω.
ἔοικεν ὡς ... : 'is like the one at Ephesos but made of cypress wood
rather than gold'; cypress wood is hard and durable. Major Greek
shrines had large temples surrounded by one or more colonnades,
with interior columns supporting the roof (sometimes partly open
to the sky). Two of the largest Doric temples - those of Zeus
at Olympia, and of Athena Parthenos at Athens (the Parthenon) -
measured roughly 100 by 220 feet; that of Zeus at Akragas in Sicily was even bigger. Inside, the cult image was huge and awe-in-
spiring; Olympian Zeus and Athena Parthenos were of gold and ivory
(chryselephantine). Also inside were other statues, trophies and
dedications. The temple of Ephesian Artemis was nearly twice as
big; it was built in the 6th century to replace an earlier, smal-
ler one; some of its many Ionic columns were unique for their
scuptured lower drums; the statue was of gold (or covered with
gold plate) and multi-breasted (as the Asiatic mother goddess);
cf. Herodotus, 1.26 and 92. Xenophon here describes a small version of this; for normal small temples see on τὸ ... τοῦ Ἀπόλλωνος, 3:5 above.

3:13 ἕστηκε παρά + acc.: 'has been set up beside', perf. (intrans.) of
ἵστημι; see on παρά ... , 3:7 above. * γράμματα ἔχουσα: 'with
an inscription'; ἔχων often = 'with'.
ΙΕΡΟΣ Ο ΧΩΡΟΣ sc. ἐστι. ἐστι: '(This) place (is) ... '. ἱερός, emphatic
position. * ΤΗΣ ΑΡΤΕΜΙΔΟΣ: 'to Artemis', possessive gen., as
often with ἱερός.
ΤΟΝ ΕΧΟΝΤΑ ... ΚΑΤΑΘΥΕΙΝ: 'he who owns it ... shall sacrifice';
inf. of command, with acc. subject. * ΤΗΝ ΔΕΚΑΤΗΝ: 'his tithe',
'the tithe' that its produce which he owes; see on 3:4 above.
ΕΚ ΔΕ ... : 'and use the residue for the maintenance of the temple';
ἐπισκευάζω, 'keep in good repair'.
ΑΝ = ἐάν. * ΠΟΙΗΙ = ποιῇ. * ΤΗΙ ΘΕΩΙ (= τῇ θεῷ) ΜΕΛΗΣΕΙ: 'the
goddess will not overlook it'; a vague threat and therefore all
the more effective. It was typical of the Greeks to combine an
act of piety with practical benefits and generosity to one's
neighbours. The management of this estate provided much material
for Xenophon's Oikonomikos (see Introduction 2).

4:1   Xenophon's narrative now follows the progress of those who
to   went by land, as he was one of them. The two tribes of the
7:35   Mossynoikoi were at war with one another. When one of these
            opposed their passage, the Greeks formed an alliance with the
            other, and their combined strength forced the enemy to yield.
            Observing their strange customs, the Greeks thought the Moss-
            ynoikoi the most barbaric of the tribes that they encountered.

            Some two weeks later the army reached Kotyora, a Greek
            city and a colony of Sinope, whose leaders, in some anxiety,
            sent an embassy to discourage the Ten Thousand from quartering
            themselves on the town. Xenophon replied that the army plun-
            dered only when cities closed their gates to it, and preferred
            to purchase provisions when markets were made available. In
            the end, the Sinopéans offered useful advice, recommending that
            the journey should be made by sea at least as far as Herakleia.
            While three officers were away at Sinope raising the required
            number of ships, the first of a series of controversies arose
            in the army. From Xenophon's account it is clear that he was
            at the centre of it. With a safe return to Greece now in pros-
            pect, it appears that three different ideas were current: to
            reach home as soon as possible, to stay in the area and some-
            how acquire wealth before returning, and to remain and found
            a permanent Greek settlement. Xenophon frankly admits that he
            favoured the last of these ideas, but that it was not generally
            popular, least of all among the inhabitants of Sinope and Her-
            akleia, who bribed Timasion to urge the departure of the whole
            army by sea, and guaranteed its pay. Xenophon did not press
            his plan any further, and spiritedly replied to accusations of
            attempted deceit. In a long speech he skilfully turned the
            controversy away from himself and discoursed at length on the
            dangers of indiscipline and failure to observe the conventions
            of war. This gave rise to a general debate on the earlier
            conduct of both officers and men.

8:1   ἔδοξε δὲ καὶ τοὺς στρατηγοὺς δίκην ὑποσχεῖν τοῦ

8:1   ἔδοξε: denoting a formal decision (+ acc. and inf. construction;
            τοὺς στρατηγούς: subject of ὑποσχεῖν).   * καὶ: besides those
            responsible for recent lawlessness in Kerasous, where 3 ambas-
            sadors had been stoned to death, contrary to the strict conven-
            tion of the inviolability of ambassadors. The aggression pre-
            viously directed against a common enemy now found other victims;
            internal tensions in the Greek army were rising to the surface.

παρεληλυθότος χρόνου. καὶ διδόντων Φιλήσιος μὲν
ὦφλε καὶ Ξανθικλῆς τῆς φυλακῆς τῶν γαυλιτικῶν χρημάτων τὸ μείωμα εἴκοσι μνᾶς, Σοφαίνετος δέ, ὅτι
ἐπιμελητὴς αἱρεθεὶς κατημέλει, δέκα μνᾶς. Ξενοφῶντος δὲ κατηγόρησάν τινες φάσκοντες παίεσθαι ὑπ' αὐ-
8:2 τοῦ καὶ ὡς ὑβρίζοντος τὴν κατηγορίαν ἐποιοῦντο. καὶ
ὁ Ξενοφῶν ἀναστὰς ἐκέλευσεν εἰπεῖν τὸν πρῶτον λέξ-
αντα ποῦ καὶ ἐπλήγη. ὁ δὲ ἀποκρίνεται· Ὅπου καὶ τῷ
8:3 ῥίγει ἀπωλλύμεθα καὶ χιὼν πλείστη ἦν. ὁ δὲ εἶπεν·

* τοῦ παρεληλυθότος χρόνου: 'their past conduct (lit. time)';
at Athens, officials faced an examination (εὔθυναι) at the end
of their year of office, as a safeguard against misconduct, including embezzlement (κλοπή); and generals whose enterprises failed risked prosecution (εἰσαγγελία) on a charge of treason (γραφὴ
προδοσίας): e.g. Perikles fined for his general conduct of the
war with Sparta in 430 B.C. (Thucydides 2.65); Thucydides himself
exiled for his failure at Amphipolis in 424 (4.103 - 106 and 5.26);
Nikias' fears of prosecution when in Sicily in 413 (7.48); 8 generals condemned to death *en masse* after failing to recover bodies
at the battle of Arginousai in 406 (Xenophon, *Hellenika* 1.6.33 - 7.
37); similarly in Sparta, the ephors could prosecute generals
(even the kings) for misconduct, before the Council of Elders (γερουσία); e.g. Klearkhos, 2.6.2 - 4 above, and the king Pausanias
in the 470s (Thucydides 1.94 - 95 and 128 - 134).
διδόντων sc. τῶν στρατηγῶν τὴν δίκην: pres. part. of δίδωμι, gen.
absolute, denoting continuing activity. * Φιλήσιος ... Ξανθικλῆς: see on 3:1 above. * τῆς φυλακῆς: 'for their failure to
guard ... properly', gen. of cause after ὦφλε. * χρημάτων:
'cargoes', which were now κοινόν (see on κοινοῦ, 4:7:27 above); presumably the generals had kept some for themselves. * τὸ μείωμα
εἴκοσι μνᾶς: 'a fine (of) 20 mnai', i.e. 2000 drakhmai, equivalent
to 19 - 20 months' pay (excluding booty); for soldiers' pay, see
on δαρεικούς, 1:1:9 above. * κατημέλει: '(had) neglected (his duty)'.
παίεσθαι 'that they had been struck'; pres. inf., for repeated action (also ὑβρίζοντος and ὕβριζον below); παίω, mostly poetic
(Introduction 6.5). * ὡς ὑβρίζοντος sc. αὐτοῦ: ὡς + part., alleged reason; for ὕβρις 'wanton assault' as a serious crime, see
on 3:1:13 above; the term was used to describe the lawless behaviour noted in 8:1 above.

8:2 καὶ ἐπλήγη: καί, 'actually'. * ἀπωλλύμεθα: imperf. mid. of ἀπόλλυμι. * τῷ ῥίγει ... : see 4:5:3 - 18 above, especially 5:16.

Ἀλλὰ μὴν εἰ χειμῶνός γε ὄντος οἵου λέγεις, σίτου δὲ
ἐπιλελοιπότος, οἴνου δὲ μηδ' ὀσφραίνεσθαι παρόν, ὑπὸ
δὲ πόνων πολλῶν ἀπαγορευόντων, πολεμίων δὲ ἐπομένων,
εἰ ἐν τοιούτῳ καιρῷ ὕβριζον, ὁμολογῶ καὶ τῶν ὄνων
ὑβριστότερος εἶναι, οἷς φασιν ὑπὸ τῆς ὕβρεως κόπον
8:4 οὐκ ἐγγίγνεσθαι. ὅμως δὲ καὶ λέξον, ἔφη, ἐκ τίνος
ἐπλήγης. πότερον ᾔτουν τί σε καὶ ἐπεί μοι οὐκ ἐδίδους

8:3 **Ἀλλὰ μὴν**: 'well, really'. * **οἵου**: attracted from acc. (object of
λέγεις) by gen. antecedent **χειμῶνος**. * **σίτου** ... **ἐπιλελοιπότος**: its uneven distribution was the problem, summarily solved by
Xenophon (4:5:5 - 8 above). * **οἴνου** ... : gen. with **ὀσφραίνεσθαι**, perhaps used idiomatically, 'get a smell of (still less
drink)' as well as literally (owing to the cold); **μηδ(έ)**: 'not even';
παρόν: lit. 'it being possible', neuter part. of impersonal **πάρεστι**, acc. absolute. * **εἰ**: picking up the earlier **εἰ** after the
sarcastically long list of participial phrases. * **ἐν τοιούτῳ
καιρῷ**: 'at a time like that'. * **καὶ τῶν ὄνων** ... : 'that I am
more "wanton" even than donkeys'; **τῶν ὄνων**, gen. of comparison,
pl. with article for the whole species. * **οἷς**: dat. with **ἐγγίγνεσθαι**; **φασιν**: 3rd pers. pl. pres. of **φημί**. * **ὑπὸ τῆς ὕβρεως**:
'because of their wantonness'. * **κόπον**: subject of **ἐγγίγνεσθαι**.
Xenophon picked up the term **ὕβρις** and, by mentioning donkeys,
suggested its weaker meaning when applied to animals, viz. 'high
spirits' (*cf.* Herodotus 4.129); in humans, it was also 'arrogance',
'insolence', or merely 'cheek', or even 'randiness' (Aristophanes,
Clouds 1068); the latter meaning is also alluded to in the saying
about the donkey (which was better known for another characteristic: stupidity) - **κόπος** also refers to sex. Xenophon used iron-
ical humour and the *double entendre* to lower the tension and dis-
arm his opponents.

8:4 **καὶ λέξον**: 'do tell us'; Xenophon's defence here becomes a counter-
attack. * **ἐκ τίνος**: 'why', 'what ... for'.
πότερον ... : 'was it because ... '; **πότερον** is usually followed
by **ἤ** 'or' and an alternative question; here further questions are
introduced by **ἀλλά**, almost = 'all right then', rejecting the previous question. * **τί**: 'something', indefinite; with an accent
τί is usually interrogative 'what?'; the accent here is due to
enclitic **σε** following. * **ἐδίδους** ... **ἔπαιον**: imperf. for continued or repeated action; **ἐδίδους**, 2nd pers. sing. imperf. of
δίδωμι.

Ἔπαιον; ἀλλ' ἀπῄτουν, ἀλλὰ περὶ παιδικῶν μαχόμεν-
8:5 ος, ἀλλὰ μεθύων παρῴνησα; ἐπεὶ δὲ τούτων οὐδὲν
ἔφησεν, ἐπήρετο αὐτὸν εἰ ὁπλιτεύοι. οὐκ ἔφη. πάλιν
εἰ πελτάζοι. Οὐδὲ τοῦτ', ἔφη, ἀλλ' ἡμίονον ἤλαυνον
8:6 ταχθεὶς ὑπὸ τῶν συσκήνων ἐλεύθερος ὤν. ἐνταῦθα δὴ
ἀναγιγνώσκει αὐτὸν καὶ ἤρετο· Ἦ σὺ εἶ ὁ τὸν κάμνοντα
ἀπαγαγών; Ναὶ μὰ Δί', ἔφη· σὺ γὰρ ἠνάγκαζες· τὰ δὲ
8:7 τῶν ἐμῶν συσκήνων σκεύη διέρριψας. Ἀλλ' ἡ μὲν διάρριψις, ἔφη ὁ Ξενοφῶν, τοιαύτη τις ἐγένετο. διέδωκα
ἄλλα ἄλλοις ἄγειν καὶ ἐκέλευσα πρὸς ἐμὲ ἀπαγαγεῖν,

ἀπῄτουν sc. τί σε: 'was I asking you for something you'd borrowed';
ἀπο- in compounds often means 'duly'; ἀπαιτέω 'ask for (something)
back'. * παιδικῶν: see on παιδικά, 2:6:6 above. * παρῴνησα:
strictly μεθύων is redundant, as παροινέω = 'act violently when
drunk' (from οἶνος).

8:5 τούτων οὐδὲν ἔφησεν sc. εἶναι: 'he said (that it was) none of these';
ἔφησεν, rare aor. of φημί (= ἔφη). * οὐκ ἔφη: 'he said "No"';
another asyndeton, speeding the exchange of questions and answers.
πάλιν sc. ἐπήρετο: 'another question - was he ... '. * συσκήνων:
lit. 'tent-fellows'; a few soldiers shared a tent, and their baggage, food, and armour had been carried in the panniers (κανθήλια)
or on the back of one mule (see on περιιὼν ἐπὶ ... , 4:5:8 above).
* ὤν: pres. part. of εἰμί 'be', concessive; Xenophon was discred-
iting the man's character, as he had been ordered to do a slave's
job (see note after 3:3:20 above).

8:6 ἀναγιγνώσκει: 'recognized', a meaning mostly confined to Homer (in
Attic prose, = 'read'; ἀναγωρίζω = 'recognize'); see Introduction
6.5. * Ἦ σὺ εἶ ... : 'surely it was you who carried off that
man who was exhausted ... ' or ' ...that casualty ... '; Xenophon
sent his youngest troops back to the casualties 'with orders to
force them to get up and proceed' (4:5:22). * Ναὶ μὰ Δί' (= Δία):
'yes, by Zeus', strong assertion.

8:7 τοιαύτη τις: 'something like this', modestly phrased.
διέδωκα: aor. of διαδίδωμι. * ἄλλα ἄλλοις: 'the items to various
men'. * ἄγειν: inf. of purpose after διέδωκα: the mule could
now have carried the casualty. * ἐκέλευσα sc. αὐτούς; ἀπαγαγεῖν
(sc. αὐτά) ... ἀπολαβὼν ... ἀπέδωκα ... ἀπέδειξας: ἀπαγαγεῖν, 'to
bring (them) back' at the next halt; ἀπο-, see on ἀπῄτουν, 8:4
above; Xenophon was labouring the point with another sarcastic
list.

καὶ ἀπολαβὼν ἄπαντα σῶα ἀπέδωκά σοι, ἐπεὶ καὶ σὺ
ἐμοὶ ἀπέδειξας τὸν ἄνδρα. οἷον δὲ τὸ πρᾶγμα ἐγένετο
8:8 ἀκούσατε, ἔφη· καὶ γὰρ ἄξιον. ἀνὴρ κατελείπετο διὰ
τὸ μηκέτι δύνασθαι πορεύεσθαι. καὶ ἐγὼ τὸν μὲν ἄνδρα τοσοῦτον ἐγίγνωσκον ὅτι εἷς ἡμῶν εἴη· ἠνάγκασα
δὲ σὲ τοῦτον ἄγειν, ὡς μὴ ἀπόλοιτο· καὶ γάρ, ὡς ἐγὼ
οἶμαι, πολέμιοι ἡμῖν ἐφείποντο. συνέφη τοῦτο ὁ ἄνθ-
8:9 ρωπος. Οὐκοῦν, ἔφη ὁ Ξενοφῶν, ἐπεὶ προύπεμψά σε,
καταλαμβάνω αὖθις σὺν τοῖς ὀπισθοφύλαξι προσιὼν βόθ-
ρον ὀρύττοντα ὡς κατορύξοντα τὸν ἄνθρωπον, καὶ ἐπι-
8:10 στὰς ἐπῄνουν σε. ἐπεὶ δὲ παρεστηκότων ἡμῶν συνέκαμ-
ψε τὸ σκέλος ἀνήρ, ἀνέκραγον οἱ παρόντες ὅτι ζῇ ἀνήρ,
σὺ δ᾽ εἶπας· Ὁπόσα γε βούλεται· ὡς ἔγωγε αὐτὸν οὐκ
ἄξω. ἐνταῦθα ἔπαισά σε· ἀληθῆ λέγεις· ἔδοξας γάρ

οἷον: 'how', introducing indir. question (lit. 'of what sort',
   agreeing with τὸ πρᾶγμα).
ἄξιον sc. ἐστιν ἀκούειν: 'it's worth it'; the following interrogat-
   tion may be compared with that of Orontas by Kyros (1:6:6 - 8).

8:8 τοσοῦτον ... ὅτι: '(only) enough (to say) that'. * ἡμῶν: 'of ours',
     either the Greeks in general or Xenophon's division in particular.
     ὡς μὴ ἀπόλοιτο: aor. opt. mid. of ἀπόλλυμι, purpose clause (see In-
     troduction 6.1).
     ὡς ἐγὼ οἶμαι: 'as I remember'. * συνέφη: imperf. of σύμφημι;
     asyndeton.
     ὁ ἄνθρωπος: 'the fellow', less complimentary than ὁ ἀνήρ (also τὸν
     ἄνθρωπον, 8:9 below; almost 'the poor fellow').

8:9 Οὐκοῦν: see on 1:6:7 above. * καταλαμβάνω: sc. σε. * ἐπιστάς:
     strong aor. part. (intrans.) of ἐφίστημι.

8:10 παρεστηκότων ἡμῶν: 'as we were standing around', perf. part. (in-
     trans.) of παρίστημι, gen. absolute. * συνέκαμψε: emphatic pos-
     ition, before subject (also ἀνέκραγον and ζῇ below). * ἀνήρ
     (ᾱ) = ὁ ἀνήρ (crasis).
     Ὁπόσα γε βούλεται sc. ζήτω: lit. '(let him be alive) as much as
     he likes at any rate' i.e. 'he can be as alive as he likes'; γε
     in replies often = 'yes'. * ὡς: lit. '(I say this) since'.
     ἀληθῆ λέγεις: 'it's true', 'you're right'. * ἔδοξας γάρ ... :
     lit. 'for you seemed to me to resemble (one) knowing ... ' i.e.
     'it looked to me as if you knew he had been alive (all along)';
                                                              (cont.)

8:11 μοι εἰδότι ἐοικέναι ὅτι ἔζη. Τί οὖν; ἔφη, ἧττόν τι
ἀπέθανεν, ἐπεὶ ἐγώ σοι ἀπέδειξα αὐτόν; Καὶ γὰρ ἡμε-
εῖς, ἔφη ὁ Ξενοφῶν, πάντες ἀποθανούμεθα· τούτου οὖν
8:12 ἕνεκα ζῶντας ἡμᾶς δεῖ κατορυχθῆναι; τοῦτον μὲν ἀνέκραγον πάντες ὡς ὀλίγας παίσειεν· ἄλλους δ᾽ ἐκέλευε
8:13 λέγειν διὰ τί ἕκαστος ἐπλήγη. ἐπεὶ δὲ οὐκ ἀνίσταντο,
αὐτὸς ἔλεγεν· ᾽Εγώ, ὦ ἄνδρες, ὁμολογῶ παῖσαι δὴ ἄνδρας
ἕνεκεν ἀταξίας ὅσοις σῴζεσθαι μὲν ἤρκει δι᾽ ὑμᾶς, ἐν
τάξει τε ἰόντων καὶ μαχομένων ὅπου δέοι, αὐτοὶ δὲ
λιπόντες τὰς τάξεις προθέοντες ἁρπάζειν ἤθελον καὶ

οἶδα, though a verb of knowing, is regularly followed by ὅτι
when the fact known is emphasized.]

8:11 Τί οὖν;: 'so what?'. * ἧττόν τι: 'any the less'.
Καὶ γὰρ ἡμεῖς: lit. 'for we also ... '; γάρ in replies means 'yes,
for', 'no, for'; here objecting to the accuser's logic, 'no (your
conclusion is wrong) for'; translate 'yes, but' (see on 2:5:40
above).
τούτου: neuter. For selfishness among the Greeks, see on ἄλλο εἴ
τι ... , 4:5:5 above.

8:12 τοῦτον μὲν ... : 'they all shouted that he had not hit him enough';
τοῦτον, subject of subordinate clause anticipated in main sentence - 'anticipatory acc.' with ἀνέκραγον (see on τὸν Καλλίμαχον,
4:7:11 above) - emphatic position, contrasted with ἄλλους 'anyone else' below; ὀλίγας sc. πληγάς '(too) few (blows)', παίσειεν,
opt., indir. statement (historic).

8:13 ἀνίσταντο: imperf. mid. of ἀνίστημι; this expression of popular
opinion had silenced further opposition. * ἔλεγεν: 'continued
speaking'.
ὦ ἄνδρες: Xenophon was addressing all the men (cf. ὑμᾶς and ὑμῶν
below). * παῖσαι δή: 'that I have indeed struck'. * ὅσοις
σῴζεσθαι ... : 'all those who were quite happy to be kept safe
thanks to you'; ὅσοις, see on ὅσος, 3:1 above. * ἰόντων sc.
ἡμῶν: pres. part. of εἶμι 'go'. * ὅπου δέοι: opt., indefinite. * αὐτοὶ δέ: Greek regularly continues after a relative
clause with a co-ordinate main sentence, where English continues
the relative clause (here begun at ὅσοις). * λιπόντες τὰς τάξεις: Xenophon's audience knew that leaving one's ranks was tanta-
mount to desertion; it rendered hoplite tactics ineffective (see
on ἐξεκύμαινέ τι τῆς φάλαγγος, 1:8:18 above). * ἁρπάζειν: 'to
go looting'.

ὑμῶν πλεονεκτεῖν. εἰ δὲ τοῦτο πάντες ἐποιοῦμεν, ἅπαντες ἂν ἀπωλόμεθα.

8:14 *Hard times, said Xenophon, had called for harsh discipline,*
to *for it is then that the worst soldiers require the most repress-*
8:26 *ive punishment. But he reminded his audience of the many occas-*
   ions on which he had praised deeds of courage, and many corrobo-
   rated his claim.

  εἰ δὲ ... : unfulfilled past condition (εἰ + past indic., past indic. + ἄν). Xenophon explicitly pointed the moral, for his audience and for us; for his responsibility as commander of the
  rearguard, see on ὀπισθοφυλακῶν, 4:5:7 above.

Greek hoplites in close formation (φάλαγξ), being piped into battle
(see on 1:8:17 and 1:10:10 above).
  From a mid-seventh century B.C. Corinthian wine jug (*olpe*) of the
black-figure style, known as the 'Chigi Vase' by the so-called 'Mac-
millan painter', in the Villa Giulia Museum, Rome.

BOOK 6

1:1　　*The Greeks made a visit by Paphlagonian ambassadors the*
to　　*occasion for festivities. There were war dances, a primitive*
1:16　*dramatic performance symbolizing the eternal conflict between*
　　　the farmer and the warrior in society and, of course, much
　　　feasting. Sufficient ships had now arrived, and the army
　　　sailed westwards to Sinope, where they stayed for 5 days.

1.17　　ὡς δὲ τῆς Ἑλλάδος ἐδόκουν ἐγγὺς γίγνεσθαι, ἤδη
　　　μᾶλλον ἢ πρόσθεν εἰσήει αὐτοὺς ὅπως ἂν καὶ ἔχοντές
1:18　τι οἴκαδε ἀφίκοιντο. ἡγήσαντο οὖν, εἰ ἕνα ἕλοιντο
　　　ἄρχοντα, μᾶλλον ἂν ἢ πολυαρχίας οὔσης δύνασθαι τὸν
　　　ἕνα χρῆσθαι τῷ στρατεύματι καὶ νυκτὸς καὶ ἡμέρας,
　　　καὶ εἴ τι δέοι λανθάνειν, μᾶλλον ἂν κρύπτεσθαι, καὶ
　　　εἴ τι αὖ δέοι φθάνειν, ἧττον ἂν ὑστερίζειν· οὐ γὰρ
　　　ἂν λόγων δεῖν πρὸς ἀλλήλους, ἀλλὰ τὸ δόξαν τῷ ἑνὶ
　　　περαίνεσθαι ἄν· τὸν δ' ἔμπροσθεν χρόνον ἐκ τῆς

1:17　τῆς Ἑλλάδος: i.e. mainland Greece; gen. with ἐγγύς.　* εἰσήει
　　　αὐτοὺς ὅπως ἂν + opt.: '(the question of) how they might ...
　　　filled their minds', indir. deliberative question in historic
　　　sequence with potential ἂν: εἰσήει, imperf. of εἴσειμι (εἶμι
　　　'go').
　　　καὶ: 'as well'.　* ἔχοντές τι: understatement; 'with plenty (of
　　　booty)'.

1:18　εἰ ... ἕλοιντο ... ἂν ... δύνασθαι: remote fut. condition in in-
　　　dir. speech (also below).　* μᾶλλον: 'better'.　* πολυαρχίας:
　　　see on στρατηγοί, 5:3:4 above.　* τὸν ἕνα: subject of δύνασθαι.
　　　εἴ τι δέοι λανθάνειν: 'if there were any need for secrecy'; τι,
　　　adverbial, with δέοι or λανθάνειν (also below).　* κρύπτεσθαι:
　　　'to hide their activities'.　* φθάνειν: 'anticipating (the en-
　　　emy)'; Xenophon, while mentioning tensions among the generals,
　　　did not emphasize these problems in Books 3 and 4.　* ἧττον:
　　　'less often'.
　　　ἂν ... δεῖν ,.. περαίνεσθαι ἄν: indir. speech continued.　* λόγ-
　　　ων ... πρὸς ἀλλήλους: 'joint discussions'; λόγων, gen. with
　　　δεῖν.　* τὸ δόξαν τῷ ἑνὶ: 'the one man's decision'; δόξαν, aor.
　　　part. with article, used as noun (see on ἔδοξε, 5:8:1 above).
　　　τὸν ... χρόνον: adverbial acc.

1:19 νικώσης ἔπραττον πάντα οἱ στρατηγοί. ὡς δὲ ταῦτα
διενοοῦντο, ἐτράποντο ἐπὶ τὸν Ξενοφῶντα· καὶ οἱ
λοχαγοὶ ἔλεγον προσιόντες αὐτῷ ὅτι ἡ στρατιὰ οὕτω
γιγνώσκει, καὶ εὔνοιαν ἐνδεικνύμενος ἕκαστός τις
1:20 ἔπειθεν αὐτὸν ὑποστῆναι τὴν ἀρχήν. ὁ δὲ Ξενοφῶν τῇ
μὲν ἐβούλετο ταῦτα, νομίζων καὶ τὴν τιμὴν μείζω οὕτως ἑαυτῷ γίγνεσθαι πρὸς τοὺς φίλους καὶ εἰς τὴν
πόλιν τοὔνομα μεῖζον ἀφίξεσθαι αὐτοῦ, τυχὸν δὲ καὶ
1:21 ἀγαθοῦ τινος ἂν αἴτιος τῇ στρατιᾷ γενέσθαι. τὰ μὲν
δὴ τοιαῦτα ἐνθυμήματα ἐπῆρεν αὐτὸν ἐπιθυμεῖν αὐτοκράτορα γενέσθαι ἄρχοντα. ὁπότε δ᾽ αὖ ἐνθυμοῖτο
ὅτι ἄδηλον μὲν παντὶ ἀνθρώπῳ ὅπη τὸ μέλλον ἕξει, διὰ

---

* ἐκ τῆς νικώσης sc. γνώμης: 'in accordance with the majority
vote'; νικάω = 'prevail', e.g. of opinions. * ἔπραττον: 'had
done'. For tension's among the generals, see e.g. 2:5:28 and 2:
5:38 above; cf. Herodotus 5.74 - 75 (between Spartan kings leading army) and Thucydides 7.47 - 49 (between Athenian generals in
Sicily in 413 B.C.)

1:19 ἡ στρατιὰ οὕτω γιγνώσκει: 'this was the army's opinion (γνώμη)';
generals were selected on the basis of popularity with the men;
see 3:1:47, where the captains' nominations were confirmed by a
general assembly. * ἔπειθεν: 'tried to persuade', imperf.
* ὑποστῆναι: strong aor. inf. act. of ὑφίστημι, lit. 'to stand
under' i.e. 'to accept' something one would rather not.

1:20 τῇ μὲν: see on 3:1:12 above; but here picked up by ὁπότε δ᾽ αὖ
(rather than τῇ δέ). * μείζω = μείζονα. * πρὸς τοὺς φίλους:
'in the eyes of his friends' in the army. For competition for
honour, see e.g. 1:9:11 and 4:7:11 - 12 above. * εἰς τὴν πόλιν ... : i.e. Athens; τοὔνομα (= τὸ ὄνομα, crasis), i.e. his reputation; αὐτοῦ = ἑαυτοῦ; for the Athenians' opinion of Xenophon,
see on ὑποπτεύσας μή τι ... , 3:1:5 and on ἔφευγεν, 5:3:7 above.
* τυχόν: lit. 'it chancing' i.e. 'with luck', 'perhaps', n.
aor. part. of τυγχάνει, used impersonally, acc. absolute.
* ἀγαθοῦ τινος: n., gen. with αἴτιος.

1:21 δή: 'so', connecting particle. * ἐπῆρεν αὐτὸν ἐπιθυμεῖν: 'roused
in him a desire'. * αὐτοκράτορα ... ἄρχοντα: 'sole commander';
αὐτοκράτωρ = entitled to act without reference to another (αὐτο-
'self' and κράτος 'power').
ἄδηλον: sc. ἐστι (or εἴη, opt., indir. statement, historic sequence).
* ὅπη ... ἕξει: 'how ... will be', adverb + ἔχω.

τοῦτο δὲ καὶ κίνδυνος εἴη καὶ τὴν προειργασμένην
1:22 δόξαν ἀποβαλεῖν, ἠπορεῖτο. ἀπορουμένῳ δὲ αὐτῷ διακρῖναι ἔδοξε κράτιστον εἶναι τοῖς θεοῖς ἀνακοινῶσαι·
καὶ παραστησάμενος δύο ἱερεῖα ἐθύετο τῷ Διὶ τῷ βασιλεῖ,
ὅσπερ αὐτῷ μαντευτὸς ἦν ἐκ Δελφῶν· καὶ τὸ ὄναρ δὴ ἀπὸ
τούτου τοῦ θεοῦ ἐνόμιζεν ἑορακέναι δ' εἶδεν ὅτε ἤρχετο ἐπὶ τὸ συνεπιμελεῖσθαι τῆς στρατιᾶς καθίστασθαι.
1:23 καὶ ὅτε ἐξ Ἐφέσου δὲ ὡρμᾶτο Κύρῳ συσταθησόμενος,
ἀετὸν ἀνεμιμνήσκετο αὐτῷ δεξιὸν φθεγγόμενον, καθήμενον μέντοι, ὅνπερ ὁ μάντις ὁ προπέμπων αὐτὸν
ἔλεγεν ὅτι μέγας μὲν οἰωνὸς εἴη καὶ οὐκ ἰδιωτικὸς

καὶ κίνδυνος εἴη: 'there was even a danger of his losing (or throwing away) even the reputation he had already won'.

1:22 διακρῖναι: inf. with ἀπορουμένῳ. * τοῖς θεοῖς ἀνακοινῶσαι: for
Xenophon's piety, see on 4:8:25 and 5:3:5 - 13 above.
παραστησάμενος: aor. part. mid. of παρίστημι. * δύο ἱερεῖα: the
second animal would be sacrificed if favourable omens were not
obtained the first time - a regular procedure (see on καὶ τὰ
ἱερὰ καλά, 1:8:15 above). * ἐθύετο: 'proceeded to sacrifice',
mid., as the actual sacrifice was performed on his behalf by the
priest. * Διὶ τῷ βασιλεῖ ... : see on θεοῖς, 3:1:6 and on Διὸς
... βασιλέως, 3:1:12 above. * ἐκ: 'at'.
τὸ ὄναρ ... : see 3:1:11; δὴ, 'of course'. * ἤρχετο ἐπὶ ... :
'he was beginning to assume his share of responsibility for the
joint supervision of the army'; ἤρχετο, imperf., showing his
tentativeness; καθίστασθαι, pres. inf. mid. of καθίστημι, lit.
'to fall in' e.g. to battle line.

1:23 συσταθησόμενος: fut. part. pass. of συνίστημι, purpose; for the
journey and its purpose, see on 3:1:4 and 3:1:8 above. * αὐτῷ
δεξιὸν: 'on his right'; αὐτῷ = ἑαυτῷ. * καθήμενον μέντοι:
'but that it had been sitting', continuing the part. construction
after ἀναμιμνήσκετο. * ὅνπερ ὁ μάντις ... ἔλεγεν ὅτι ... εἴη:
'which the soothsayer ... said was'; ὅνπερ, anticipatory acc.,
see on τὸν Καλλίμαχον, 4:7:11 and on τοῦτον μὲν, 5:8:12 above.
* ὁ προπέμπων: whom Xenophon consulted before setting out; προ-
πέμπω, 'send off' a departing traveller. * μέγας μὲν οἰωνὸς ... :
lit. 'it was a great bird (of prey) ... ' i.e. 'an important om-
en'; for augury and soothsayers see on εὐώνυμον, 1:8:4 and on
μάντεων, 4:5:4 above (Aeschylus, Prometheus Bound 488 - 492 and
Aristophanes, Birds 716 - 722, where ὄρνις = 'bird' and 'omen').
* οὐκ ἰδιωτικὸς: i.e., as Xenophon understood it, referring to
royalty and to Persia; the eagle was associated with Zeus, king
of the gods.

καὶ ἔνδοξος, ἐπίπονος μέντοι· τὰ γὰρ ὄρνεα μάλιστα
ἐπιτίθεσθαι τῷ ἀετῷ καθημένῳ· οὐ μέντοι χρηματιστι-
κὸν εἶναι τὸν οἰωνόν· τὸν γὰρ ἀετὸν περιπετόμενον
1:24 μᾶλλον λαμβάνειν τὰ ἐπιτήδεια. οὕτω δὴ θυομένῳ αὐτῷ
διαφανῶς ὁ θεὸς σημαίνει μήτε προσδεῖσθαι τῆς ἀρχῆς
1:25 μήτε εἰ αἱροῖντο ἀποδέχεσθαι. τοῦτο μὲν δὴ οὕτως
ἐγένετο. ἡ δὲ στρατιὰ συνῆλθε, καὶ πάντες ἔλεγον
ἕνα αἱρεῖσθαι· καὶ ἐπεὶ τοῦτο ἔδοξε, προυβάλλοντο
αὐτόν.

τὰ ὄρνεα ἐπιτίθεσθαι: acc. and inf., indir. statement (also εἶναι
τὸν οἰωνόν and τὸν ... ἀετὸν λαμβάνειν below).
τὰ ἐπιτήδεια: lit. 'supplies', a military term for food. Note the
typical ambiguity of the prophecy.

1:24 οὕτω δὴ: 'so this was how ... '. * σημαίνει μήτε + inf.: 'indic-
ated that he should neither'; μή + inf., indir. command.
* προσδεῖσθαι: in addition to (προσ-) the command he already
had. * εἰ αἱροῖντο: opt., remote fut. condition.

1:25 πάντες ἔλεγον ... αἱρεῖσθαι: 'everyone spoke in favour of choosing';
αἱρεῖσθαι, indir. command.
ἔδοξε: see on 5:8:1 and on τὸ δόξαν ... , 1:18 above.

1:25   *Xenophon declined the command, arguing that it should go
to   to a Spartan, and saying that the gods had advised him in a
6:38   sacrifice against accepting it; Kheirisophos was therefore el-
            ected. The next stage of the sea journey, to Herakleia, was
            completed. There, with the disapproval of both Xenophon and
            Kheirisophos, the army sent delegates to demand money from the
            Herakleians, who responded by closing the gates of their city.
            This led to dissension among the Greek leaders, and the army
            was divided under three commanders, with Xenophon commanding
            the only cavalry.*

            *The largest contingent was that of the Akhaians and Ark-
            adians, comprising about half the total force. They set off
            to plunder the land of the Thracians, but were surrounded on
            a hill and had to be rescued by Xenophon and his contingent,
            who approached the Thracian positions by night and lit many
            fires in order to deceive them about the size of their force.
            The ruse worked, and they withdrew without a fight. After
            this escape the army was reunited at Kalpēs Limēn, and resol-
            ved not to break up again. But there were no ships to take
            them home, and in gathering supplies they suffered severe cas-
            ualties at the hands of the Bithynians and the cavalry of the
            Persian satrap Pharnabazos. They went in pursuit of the enemy,
            and, in a battle in which, on Xenophon's suggestion, a reserve
            force was kept back in three formations, they won a crushing
            victory. The cohesion of the hoplites was the deciding factor,
            as in previous engagements. They advanced in an unbroken line,
            levelling their spears at the enemy on the trumpet's signal,
            moving slowly at first then quickening to the double and chant-
            ing the battle-cry. The enemy had no effective answer to this
            bristling line of armour, and the battle ended with the extra-
            ordinary spectacle of Pharnabazos' cavalry fleeing from the
            Greek infantry.*

            *In the meantime a rumour had gone round the countryside
            that the Greeks, who appeared to have no intention of contin-
            uing their homeward march, were founding a city. The inhabit-
            ants of the surrounding area now brought supplies to sell to
            the colonizers, and passing ships called in. This was the
            situation when Kleandros the Spartan harmost (governor) of
            Byzantion arrived with two triremes, but no transports. A dis-
            pute over booty gave him a bad impression of the Ten Thousand,
            but he was persuaded by Xenophon and the other officers to
            assist the army's journey by land to Byzantion. The army made
            a six-day march to Khrysopolis in Khalkedonia, and stayed there
            for 7 days to sell their booty. They were still close to the
            province of the satrap Pharnabazos. Anaxibios, who was in
            overall command of Spartan forces in the Hellespontine region,
            was as anxious as Pharnabazos that the Ten Thousand should be
            disbanded, since at this time Sparta was at peace with Persia.*

                            * * * * * * *

BOOK 7

1:2 ἐκ τούτου δὲ Φαρνάβαζος φοβούμενος τὸ στράτευμα
μὴ ἐπὶ τὴν αὐτοῦ ἀρχὴν στρατεύηται, πέμψας πρὸς Ἀναξίβιον τὸν ναύαρχον (ὁ δ' ἔτυχεν ἐν Βυζαντίῳ ὤν)
ἐδεῖτο διαβιβάσαι τὸ στράτευμα ἐκ τῆς Ἀσίας, καὶ
1:3 ὑπισχνεῖτο πάντα ποιήσειν αὐτῷ ὅσα δέοιτο. καὶ ὁ
Ἀναξίβιος μετεπέμψατο τοὺς στρατηγοὺς καὶ λοχαγοὺς
τῶν στρατιωτῶν εἰς Βυζάντιον, καὶ ὑπισχνεῖτο, εἰ
διαβαῖεν, μισθοφορὰν ἔσεσθαι τοῖς στρατιώταις.

1:4   *Xenophon now wished to leave the army and return home,*
to   *but was persuaded by Anaxibios to stay on. He was also app-*
1:6   *roached by the Thracian king Seuthes, who wished to hire mer-*
      cenaries for an internal war of his own. At first Xenophon
      was not tempted.

1:2 ἐκ τούτου: 'then' (also 1:7 below). * τὴν αὐτοῦ ἀρχὴν: Bithynia
and Lesser Phrygia; αὐτοῦ = ἑαυτοῦ. * πέμψας ... ἐδεῖτο: 'sent
word ... asking (him)'; πέμψας sc. ἄγγελον, see on πέμπων, 1:1:8
above. * Ἀναξίβιον: see on ἐπεὶ δὲ ... , 5:3:1 above. * διαβιβάσαι: across the Bosporos to Byzantion; Byzantion controlled
the corn route from the Black Sea (Εὔξεινος Πόντος) to Greece
(cf. Herodotus 6.26); Kleandros, as its harmost, was concerned
for its security; he and Xenophon had become ξένοι (see on ξένος, 1:1:10 above).

1:3 τοὺς στρατηγούς: see on 5:3:4 above; but Kheirisophos had recently
died as the result of a drug taken to cure a fever; this is only
mentioned in passing in Book 6 (contrast the detailed obituaries
in Books 1 and 2); his division was taken over by Neon of Asine,
his lieutenant. In general Xenophon tends to underplay the rôle
played by Kheirisophos and they were not always on good terms;
see on Χειρίσοφος, 2:5:37, ἐγὼ οὖν ... , 3:1:14 and ἐπορεύοντο
τεταγμένοι, 3:3:6 above. * μισθοφοράν: '(regular) pay'; Anaxibios would assume Kyros' rôle as μισθοδότης 'paymaster'; this
was a radical change of Spartan policy after their previous support for Kyros against the King (see on Λακεδαιμονίοις, 3:1:5 above).

1:7   ἐκ τούτου διαβαίνουσι πάντες εἰς τὸ Βυζάντιον οἱ
στρατιῶται.   καὶ μισθὸν μὲν οὐκ ἐδίδου ὁ Ἀναξίβιος,
ἐκήρυξε δὲ λαβόντας τὰ ὅπλα καὶ τὰ σκεύη τοὺς στρατιώτας ἐξιέναι, ὡς ἀποπέμψων τε ἅμα καὶ ἀριθμὸν ποιή-
σων.   ἐνταῦθα οἱ στρατιῶται ἤχθοντο, ὅτι οὐκ εἶχον
ἀργύριον ἐπισιτίζεσθαι εἰς τὴν πορείαν, καὶ ὀκνηρῶς
συνεσκευάζοντο.

1:8   *Even now Seuthes' offer was not attractive enough to change*
to   *Xenophon's plans. But he was once more persuaded, this time*
1:11   *by Kleandros, to continue to act as the army's spokesman in neg-*
           otiations about pay and supplies with Anaxibios, who undertook
           to provide for their homeward passage if they would leave the
           city of Byzantion.

1:12   ἐντεῦθεν ἐξῆσαν οἵ τε στρατηγοὶ πρῶτοι καὶ οἱ ἄλλοι.   καὶ ἄρδην πάντες πλὴν ὀλίγων ἔξω ἦσαν, καὶ Ἐτεόνικος εἰστήκει παρὰ τὰς πύλας ὡς ὁπότε ἔξω γένοιντο

1:7   οὐκ ἐδίδου: 'would not give', 3rd pers. sing. imperf. indic. of
       δίδωμι.   *   λαβόντας ... τοὺς στρατιώτας ἐξιέναι: 'that the sol-
       diers had to take ... and get out', indir. command.   *   ὡς ἀπο-
       πέμψων ... ποιήσων: fut. part., purpose as stated by Anaxibios;
       ἀριθμὸν ποιέω 'count', 'ascertain the strength' of an army, osten-
       sibly as a preliminary to distributing pay (see on ἀριθμός, 5:3:3).

1:12   ἐξῆσαν: imperf. of ἔξειμι (εἶμι 'go').   *   καὶ οἱ ἄλλοι: 'and (then)
       the rest'.
       Ἐτεόνικος: a Spartan officer, naval commander, and former harmost
       of Thasos (cf. Thucydides 8:23, Xenophon, Hellenika 1.1.32 and 1.
       6.26).   *   εἰστήκει: 'had stationed himself', pluperf. (intrans.)
       of ἵστημι.   *   παρά + acc.: see on παρὰ τὴν Ὀλυμπίαν, 5:3:7 and
       on ἕστηκε παρά, 5:3:13 above.   *   ὡς: see over.   *   ὁπότε + opt.:
       'when', indefinite in the future.

πάντες συγκλείσων τὰς πύλας καὶ τὸν μοχλὸν ἐμβαλ-
1:13 ῶν. ὁ δὲ Ἀναξίβιος συγκαλέσας τοὺς στρατηγοὺς καὶ
τοὺς λοχαγοὺς ἔλεγε· Τὰ μὲν ἐπιτήδεια, ἔφη, λαμβάνετε
ἐκ τῶν Θρᾳκίων κωμῶν· εἰσὶ δὲ αὐτόθι πολλαὶ κριθαὶ
καὶ πυροὶ καὶ τἄλλα τὰ ἐπιτήδεια· λαβόντες δὲ πορεύ-
εσθε εἰς Χερρόνησον, ἐκεῖ δὲ Κυνίσκος ὑμῖν μισθοδοτ-
1:14 ήσει. ἐπακούσαντες δέ τινες τῶν στρατιωτῶν ταῦτα ἢ
καὶ τῶν λοχαγῶν τις διαγγέλλει εἰς τὸ στράτευμα. καὶ
οἱ μὲν στρατηγοὶ ἐπυνθάνοντο περὶ τοῦ Σεύθου πότερα
πολέμιος εἴη ἢ φίλος, καὶ πότερα διὰ τοῦ Ἱεροῦ ὄρους
1:15 δέοι πορεύεσθαι ἢ κύκλῳ διὰ μέσης τῆς Θρᾴκης. ἐν ᾧ
δὲ οὗτοι ταῦτα διελέγοντο οἱ στρατιῶται ἀναρπάσαντες
τὰ ὅπλα θέουσι δρόμῳ πρὸς τὰς πύλας, ὡς πάλιν εἰς τὸ
τεῖχος εἰσιόντες. ὁ δὲ Ἐτεόνικος καὶ οἱ σὺν αὐτῷ
ὡς εἶδον προσθέοντας τοὺς ὁπλίτας, συγκλείουσι τὰς
1:16 πύλας καὶ τὸν μοχλὸν ἐμβάλλουσιν. οἱ δὲ στρατιῶται
ἔκοπτον τὰς πύλας καὶ ἔλεγον ὅτι ἀδικώτατα πάσχοιεν
ἐκβαλλόμενοι εἰς τοὺς πολεμίους· κατασχίσειν τε τὰς

---

* ὡς ... συγκλείσων ... ἐμβαλῶν: fut. part., purpose. * τὸν
μοχλὸν ἐμβαλῶν: 'to put the bar across'; gates were fastened by a
horizontal bar (μοχλός) passed through staples on each leaf, insert-
ed into a socket in one gatepost, and secured by a bolt (βάλανος).

1:13 κριθαὶ καὶ πυροὶ ... : see on κρέα ... ἐσθίοντες, 1:5:6 above.
* τἄλλα = τὰ ἄλλα, crasis.
Χερρόνησον: see on 1:1:9 above. * Κυνίσκος: a Spartan general
campaigning against the native Thracians.

1:14 Ἱεροῦ ὄρους: a natural barrier between Thrace and the Chersonese.
* κύκλῳ: (march) 'by a roundabout route'; the choice was between
a shorter but harder coastal route and a longer but easier one
inland.

1:15 ἐν ᾧ: 'while'. * θέουσι δρόμῳ: 'ran'. * ὡς εἰσιόντες: part. of
εἴσειμι (εἶμι 'go') in fut. sense, purpose.

1:16 ἀδικώτατα πάσχοιεν: 'they were being treated very unfairly'.
* εἰς τοὺς πολεμίους: 'into enemy country', a usage of the Ionic dialect.

1:17 πύλας ἔφασαν, εἰ μὴ ἐκόντες ἀνοίξουσιν. ἄλλοι δὲ
ἔθεον ἐπὶ θάλατταν καὶ παρὰ τὴν χηλὴν τοῦ τείχους
ὑπερβαίνουσιν εἰς τὴν πόλιν, ἄλλοι δὲ οἱ ἐτύγχανον
ἔνδον ὄντες τῶν στρατιωτῶν, ὡς ὁρῶσι τὰ ἐπὶ ταῖς πύ-
λαις πράγματα, διακόψαντες ταῖς ἀξίναις τὰ κλεῖθρα
1:18 ἀναπεταννύασι τὰς πύλας, οἱ δ' εἰσπίπτουσιν. ὁ δὲ
Ξενοφῶν ὡς εἶδε τὰ γιγνόμενα, δείσας μὴ ἐφ' ἀρπαγὴν
τράποιτο τὸ στράτευμα καὶ ἀνήκεστα κακὰ γένοιτο τῇ
πόλει καὶ αὑτῷ καὶ τοῖς στρατιώταις, ἔθει καὶ συνεισ-
1:19 πίπτει εἴσω τῶν πυλῶν σὺν τῷ ὄχλῳ. οἱ δὲ Βυζάντιοι
ὡς εἶδον τὸ στράτευμα βίᾳ εἰσπῖπτον, φεύγουσιν ἐκ
τῆς ἀγορᾶς, οἱ μὲν εἰς τὰ πλοῖα, οἱ δὲ οἴκαδε, ὅσοι
δὲ ἔνδον ἐτύγχανον ὄντες ἔξω, οἱ δὲ καθεῖλκον τὰς
τριήρεις, ὡς ἐν ταῖς τριήρεσι σῴζοιντο, πάντες δὲ
1:20 ᾤοντο ἀπολωλέναι, ὡς ἐαλωκυίας τῆς πόλεως. ὁ δὲ

εἰ μὴ ... ἀνοίξουσιν: see on τῇ στρατιᾷ ... , 4:7:3 above.
* ἐκόντες: 'voluntarily'; ἑκών is often used adverbially.

1:17 θάλατταν: no article, as often with natural objects; see on ὥσπερ
θάλαττα, 1:5:1 above. * παρὰ τὴν χηλὴν ... : 'used the breakwater which ran along the wall to climb over ... '; χηλήν, lit.
'hoof', i.e. a breakwater made of stones piled against the base
of the wall, to protect it from the waves (cf. Aristeus' action
at Poteidaia, Thucydides 1.63). * τῶν στρατιωτῶν: partitive gen.
after ἄλλοι. * ὡς: 'when'. * τὰ ... πράγματα: 'what was going
on' or 'the trouble'. * ταῖς ἀξίναις: 'with their axes'; chopping
wood was a regular fatigue; see on ἄλλην τινὰ ἀτέλειαν, 3:3:18
above. * τὰ κλεῖθρα: 'the bar' and its associated mechanism (see
on τὸν μοχλὸν ... , 1:12 above). * ἀναπεταννύασι: 3rd pers. plur.
of ἀναπετάννυμι. * οἱ δ(έ): 'and they' (see e.g. on ὁ δὲ πείθεται, 1:1:3 above).

1:18 αὑτῷ: Xenophon does not always use reflexive pronouns.

1:19 οἱ μὲν ... οἱ δέ: 'some ... others'. * ὅσοι: 'all those who';
ὅσος (ὅσοι) often means 'all that which', 'all those who'.
* ἔνδον: 'indoors'. * τριήρεις: undecked war-ships, measuring
about 120 by 20 feet, manned by up to 200 oarsmen, probably three
to a bench. * ὡς + opt.: purpose (Introduction 6.1); i.e. to
escape, not to launch an attack. * ἀπολωλέναι: 'that they were
done for', perf. inf. (mid. sense) of ἀπόλλυμι. * ὡς ἐαλωκυίας:
f. gen. perf. part. of ἁλίσκομαι, alleged reason.

Ἐτεόνικος εἰς τὴν ἄκραν ἀποφεύγει. ὁ δὲ Ἀναξίβιος
καταδραμὼν ἐπὶ θάλατταν ἐν ἀλιευτικῷ πλοίῳ περιέπλει
εἰς τὴν ἀκρόπολιν, καὶ εὐθὺς μεταπέμπεται ἐκ Καλχηδ-
όνος φρουρούς· οὐ γὰρ ἱκανοὶ ἐδόκουν εἶναι οἱ ἐν τῇ
1:21 ἀκροπόλει σχεῖν τοὺς ἄνδρας. οἱ δὲ στρατιῶται ὡς
εἶδον Ξενοφῶντα, προσπίπτουσι πολλοὶ αὐτῷ καὶ λέγ-
ουσι· Νῦν σοι ἔξεστιν, ὦ Ξενοφῶν, ἀνδρὶ γενέσθαι.
ἔχεις πόλιν, ἔχεις τριήρεις, ἔχεις χρήματα, ἔχεις
ἄνδρας τοσούτους. νῦν ἄν, εἰ βούλοιο, σύ τε ἡμᾶς
ὀνήσαις καὶ ἡμεῖς σὲ μέγαν ποιήσαιμεν.

1:22   *Xenophon's leadership and persuasive powers now became*
to   *more indispensable than ever. Finding himself master of Byz-*
8:9   *antion, he viewed with alarm the possibility of being at war*
        with Sparta and Persia at the same time. On his advice, the
        army resumed negotiations with Anaxibios and the successor
        to his command, Aristarkhos; but the latter had apparently
        brought instructions with him from Sparta to co-operate with
        Pharnabazos. Perhaps recalling the earlier fate of the gen-
        erals who negotiated with a Persian satrap, and mistrusting
        Aristarkhos, Xenophon and the army decided to take up Seuthes'
        offer of service in his pay.

        Xenophon gives a clear account of the meeting at which
        Seuthes made definite promises concerning payment of the Ten
                                                    (cont. over)

1:20 ἄκραν = ἀκρόπολιν: see on 1:6:6 above.
      Καλχηδόνος: Kalkhedon, perhaps named after the local murex (κάλχη,
      = πορφύρα, see on τοὺς πορφυροῦς κάνδυς, 1:5:8 above). * φρου-
      ρούς: see on διαβιβάσαι, 1:2 above.
      σχεῖν τοὺς ἄνδρας: 'to stop the soldiers'.

1:21 ἀνδρὶ: 'a (real) man' i.e. 'a hero', dat. agreeing with σοι; for
      the complimentary use of ἀνήρ, see on ὁ ἄνθρωπος, 5:8:8 above.
      ἔχεις: asyndeton and anaphora (see Introduction 6).
      ἄν ... ὀνήσαις ... ποιήσαιμεν: 'could (would) benefit ... could
      make'; potential opt. + ἄν.

      It is ironic that the Ten Thousand, after surviving the hostility
      of barbarian nations, should prove to be so unpopular with the
      Greek cities they encountered.

Thousand, and undertook to let them take refuge in his kingdom if the Spartans threatened their security. He also promised that the Greeks would never be more than 7 days' march
from the sea. Xenophon mentions more than once that his personal funds at this time were very low. After a feast cele-
brating their alliance, Seuthes and his new army set out on
a campaign against the neighbouring Thynoi and other tribes,
and won several engagements on both sides of the Bosporos,
taking much booty. But Seuthes gave the soldiers only 20 days'
pay after a month's campaigning. Relations between Xenophon
and Seuthes became cool, and the king evaded his attempts to
obtain an audience.

Meanwhile in Asia the Spartans under a new commander,
Thibron, were about to fight Tissaphernes, and needed as many
troops as they could muster. This change of Spartan policy
was welcomed by Seuthes, who hoped that the Ten Thousand would
be needed for the new war, and would thus cease to be his responsibility. Xenophon significantly records a conversation
between Seuthes and some Spartan envoys, in which the latter
asked what sort of a man Xenophon was, and Seuthes replied
that he was not a bad man, but was too much a friend of the
common soldier, with the consequence that he was not as well
off as he might have been. With this unsolicited testimonial
to his honesty and open-handedness, Xenophon prepares his readers for the verbal attacks on him which follow. As reported
by him, these attacks seem wholly unreasonable. They were led
by an unnamed Arkadian, who accused him of detaining the army
for his own gain. Xenophon was able to rebut this and other
charges easily by reminding his audience of the previous events.
He said frankly that he, like they, had hoped for enrichment
from his service with Seuthes; but, like them, he had been
frustrated by Seuthes' deceit.

Finally Xenophon, with a slightly improbable moral homily,
persuaded Seuthes to settle his debt in part; he paid 6000 drakhmai, six hundred oxen, and about four thousand sheep, which Xenophon handed over to the army. At their own request, he agreed
to lead them out of Thrace to join Thibron. He came first to
Lampsakos. There he was advised by Eukleides the soothsayer
that if he made a timely sacrifice to Zeus things would turn
out well for him. Soon after this his horse, which he had been
forced to sell in Lampsakos, was returned to him by two of his
fellow-officers. The army then marched over the Trojan Plain
and reached Pergamos in Mysia.

8:8   ἐνταῦθα δὴ ξενοῦται Ξενοφῶν παρ' Ἑλλάδι τῇ Γογγ-
       ύλου τοῦ Ἐρετριέως γυναικί καί Γοργίωνος καί Γογγύ-
8:9   λου μητρί. αὕτη αὐτῷ φράζει ὅτι Ἀσιδάτης ἐστίν ἐν
       τῷ πεδίῳ ἀνήρ Πέρσης· τοῦτον ἔφη αὐτόν, εἰ ἔλθοι τῆς
       νυκτός σύν τριακοσίοις ἀνδράσι, λαβεῖν ἄν καί αὐτόν
       καί γυναῖκα καί παῖδας καί τά χρήματα· εἶναι δέ πολ-
       λά. ταῦτα δέ καθηγησομένους ἔπεμψε τόν τε αὐτῆς ἀν-
       εψιόν καί Δαφναγόραν, ὅν περί πλείστου ἐποιεῖτο.
8:10   ἔχων οὖν ὁ Ξενοφῶν τούτους παρ' ἑαυτῷ ἐθύετο. καί
       Βασίας ὁ Ἡλεῖος μάντις παρών εἶπεν ὅτι κάλλιστα
8:11   εἶεν τά ἱερά αὐτῷ καί ὁ ἀνήρ ἄν ἁλώσιμος εἴη. δειπ-
       νήσας οὖν ἐπορεύετο τούς τε λοχαγούς τούς μάλιστα

8:8   ξενοῦται: see on ξένος, 1:1:10 above.
       παρ' Ἑλλάδι: 'at the house of Hellas' (παρά here = French chez).
       The elder Gongylos had been 'the only Eretrian to support Per-
       sia'; he was exiled, and given several Mysian towns by Xerxes;
       in about 477 B.C. he helped the renegade Spartan general Pausan-
       ias who was plotting to bring Greece under Persian control, with
       himself as ruler; he was now dead, and his wife Hellas lived on
       in Pergamos; one of his sons ruled Gambrion and Palaigambrion;
       the other Myrina and Gryneion (cf. Thucydides 1.128 and Xenophon,
       Hellenika 3.1.6).

8:9   πεδίῳ: the Kaïkos valley.
       τοῦτον: object of λαβεῖν. * αὐτόν, εἰ ἔλθοι ... λαβεῖν ἄν: remote
       fut. condition (in indir. speech). * εἶναι δέ πολλά: indir.
       speech continued.
       ταῦτα: 'in this enterprise', internal (adverbial) acc. * καθηγη-
       σομένους: fut. part., purpose. * αὐτῆς = ἑαυτῆς. * περί πλεί-
       στου ἐποιεῖτο: 'she thought very highly of'.

8:10   ἔχων: 'taking'. * ἐθύετο: 'proceeded to sacrifice', mid.; see on
       6:1:22 above. He sacrificed to Zeus the Gracious (Μειλίχιος) as
       one atoning for sin, in accordance with the advice of Eukleides.
       εἶεν: neuter plur. subject + plur. verb, irregular (see on ἅπαντα
       ἦσαν ... , 1:5:1, and on ἅρματα ἐφέροντο, 1:8:20 and on ὅπλα
       ἦσαν 2:5:38 above); τά ἱερά, see on καί τά ἱερά καλά, 1:8:15
       above. * ἄν ... εἴη: potential (in indir. speech).

8:11   δειπνήσας: δεῖπνον was the main meal of the day, eaten in the even-
       ing, or (probably as here) at mid-day.

φίλους λαβὼν καὶ πιστοὺς γεγενημένους διὰ παντός,
ὅπως εὖ ποιῆσαι αὐτούς. συνεξέρχονται δὲ αὐτῷ καὶ
ἄλλοι βιασάμενοι εἰς ἑξακοσίους· οἱ δὲ λοχαγοὶ ἀπήλαυνον, ἵνα μὴ μεταδοῖεν τὸ μέρος, ὡς ἑτοίμων δὴ
8:12 χρημάτων. ἐπεὶ δὲ ἀφίκοντο περὶ μέσας νύκτας, τὰ
μὲν πέριξ ὄντα ἀνδράποδα τῆς τύρσιος καὶ χρήματα τὰ
πλεῖστα ἀπέδρα αὐτοὺς παραμελοῦντας, ὡς τὸν Ἀσιδάτην
8:13 αὐτὸν λάβοιεν καὶ τὰ ἐκείνου. πυργομαχοῦντες δὲ ἐπεὶ
οὐκ ἐδύναντο λαβεῖν τὴν τύρσιν (ὑψηλὴ γὰρ ἦν καὶ μεγάλη καὶ προμαχεῶνας καὶ ἄνδρας πολλοὺς καὶ μαχίμους
8:14 ἔχουσα), διορύττειν ἐπεχείρησαν τὸν πύργον. ὁ δὲ
τοῖχος ἦν ἐπ' ὀκτὼ πλίνθων γηίνων τὸ εὖρος. ἅμα δὲ

---

* **λαβών**: 'with'; cf. ἔχων, 8:15, 8:17 and 8:19 below. * **διὰ**
παντός: 'throughout'. * **ποιῆσαι**: 3rd pers. sing. aor. opt. act.
(= ποιήσειε); they would receive a share of the booty.
βιασάμενοι: 'who had forced themselves (on him)'. * **εἰς**: 'up to',
'about', with numbers.
ἀπήλαυνον: imperf., repeated action. * **ἵνα μὴ** ... : lit. 'in order that they might not give the share, as though of actually
assured property' i.e. 'to avoid giving them their share of the
booty, as if they actually possessed it'; **μεταδοῖεν**, 3rd pers.
plur. aor. opt. of **μεταδίδωμι**; **ἑτοίμων** ... **χρημάτων**, partitive
gen. with μεταδοῖεν τὸ μέρος; **δή**, almost = 'already'.

8:12 **πέριξ** ... **τῆς τύρσιος**: **πέριξ**, strengthened form of **περί**, rare in
Attic prose (mostly Ionic); **τῆς τύρσιος**, Ionic gen. form (= Attic gen. -εως); he lived in a stronghold with a tower built on
to the wall. * **ἀνδράποδα** ... see on **ἀνδραπόδων**, 4:5:4 above;
χρήματα, 'livestock'. * **ἀπέδρα** ... : 3rd pers. sing. aor. indic. of **ἀποδιδράσκω**: this verb, which implies 'bolt' (as a run-
away slave), takes a dir. object of the thing one runs from;
παραμελοῦντας, 'as they took no notice of them'. * **ὡς** + opt.:
purpose (see Introduction 6.1). * **τὰ ἐκείνου**: 'his (personal)
property (or belongings).

8:13 **πυργομαχοῦντες δὲ** ... : **μεγάλη**, 'broad' or 'massive'; the Greeks
usually found siege warfare difficult (see *Oxford Classical Dictionary*, 'Siegecraft, Greek'); but see 4:7:1 - 12 above. Clearly
the Mysians were not always unwarlike; see on **ἀποστὰς εἰς Μυσούς**,
1:6:7 above.

8:14 **τοῖχος**: 'wall' of a building, as opposed to **τεῖχος** (town wall).
* **ἦν ἐπ' ὀκτὼ** ... : lit. 'was on eight earthen bricks in respect of thickness' i.e. 'had a thickness of eight clay bricks';
(cont.)

τῇ ἡμέρᾳ διωρώρυκτο· καὶ ὡς τὸ πρῶτον διεφάνη, ἐπάταξεν ἔνδοθεν βουπόρῳ τις ὀβελίσκῳ διαμπερὲς τὸν μηρὸν
τοῦ ἐγγυτάτω· τὸ δὲ λοιπὸν ἐκτοξεύοντες ἐποίουν μηδὲ
8:15 παριέναι ἔτι ἀσφαλὲς εἶναι. κεκραγότων δὲ αὐτῶν καὶ
πυρσευόντων ἐκβοηθοῦσιν Ἰταμένης μὲν ἔχων τὴν ἑαυτοῦ
δύναμιν, ἐκ Κομανίας δὲ ὁπλῖται Ἀσσύριοι καὶ Ὑρκάνιοι ἱππεῖς καὶ οὗτοι βασιλέως μισθοφόροι ὡς ὀγδοήκοντα, καὶ ἄλλοι πελτασταὶ εἰς ὀκτακοσίους, ἄλλοι δ'
ἐκ Παρθενίου, ἄλλοι δ' ἐξ Ἀπολλωνίας καὶ ἐκ τῶν πλη-
8:16 σίον χωρίων καὶ ἱππεῖς. ἐνταῦθα δὴ ὥρα ἦν σκοπεῖν πῶς
ἔσται ἡ ἄφοδος· καὶ λαβόντες ὅσοι ἦσαν βόες καὶ πρόβατα
ἤλαυνον καὶ τὰ ἀνδράποδα ἐντὸς πλαισίου ποιησάμενοι, οὐ
τοῖς χρήμασιν ἔτι προσέχοντες τὸν νοῦν, ἀλλὰ μὴ φυγὴ εἴη ἡ

bricks were made of clay (γήιναι, κεραμεαί), sun-dried or fire-
baked (ὀπταί); τὸ εὖρος, acc. of respect.]
διωρώρυκτο: pluperf. pass. of διορύττω.
ὡς τὸ πρῶτον διεφάνη: 'as soon as the light showed through'.
* ἐπάταξεν: emphatic position. * διαμπερὲς: mostly poetic
(Introduction 6.5).
τὸ λοιπὸν: adverbial acc. * ἐποίουν μηδὲ ... : 'made it no longer
safe even to go past'.

8:15 κεκραγότων ... : perf. with pres. meaning, gen. absolute; αὐτῶν,
Asidates and his household; πυρσευόντων: from πυρσός 'beacon',
the best means of long-distance communication in a siege (e.g.
at Plataia in 431 B.C.; Thucydides 3.22, where φρυκτός and its
compounds are used). * ἐκβοηθοῦσιν: from his own stronghold.
* Ἀσσύριοι καὶ Ὑρκάνιοι: these peoples had also accompanied
Xerxes' invading army in 480 B.C.; cf. Herodotus 7.62 - 63: 'The
Hyrkanoi, armed in the Persian manner, were led by Megapanos ...
The Assyrians ... had on their heads bronze helmets twisted after
a barbarian fashion not easy to describe; and they carried shields
and spears and daggers like the Egyptians', and wooden clubs as
well, studded with iron, and they wore corslets made of linen.'
* ὡς: 'about', with numbers (also εἰς, see on 8:11 above).
* καὶ ἱππεῖς: 'including cavalry'.

8:16 καὶ ἀνδράποδα: 'as well as slaves', previously ignored (see on 8:
12, and 4:5:4 above). * ἐντὸς πλαισίου ποιησάμενοι: 'putting
(them) inside a square formation'; see on ἐπορεύοντο τεταγμένοι,
3:3:6 above. * τοῖς χρήμασιν: 'the booty (itself)', emphatic
position. * μὴ ... εἴη ... εἶεν: opt., fear clauses after
προσέχοντες τὸν νοῦν. * φυγὴ: complement - no article (cont.)

ἄφοδος, εἰ καταλιπόντες τὰ χρήματα ἀπίοιεν, καὶ οἵ
τε πολέμιοι θρασύτεροι εἶεν καὶ οἱ στρατιῶται ἀθυμ-
ότεροι· νῦν δὲ ἀπῆσαν ὡς περὶ τῶν χρημάτων μαχούμενοι.

8:17 ἐπεὶ δὲ ἑώρα Γογγύλος ὀλίγους μὲν τοὺς ῞Ελληνας, πολλοὺς δὲ τοὺς ἐπικειμένους, ἐξέρχεται καὶ αὐτὸς βίᾳ
τῆς μητρὸς ἔχων τὴν ἑαυτοῦ δύναμιν, βουλόμενος συμ-
μετασχεῖν τοῦ ἔργου· συνεβοήθει δὲ καὶ Προκλῆς ἐξ

8:18 Ἀλισάρνης καὶ Τευθρανίας ὁ ἀπὸ Δαμαράτου. οἱ δὲ περὶ
Ξενοφῶντα ἐπεὶ πάνυ ἤδη ἐπιέζοντο ὑπὸ τῶν τοξευμάτων

(ἡ ἄφοδος is subject of εἴη).⌉ * εἰ ... ἀπίοιεν: 3rd pers. pl.
opt. of ἄπειμι (εἶμι 'go'), fut. condition in virtual indir.
speech, depending on idea of 'fear' (historic sequence), = ἐάν
ἀπίωμεν of dir. speech. The men would have to keep their ranks
and march steadily - they had something to lose by running; for
Xenophon's experience of morale and discipline in retreat, cf.
Books 3 and 4.
νῦν δέ: 'but as it was'. * ὡς μαχούμενοι:'like (men) ready to
fight' (fut. part.).

8:17 ὀλίγους: sc. ὄντας, acc. and part. construction after ἑώρα.
* ἐπικειμένους: 'at their heels'; ἐπίκειμαι 'attack' a retreat-
ing enemy (lit. 'lie upon'). * καὶ αὐτὸς βίᾳ ... : 'he himself
also ... against his mother's will'.
ὁ ἀπὸ Δαμαράτου: 'the descendant of Damaratos', mentioned in Book
2 as having informed the Ten Thousand at Kounaxa that Kyros had
been killed. Damaratos, joint king of Sparta with Kleomenes
(Sparta had a dual kingship), had opposed his colleague's inter-
ference in Athenian affairs and his hostility to Dareios I (Herodotus 5.70 - 75 and 6.50 - 51); Kleomenes got him dethroned and
he fled to Persia in 491 B.C. (Herodotus 6.61 - 67), where Dareios
'gave him land and cities' (Herodotus 6.70). On his advice Dareios made Xerxes heir to the throne; he warned the Greeks of Dareios' invasion plans, but in 480 accompanied Xerxes, no doubt hoping to regain the throne, and gave him useful advice (Herodotus
7.101 - 104, 209, 234 - 235 and 239). He and his descendants
lived on in Asia, including Prokles and his co-ruler Eurysthenes;
Teuthrania and Halisarna were towns given to Damaratos as a reward
by Xerxes (cf. Xenophon, Hellenika 3.1.6); for a somewhat similar
career, see on παρ᾽ ῾Ελλάδι, 8:8 above.

8:18 οἱ ... περὶ Ξενοφῶντα: 'Xenophon and his men'. * τοξευμάτων ...
σφενδονῶν: for archers and slingers, see especially 3:3:6 - 18
above.

καὶ σφενδονῶν, πορευόμενοι κύκλῳ, ὅπως τά ὅπλα ἔχοιεν πρὸ τῶν τοξευμάτων, μόλις διαβαίνουσι τὸν Κάρ-
8:19 κασον ποταμόν, τετρωμένοι ἐγγὺς οἱ ἡμίσεις. ἐνταῦθα
καὶ Ἀγασίας ὁ Στυμφάλιος λοχαγὸς τιτρώσκεται, τὸν
πάντα χρόνον μαχόμενος πρὸς τοὺς πολεμίους. καὶ δια-
σῴζονται ἀνδράποδα ὡς διακόσια ἔχοντες καὶ πρόβατα
8:20 ὅσον θύματα. τῇ δὲ ὑστεραίᾳ θυσάμενος ὁ Ξενοφῶν ἐξ-
άγει νύκτωρ πᾶν τὸ στράτευμα, ὅπως ὅτι μακροτάτην
ἔλθοι τῆς Λυδίας, εἰς τὸ μὴ διὰ τὸ ἐγγὺς εἶναι φοβ-
8:21 εῖσθαι, ἀλλ' ἀφυλακτεῖν. ὁ δὲ Ἀσιδάτης ἀκούσας ὅτι
πάλιν ἐπ' αὐτὸν τεθυμένος εἴη ὁ Ξενοφῶν καὶ παντὶ τῷ
στρατεύματι ἥξοι, ἐξαυλίζεται εἰς κώμας ὑπὸ τὸ Παρ-
8:22 θένιον πόλισμα ἐχούσας. ἐνταῦθα οἱ περὶ Ξενοφῶντα

* πορευόμενοι κύκλῳ: 'wheeling round'. * ὅπλα: 'shields';
see on ἐξοπλίζεσθαι, 1:8:3 above. * πρὸ: 'facing', 'as a defence against', a rare usage. * οἱ ἡμίσεις: with οἱ ... περὶ
Ξενοφῶντα, nom. of whole and part.

8:19 καὶ Ἀγασίας: 'Agasias ... also'; for Agasias, see 4:7:9 - 12 above.
* τὸν πάντα χρόνον: acc. of time throughout which.
πρόβατα ὅσον θύματα: lit. 'sheep as much as sacrificial victims'
i.e. 'enough sheep for sacrifices'.

8:20 ὅπως ὅτι ... : 'in order to get as far as possible into Lydia';
see on ὅτι ἀπαρασκευότατον, 1:1:6 above; μακροτάτην, sc. ὁδόν,
acc. of extent of space; τῆς Λυδίας, partitive gen. * εἰς τὸ
... : lit. 'for the purpose of (Asidates') not fearing (them)
because of (their) being near, but being off his guard' i.e.
'hoping that Asidates would stop worrying about their proximity
and drop his guard'; τό + inf., verbal noun.

8:21 ἀκούσας: 'on being told'; ἀκούω, although a verb of perceiving
(usually + acc. and part.), regularly takes ὅτι construction
(indir. statement) in this sense. * ἐπ' αὐτὸν τεθυμένος εἴη:
'had made the sacrifices preliminary to attacking him'; ἐπί(ὶ),
indicating both intention and hostility; τεθυμένος εἴη, perf.
opt. mid. of θύω (see on ἐθύετο, 6:1:22 above). * παντὶ τῷ
στρατεύματι: 'with ... ', dat. of association. * ἥξοι: 'would
(soon) be there', fut. opt. of ἥκω. * ἐχούσας: 'situated';
cf. adverb + ἔχω 'be in ... condition'.

περιτυγχάνουσιν αὐτῷ καὶ λαμβάνουσιν αὐτὸν καὶ γυν-
αῖκα καὶ παῖδας καὶ τοὺς ἵππους καὶ πάντα τὰ ὄντα·
8:23 καὶ οὕτω τὰ πρότερα ἱερὰ ἀπέβη. ἔπειτα πάλιν ἀφικνοῦνται εἰς Πέργαμον. ἐνταῦθα τὸν θεὸν ἠσπάσατο Ξε-
νοφῶν· συνέπραττον γὰρ καὶ οἱ Λάκωνες καὶ οἱ λοχαγοὶ
καὶ οἱ ἄλλοι στρατηγοὶ καὶ οἱ στρατιῶται ὥστ' ἐξαίρετα
λαβεῖν καὶ ἵππους καὶ ζεύγη καὶ τἄλλα, ὥστε ἱκανὸν εἶναι καὶ ἄλλον ἤδη εὖ ποιεῖν.
8:24 ἐκ τούτου Θίβρων παραγενόμενος παρέλαβε τὸ στράτευμα καὶ συμμείξας τῷ ἄλλῳ Ἑλληνικῷ ἐπολέμει πρὸς
Τισσαφέρνη καὶ Φαρνάβαζον.

8:22 περιτυγχάνουσιν: implies 'accidentally', 'luckily'. * τὰ πρότερα
ἱερὰ ἀπέβη: 'the omens from the earlier sacrifice turned out to
be right'; see on ἐθύετο, 8:10 above.

8:23 ἠσπάσατο: i.e. hailed him as truly Μειλίχιος (see on ἐθύετο, 8:10
above).
συνέπραττον: 'arranged between them', emphatic position. * καὶ
οἱ Λάκωνες: 'both the Spartans'; Xenophon had not always been on
the best of terms with them (see on προδῶ, 3:1:14 above), and
there had been tension between him and Kheirisophos (see on τοὺς
στρατηγούς, 1:3 above and references given there). * ὥστ' ἐξαίρετα ... : lit. 'so that (he) got (as) selected (things) both
... ' i.e. (arranged) 'that he got the pick both of the ... ';
normally booty was assigned by lot, and shared equally among men
of the same rank. * ζεύγη: pairs of mules or oxen, with or
without their carts. * τἄλλα = τὰ ἄλλα (crasis). * ἱκανὸν
εἶναι ... : 'he was now able to benefit someone else as well';
it was shameful to end a campaign no richer than one began; for
wealth enabling one to benefit others (and fulfil one's obliga-
tions), see on ἀλεξόμενος, 1:9:11 and τὸ μὲν τὰ μεγάλα, 1:9:24
above (Kyros), on ἱκανὸς νομίσας, 2:6:17 above (Proxenos), and
5:3:9 - 12 above (Xenophon himself); cf. also Thucydides 2.40
(Funeral Speech) and Plato, Republic 1.331 a - b).

8:24 ἐκ τούτου: 'then'. * Θίβρων: see link passage introducing 8:8 ff.
above. * παραγενόμενος παρέλαβε: 'arrived and took over'.
τῷ ἄλλῳ Ἑλληνικῷ: 'his other Greek forces', another radical change
of Spartan policy (see on μισθοφοράν, 1:3 above). Thibron also
gained the alliance of Gorgion and Gongylos.

For Xenophon's service under Thibron, see Hellenika 3.1.3 - 8; and for his later career, see on 5:3:5 - 13 above and Hellenika 3.1.9 - 4.4.1.

Finally, for two contrary assessments of the march of the Ten Thousand, contrast the following: (a) C. L. Brownson (Loeb translation, 1922): 'Defeating with scarcely an effort Persian forces many times their number, and accomplishing a safe return despite all the efforts of Artaxerxes to hinder them, they revealed to all men the utter weakness of the ... Persian Empire ... . Xenophon's account reveals to us most clearly the fine qualities of these Greek soldiers of fortune - their courage and endurance, piety and humanity, independence and reasonableness'.
(b) G. Cawkwell (Introduction to R. Warner's Penguin Translation, 1972): 'Tissaphernes made no real attempt to block their passage. So their march from the Zab up the Tigris was no great feat and proved nothing about Persian military power ... . The Ten Thousand were a gang of roughs ... (who) took to war out of poverty, and menaced the peace and prosperity of Greece'.

Gold daric (δαρεικός, see on 1:1:9 above) showing archer with bow and spear. He wears a long robe (κάνδυς, see on 1:5:8 above) and notched head-dress (cidaris or tiara; see on 1:8:6 above), which suggests that he represents the King.

Coin probably minted in the reign of Dareios III (337 - 330 B.C.) but the type had remained very similar since the early 5th century.

VOCABULARY

*Abbreviations used are the same as those in the Notes and are
listed after the Preface. The Latinized form of proper names has sometimes been added in brackets, when it is commonly found in reference
books and differs significantly from the Greek form.*

A

Ἄβυδος -ου f., Abydos
ἀγαθός, good; brave; noble;
  ἀγαθὸν ποιέω + acc., benefit.
ἀγάλλομαι ἐπί + dat., glory in,
  take pleasure in.
ἄγαμαι, ἠγάσθην, admire.
ἀγαστός, admirable.
ἀγείρω, ἤγειρα, assemble.
ἀ-γένειος -ον, beardless, boyish.
Ἀγησίλαος, Agesilaos.
Ἀγίας, Agias.
ἀγνοέω, not know.
ἀγορά, market; market-place.
ἀγρεύω, catch (by hunting).
ἄγριος, wild.
ἀγρός, land.
ἄγω, ἄξω, ἤγαγον, bring, carry,
  lead, take;
  εἰρήνην ἄγω, be at peace, live
  peaceably;
  ἡσυχίαν ἄγω, be at peace, live
  quietly.
ἀγών -ῶνος m., contest, games,
  sports.
ἀγωνίζομαι, compete in.
ἀδεῶς, fearlessly.
ἀδελφός, brother.
ἄ-δηλος -ον, uncertain.
ἀδικέω, do harm to, injure; be a
  lawbreaker, do wrong.
ἀδικία, injustice;
  μετὰ ἀδικίας, unjustly.
ἄ-δικος -ον, unfair, unjust, harm-
  ful;
  ἐκ τοῦ ἀδίκου, by unjust means,
  illegally.
ἀεί, always; at any one time.
ἀετός, eagle.
ἄ-θεος -ον (sup. -ώτατος), godless.
Ἀθῆναι, Athens.
Ἀθηναῖος, Athenian, of Athens.

ἀθροίζω, gather, recruit; (mid.)
  be gathered, muster.
ἀθρόος, keeping together, in a
  group.
ἀθυμία, despondency.
ἄ-θυμος -ον (comp. -ότερος; adv.
  -ως), despondent, disheartened.
Αἰγύπτιος, Egyptian.
αἰδήμων (sup. αἰδημονέστατος),
  modest, well-behaved.
αἰδώς -οῦς f., shame; respect.
αἴθω, burn.
αἰκίζομαι, ἠκίσθην, torture.
Αἰνέας, Aineas (Aeneas).
αἴξ, αἰγός m./f., goat.
αἱρέω, εἷλον (ἑλ-), ᾑρέθην, capture;
  (mid.) choose.
αἴρω, hoist, lift, raise.
αἰσθάνομαι, αἰσθήσομαι, ᾐσθόμην, be/
  become aware, notice, realise, see.
αἰσχρός, disgraceful, shameful.
αἰσχύνη, shame.
αἰσχύνομαι + acc., be ashamed/feel
  shame before.
αἰτέω (+ double acc.), ask for.
αἰτιάομαι, criticise, find fault
  with, reproach, reprove.
αἴτιος + gen., responsible for.
αἰχμ-άλωτος -ον, captured.
ἀκινάκης, dagger.
ἀκινδύνως, without danger.
ἀ-κόλαστος -ον, unpunished, undisciplined.
ἀκοντίζω, throw javelin at, strike.
ἀκόντισις -εως f., throwing the
  javelin.
ἀκοντιστής, javelin-thrower.
ἀκούω (+ gen. of source), hear;
  hear about; listen to, obey.
ἄκρα, citadel.
ἄκρον, top.
ἀκρόπολις -εως f., citadel.
ἄκων -ουσα -ον, unwilling (accidentally).

ἀλέξομαι, requite, give like for like.

ἀλέτης, grinder.

ἄλευρα n.pl., wheat flour.

ἀλήθεια, truth.

ἀλήθης, true.

ἀληθινός, genuine, real.

ἀλιευτικός, for fishing.

Ἀλίσαρνα, Halisarna.

ἀλίσκομαι, ἑάλωκα, be caught, be captured.

ἀλλά, but;
  ἀλλὰ μήν, well, really.

ἀλλαχοῦ, elsewhere.

ἀλλήλους, each other, one another.

ἄλλοθεν, from another side.

ἄλλος -η -ο, other; another; else; rest (of); (pl. as noun) others.

ἄλσος -ους n., grove.

ἄλφιτα n.pl., barley meal.

ἁλώσιμος, easy to capture.

ἅμα, at the same time;
  ἅμα τῇ ἡμέρᾳ, at daybreak.

ἅμαξα, cart; cart-load.

ἀμύνομαι, ἀμυνοῦμαι, defend oneself.

ἀμφί + acc., about, around;
  + gen., about, concerning.

ἀμφι-γνοέω, ἠμφ-εγνόουν, be puzzled.

Ἀμφιπολίτης, (citizen) of Amphipolis.

ἀμφότερος, both; (pl.) both sides.

ἀμφοτέρωθεν, on both sides.

ἄμφω, both.

ἄν + subj., ever (indefinite);
  + opt., would (potential).

ἄν (= ἐάν) + subj., if.

ἀνά + acc., up;
  ἀνὰ κράτος, with all one's strength.

ἀνα-βαίνω, -έβην (part. -βάς), go up, go inland; get up, mount.

ἀνα-βιβάζω, lead up.

ἀνα-γιγνώσκω -έγνων (part. -γνούς), read; recognise.

ἀναγκάζω, compel, force.

ἀναγκαῖος, necessary.

ἀνάγκη, necessity, compulsion.
  ἀνάγκη ἐστι, it is necessary.

ἀν-άγω, -ήχθην, lead (up).

ἀνάθημα -ατος n., votive offering.

ἀν-αιρέω, -εῖλον, (of oracle) answer, give response, ordain.

ἀνα-κοινάω, (& mid.) + dat., communicate with, consult.

ἀνα-κομίζομαι, -κεκόμισμαι, take away with one.

ἀνα-κράζω, -έκραγον, shout.

ἀνα-λαμβάνω, -έλαβον, pick up, take with one.

ἀν-αλίσκω, -αλώσω, -ήλωσα, use up, exhaust supply of.

ἀνα-μένω, wait for.

ἀνα-μιμνήσκω, -μνήσω (+ double acc.), remind of; (pass.) remember.

ἄν-ανδρος -ον, unmanly.

Ἀναξίβιος, Anaxibios.

ἀναξυρίδες f.pl., trousers.

ἀνα-πετάννυμι, throw open.

ἀνα-πτύσσω, deploy.

ἀν-αρίθμητος -ον, countless.

ἀν-αρπάζω, -ήρπασα, grab.

ἀνα-στρέφω, -έστρεψα, -εστράφην, turn/wheel round; (pass.) rally.

ἀνα-τείνω, stretch out, extend;
  ἀνατεταμένος, spread.

ἀνα-τίθημι, offer up, dedicate.

ἀνα-χάζομαι, draw back.

ἀνα-χωρέω, retreat.

ἀνδράποδον, slave.

ἀν-εγείρω, -ηγέρθην, wake up (trans.); (pass.) wake up (intrans.).

ἄνεμος, wind.

ἄνευ + gen., without.

ἀν-έχομαι, ἠν-εσχόμην, face boldly, face up to; contain oneself.

ἀνεψιός, cousin.

ἀν-ήκεστος -ον, irreparable.

ἀνήρ, ἀνδρός m., man; (pl.) soldiers, troops.

ἄνθρωπος, man, mortal; (pl.) inhabitants, population, people.

ἀνιάω, annoy; hurt.

ἀν-ίστημι, put up, flush; (mid. & intrans.) stand up, recover.

ἀν-οίγνυμι, -οίξω, open.

ἀντ-αγοράζω, buy in exchange.

ἀντί + gen., instead of; facing.

ἀντι-δίδωμι, replace with.

ἀντι-καθ-ίστημι, appoint instead.

ἀντι-λέγω μή + inf., object to.

ἀντίος, (adj.) opposite; facing; to meet; (pl. as noun) the other side, the enemy;
  ἐκ τοῦ ἀντίου, in front.

ἀντίπερας: κατ' ἀντίπερας + gen., opposite.

ἀντι-ποιέω, do in return; (mid. + gen.) be a rival for.

ἀντιστασιώτης, political opponent.

ἀντι-τάττω, -ετάχθην, draw up against.

ἀντι-τοξεύω, shoot back.

ἀνυστός -ον, possible.

ἄνω, up, inland.

ἄνωθεν, from above.

ἀξίνη, axe.

ἄξιος, worthy.

ἀξιόω, ask, claim, expect, maintain; (+ inf.) think worthy.

ἄξω: ἄγω.

ἄξων -ονος m., axle.

ἀπ-αγγέλλω, -ήγγειλα, report (back), deliver (message).

ἀπ-αγορεύω, tire, get tired.

ἀπ-άγω, -ήγαγον, lead off; carry off; bring back.

ἀ-παίδευτος -ον, uneducated, ignorant.

ἀπ-αιτέω, demand; ask for (something) back.

ἀπ-αλλάττομαι, -ηλλάγην, come off.

ἁπαλος, tender.

ἅπαξ, once.

ἀ-παρασκεύαστος -ον, unprepared.

ἀ-παράσκευος -ον, unprepared.

ἅπας ἅπασα ἅπαν, all, entire.

ἀπ-έδρα: ἀπο-διδράσκω.

ἀπειθέω, disobey.

ἄπ-ειμι (εἰμί 'be'), be away.

ἄπ-ειμι (εἶμι 'go'), depart, go away; desert.

ἀπ-ελαύνω, drive off; ride off.

ἀπ-έρχομαι, -ῆλθον (-ελθ-), depart, go away, leave; desert.

ἀπ-εχθάνομαι, be hated.

ἀπ-έχομαι, ἀφ-έξομαι + gen., keep one's hands off.

ἀπ-ῄτουν: ἀπ-αιτέω.

ἀπιστέω + dat., disobey.

ἀπιτέον ἐστι, one must depart.

ἁπλοῦς -ῆ -οῦν (-όος), frank, sincere, straightforward.

ἀπό + gen., from;
    ἀπό τούτου, from that time on.

ἀπο-βαίνω, -έβην, succeed, prove true.

ἀπο-βάλλω, -έβαλον, throw away, lose.

ἀπο-βλέπω (εἰς + acc.), look (at).

ἀπο-δείκνυμι, -έδειξα, appoint; show, produce.

ἀπο-δέχομαι, accept.

ἀπο-διδράσκω, -έδραν + acc., run away from.

ἀπο-δίδωμι, give back.

ἀπο-θνῄσκω, -θανοῦμαι, -έθανον, die; be killed; be put to death.

ἀπο-θύω, duly offer up (sacrifice).

ἄποικος, colony.

ἀπο-καίω, (of cold) blast, penetrate.

ἀπο-κάμνω, be tired out.

ἀπο-κρίνομαι, -εκρινάμην, answer, reply.

ἀπο-κτείνω, -κτενῶ, -έκτεινα, kill, put to death.

ἀπο-λαμβάνω, -έλαβον, get back.

ἀπο-λείπω, leave (behind).

ἀπ-όλλυμι, -ώλεσα, -ολώλεκα, destroy, kill, ruin; (mid. & intrans.) -ωλόμην, -όλωλα, die, perish.

Ἀπόλλων -ωνος acc. -ω m., Apollo.

Ἀπολλωνία, Apollonia.

ἀπο-πέμπω, -πέμψω, dismiss, send away; remit; (mid.) get rid of.

ἀπορέομαι, be unsure what to do; (+ inf.) be unsure how to.

ἀπορία, difficulty, difficult situation.

ἀπό-ρ-ρητος -ον, secret.

ἀπο-σήπομαι, -σέσηπα, lose through gangrene.

ἀπο-σπάω, draw away.

ἀπο-στρέφω, turn back.

ἀπο-τείνομαι, extend (intrans.); ἀποτεταμένος, extending.

ἀπο-τέμνω, -ετμήθην, cut off.

ἀπό-τομος -ον, precipitous, steep.

ἀπο-φαίνω, -έφηνα, declare, disclose.

ἀπο-φεύγω, escape.

ἀπο-χωρέω, withdraw.

ἀπροφασίστως, without making excuses.

ἀπ-ών: ἄπ-ειμι (εἰμί 'be').

Ἀραβία, Arabia.

ἀργυροῦς -ᾶ -οῦν (-εος), silver.

ἀργύριον, money.

ἄρδην, utterly;
ἄρδην πάντες, all together.
ἀρετή, courage, valour.
ἀρήγω, relieve.
Ἀριαῖος, Ariaios (Ariaeus).
ἀριθμός, a count.
ἀριστάω, have breakfast.
Ἀρίστιππος, Aristippos.
ἄριστος (sup. of ἀγαθός), best, noblest; (pl. as noun) nobles.
Ἀριστώνυμος, Aristomymos.
Ἀρκάς -άδος, Arkadian, of Arkadia.
ἀρκεῖ + dat. or πρός + acc., it is enough for.
ἄρκτος -ου f., bear.
ἅρμα -ατος n., chariot.
ἁρπαγή, looting.
ἁρπάζω, loot; seize.
Ἀρταγέρσης, Artagerses.
Ἀρταξέρξης, Artaxerxes.
Ἀρτάοζος, Artaozos.
Ἀρταπάτης, Artapates.
Ἄρτεμις -ιδος f., Artemis.
ἄρτος, loaf.
ἀρχαῖος, old;
τὸ ἀρχαῖον (adv.), formerly, originally.
ἀρχή, command; province; empire.
ἀρχικός, able to command.
ἄρχω, ἄρξω + gen., begin, open; command, be in command of, rule; (mid.) begin.
ἄρχων -οντος m., commander, general, ruler.
ἄρωμα -ατος n., spice.
ἀσθενέω, be ill.
ἀσθενής, weak.
Ἀσία, Asia (Minor).
Ἀσιδάτης, Asidates.
Ἀσιναῖος, of Asine.
ἀσπάζομαι, ἠσπασάμην, greet, pay one's respects to.
ἀσπίς -ίδος f., shield.
Ἀσσύριος, Assyrian, from Assyria.
ἀστράπτω, flash.
ἀσφαλής (sup. -έστατος), safe.
ἄ-τακτος -ον, in disorder, not drawn up.
ἀταξία, indiscipline, bad discipline.
ἅτε + part., because.
ἀτέλεια, exemption.

ἀτιμάζω, dishonour, insult.
ἀτμίζω, steam.
Ἀττικός, Attic, Athenian.
αὖ, again; also, as well, too; on the other hand, in one's turn, for one's part.
αὖθις, again.
αὐτίκα, at once, immediately.
αὐτόθεν, from there.
αὐτόθι, right here.
αὐτοκράτωρ -ορος adj., (of power) absolute, unrestricted.
αὐτομολέω, desert.
αὐτόν etc. = ἑαυτόν etc.
αὐτός (pron. & adj.), (he) himself etc.;
(pron., all cases but nom.), him etc., (gen.) his etc.;
ὁ αὐτός (+ dat.), the same (as).
αὐτόσε, to that (very) place, there.
ἀφανής, unseen; secret; doubtful.
ἀφανίζω, ἀφανιῶ, wipe out.
ἀφειδής (sup. adv. -έστατα), unsparing, merciless, ruthless.
ἀφ-έξεσθαι: ἀπ-έχομαι.
ἀφθονία, abundance.
ἀφ-ικνέομαι -ίξομαι -ικόμην, come; (ἐπί, εἰς, πρός + acc.) arrive at.
ἀφ-ίσταμαι, revolt, go over; (+ gen.) leave.
ἄφοδος -ου f., retreat.
ἀφυλακτέω, be off one's guard.
ἀ-φύλακτος -ον, unguarded.
Ἀχαιός, Akhaian, of Akhaia (Achaea).
ἄχθομαι, be annoyed, object.
ἀψίνθιον, wormwood.

B

Βαβυλών -ῶνος f., Babylon.
βάδην, at a walk.
βάθος -ους n., depth.
βακτηρία, stick.
βάλλω, hit (with missile).
βαρβαρικός, non-Greek, native.
βάρβαρος -ον, non-Greek, native.
Βασίας, Basias.
βασιλεία, kingdom.
βασίλειος, royal.
βασιλεύς, king; (no article) the King (of Persia).
βασιλεύω, be king.

βασιλικός (sup. -ώτατος), kingly.
βέβαιος, reliable.
βέλος -ους n., missile.
βελτιστός (sup. of ἀγαθός), best.
βῆμα -ατος n., step.
βία, force;
   βίᾳ + gen., against the will of.
βιάζομαι, ἐβιασάμην, force one's
   way.
βιαίως adv., hard.
βῖκος, cask.
βίος, life.
βλάβη, harm, injury.
βλάπτω, ἔβλαψα, damage, harm.
βλέπω (εἰς + acc.), face, point
   (towards).
βοάω, shout.
βόες: βοῦς.
βοή, shout.
βοηθέω, come and help.
βόθρος, hole.
Βοιώτιος, Boiotian (Boeotian), of
   Boiotia (Boeotia).
Βοιωτός, a Boiotian (Boeotian).
βορρᾶς -ᾶ m., north wind.
βουλεύομαι, consider, consult,
   discuss.
βουλιμιάω, suffer from starvation.
βούλομαι, want, wish, be willing.
βου-πόρος -ον, for roasting oxen.
βοῦς βοός m./f., ox; cow; (pl.)
   cattle.
βραδέως, slowly.
βραχύς (comp. -ύτερος), short.
βροντή, thunder.
βρωτός, edible.
Βυζάντιον, Byzantion (Byzantium).
Βυζάντιος, Byzantine.
βωμός, altar.

Γ

γάρ (2nd word), for;
   καὶ γάρ, for in fact;
   καὶ γὰρ οὖν, and consequently.
γαστήρ γαστρός f., stomach.
γαυλιτικός, of merchant ships.
γε (enclitic), at any rate;
   ὅς γε, since he;
   γε μήν, furthermore;
   μήν ... γε, all the same.
γέλως -ωτος m., laughter.

γενεά, birth.
γενειάω, get a beard.
γένος -ους n., birth.
γέρρον, wicker shield.
γερροφόροι, troops with wicker
   shields.
γεύομαι + gen., taste, have a
   taste of.
γῆ, ground; land.
γήινος, made of earth, clay.
γήλοφος, hill.
γίγνομαι, γενήσομαι, ἐγενόμην, γέ-
   γονα, γεγένημαι, be born; accrue,
   become, come, ensue, form, get;
   happen, occur, proceed, prove; be;
   γίγνεται, it is possible.
γιγνώσκω, ἔγνων, know; learn; recognise; think, be of an opinion.
Γλοῦς -ου m., Glous (Glus).
γνώμη, intention, plan; opinion; inclination; thought;
γνώμῃ, deliberately.
Γογγύλος, Gongylos.
Γοργίας, Gorgias.
Γοργίων -ωνος m., Gorgion.
γράμματα n.pl., words, inscription.
γράφω, γέγραμμαι, write.
Γυμνίας, Gymnias.
γυμνικός, athletic, sporting.
γυμνός, not fully dressed.
γυνή γυναικός f., woman; wife.

Δ

δακρύω, weep.
δακτύλιος, ring.
δάκτυλος, finger.
Δαμάρατος, Damaratos (Demaratus).
δαπανάω ἀμφί/εἰς + acc., spend
   money on.
δάπεδον, ground.
Δαρδανεύς, of Dardanos.
δαρεικός, daric (coin).
Δαρεῖος, Dareios (Darius).
δασμός and pl., tribute.
δασύς, hairy; thickly covered;
   overgrown; τὸ δασύ, thicket.
Δαφναγόρας, Daphnagoras.
δέ (2nd word), and; but; whereas,
   on the other hand.
δέδοικα or δέδια (perf. form; no
   pres.), ἔδεισα, fear, become

178

afraid.
δεῖ (subj. δέη) + acc. & inf., it is necessary (have to, must); + gen., there is need of.
δείκνυμι, ἔδειξα, point out.
δείλη, late afternoon.
δεινός, dreadful, terrible; τὸ δεινόν, danger.
δειπνέω, have dinner.
δέκα, ten.
δεκατεύω, pay as tithe.
δέκατος, tenth; δεκάτη (sc. μερίς), tithe.
Δελφοί, Delphoi (Delphi).
δένδρον, tree.
δεξιός, right; ἡ δεξιά (sc. χείρ), right hand, right.
δέομαι, ἐδεήθην, need; request; (+ gen.) be in need of.
δέρμα -ατος n., hide.
δεσπότης, master.
δεῦρο, here (to this place).
δεύτερον adv., for the second time.
δέχομαι, accept; receive; wait for.
δή (emphasising preceding word), indeed, of course; ὅστις δή, someone or other; (connecting particle), so.
δῆλος, clear, evident.
δηλόω, demonstrate, show.
διά + acc., because of; + gen., across, through.
Δί-α -ί -ός: Ζεύς.
δια-βαίνω -έβην, cross (over).
δια-βάλλω, accuse falsely; slander.
δια-βιβάζω -εβίβασα, carry across.
δι-αγγέλλω -ήγγειλα, report back.
δια-γελάω, laught at, mock.
δια-γίγνομαι -εγενόμην, get through, live, survive; (+ part.) continue.
δι-αγωνίζομαι πρός + acc., compete with.
δια-δέχομαι, recieve in succession.
διαδεχόμενοι, in relays.
δια-δίδωμι, distribute.
δι-έρχομαι -ήλθον (-ελθ-), cross.
διά-κειμαι (+ adv.), be in a certain state, feel.

δια-κελεύομαι + dat., direct, urge.
δια-κόπτω, cut to pieces; cut through.
διακόσιοι, two hundred.
δια-κρίνω, -έκρινα, decide.
δια-λαμβάνω, -έλαβον, divide up.
δια-λέγομαι, -ελέχθην (+ dat.), discuss (with).
δια-λείπω, leave intervals between.
διαμπερές, right through.
δια-νοέομαι, think over.
δια-πέμπω, send in all directions; (+ dat.) distribute among.
δια-πράττομαι, -επραξάμην + acc. & inf., obtain one's aim, manage to get.
δι-αρπάζω, loot.
δια-ρ-ρέω, flow through.
δια-ρ-ρίπτω, -έρριψα, throw in all directions.
διάρριψις -εως f., a throwing in all directions.
δια-σπάω, -έσπασμαι, disperse, separate.
δια-σπείρω, scatter, separate.
δια-σῴζομαι, come through safely.
δια-τελέω, continue, press on.
δια-τήκομαι, melt away.
δια-τίθημι, treat, deal with.
δια-τρίβω, delay.
δια-φαίνομαι, -εφάνην, show through.
διαφανῶς, distinctly, quite clearly.
δια-φέρομαι, quarrel.
διαφερόντως, especially.
δια-φθείρω, -έφθαρμαι, destroy.
δια-χειρίζομαι, administer, manage.
διδάσκαλος, teacher.
δίδωμι, give; (cf. δίκη).
δι-ελαύνω, -ήλασα, ride through.
δι-έρχομαι, -ήλθον, cover (distance).
δι-έχω, -εῖχον, -έσχον (+ gen.), be distant (from).
δι-ίσταμαι, be placed at intervals; open ranks.
δίκαιος, just, right.
δικαιοσύνη, justice.
δίκη, punishment, deserts; δίκην δίδωμι, pay the penalty, be punished; δίκην ὑπέχω + gen., be called to account for; give an account of.
δι-ορύττω, -ορώρυγμαι, dig through.

διπλάσιον *adv.*, twice as far.
δισχίλιοι, two thousand.
δίφρος, driver's platform.
διώκω, chase, give chase, pursue.
δοκέω, ἔδοξα + *inf.*, seem; have a
reputation, be thought; believe,
think; [decide.
δοκεῖ + *dat.*, it seems good,
δοκιμάζω, examine; *(pass.)* be examined and approved.
δόλιχος, long distance race.
δόξα, reputation.
δορκάς -άδος *f.*, gazelle.
δόρυ, δόρατος *n.*, spear.
δοῦλος, slave.
δουπέω, bang.
Δαρκόντιος, Drakontios.
δρεπανη-φόρος -ον, scythed.
δρέπανον, scythe.
δρόμος, running; foot-race; running track.
δύναμαι, δυνήσομαι, be able (can);
be powerful.
δύναμις -εως *f.*, force; power.
δυνατός, able; possible.
δύο, two.
δυσ-πόρευτος -ον, hard to get
through.
δύομαι, set.
δῶρον, gift.

E

ἔ *(acc.)*, *dat.* οἷ, *dat. pl.* σφίσιν
(reflexive), himself, etc.
ἑαλωκυίας: ἁλίσκομαι.
ἐάν + *subj.*, if.
ἑαυτόν *(reflexive)*, him, himself
etc.; *(gen.)* his (own).
ἐάω, *imperf.* εἴων, allow.
ἑβδομήκοντα, seventy.
ἐγ-γίγνομαι + *dat.*, occur in.
ἔγγυς *(comp.* -ύτερον, *sup.* -ύτατω)
adv., near, nearly; *(+ gen.)* near.
ἐγενόμην: γίγνομαι.
ἔγνως -ωσαν: γιγνώσκω.
ἐγ-κλίνω, (of a line) swerve,
turn aside, break.
ἐγώ, ἐμέ etc., I *(emphatic)*;
ἔγωγε, I for my part.
ἔδεισαν: δέδοικα.
ἔδραμον: τρέχω.
ἐθελοντής, volunteer.

ἐθέλω, be willing, wish.
ἔθνος -ους *n.*, nation;
κατὰ ἔθνη, by nations.
εἰ, if, whether;
εἰ μή, unless, except, if not.
εἶ, εἴη, εἶεν: εἰμί *('be')*.
εἶδον: ὁράω.
εἰδ-ώς -ότος: οἶδα.
εἰκάζω, *imperf.* ἤκαζον, ἤκασμαι,
portray; guess.
εἰκός: ἔοικα.
εἴκοσι, twenty.
εἴλοντο: αἱρέω.
εἰμί *(subj.* ὦ, *opt.* εἴην, *inf.* εἶναι, *part.* ὤν)*, ἔσομαι, ἦν, be;
ἔστι, it is possible;
τὰ ὄντα, property, belongings.
εἶμι *(fut. indic; inf.* ἰέναι, *part.*
ἰών, *pres. sense)*, go.
εἰ-πεῖν: λέγω.
εἵποντο: ἕπομαι.
εἴργω, shut in; *(ὥστε μή + inf.)*
prevent (from).
εἰρήνη, peace; *(cf.* ἄγω).
εἰς + *acc.*, into; to; on to; for
(the purpose of), towards; regarding; *(+ number)* up to, about.
εἷς *(ἕν-)* μία ἕν, one;
καθ' ἕνα, singly.
εἰσ-άγω, -ήχθην, lead into, take into.
εἰσ-βιβάζω, send on board.
εἰσ-δύομαι, sink into, cut into.
εἰσ-ειμι *(εἶμι 'go')*, enter.
εἰσ-έρχομαι, -ῆλθον *(-ελθ-)*, enter.
εἰσ-πηδάω, jump into.
εἰσ-πίπτω, rush in/into.
εἰσ-τρέχω, -έδραμον, charge in,
rush in.
εἴσω, in, inside; *(+ gen.)* inside.
εἶτα, next, then.
εἶχον: ἔχω.
ἐκ + *gen.*, out of, from; by;
ἐκ τούτου, at this, then, as a
result.
ἐκ τίνος, why.
ἕκαστος, each; *(pl.)* each and every.
ἑκάτερος, each (of two). [side.
ἑκατέρωθεν, on both sides, on either
ἑκατέρωσε, each way, in either direction.
ἐκ-βάλλω, -έβαλον, banish, exile,
expel, throw out.
ἐκ-βοηθέω, come out to help.

ἐκεῖ, there.
ἐκεῖνος -η -ο, that; he etc.;
(gen.) his.
ἐκ-κομίζω, carry out, carry to
safety.
ἐκ-κυμαίνω, billow out.
ἐκ-λέγω, -έλεξα, pick out.
ἐκ-λείπω, -λέλοιπα, disappear.
ἐκ-πίνω, -έπιον, drink up.
ἐκ-πίπτω, -πέπτωκα, be banished,
be expelled.
ἐκ-πλέω, sail out.
ἐκ-πλήττω, -πέπληγμαι, -επλάγην,
strike with panic, alarm.
ἐκποδών, out of the way;
ἐκποδὼν ποιέομαι, get rid of.
ἐκ-τοξεύω, shoot arrows out.
ἐκ-τρέπω, -έτραπον, turn aside
(trans.); *(mid. & pass.)* turn
aside *(intrans.)*.
ἐκ-φέρω, tell of.
ἐκ-φεύγω, escape.
ἐκών -οῦσα -όν, willing (willingly, voluntarily).
ἐλαύνω, ἐλῶ, ἤλασα, drive (forward); ride; march.
ἐλάφειος, of deer;
ἐλάφεια *(sc. κρέα n.pl.)*, ven-
ison.
ἔλαφος, deer.
ἐλαφρός, nimble.
ἐλέγχω, ἠλέγχθην *(+ part.)*, con-
vict (of), find guilty (of).
ἐλελίζω, raise battle cry.
ἐλευθερία, freedom.
ἐλεύθερος, free.
ἐλήφθησαν: λαμβάνω.
ἐλθεῖν: ἔρχομαι.
Ἑλλάς -άδος f., Greece; (as a
woman's name) Hellas.
Ἕλλην -ηνος m., a Greek.
Ἑλληνικός, Greek.
Ἑλληνίς -ίδος f. adj., Greek.
Ἑλλησποντιακός, Hellespontine.
Ἑλλήσποντος, the Hellespont.
ἔλ-οι -οιντο: αἱρέω.
ἐλπίς -ίδος f., hope.
ἐλῶντα: ἐλαύνω.
ἐμαυτόν *(reflexive)*, myself.
ἐμ-βάλλω, -βαλῶ, -έβαλον, attack,
invade; *(+ dat.)* throw (fodder)
to, put (bar) across.

ἐμ-βιβάζω, -εβίβασα *(εἰς + acc.)*,
put on board.
ἐμός, my.
ἐμπεδόω, abide by.   with.
ἔμ-πειρος -ον + *gen.*, acquainted
ἐμ-πίπλημι, -επλήσθην + *gen.*, fill
with, crowd with.   press upon.
ἐμ-πίπτω + *dat.*, produce in; im-
ἔμπροσθεν, ahead, before; *(+ gen.)*
in front of.
ἐμ-φάγοιεν: ἐν-έφαγον.
ἐν + *dat.*, in, on, among, at; ἐν
τούτῳ, meanwhile; ἐν ᾧ, while.
ἕνα: εἷς.
ἐνάντιος *(+ dat.)*, facing; opposed
(to); ἐκ τοῦ ἐναντίου, opposite.
ἐν-δείκνυμαι, demonstrate.
ἔν-δηλος -ον, clear, evident.
ἔνδοθεν, from inside.
ἔνδον, inside; indoors.
ἔν-δοξος -ον, glorious; signifying
glory.
ἐν-δύω, -έδυν, put on.
ἐνέδρα, ambush.
ἐν-εδρεύω, ambush.
ἔν-ειμι *(εἰμί 'be')*, be in, be on.
ἕνεκα *(after gen.)*, -κεν *(+ gen.)*,
for (the purpose of); because of.
ἐνενήκοντα, ninety.
ἐν-επλήσθη: ἐμ-πίπλημι.
ἐν-έφαγον *(aor.; no present in use)*,
eat.
ἐν-ῆν: ἔν-ειμι.
ἔνθα, then; there; where.
ἔνθαπερ, just where.
ἔνθεν, from which.
ἐν-θυμέομαι, reflect.
ἐνθύμημα -ατος n., consideration,
argument.
ἔνι *(= ἔν-εστι)*: ἔν-ειμι.
ἕνι: εἷς.
ἐνιαυτός, year.
ἔνιοι, some.
ἐνίοτε, sometimes.
ἐν-νοέω, think of.
ἔν-νοια, thought.
ἐν-οικέω, live in; inhabit.
ἐνταῦθα, there; at this/that point.
ἐν-τέλλω -τέταλμαι & mid., order.
ἔντερα n.pl., guts, intestines.
ἐν-τεταλμένῳ: ἐν-τέλλω.

ἐντεῦθεν, from here, from there.
ἐντός + gen., inside, within.
ἐν-τυγχάνω + dat., come across, meet.
'Ενυάλιος, Enyalios (= Ares).
ἕξ, six.
ἐξ-άγω, -ήχθην, lead out.
ἐξ-αίρετος -ον, choice, specially selected.
ἐξ-αιρέω -εῖλον, set aside.
ἐξ-αιτέομαι, intercede, secure someone's release.
ἐξακόσιοι, six hundred.
ἐξ-αν-ίσταμαι, go into action.
ἐξ-απατάω, deceive.
ἐξαπίνης, suddenly.
ἐξ-αυλίζομαι, decamp.
ἔξει: ἔχω.   out.
ἐξ-ειμι (εἶμι 'go'), leave, get
ἐξ-ελαύνω, advance, march on.
ἐξ-έρχομαι, -ἦλθον (-ελθ-), come out, go out.
ἐξ-εστι + (dat. &) inf., it is permitted, it is possible.
ἐξέτασις -εως f., inspection.
ἐξήκοντα, sixty.
ἐξ-ικνέομαι (+ gen.), reach.
ἐξ-όν: ἐξ-εστι.
ἐξ-οπλίζομαι, get fully armed.
ἔξω, outside; (+ gen.) beyond, outside.
ἔοικα (inf. -έναι), seem (likely); (+ dat.) resemble.
εἰκός (n. part. sc. ἐστι), it is likely.
ἐορακέναι: ὁράω.
ἑορτή, festival.
ἐπ-αγγέλλομαι, -ηγγειλάμην, offer.
ἐπ-αινέω, praise.
ἐπ-αίρω, rouse, stir.
ἐπ-ακούω, overhear.
ἐπ-ανα-χωρέω, retreat.
ἐπάταξεν: πατάσσω.
ἐπεί (ἐπειδή), after, when; since.
ἐπειδάν + subj., whenever, when;
    ἐπειδὰν τάχιστα, as soon as.
ἐπείπερ, since in fact, seeing that.
ἐπ-ειμι (εἶμι 'go'), advance (against); follow (in time).
ἔπειτα, subsequently, then; secondly.

ἐπ-ερωτάω, -ηρόμην, ask.
ἐπ-ήκοος -ον adj., hearing;
    εἰς ἐπήκοον, within earshot.
ἐπ-ήνουν: ἐπ-αινέω.
ἐπ-ῆρεν: ἐπ-αίρω.
ἐπί + acc., against, at, on to, over, to;
    ὡς ἐπὶ τὸ πολύ, generally;
    + gen., on, in the time of,
    (with number) ... deep;
    + dat., on top of, on, at, in the power of, for.
ἐπι-βουλεύω + dat., plot against.
ἐπιβουλή, plot.
ἐπι-γράφω -έγραψα, inscribe.
ἐπι-δείκνυμαι, distinguish oneself; show, demonstrate.
ἐπι-διώκω, give chase.
ἐπ-ιδόντας: ἐφ-οράω.
ἐπι-θυμέω, be eager, desire; (+ gen.) desire.
ἐπιθυμία, desire.
ἐπι-κάμπτω, wheel round.
ἐπι-κατα-ρ-ριπτέω, throw down after.
ἐπί-κειμαι, attack.
ἐπικούρημα -ατος n., help, protection.
ἐπι-κρύπτομαι, disguise, keep secret.
ἐπι-λαμβάνομαι + gen., catch hold of.
ἐπι-λέγω, add (message).
ἐπι-λείπω, -έλιπον, -λέλοιπα, run out; wear out.
ἐπιμέλεια, attention, care, diligence.
ἐπι-μελέομαι, observe carefully;
    (+ gen.) pay attention to; supervise; (+ ὅπως) see to it that.
ἐπιμελητής, supervisor.
ἐπι-νοέω, intend, think of.
ἐπι-ορκέω, break one's oath.
ἐπί-ορκος -ον, forsworn, perjured.
ἐπι-πίπτω, -πεσοῦμαι, -έπεσον + dat., attack, fall upon.
ἐπί-πονος -ον, signifying pain/ trouble.
'Επισθένης -ους, Episthenes.
ἐπι-σιτίζομαι, get food, get provisions.
ἐπισιτισμός, getting provisions.
ἐπι-σκευάζω, repair.

ἐπι-σκοπέω, -εσκεψάμην, inspect (troops).

ἐπι-σπάομαι, drag after one.

ἐπίσταμαι (+ inf.), know, understand (how to).

ἐπι-στέλλω, -έστειλα, instruct, order.

ἐπιστολή, letter.

ἐπι-σφάττω, -έσφαξα, slaughter on top of; (mid.) cut one's throat on, stab oneself on.

ἐπιτήδειος, necessary; τὰ ἐπιτήδεια, provisions, supplies.

ἐπι-τίθεμαι (+ dat.), attack.

ἐπι-τυγχάνω, -έτυχον + dat., come across.

ἐπι-φαίνομαι, appear.

ἐπι-φέρομαι, charge, rush at.

ἐπίχαρις -ι gen. -ιτος, pleasant, attractive.

ἐπι-χειρέω, attempt.

ἕπομαι, imperf. εἱπόμην, follow.

ἑπτά, seven.

ἔργον, action, activity; (pl.) conduct.

Ἐρετριεύς, an Eretrian.

ἔρημος, abandoned; in/through the desert.

ἐρίζω, compete.

ἑρμηνεύς, interpreter.

ἐρρωμένος: ῥώννυμι.

ἔρχομαι, ἦλθον (ἐλθ-), come, go, advance, return.

ἐρωτάω, ἠρόμην, ask, question.

ἔσεσθαι: εἰμί 'be'.

ἐσθίω, ἔφαγον, eat.

ἑσπέρα, evening.

ἐστε: εἰμί 'be'.

ἔστε, until. ⌐ily.

ἐσχάτως, extremely, extraordinar-

ἔσχε: ἔχω.

ἑταίρα, girl friend, mistress.

ἑταῖρος, comrade, friend.

Ἐτεόνικος, Eteonikos.

ἕτεροι, others.

ἔτι, after this, in the future; still; (after negative) again, any more, any longer.

ἔτι καὶ νῦν, to this day, even now.

ἑτοῖμος, ready; assured.

ἔτος -ους n., year.

ἐτραπόμην: τρέπω.

ἐτράφητε: τρέφω.

εὖ (adv. of ἀγαθός), well; εὖ ποιέω + acc., treat well, benefit.

εὐδαίμων -ον, prosperous, wealthy.

εὐεργεσία, act of kindness, service.

εὐεργέτεω, benefit.

εὖ-ζωνος -ον, ready for action.

εὔ-θυμος -ον, cheerful.

εὐθύς, immediately.

εὐ-μεταχείριστος -ον, easy to manipulate, manageable.

εὔνοια, good will.

εὐνοϊκός, well-disposed.

εὔ-νους -νουν (-οος), well-disposed.

εὐπετῶς, easily, without trouble.

εὑρίσκω, ηὗρον, find.

εὖρος -ους n., width, thickness.

Εὐρύλοχος, Eurylokhos (Eurylochus).

εὔ-τακτος -ον, well-disciplined.

εὐταξία, (good) discipline.

Εὐφράτης, the Euphrates.

εὐχή, prayer.

εὔχομαι, pray; vow.

εὐώδης -ες, aromatic, sweet-smelling.

εὐ-ώνυμος -ον, left.

εὐωχέομαι, have a feast.

ἐφ-έπομαι, imperf. -ειπόμην, follow, be after.

Ἐφέσιος, Ephesian.

Ἔφεσος, Ephesos.

ἐφ-ίστημι, set over; (sc. ἵππον) pull up; (mid. & intrans.) halt, take up position (near).

ἐφ-οράω -εῖδον (-ιδ-), witness.

ἔφορος, ephor (Spartan official).

ἔφυγε(ν): φεύγω.

ἐχθρός, hostile; (as noun) enemy.

ἔχω, ἕξω, imperf. εἶχον, ἔσχον, get, have, hold; occupy; stop; wear; (+ adv.) be; ἐχόμενος, com-

ἑώρων: ὁράω. ⌐ing next.

ἕως, while, as long as.

Z

Ζαπάτας -ου, Zapatas (Zab).

ζάω, live, be alive; get one's living.

ζεῦγος -ους n., pair of draught animals.
Ζεῦς Διός m., Zeus.
ζωγρέω, take prisoner.
ζῶν ζῶντος (part. ζάω), alive.
ζώνη, belt.

H

ἤ, or; (after comparative) than; ἤ ... ἤ, either ... or.
ἤ, certainly, truly.
ἤ: ὅς.
ἤ: εἰμί 'be'.
ἤ sc. ὁδῷ, by which (route); where.
ἡγεμόσυνα sc. ἱερά, thank-offerings for safe conduct.
ἡγεμών -όνος m., commander; guide.
ἡγέομαι, think; (+ gen.) lead, be in command of.
ᾔδει: οἶδα.
ἤδη, already; now; immediately.
ἤδομαι, ἤσθην, be pleased; (+ dat.) enjoy.
ἡδονή, pleasure.
ἡδύς (comp. ἡδίων, sup. ἥδιστος), pleasant, delicious. [back.
ἥκω, ἥξω, have come, have arrived
Ἠλεῖος, Elean, from Elis.
ἦλθον: ἔρχομαι.
ἠλίθιος, foolish, simple-minded.
ἡλικία, age, time of life.
ἡλικιώτης, contemporary, someone of one's own age.
ἥλιος, the sun.
ἡμεῖς -ᾶς -ῶν -ῖν, we (emphatic), us; (gen.) our.
ἡμέρα, day.
ἥμερος, tame, cultivated.
ἡμέτερος, our.
ἡμί-βρωτος -ον, half-eaten.
ἡμι-δεής, half-empty.
ἡμίονος, mule.
ἡμίπλεθρον, half a plethron (50 feet).
ἥμισυς adj., half.
ἡμιωβέλιον, half-obol (coin).
ἡμφ-εγνόουν: ἀμφι-γνοέω.
ἦν = ἐάν.
ἦν: εἰμί 'be'.
ἥν: ὅς.

ἠνέχθη: φέρω.
ἡνίκα, when.
ἡνίοχος, charioteer, driver.
ἤξοι: ἤκω.
ἤσθη: ἤδομαι.
ἡσυχῇ adv., calmly, unhurriedly.
ἡσυχία, rest, quiet; (cf. ἄγω).
ἦτε: εἰμί 'be'.
ἡττάομαι + gen., be inferior to.
ἥττων -ον (adv. -ον), less.

Θ

θάλαττα, sea.
θάνατος, death.
θανατόω, condemn to death.
θαρραλέως, confidently.
Θαρύπας, Tharypas.
θᾶττον: ταχύς.
θαυμάζω, wonder (at).
θαυμαστός, surprising.
θέα, spectacle, sight.
θέαμα -ατος n., sight.
θεάομαι, see, witness, watch.
θέλω = ἐθέλω.
θεός m./f., god; goddess.
θεοσέβεια, fear/worship of the gods.
θεραπεύω, serve; give one's attentions to, flatter.
θεράπων -οντος m., attendant.
Θετταλία, Thessaly.
Θετταλός, Thessalian.
θέω, run.
θεωρέω, be a spectator.
Θήχης, Thekhes (Theches).
θήρα, hunting.
θηράω & -εύω, hunt.
θηρίον, (wild) animal; (pl.) game, wildlife.
θησαυρός, treasury.
Θίβρων -ωνος m., Thibron.
θνῄσκω, τέθνηκα (inf. τεθνάναι), die (perf., be dead); be put to [death.
θόρυβος, noise.
Θρᾴκη, Thrace, Θρᾴκιος, Thracian.
Θρᾷξ -ᾳκός m., a Thracian.
θρασύς (comp. -ύτερος), bold.
θῦμα -ατος n., sacrificial victim, sacrifice. [ace.
θύραι f. pl., entrance; court, pal-
θυσία, sacrifice.

184

θύω & mid., sacrifice.
θωρακίζομαι, put on one's cuirass;
τεθωρακισμένος, wearing a cuirass.
θώραξ -ακος m., breast-plate,
cuirass.

I

ἰάομαι, treat.
ἰατρός, doctor.
ἰδεῖν: ὁράω.
ἰδιωτικός, of private significance,
referring to a private individual.
ἱδρόω, sweat.
ἱερεῖον, sacrificial victim.
ἱερός (+ gen.), sacred (to);
ἱερόν n.s., temple;
ἱερά n.pl., omens.
ἵημι, throw, fling, hurt; (mid.)
rush.
ἱκανός, enough; (+ inf.) able to.
ἱμάς -άντος m., strap.
ἵνα + subj./opt., in order that/
to.
ἵππαρχος, cavalry-commander.
ἱππασία, riding.
ἱππεύς, horseman; (pl.) cavalry.
ἱππικός adj., of the cavalry;
τὸ ἱππικόν, the cavalry.
ἱππόδρομος, racecourse.
ἵππος, horse.
ἴσασι: οἶδα.
Ἰσθμός, the Isthmus (of Corinth).
ἴσος, equal;
ἐν ἴσῳ, evenly, in step;
ἴσως, perhaps, probably.
ἵστημι, halt (trans.); (mid. &
intrans.) stand (still), halt,
be positioned, stand one's
ground.
ἱστίον, sail.
ἰσχυρός, strong; (of punishment)
severe; vehement.
ἰσχύς -ύος f., strength, forces.
Ἰταμένης, Itamenes.
ἰτέον ἐστι + dat., one must go.
ἴτυς -υος f., rim (of shield).
ἰχθύς -ύος m., fish.
ἴχνιον, track.
Ἰωνικός, Ionian, of Ionia.

K

καθ-έλκω, imperf. -εῖλκον, launch.
καθέζομαι, halt.
καθεύδω, sleep.
καθ-ηγέομαι, act as guide.
καθ-ίστημι, position; (mid.) appoint for oneself; (mid. & intrans.) be established, (of troops)
fall in, (εἰς/ἐπί + acc.) go.
κάθημαι, sit (down).
καθ-οράω, -εῖδον (-ιδ-), catch sight
of; look down on.
καί, and; also; even;
καί ... καί, both ... and;
καί γάρ, for (in fact).
καίπερ + part., although.
καιρός, critical time;
ἐν καιρῷ, usefully.
καίω, burn.
κακό-νους -νουν (-οος) + dat., ill-
disposed towards; (as noun) enemy
of.
κακός (sup. -ιστος), bad, evil;
cowardly; κακόν (& pl.), harm.
κακ-ὸν/-ῶς ποιέω (+ acc.), harm.
κακ-οῦργος -ον, (adj. as noun)
criminal.
κάλαμος, reed.
καλέω, ἐκάλεσα, call; call together; καλούμενος, so-called.
καλινδέομαι, roll over and over.
Καλλίμαχος, Kallimakhos (Calli-
machus).
καλλωπισμός, adornment.
καλός, (sup. κάλλιστος), beautiful,
handsome, fine; good; honourable;
(of omens) favourable.
Καλχεδών -όνος f., Kalkhedon
(Chalcedon).
κάμνω, be exhausted; be ill.
κάνδυς -υος m., caftan.
καπίθη, kapithe (dry measure).
καρβάτιναι f.pl., raw-hide sandals.
Κάρκασος, the Karkasos (Carcasus).
καρπόομαι, gather fruit, reap crops.
Καστωλός, Kastolos (Castolus).
κατά + acc., on, down upon, against,
opposite; according to; κατὰ γῆν/
θάλατταν, by land/sea; καθ' ἕνα,
singly; κατ' ἐνιαυτόν, every year;

+ gen., down, down from.
κατα-βαίνω, -έβην, enter (contest).
κατ-αγγέλλω -ήγγειλα, denounce.
κατα-γελάω (+ gen.), jeer, laugh
  scornfully (at); scorn, mock.
κατ-άγω, get back, restore (from
  exile).
κατα-δραμών: κατα-τρέχω.
κατα-θεάομαι, survey the scene.
κατα-θύω, sacrifice.
κατα-καίνω, -έκανον, kill.
κατά-κειμαι, lie (down).
κατα-κλείω -κέκλειμαι, shut up.
κατα-κόπτω -έκοψα -εκόπην, cut to
  pieces, cut down.
κατα-λαμβάνω -ελήφθην, catch,
  overtake.
κατα-λέγω, count, reckon.
κατα-λείπω -έλιπον -ελείφθην -λέ-
  λειμμαι, leave (behind).
κατ-αλλάττω -ηλλάγην, reconcile.
κατα-λύω, break off; (sc. ὁδόν)
  halt; (sc. πόλεμον) cease hostilities.
κατα-μανθάνω -έμαθον, learn well,
  observe well.
κατ-αμελέω, neglect.
κατα-πηδάω, jump down.
κατα-πίπτω -έπεσον, fall down.
κατα-σκευάζομαι -εσκευασάμην,
  equip.
κατα-σπάω, drag down.
κατα-στρέφομαι, subdue, make sub-ject.
κατα-σχίζω -σχίσω, smash open.
κατα-τείνω -έτεινα, insist (against opposition).
κατα-τέμνω, cut up.
κατα-τρέχω -έδραμον, run down.
καταφανής, visible.
κατ-εῖδον -ιδόντας: καθοράω.
κατ-εργάζομαι, accomplish, achieve.
κατ-έχω, restrain.
κατ-ηγορέω + gen., accuse.
κατηγορία, accusation.
κατ-οικέω, live.
κατ-ορύττω -ορύξω -ωρύχθην, bury.
κάτω, downwards, on the way down.
κεῖμαι, lie (dead).
κελεύω, command, direct, instruct,
  tell.
κενός, empty; (+ gen.) without.

κέρας -ατος n., flank, wing (of
  army).
Κερασοῦς -οῦντος m., Kerasous
  (Cerasus).
κερδαίνω, gain, profit.
κερδαλέος, profitable.
κέρδος -ους n., gain, profit.
κεφαλή, head.
κηρύττω, ἐκήρυξα, announce, pro-
  claim.
Κιλικία, Kilikia (Cilicia).
κινδυνεύω, be in danger, run risks.
κίνδυνος, danger.
κινέω, move (trans.); (pass.) keep
  moving.
Κλεάνωρ -ορος m., Kleanor (Cleanor).
Κλέαρχος, Klearkhos (Clearchus).
κλεῖθρον & pl., bar.
κόγχη, mussel.
κοιμάομαι, go to sleep.
κοινός, common;
  τὸ κοινόν, the common store;
  κοινῇ, together.
κολάζω, punish.
Κολχίς -ίδος f.adj., Kolkhian, of
  Kolkhis (Colchis).
κολωνός, heap, pile.
Κομανία, Komania (Comania).
κονιορτός, dust-cloud.
κόπος, fatigue, weariness.
κόπρος -ου f., dung.
κόπτω, hammer on.
Κορσωτή, Korsote (Corsote).
κοσμέω, adorn.
κόσμος, adornment, ornament.
κράζω, κεκράγα (perf. with pres.
  meaning), scream.
κράνος -ους n., helmet.
κράτιστος, best; noblest.
κράτος -ους n., strength.
κραυγή, shouting.
κρεας, κρέως n., & pl. κρέα, flesh,
  meat.
κρείττων, better.
κρήνη, spring.
Κρής, Κρητός m., a Cretan.
κριθαί f.pl., barley.
κρίνω, ἔκρινα, judge; decide; in-
  terpret.
κρίσις -εως f., trial.
κρούω, beat.
κρύπτω, hide; (pass.) act secretly.

κτάομαι, acquire, obtain.
κτῆμα -ατος n., possession; (pl.) property.
κτῆνος -ους n., head of cattle; (pl.) herds, flocks, cattle.
Κτησίας, Ktesias (Ctesias).
κύκλος, circle.
κυκλόω, surround.
κύκλωσις -εως f., encircling movement.
κυλινδέω (κυλίνδω), roll.
Κυνίσκος, Kyniskos (Cyniscus).
κυπαρίττινος, made of cypress wood.
Κύρειος, of Kyros.
Κῦρος, Kyros (Cyrus).
κωλύω (+ gen. & inf.), prevent (from).
κώμη, village.

Λ

λαγχάνω, ἔλαχον, get.
Λακεδαιμόνιος, Spartan (Lacedaemonian).
Λακεδαίμων -ονος f., Sparta (Lacedaemon).
Λάκων -ωνος m., a Spartan.
λαμβάνω, λήψομαι, ἔλαβον, ἐλήφθην, capture, catch, get, obtain, receive, take.
λάμπομαι, shine.
λανθάνω + part., escape notice (secretly).
λάχος -ους n., share.
λέγω, ἔλεξα & εἶπον (εἰπ-), say, speak, tell;
λεγόμενος, reckoned.
λειμών -ῶνος m., meadowland.
λείπω, ἔλιπον, leave (behind).
Λεοντῖνος, of Leontinoi (Leontini).
λευκοθώραξ -ακος, with white cuirasses.
λευκός, white. [end.
λήγω, ἔληξα, cease, come to an
ληφθ-έντες, -εῖσα, λήψομαι: λαμβάνω.
λίθος, stone, boulder.
λιμός, hunger, starvation.
λιπόντες: λείπω.
λόγος, word; argument; conference, discussion.
λόγχη, lance.
λοιπός, remaining.

τὸ λοιπόν, the remainder; (acc. as adv.) from then on.
Λουσιεύς, (native) of Lousoi/Lousia (Lusian).
λόφος, hill-top.
λοχαγός, captain.
Λύδιος, Lydian.
Λύκιος, Lykios (Lycius).
λυπέω, distress.
λύω, break, violate.
λωφάω, abate, slacken.
λώων, λῷον, better.

M

μά, by (in oaths).
μακαριστός, to be envied.
μακρός, long.
Μάκρωνες, the Makrones.
μάλα, very;
μᾶλλόν, more, rather;
μάλιστα, very much, most, mostly, in particular.
μανθάνω, ἔμαθον, learn; hear (news).
μαντεία, answer of an oracle.
μαντευτός, prescribed by an oracle.
μάντις -εως m., soothsayer.
μαρτυρέω, bear witness, provide evidence.
μαρτύριον, evidence, proof.
Μάσκας -α m., the Maskas.
μάχαιρα, sabre.
μάχη, battle.
μάχιμος, good at fighting.
μάχομαι, μαχοῦμαι (+ dat. or πρός + acc.), fight (with).
Μεγάβυζος, Megabyzos.
μέγας μεγάλη μέγα (comp. μείζων, sup. μέγιστος, adv. μέγα), great; tall; loud.
Μεθρυδριεύς, of Methydrion.
μεθύω, be drunk.
μεῖζ-ων -ον: μέγας.
μειράκιον, youth, teenager.
μείωμα -ατος n., fine. [worse.
μείων -ον (comp. of μικρός), less;
μελανία, blackness, darkness.
μέλας -αινα -αν, black, dark.
μέλει, μελήσει + dat., it is a concern (take care, heed).
μελετηρός, diligent in practising.
μέλλω + inf., be about to, intend

to; *(+ fut. inf.)* be likely to;
τὸ μέλλον, the future.
μέμφομαι, find fault with.
μέν *(2nd word)*, on the one hand
(followed by δέ);
μὲν οὖν, anyway.
μέντοι *(2nd word)*, however, yet.
μένω, ἔμεινα, remain, stay, wait.
Μένων -ωνος *m.*, Menon (Meno).
μέρος -ους *n.*, amount, sample,
share; detachment.
μέσος, at/in the centre;
μέσον ἡμέρας, midday;
μέσαι νύκτες, midnight.
μεστός + *gen.*, full of, covered in.
μετά + *acc.*, after;
+ *gen.*, with, in company with.
μετα-γιγνώσκω -έγνων *(part.*
-γνούς)*, change one's mind.
μετα-δίδωμι + *dat.*, give (a share)
to, share with.
μετα-μέλει + *dat.*, it repents (be
sorry).
μετα-πέμπομαι -επεμψάμην, send for.
μετ-έχω + *gen.*, join in.
μετ-έωρος -ον, lifted up.
μετρέω, measure.
μέχρι, until; *(+ gen.)* as far as.
μή, not; (fear) that.
μηδέ, and not, nor; not even.
μηδ-είς, μηδε-μία, μηδ-εν, no-one;
(n.) nothing.
μηδέποτε (μήποτε), never.
μηκέτι, no longer.
μῆκος -ους *n.*, length.
μήν μηνός *m.*, month.
μήν, really;
μήν ... γε, however, all the
same.
μηρός, thigh.
μήτε ... μήτε, neither ... nor.
μήτηρ -τρός *f.*, mother.
μηχανάομαι, contrive, devise.
μηχανή, instrument, means.
μία: εἷς.
Μιθραδάτης, Mithradates.
μικρός *(comp.* μείων), little, small.
Μιλήσιος, Milesian.
Μίλητος -ου *f.*, Miletos (Miletus).
μισθοδοτέω, pay wages.
μισθός, pay.
μισθοφορά, pay.

μισθοφόρος, mercenary.
μνᾶ, mna (mina) = 100 drakhmai
(drachmae).
μόλις, hardly, scarcely, with
difficulty.
μολυβδίς -ίδος *f.*, lead bullet.
μόνος *(adv.* μόνον), unique; alone.
μοχλός, bar.
μύριοι, ten thousand.
Μυσοί, Mysians.

N

ναί, yes.
ναός = νεώς.
νάπη, dell.
νεό-δαρτος -ον, newly-flayed.
νέος, young.
νεφέλη, cloud.
νεωκόρος, warden.
Νέων -ωνος *m.*, Neon.
νεώς -ώ *m.*, temple.
Νίκαρχος, Nikarkhos (Nicarchus).
νικάω, defeat, surpass.
νίκη, victory.
νομή, pasture.
νομίζω, νομιῶ, ἐνόμισα, consider,
think.
νόσος -ου *f.*, disease.
νοῦς, νοῦ *(-δος)*, mind; *(cf.* προσ-
έχω).
νύκτωρ *adv.*, by night.
νῦν, now.
νύξ, νυκτός *f.*, night.

Ξ

Ξανθικλῆς, Xanthikles.
Ξενίας, Xenias.
ξένος, guest-friend; mercenary.
Ξενοφῶν -ῶντος *m.*, Xenophon.
ξενόω, entertain.
Ξέρξης, Xerxes.
ξόανον, image (of a deity).
ξυήλη, dagger.
ξυλινός, wooden.
ξύλον, piece of wood; *(pl.)* wood.

O

ὁ ἡ τό, the; his etc.;
οἱ + *phrase*, those;

188

ὁ δέ, and he, but he *(change of subject)*;
οἱ μέν ... οἱ δέ, some ... others.
τῇ μέν, in some ways.
τό + *inf.*, (= *verbal noun*).
ὃ τι: ὅστις.
ὀβελίσκος, small spit, skewer.
ὀβολός, obol (coin).
ὀγδοήκοντα, eighty.
ὅ-δε, ἥ-δε, τό-δε, this; the following.
ὁδοποιέω, make (road) passable, clear of obstacles.
ὁδός -οῦ *f.*, road; way, journey; expedition.
ὅθεν, from which, from where.
οἷ: ἕ.
οἶδα, ᾔδειν *(part. εἰδώς)*, know (about).
οἴκαδε *(adv. of direction)*, home.
οἰκεῖος + *dat.*, intimate with, close to.
οἰκέω, live (in), inhabit.
οἰκία, house.
οἰκίζω, ᾠκίσθην, settle *(trans.)*.
οἴκοθεν, from home.
οἴκοι *adv.*, at home.
οἶνος, wine.
οἴομαι *(& οἶμαι)*, ᾠήθην, believe, suppose, think.
οἷος, (such) as;
  οἷον, the kind of (thing) that, (+ *indir. question*) how;
  οἷόν τέ ἐστι, it is possible.
οἴχομαι, have gone.
οἰωνός, bird; omen.
ὀκνηρῶς, reluctantly.
ὀκτακισχίλιοι, eight thousand.
ὀκτακόσιοι, eight hundred.
ὀκτώ, eight.
ὀλίγος, small; *(pl.)* (a) few, a small number.
ὅλος, entire, whole.
Ὀλυμπία, Olympia.
ὁμαλής, even, level.
ὄμνυμι, ὤμοσα, swear.
ὁμολογέω, admit; agree;
  ὁμολογουμένως, admittedly.
ὁμο-τράπεζος -ον, *(adj. as noun)* table-companion, messmate.
ὁμοῦ, together.
ὅμως, nevertheless, still.

ὄναρ *n.*, dream.
ὀνίνημι, ὤνησα, benefit.
ὄνομα -ατος *n.*, name; reputation.
ὄνος, ass, donkey;
  ὄνος ἀλέτης, upper mill-stone.
ὅπῃ *sc.* ὁδῷ, where, by what road.
ὄπισθεν, behind, in/from the rear.
ὀπισθοφυλακέω, guard the rear, be in the rearguard.
ὀπισθοφύλαξ -ακος *m.*, one of the rearguard; *(pl.)* the rearguard.
ὁπλίζω, arm; *(mid.)* arm oneself; *(pass.)* be armed.
ὁπλιτεύω, be a hoplite.
ὁπλίτης, hoplite, heavy-armed soldier.
ὅπλον, weapon, (hoplite) shield; *(pl.)* arms; camp; hoplite lines.
ὁποῖος, of what kind.
ὁπόσος, as much as; *(pl.)* as many as, all those who; *(indir. question)* how many;
ὁπόσον *(adv.)*, as far as.
ὁπότε + *indic.*, when; (+ *subj.* & ἄν/opt.) whenever.
ὁπότερος, which of the two; *(pl.)* which of the two sides.
ὅπου + *indic.*, where; (+ *subj.* & ἄν/opt.) wherever;
ὅπου μή, except where.
ὅπως + *fut.*, *(after verb of precaution)* how; (+ *subj./opt.*) in order that/to.
ὁράω, ὄψομαι, *imperf.* ἑώρων, εἶδον *(ἰδ-)*, ἑόρακα, see; have a look; have (dream).
ὀργή, anger.
ὀργυιά, fathom (6 ft.).
ὄρθιος, uphill.
ὀρθῶς, accurately, correctly.
ὅρκος & *pl.*, oath.
ὁρμάω, rush off, be eager; *(mid.)* set out, use (a place) as a base.
ὁρμή, attack.
ὄρνεον, bird.
Ὀρόντας -α, Orontas.
ὄρος -ους *n.*, mountain, hill.
ὀρύττω, dig; quarry.
Ὀρχομένιος, Orkhomenian, of Orkhomenos (Orchomenus).
ὅς ἥ ὅ, who, which;
  ὅς γε, since he;

καὶ ὅς, and he;
ᾗ (sc. ὁδῷ), by which (route),
where;
ἐν ᾧ, while.
ὅσιος, pious.
ὅσος, as much as; (pl.) as many
as, all those who;
ὅσον, as far as, as much as, (+
number) about;
ὅσῳ + comp. ... τοσούτῳ + comp.,
the more ... , the more.
ὅσ-περ, ἥ-περ, ὅ-περ, the very
one who/which.
ὅσ-τις, ἥ-τις, ὅ τι, anyone who,
whoever, anything which, whatever;
ὅστις δή, someone or other.
ὀσφραίνομαι + gen., smell.
ὅταν + subj., whenever.
ὅτε, when.
ὅτι, because;
+ indir. statement, that;
+ sup., as ... as possible.
ὅ τι: ὅσ-τις.
οὐ, οὐκ, οὐχ(ί), not; (in replies)
no.
οὗ (gen. of ὅς), where; of whom.
οὐδαμοῦ, nowhere.
οὐδέ, nor, and not; not even.
οὐδ-εἷς, οὐδε-μία, οὐδ-έν, (adj.)
no; (pron.) no-one, nothing, none;
οὐδέν (adv.), not at all.
οὐδέποτε, never.
οὐκέτι, no longer.
οὐκοῦν, is it not true that ...
οὖν (2nd word), so, then, therefore.
οὗπερ, exactly where.
οὔπω, not yet.
οὔτε ... οὔτε, neither ... nor.
οὗτος, αὕτη, τοῦτο, this, that;
he; (gen.) his;
οὑτοσ-ί, this (man) here;
ταύτῃ (sc. ὁδῷ), here, there,
this/that way.
οὕτω(ς), in such a way, in this
way; so.
ὄφελος n. (nom. & acc. s. only),
advantage, help, use.
ὀφθαλμός, eye.
ὀφλισκάνω, ὦφλον + gen., incur
(penalty) for.
ὄχλος, crowd; camp-followers.

ὀψέ, late.
ὀψίζω, come late.
ὄψομαι: ὁράω.

Π

παγκράτιον, all-in combat.
παγχαλέπως, with great difficulty/
danger, in very difficult circumstances.
παθ-εῖν: πάσχω.
πάθος -ους n., illness.
παιανίζω, sing the paean, sing
battle-hymn.
παιδεύω, educate.
παιδικά (n.pl. adj. as noun), boy-friend.
παιδίον, little child.
παῖς παιδός m./f., boy; son; child.
παίω, hit, strike.
πάλαι, before.
παλαίω, wrestle.
πάλη, wrestling.
πάλιν, again, back.   [cubine.
παλλακίς -ίδος f., mistress, con-
παλτόν, javelin.
πομπληθής, in full force.
πᾶν, πάντας: πᾶς.
παν-οῦργος -ον, wicked.
παντάπασιν, altogether, completely.
πανταχοῦ, everywhere.
πάντοθεν, on all sides.
παντοῖος, of every kind.   [very.
πανύ, very; οὐ πανύ, not at all, not
παρά + acc., along, beside, past,
to, in violation of (oath);
+ gen., from, by (agent);
+ dat., with, at the house of.
παρα-βοηθέω, go to the rescue.
παρ-αγγέλλω -ήγγειλα, issue orders.
παρα-γίγνομαι -εγενόμην, come and
παρα-δίδωμι, hand over. [help/join.
παρα-δραμεῖν: παρα-τρέχω.
παρα-θαρρύνω, encourage.
παρα-θέω, run past, overtake.
παρα-καλέω -εκάλεσα -εκλήθην, invite.
παρα-κατα-θήκη, deposit (money).
παρα-κελεύομαι + dat., urge.
παρακέλευσις -εως f., cheering.
παρα-λαμβάνω -έλαβον, take over.
παρα-λυπέω, make (extra) trouble.
παρ-αμείβομαι -ημειψάμην, by-pass.
παρα-μελέω, take no notice.

παρα-μένω + *dat.*, stay with.
παραμηρίδια *n.pl.*, thigh armour.
παρα-πλήσιος + *dat.*, very like.
παρα-ρ-ρέω, flow past.
παρασάγγης, parasang (measure of distance travelled).
παρα-σκευάζω, prepare; provide; *(mid.)* equip oneself; obtain.
παρα-τάττω -τέταγμαι, draw up alongside (each other).
παρα-τρέχω -έδραμον, run along; run across.
παρ-εγγυάω, pass (word) along, issue order.
πάρ-ειμι *(εἰμί 'be')*, be present, be there; *(+ dat.)* be near; πάρεστι, it is possible.
πάρ-ειμι *(εἶμι 'go')*, enter; go past.
παρ-ελαύνω, ride along.
παρ-έρχομαι -ῆλθον -ελήλυθα, pass (along), go past; παρεληλυθώς -ότος, past.
παρ-έχω, *imperf.* -εῖχον, cause, make, provide.
Παρθένιον, Parthenion.
παρ-ίστημι, *(mid.)* produce, bring (victim) to the altar; *(mid. & intrans.)* stand near.
πάροδος -ου *f.*, approach, entrance.
παρ-οινέω, do violence to (when παρ-όν: πάρ-ειμι. drunk).
Παρράσιος, Parrhasian.
Παρύσατις -ιδος, Parysatis.
πᾶς, πᾶσα, πᾶν, whole; *(pl.)* all, everybody; πάντα *(adv.)*, in every way.
πάσχω, πείσομαι, ἔπαθον, suffer, be hurt, have something happen to one.
πατάσσω, ἐπάταξα, strike, stab.
Πατηγύας, Pategyas.
πατήρ -τρός *m.*, father.
πατρίς -ίδος *f.*, one's (native) country.
πατρῷος, paternal.
παύομαι *(+ gen.)*, give up, stop.
Παφλαγών -όνος, Paphlagonian.
πεδίον, plain.
πεζός *(adj.)*, on foot; *(as noun)* foot-soldier; *(pl.)* infantry.
πείθω, ἔπεισα, persuade, win over;

(mid.) believe; *(+ dat.)* be obedient (to), obey.
πεινάω, be hungry.
πεῖρα, personal experience; ἐν πείρᾳ γίγνομαι + *gen.*, know personally.
πειράομαι, attempt, endeavour, try.
πείσας: πείθω.
πείσονται: πάσχω.
Πελοποννήσιος, Peloponnesian, from the Peloponnese.
πελτάζω, be a peltast.
πελταστής, peltast, light-armed soldier.
πελταστικός, of peltasts.
πέλτη, small shield.
πέμπτος, fifth.
πέμπω, ἔπεμψα, send; send word.
πεντακόσιοι, five hundred.
πέντε, five.
πεντήκοντα, fifty.
πέπαμαι *(perf. form; no pres.)*, have, possess.
πεπτωκότα: πίπτω.
περαίνω, carry out (decision).
πέρδιξ -ικος *f.*, partridge.
περί + *acc.*, round, around; *(time)* about; + *gen.*, about, concerning; + *dat.*, round.
περι-βάλλω, embrace.
περι-γίγνομαι -εγενόμην + *gen.*, get the better of, overcome.
περί-ειμι *(εἰμί 'be')*, be superior; *(+ gen.)* surpass.
περί-ειμι *(εἶμι 'go')*, go round.
περι-ίσταμαι, surround.
Πέρινθος -ου *f.*, Perinthos (Perinthus).
πέριξ + *gen.*, all round.
περι-πέτομαι, fly around.
περι-πήγνυμαι, freeze round.
περι-πίπτω -έπεσον + *dat.*, fall upon, embrace.
περι-πλέω, sail round.
περι-πτύσσω -έπτυξα, outflank.
περι-ρ-ρέω, surround.
περιττός, more than enough; τὸ περιττόν, the surplus.
περι-τυγχάνω + *dat.*, come across.
περιφανῶς, clearly, noticeably.
περί-φοβος -ον, in great fear.
Πέρσης, a Persian; *(as adj.)* Persian.

Περσικός, Persian.
πεσεῖν: πίπτω.
πέτομαι, fly.
πέτρα, boulder, rock, crag.
πέτρος, stone.
πήγνυμι, freeze.
πηλός, mud.
Πίγρης, Pigres.
πιέζομαι, be hard pressed.
πίπτω, ἔπεσον, πέπτωκα, fall.
Πίσιδαι, Pisidiai (Pisidians).
πιστεύω + dat., trust.
πίστις -εως f., loyalty.
πιστός, faithful, loyal, trust-
  worthy;
  πιστά n.pl., pledges.
πιστότης -ητος f., loyalty.
πίτυς -υος f., pine tree.
πλάγιος, slanting;
  εἰς πλάγιον, at an angle, obliquely.
πλαίσιον, (military) square, hollow square.
πλάττομαι, ἐπλασάμην, fabricate
  for oneself.
πλεθριαῖος (adj.), a plethron wide.
πλέθρον, plethron (100 ft.).
πλεῖστος (sup.), πλείων and πλέων
  (comp.): πολύς.
πλέκω, plait.   [tage of.
πλεονεκτέω + gen., get the advan-
πλευρά, rib, side.
πλέω, ἔπλευσα, sail.
πλῆθος -ους n., amount, extent,
  number(s).
πλήθω, be full.
πλήν, except that; (+ gen.) except.
πλήρης + gen., full of.
πλησιάζω, get close/near.
πλησίος (sup. -αίτατος), near;
  πλησίον (adv.), near, nearly.
πλήττω, ἐπλήγην, strike.
πλίνθος -ου f., brick.
πλοῖον, boat, ship.
πλούσιος, rich.
πλουτέω, be rich.
πνεῦμα -ατος n., wind.
πνέω, blow.
ποδήρης adj., down to the feet.
ποιέω, do; make, cause, produce,
  appoint; work; (mid.) get, make,

have made;
  ποιέω ὥστε + inf., make sure
  that, see to it that;
  περὶ παντὸς ποιέομαι, consider of
  great importance.
ποικίλος, multicoloured.
ποῖος, (of) what (sort).
πολεμέω, be at war, fight; (+ dat.
  or πρός + acc.) make war on.
πολεμικός, expert in war; (n.pl. as
  noun) warfare.
πολέμιος, hostile; (as noun, & pl.)
  enemy; (n.pl.) military matters.
πόλεμος, war.
πολιορκέω, besiege, blockade.
πόλις -εως f., city; state, country.
πόλισμα -ατος n., town.
πολίτης, citizen.
πολλάκις, often.
πολυαρχία, divided command.
πολύς, πολλή, πολύ, much; great,
  large, (of time) long; (of distance) far; (pl.) many; (comp.
  πλείων/πλέων, sup. πλεῖστος).
  ὡς ἐπὶ τὸ πολύ, generally.
Πολύστρατος, Polystratos.
πολυτελής, very costly.
πονέω, work.
πονηρός, (adj. as noun) villain.
πόνος, hardship.
πορεία, journey.
πορεύομαι, advance, march, walk;
  travel.
πορίζω, provide.
πορφυροῦς -ᾶ -οῦν (-εος), purple.
πόσι: πούς.
ποταμός, river.
ποτε, ever, once, on one occasion.
πότερα, πότερον (+ direct question),
  (not translated); (+ indir. alternative question) whether.
ποῦ (+ question), where.
που, anywhere.
πούς, ποδός m., foot.
πρᾶγμα -ατος n., thing, affair;
  (pl.) trouble.
πρανής, precipitous, steep.
πρᾶξις -εως f. (and pl.), affair,
  business, enterprise, undertaking.
πράττω, πράξω, ἔπραξα, do.
πρέπει + dat., it suits.
πρεσβύτερος, comp. adj. (sup. -ύτατος).

elder, older.
πρίασθαι: ὠνέομαι.
πρίν + indic., until;
+ inf., before; (after negative)
until.
πρό + gen., in front of.
προ-αισθάνομαι, find out in time.
προ-βαίνω, advance.
προ-βάλλομαι, propose.
πρόβατον, sheep.
πρόγονος, ancestor.
προ-δίδωμι, betray, give up.
προ-διώκω, προυδίωξα, advance in
pursuit.
προδότης, traitor.
προδρομή, sally.
πρό-ειμι (εἶμι 'go'), advance; go
in front.
προ-εργάζομαι -είργασμαι, do be-
forehand.
προ-έρχομαι -ῆλθον (-ελθ-) -ελήλυθα,
advance, come forward.
προ-θέω, run on ahead.
προ-θυμέομαι, be eager, be ready.
πρό-θυμος -ον, eager, ardent.
προ-ἵεμαι, give freely.
προ-κατα-καίω, burn the land ahead.
Προκλῆς, Prokles.
προμαχεών -ῶνος, battlement.
προ-μετ-ωπίδιον, frontlet.
Πρόξενος, Proxenos.
προ-οράω -εἶδον (-ιδ-), see (something) ahead.
προ-πέμπω, προύπεμψα, send on ahead; send off (departing traveller).
πρός + acc., to; against;
πρὸς ταῦτα, accordingly, in reply;
+ gen., in the sight of;
+ dat., near.
προσ-άγω, lead against.
προσ-βάλλω, attack.
προσ-δέομαι + gen., ask for in
addition.
προσ-δοκάω (+ acc. & fut. inf.),
expect.
πρόσ-ειμι (εἶμι 'go'), approach,
come on, come up.
προσ-έρχομαι -ῆλθον (-ελθ-), approach, come.
προσ-έχω, apply;

προσέχω τὸν νοῦν + dat., observe
carefully, be concerned about.
προσ-ήκω + dat., be related to;
προσήκει (impersonal), it befits.
πρόσθεν, before(hand), previously;
εἰς τὸ πρόσθεν, ahead.
προσ-θέω, run towards.
προσ-ίημι, allow near.
προσ-καλέω, call to oneself.
προσ-κυνέω, make obeisance to.
προσ-πίπτω + dat., rush up to.
προσ-πολεμέω + acc., fight.
προστατέω + gen., preside over.
προσ-τάττω -ετάχθην, give orders.
προστερνίδιον, chest armour.
προσ-τίθεμαι + dat., agree with.
πρόσ-χωρος -ον, local.
πρόσωπον, face.
πρότερος, earlier.
προ-τιμάω + gen., honour (someone)
above; (pass.) be held in greater
honour than.
προ-τρέχω, προύδραμον, run forward,
run ahead.
προ-φαίνομαι, appear, come into
sight.
πρόφασις -εως f., excuse, pretext.
προ-χωρέω, advance; go well; suit.
πρωτεύω, be first.
πρῶτος, first;
πρῶτον (adv.), first(ly), to begin
with, in the first place.
πτέρυξ -υγος f., wing.
πυγμή, boxing.
πύλη, gate; (pl.) border pass.
πυνθάνομαι, inquire.
πῦρ, πυρός n., fire.
πυργομαχέω, attack (a tower).
πύργος, tower.
πυροί m.pl., wheat.
πυρσεύω, light beacon-fires.
πωλέω, sell.
πώποτε, ever.
πῶς, how.

P

ῥάδιος (sup. ῥᾷστος), easy.
ῥᾳθυμέω, be idle.
ῥᾳθυμία, idleness.
ῥῖγος -ους n., cold.
ῥίπτω, ἔρριψα (ῥίψ-), throw, throw
down/off.

Ῥόδιος, Rhodian.
ῥῦμα -ατος n., drawing (of bow);
τόξου ῥῦμα, bowshot.
ῥώμη, strength.
ῥώννυμι, strengthen;
ἐρρωμένος (comp. -έστερος),
strong, vigorous.

Σ

Σάρδεις -εων f.pl., Sardeis (Sardis).
σατράπης, satrap, governor.
σαφής (adv. -ῶς), clear.
σεαυτόν (reflexive), yourself;
(gen.) your.
Σελινοῦς -οῦντος m., the Selinous
(Selinus).
Σεύθης, Seuthes.
σημαίνω, indicate.
σημεῖον, signal; standard.
σιγή, silence.
σίγλος, siglos (coin).
Σινωπεύς, Sinopean, citizen of
Sinope.
σῖτος, grain; provisions.
σκέλος -ους n., leg.
σκευή, robe.
σκεῦος -ους n., item of equipment;
(pl.) equipment, baggage.
σκευοφορέω, carry baggage.
σκευο-φόρος -ον, baggage-carrying;
τὰ σκευοφόρα, the pack animals.
σκηνέω, encamp, be quartered.
σκηνή, tent.
σκηπτός, thunderbolt.
σκηπτοῦχος, sceptre-bearer.
Σκιλλοῦς -οῦντος m., Skillous
(Scillus).
σκληρός, hard.
σκοπέω, consider; (πρός + acc.)
have regard for.
σκότος, darkness.
Σοφαίνετος, Sophainetos (Sophaenetus).
σοφός, intelligent.
σπάνιος, scarce.
Σπάρτη, Sparta.
Σπαρτιάτης, a Spartiate, Spartan
noble.
σπάομαι, draw (sword).
σπεύδω, hurry.

σπολάς -άδος f., leather jerkin.
σπονδαί f.pl., truce.
σπουδαιολογέομαι, have an earnest
conversation.
σπουδή, haste.
στάδιον, stade, furlong (607 ft.).
σταθμός, stopping place, stage;
day's march.
στασιάζω + dat., rebel against.
στείβω, tread;
στειβόμενος, well trodden.
στενοχωρία, narrow pass/place.
στέργω, feel affection for.
στέρνον, chest.
στέρομαι + gen., be deprived of.
στήλη, monument, pillar, tablet.
στίβος, trail.
στῖφος -ους n., compact mass, men
in close array.
στολή, clothes.
στόλος, (military) preparations,
expedition.
στρατεία, campaign.
στράτευμα -ατος n., army.
στρατεύω & mid., serve as a soldier;
go an a campaign.
στρατηγέω + gen., be in command of.
στρατηγός, general.
στρατιά, army.
στρατιώτης, soldier.
στρατόπεδον, camp.
στρατός, army.
στρεπτός, torque.
στρέφω, ἐστράφην, turn.
στρουθός -οῦ f., (kind of) sparrow;
ἡ μεγάλη στρουθός, ostrich.
στυγνός, gloomy, sullen.
Στυμφάλιος, Stymphalian, of Stymphalos.
σύ, σέ (σε), σου, σοί, you (s.).
συγγενής, related; (pl. as noun)
relatives.
συγ-γίγνομαι -γεγένημαι + dat.,
meet; associate with.
συγ-καλέω -εκάλεσα, call together.
συγ-κάμπτω -έκαμψα, bend.
συγ-κλείω, shut.
συλ-λαμβάνω, arrest.
συλ-λέγω -έλεξα -είλεγμαι, collect,
recruit; assemble.
συλλογή, recruitment (of troops).
συμ-βαίνω -έβην, happen;

τὰ συμβάντα, events.
συμ-βάλλομαι, contribute.
συμ-βοηθέω + dat., also come to the rescue.
συμ-βουλεύω, advise; (mid. + dat.) discuss with.
σύμβουλος, adviser.
σύμμαχος, ally.
συμ-μείγνυμι -έμειξα + acc. & dat., join to, add to.
συμ-μετ-έχω -έσχον + gen., take part in as well.
σύμ-πας -πασα -παν, all together; τὸ σύμπαν (adv.), in general.
συμ-πίπτω, -έπεσον, grapple with.
συμ-πολεμέω + dat., fight on the same side as.
συμ-πράττω, co-operate with someone (dat.) in something (acc.).
συμ-προθυμέομαι, be equally eager.
σύμ-φημι, agree with.
σύν + dat., with; with the help of.
συν-αγείρω, collect.
συν-αδικέω + dat., join (someone) in doing wrong.
συν-αιρέω -εῖλον (-ελ-), sum up.
συν-ακολουθέω, go with, accompany.
συν-αντάω, meet.
συν-ειλεγμένοι: συλ-λέγω.
σύν-ειμι (εἰμί 'be'), associate with.   [meet.
σύν-ειμι (εἶμι 'go'), advance to
συν-εις-πίπτω, rush in with.
συν-εκ-βιβάζω, help to pull out.
συν-εξ-έρχομαι, go out with.
συν-επι-μελέομαι + gen., supervise jointly.
συν-έρχομαι -ῆλθον (-ελθ-) -ελήλυθα, assemble, gather.
σύνθημα -ατος n., war-cry.
συν-θηράω, join in hunting.
συν-ίστημι, introduce.
σύνοδος -ου f., encounter.
συν-οράω -εῖδον (-ιδ-), see at a glance.
συν-τάττω -έταξα, draw up, marshal; (mid.) form one's battle line.
σύν-τομος -ον, short.
συντράπεζος, table-companion, messmate.
συν-τρίβω -τέτριμμαι, crush.
συν-τυγχάνω + dat., come upon.

Συρακόσιος, Syracusan, of Syracuse.
σύς, συός m./f., boar, pig.
σύσκηνος, comrade.
συ-σπειράομαι, roll up; form up in close order;
συν-εσπειραμένος, in close order.
συστράτηγος, fellow-general.
συχνός, long (of time); συχνόν, considerably.
σφαγιάζομαι, sacrifice.
σφάγιον, (sacrificial) victim.
σφάττω, slaughter, cut the throat.
σφενδονάω, sling, hurl sling-shot.
σφενδόνη, sling; sling-shot.
σφενδονήτης, slinger.
σφόδρα, vehemently, very much.
σχεδόν, about; mainly.
σχεῖν: ἔχω.
σχῆμα -ατος n., formation.
σχολαίως (comp. -αίτερον), slowly, lazily.
σχολή, leisure; respite; freedom.
σῴζω, ἔσωσα, ἐσώθην, save, keep safe.
Σωκράτης, Sokrates.
σῶμα -ατος n., one's person.
σῶς, σῶν, in good condition.
σωτήρ -ῆρος m., saviour.
σωτηρία, safety.
σωτήριος, bringing safety.
σωφροσύνη, good behaviour, discretion, self-control.

T

τάξις -εως f., position; line (of battle).
Τάοχοι, Taokhoi (Taochi).
τάραχος, confusion.
τάττω, ἔταξα, τέταγμαι, ἐτάχθην, order; draw up (troops); station.
τάφος, grave.
τάχα, quickly, straight away.
ταχύς (comp. θάττων, sup. τάχιστος), fast, quick;
διὰ ταχέων, with speed;
τὴν ταχίστην (sc. ὁδόν), as quickly as possible;
ταχύ (comp. θᾶττον, sup. τάχιστα), quickly, soon;
ἐπειδὰν τάχιστα + subj., as soon as.

τε (enclitic), and;
τε ... καί (& τε ... τε), both
... and.
τεθν-άναι -ηκε -ηκότα: θνήσκω.
τεῖχος -ους n., wall.
τεκμήριον, proof.
τελέω, pay.
τελευτάω, end; die.
τελευτή, end.
τέλος -ους n., end;
τέλος (adv.), at last, finally;
τὰ τέλη, the authorities.
τετρακισχίλιοι, four thousand.
τετρακόσιοι, four hundred.
τετρωμένος: τιτρώσκω.
τεττάκοντα, forty.
τέτταρες -α, four.
τέχνη, skill; means.
τήκομαι, τέτηκα (intrans.), melt.
τήμερον, today.
τίθεμαι, rest (arms).
Τιμασίων -ωνος m., Timasion.
τιμάω, honour.
τιμή, honour; reward.
τιμωρέομαι, (mid.) punish, take
vengeance on; (pass.) be punished.
τιμωρία, punishment.
τις, τι (indefinite pron.), some-,
any-one, -thing; one; (as adj.) a
certain, a considerable.
τι (adv.), somewhat.
τίς, τί (interrogative), who, what;
τί & διὰ τί, why.
Τισσαφέρνης -ους, Tissaphernes.
τιτρώσκω, τέτρωμαι, wound, cause
injury.
τοιγαροῦν, as a result, consequently.
τοίνυν (2nd word), so, then.
τοι-οῦτος -αύτη -οῦτο(ν), such, of
such a kind.
τοῖχος, wall.
τολμάω, have the courage.
τόξευμα -ατος n., arrow.
τοξεύω, shoot, hit (with arrow).
τοξικός, of archery;
τοξική (sc. τέχνη), archery.
τόξον, bow.
τοξότης, archer.
τόπος, place, spot.
τοσ-οῦτος -αύτη -οῦτο(ν), so much;
(pl.) so many; as many;
τοσοῦτον (adv.), so far, so much;

ὅσῳ + comp. ... τοσούτῳ + comp.,
the more ... , the more.
τότε, then, at that time, on that
occasion.
τράγημα -ατος n., sweet, sweetmeat.
τραῦμα -ατος n., wound.
τράχηλος, neck.
τραχύς, harsh.
τρεῖς, τρία, three.
τρέπω, ἔτρεψα, aor. mid. ἐτραπόμην,
turn (trans.); (mid.) turn (intrans.).
τρέφω, ἐτράφην, bring up; rear;
maintain.
τρέχω, ἔδραμον, run; (εἰς + acc.)
charge.
τρέω, ἔτρεσα, be afraid; run away.
τριάκοντα, thirty.
τριακόσιοι, three hundred.
τριήρης -ους f., trireme, warship.
τρισχίλιοι, three thousand.
τριταῖος, on the third day.
τρίτος, third.
τρόπαιον, trophy.
τροπή, rout.
τρόπος, character, temperament;
manner, way; taste.
τροφή, maintenance.
τρωκτός, edible.
τυγχάνω, ἔτυχον + part., happen
to; (+ gen.) get, obtain; meet;
τυχόν (acc. absolute), perhaps,
with luck.
τύρσις -ιος f., tower.

Υ

ὑβρίζω, maltreat.
ὕβρις -εως f., wantonness.
ὕβριστος, wanton.
ὑγιαίνω, be healthy.
ὕδωρ, ὕδατος n., water.
ὕλη, shrub, brushwood, wood.
ὑμεῖς -ᾶς -ῶν -ῖν, you (pl.).
ὑμέτερος, your.
ὑπ-αίτιος -ον, reprehensible.
ὕπαρχος, second-in-command.
ὑπ-άρχω + dat., be on the side of.
ὑπ-ελαύνω -ήλασα, ride up to.
ὑπέρ + acc., beyond, over;
+ gen., for, on behalf of; above,
over; beyond.

ὑπερ-βαίνω, climb over.
ὑπερ-έχω, overhang.
ὑπ-έχω -έσχον, undergo; (cf. δίκ-ην).
ὑπ-ήκοος -ον, subject.
ὑπηρέτης, servant.
ὑπ-ισχνέομαι + fut. inf., promise to.
ὕπνος, sleep.
ὑπό + acc., below, under; at the foot of;
+ gen., by, at the hands of, because of;
+ dat., under.
ὑποδεής (comp. -έστερος), inferior.
ὑπο-δέχομαι, welcome.
ὑπο-δέω -δέδεμαι, put on sandals.
ὑπόδημα -ατος n., sandal.
ὑποζύγιον, pack animal.
ὑπο-λαμβάνω -έλαβον, take under one's protection.
ὑπο-λείπω, leave behind.
ὑπο-λύομαι, take off one's sandals.
ὑπόμνημα -ατος n., reminder.
ὑπ-οπτεύω, suspect.
Ὑρκάνιος, Hyrkanian, from Hyrkania.
ὑστεραῖος, following, next;
τῇ ὑστεραίᾳ (sc. ἡμέρᾳ), (on) the following/next day.
ὑστερίζω, be too late.
ὕστερον adv., afterwards, later.
ὑφ-ίσταμαι, accept, consent to; (+ dat.) hold our against.
ὑψηλός, high.

Φ

φάγωσιν: ἐσθίω.
φαιδρός, cheerful.
φαίνομαι, φανοῦμαι, ἐφάνην, appear be seen; (+ part.) be evidently.
φάλαγξ -αγγος f., line (of battle).
φανερός, evident, shown up.
Φαρνάβαζος, Pharnabazos.
φάσκω, allege.
φέρω, ἠνέχθην, bring, carry; (pass.) be swept along.
φεύγω, ἔφυγον, run away, flee; be exiled.
φημί, say; say yes.
φθάνω, anticipate.

φθέγγομαι, ἐφθεγξάμην, shout, utter; (of eagle) screech, scream.
φθείρω, destroy.
φιάλη, bowl.
φιλέω, love.
Φιλήσιος, Philesios.
φιλία, friendship.
φιλικός (and φίλιος), friendly.
φίλ-ιππος -ον, keen on horses.
φιλό-θηρος -ον, keen on hunting.
φιλοκερδέω, be greedy to make money.
φιλο-κίνδυνος -ον, fond of danger, adventurous.
φιλομαθής + gen., eager to learn.
φιλονικία, competitiveness.
φιλο-πόλεμος -ον, keen on war.
φίλος (comp. -αίτερος), friendly; (+ dat.) on friendly terms with; (as noun) friend, ally.
φοβέω, frighten; (mid. & pass.) fear, be afraid (of).
φόβος, fear;
φόβον ποιέω + dat., frighten.
Φολόη, (Mount) Pholoë.
φορέω, wear.
φράζω, ἔφρασα, tell; order.
φρόνιμος, prudent, sensible.
φροντίζω, consider, think.
φρούραρχος, garrison commander.
φρουροί m.pl., garrison troops.
φυγάς -άδος m., an exile.
φυγή, flight, rout.
φυλακή, guarding; guard, garrison; guard/sentry duty, watch.
φυλάττω, φυλάξω, guard, protect; (mid.) be on one's guard (against), be cautious.
φυτεύω, plant.
Φωκαΐς -ίδος f., Phokaian woman, woman from Phokaia (Phocaea).
φωνή, voice.
φῶς, φωτός n., light.

X

χαλεπαίνω, be angry.
χαλεπός, hard, difficult; harsh, severe; painful.
χαλκός, bronze.
χάρις -ιτος f., thanks.
χαρίζομαι, χαριοῦμαι, show favour; gratify, please.

χειμών -ῶνος m., cold weather.
χείρ, χειρός f., hand; wrist.
Χειρίσοφος, Kheirisophos (Chiri-
sophus).
χειροπληθής, hand-sized.
Χερρόνησος -ου f., Peninsula,
Chersonese.
χηλή, breakwater.
χήν, χηνός m., goose.
χίλιοι, a thousand.
χιλός, fodder.
χίμαιρα, she-goat.
χιτών -ῶνος m., tunic.
χιών -όνος f., snow.
χοῖνιξ -ικος f., khoinix (choenix,
dry measure, 1¼ pints).
χόρτος, grass.
χράομαι + dat., use, obtain the
services of; manage; treat; have
dealings with.
χρή + acc. & inf., it is necessary.
χρῄζω, need, want.
χρῆμα -ατος n., thing; (pl.) money,
property, cargo(es), livestock.
χρηματιστικός, signifying money/
gain.
χρήσιμος, of use, useful.
χρηστός, brave, good.
χρόνος, time.
χρυσίον, gold; money.
χρυσοῦς -ῆ -οῦν (-εος), made of
gold, golden.
χώρα, area, country, land,
territory; position.
χωρέω, advance; contain, be equivalent to.
χωρίον, place; space; estate.
χῶρος, area.

Ω

ὦ + vocative, (not translated).
ὧδε, in this way, as follows.
ὠμοβόειος, of undressed ox-hide.
ὠμός, cruel, fierce, rough, savage.
ὠνέομαι, ἐπριάμην, buy.
ὥρα, (high) time.
ὡραῖος, in season; in the bloom of
youth;
τὰ ὡραῖα, produce (fruits) of the
season.
ὡς + noun, as, as though;
+ sup. adj. or adv., as ... as
possible;
+ number, about, nearly;
+ part., in the belief that, on
the pretext that;
+ fut. part., intending to;
+ indic./opt., that, as, since,
when, how;
+ subj./opt., in order that/to
(purpose);
+ inf., so that, so as to (result).
ὥς, so, in these circumstances.
ὡσαύτως, likewise.
ὥσπερ, (just) like; as if; just
as (when).
ὥστε + indic., and so, as a result;
+ inf., (so) that, so as to.
ὠτειλή, scar.
ᾧ-τινι: ὅσ-τις.
ὠτίς -ίδος f., bustard.
ὠφελέω, help.
ὠφέλιμος, advantageous, helpful.
ὤφλε: ὀφλισκάνω.

Ψ

ψέλιον, bracelet.
ψευδής, false; (n. pl. as noun)
lies.
ψεύδομαι, ἐψεύσθην, tell lies; be
mistaken.
ψιλός, bare, exposed, unprotected.
ψιλόω, strip.
ψυχή, heart, spirit.
ψῦχος -ους n., cold.

SELECTIVE BIBLIOGRAPHY

Specialized and foreign works are included since an adequate full bibliography is not conveniently available elsewhere. Works which may be suitable for students at the early stages are marked with an asterisk.

TRANSLATIONS

Warner, R.:
Xenophon - The Persian Expedition (Penguin, 1949: revised edition with Introduction by G. Cawkwell, 1972).

Brownson, C. L.:
Xenophon - Anabasis (Loeb Classical Library, 1922).

BOOKS AND ARTICLES

Anderson, J. K.:
Military Theory and Practice in the Age of Xenophon (California, 1970).

*Anderson, J. K.:
Xenophon (London, 1974).

Barnett, R. D.:
Xenophon and the Wall of Media, *Journal of Hellenic Studies* 83 (1963) 1 - 26.

Breitenbach, H. R.:
Xenophon, in *Realencyclopädie der Altertumswissenschaft* IX A2 (1967) 1569 - 2052.

Bury, J. B.:
The Ancient Greek Historians (London, 1909: reprinted by Dover, New York, 1958).

Cawkwell, G.:
A Diet of Xenophon, *Didaskalos* 12 (1967) 50 - 58.

Chroust, A. H.:
Socrates, Man and Myth (London, 1957).

Colin, G.:
En lisant Xénophon, *Revue des Etudes Grecques* 32 (1919) 72 - 95.

Croiset, A.:
Xénophon, son caractère et son talent (Paris, 1873).

Dakyns, H. G.:
Xenophon, in *Hellenica Essays* - ed. E. Abbott (London, 1880).

Delebecque, E.:
Essai sur la vie de Xénophon (Paris, 1957).

Dürrbach, F.:
L'apologie de Xénophon dans l'Anabase, *Revue des Etudes Grecques* 6 (1893) 343 - 386.

Erbse, H.:   Xenophons Anabasis, *Gymnasium* 73 (1966) 485 -
                           505.

Farrell, W. J.:   A Revised Itinerary of the Route followed by
                           Cyrus the Younger through Syria in 401 B.C.,
                           Journal of Hellenic Studies 81 (1961) 153 -
                           155.

*Finley, M. I.:   The Greek Historians (London, 1959), especial-
                           ly pp. 13 - 15 and 381 - 439.

Grant, A.:   *Xenophon* (Edinburgh, 1914).

*Grant, M.:   The Ancient Historians (London, 1970), pp.
                           125 - 135.

Gwynne, A.:   Xenophon and Sophaenetus, *Classical Review*
                           43 (1929) 38 - 39.

Higgins, W. E.:   *Xenophon the Athenian* (New York, 1977).

Hoeg, C.:   Kyrou Anabasis, oeuvre anonyme ou pseudonyme
                           ou orthonyme?, *Classica et Mediaevalia* 11
                           (1950) 151 - 179.

Jacks, L. V.:   *Xenophon, Soldier of Fortune* (London, 1930).

Jaeger, W.:   *Paedeia*, Vol. III (Oxford, 1945) especially
                           pp. 156 - 181.

Lendle, O.:   Der Bericht Xenophons über die Schlacht von
                           Kunaxa, *Gymnasium* 73 (1966) 429 - 452.

Luccioni, J.:   *Les idées sociales et politiques de Xénophon*
                           (Paris, 1948).

*Moorey, P. R. S.:   Biblical Lands (Oxford, 1975), especially pp.
                           117 - 136 (on Persia).

Münscher, K.:   Xenophon in der Griechische-Römische Literatur,
                           Philologus Supplement, 1920.

Nestle, W.:   Xenophon und die Sophistik, *Philologus* (1941)
                           31 - 51.

Nussbaum, G.:   *The Ten Thousand* (Leiden, 1967).

*Parke, H. W.:   *Greek Mercenary Soldiers* (Oxford, 1933).

*Parker, M: *Socrates and Athens* (London, 1973).

Rahn, P. J.:   Xenophon's Developing Historiography, *Trans-*

actions of the American Philological Association 102 (1971) 497 - 508.

Roy, J.: The Mercenaries of Cyrus, Historia 16 (1967)
287 - 323; Phoenix 22 (1968) 158 - 159 and
Athenaeum 46 (1968) 37 - 46.

Snodgrass, A. M.: Arms and Armour of the Greeks (London, 1967).

*Usher, S.: The Historians of Greece and Rome (London,
1969 and 1970) especially pp. 66 - 99.

*Usher, S.: Xenophon, History Today, July 1962.

Westlake, H. D.: Essays on Greek Historians and Greek History,
(Manchester, 1969) 203 - 225.

Wood, N.: Xenophon's Theory of Leadership, Classica et
Mediaevalia 25 (1964) 33 - 66.

Greek killing Persian, from an Athenian vase in the red-figure
style, mid fifth century.